Lecture Notes in Computer Science 8551

Commenced Publication in 1973
Founding and Former Series Editors:
Gerhard Goos, Juris Hartmanis, and Jan van Leeuwen

Stephen Jarvis · Steven Wright
Simon Hammond (Eds.)

High Performance Computing Systems

Performance Modeling, Benchmarking and Simulation

4th International Workshop, PMBS 2013
Denver, CO, USA, November 18, 2013
Revised Selected Papers

 Springer

Editors
Stephen Jarvis
Steven Wright
University of Warwick
Coventry, West Midlands
UK

Simon Hammond
Sandia National Laboratories CSRI
Albuquerque, NM
USA

ISSN 0302-9743   ISSN 1611-3349   (electronic)
ISBN 978-3-319-10213-9   ISBN 978-3-319-10214-6   (eBook)
DOI 10.1007/978-3-319-10214-6

Library of Congress Control Number: 2014952188

LNCS Sublibrary: SL1 – Theoretical Computer Science and General Issues

Springer Cham Heidelberg New York Dordrecht London

Printed on acid-free paper

Springer is part of Springer Science+Business Media (www.springer.com)

4th International Workshop on Performance Modeling, Benchmarking and Simulation of High-Performance Computing Systems (PMBS 2013)

This volume contains the 14 papers that were presented at the 4th International Workshop on Performance Modeling, Benchmarking and Simulation of High-Performance Computing Systems (PMBS 2013), which was held as part of the 25th ACM/IEEE International Conference for High-Performance Computing, Networking, Storage and Analysis (SC 2013) at the Colorado Convention Center in Denver during November 17–22, 2013.

The SC conference series is the premier international forum for high-performance computing, networking, storage, and analysis. The conference is unique in that it hosts a wide range of international participants from academia, national laboratories, and industry; this year's conference attracted over 10,000 attendees and featured over 350 exhibitors in the industry's largest HPC technology fair.

This year's conference was themed *HPC Everywhere, Everyday*, recognizing the impact that high-performance computing has on all aspects of society around the world, from weather forecasting, drug design, and finance, to aerospace, national security, and commerce.

SC offers a vibrant technical program, which includes technical papers, tutorials in advanced areas, birds of a feather sessions (BoFs), panel debates, a doctoral showcase, and a number of technical workshops in specialist areas (of which PMBS is one).

The focus of the PMBS 2013 workshop was comparing high-performance computing systems through performance modeling, benchmarking, or the use of tools such as simulators. We were particularly interested in receiving research papers that reported the ability to measure and make trade-offs in hardware/software co-design to improve sustained application performance. We were also keen to capture the assessment of future systems, for example, through work that ensured continued application scalability through peta- and exa-scale systems.

The aim of the PMBS 2013 workshop was to bring together researchers from industry, national labs, and academia, who were concerned with the qualitative and quantitative evaluation and modeling of high-performance computing systems. Authors were invited to submit novel research in all areas of performance modeling, benchmarking, and simulation, and we welcomed research that combined novel theory and practice. We also expressed an interest in submissions that included analysis of power consumption and reliability, and were receptive to performance modeling research that made use of analytical methods as well as those based on tracing tools and simulators.

Technical submissions were encouraged in areas including: performance modeling and analysis of applications and high-performance computing systems; novel techniques and tools for performance evaluation and prediction; advanced simulation techniques and tools; micro-benchmarking, application benchmarking, and tracing; performance-driven code optimization and scalability analysis; verification and validation of performance models; benchmarking and performance analysis of novel hardware; performance concerns in software/hardware co-design; tuning and auto-tuning of HPC applications and algorithms; benchmark suites; performance visualization; real-world case studies; studies of novel hardware such as Intel Xeon Phi coprocessor technology, NVIDIA Kepler GPUs, and AMD Fusion APU.

PMBS 2013

We received an excellent number of submissions for this year's workshop. This meant that we were able to be very selective in those papers that were chosen; the acceptance rate for full papers was approximately 30%. The resulting papers show worldwide programs of research committed to understanding application and architecture performance to enable peta-scale computational science.

Contributors to the workshop included Argonne National Laboratory, ETH Zurich, Georgia Institute of Technology, Inria, Indiana University, Lawrence Berkeley National Laboratory, NASA, Oak Ridge National Laboratory, San Diego Supercomputer Center, Sandia National Laboratories, Tokyo Institute of Technology, University of Grenoble, University of Tennessee, US National Energy Research Scientific Computing Center, amongst others.

Several of the papers are concerned with performance benchmarking and analysis (see Sect. A). The paper by Jeffrey Vetter et al. quantifies the architectural requirements of contemporary extreme-scale scientific applications. The paper by Subhash Saini et al. presents a performance evaluation of NASA's Pleiades, one of the world's most powerful supercomputers, using scientific and engineering applications. Matthew Cordery and colleagues document an analysis of the performance of the Cray XC30 using NERSC benchmarks, and contrast these results with those from the Cray XE6 and an IBM BG/Q. The paper by Pericàs et al. proposes a low-overhead methodology with which to benchmark data reuse in task-parallel runtimes, and in so doing correlates reuse distance with processor and memory configuration.

Section B of the proceedings collates papers concerned with performance modeling and simulation. Scott Levy and colleagues use simulation to identify system characteristics necessary for the exploration of resiliency in high-performance computing systems and applications. The paper by Collin McCurdy et al. introduces two analytic techniques with which to characterize and understand the impact of hardware and software data prefetching on scientific application performance. The performance modeling of the 3D gyrokinetic toroidal code GTC is examined by Matthew Anderson et al. in order to improve the efficiency and scalability of this code on many-tasking runtime systems. A novel flow-based hybrid network model for accurately simulating MPI applications on Ethernet/TCP networks is proposed by Paul Bédaride et al. The paper by Joo Hwan Lee et al. presents a model-driven co-design framework for high-performance computing architectures employing GPUs. Guillaume Aupy and colleagues provide a model and mathematical foundation for exploring the optimal checkpointing period for future exascale systems.

The final section of the proceedings, Sect. C, is concerned with performance optimization. The paper by Abhinav Sarje et al. presents the optimization and tuning of HipGISAXS, a parallel X-ray scattering simulation code, on general-purpose multi-core architectures as well as those with many-core accelerators. Prasanna Balaprakash and colleagues document a multi-objective optimization of HPC kernels for performance, power, and energy, with validation on three key architectures, an IBM BG/Q, hardware comprising Intel Xeon Phis, and a current generation Intel Xeon platform. Hongzhang Shan et al. present the performance tuning of fock matrix and two-electron integral calculations for NWChem, a computational chemistry package, on the Cray XE6, the Cray XC30, and the IBM BG/Q. The final paper by Priyanka Ghosh et al. reports on a performance analysis of NWChem's Tensor Contraction Engine module, exploring alternative communications patterns through a new proxy application.

Acknowledgments

The PMBS 2013 workshop was extremely well attended and we thank the participants for the lively discussion and positive feedback received throughout the workshop. We hope to be able to repeat this success in future years.

The SC conference series was sponsored by the IEEE Computer Society and the ACM (Association for Computing Machinery). We are extremely grateful for the support we received from the SC 2013 Steering Committee, and in particular from Barbara Chapman and Wolfgang Nagel, the SC 2013 workshop chairs.

The PMBS 2013 workshop was only possible thanks to significant input from AWE in the UK, and from Sandia National Laboratories and the Lawrence Livermore National Laboratory in the US. We acknowledge the support of the AWE Technical Outreach Programme (project CDK0724) and the Royal Society Industry Fellowship scheme (IF090020).

We are also grateful to LNCS for their support, and to Alfred Hofmann and Anna Kramer for assisting with the production of this volume.

May 2014

Stephen A. Jarvis
Steven A. Wright
Simon D. Hammond

Organization

Program Committee

Workshop Chairs

Stephen Jarvis   University of Warwick, UK
Simon Hammond   Sandia National Laboratories (NM), USA

Workshop Technical Program Committee

Pavan Balaji	Argonne National Laboratory, USA
Patrick Carribault	CEA, France
Todd Gamblin	Lawrence Livermore National Laboratory, USA
Jeff Hammond	Argonne National Laboratory, USA
Andrew Jones	NAG Ltd., UK
Darren Kerbyson	Pacific Northwest National Laboratory, USA
David Lecomber	Allinea Software Ltd., UK
John Pennycook	Intel, UK
Karthik Raman	Intel Corporation, USA
Rolf Riesen	IBM Research, Dublin, Ireland
Arun Rodrigues	Sandia National Laboratory (NM), USA
Ali Saidi	ARM Research and Development, USA
Christian Trott	Sandia National Laboratories (NM), USA
Ash Vadgama	UK Atomic Weapons Establishment, UK
Meghan Wingate-McClelland	Xyratex, USA
Steven Wright	University of Warwick, UK
Yunquan Zhang	Chinese Academy of Sciences, China

Contents

Section C: Performance Optimization

Performance Benchmarking and Analysis

Quantifying Architectural Requirements of Contemporary Extreme-Scale Scientific Applications

Jeffrey S. Vetter[1,2(✉)], Seyong Lee[1], Dong Li[1], Gabriel Marin[3],
Collin McCurdy[1], Jeremy Meredith[1], Philip C. Roth[1], and Kyle Spafford[1]

[1] Oak Ridge National Laboratory, Oak Ridge, TN 37831, USA
vetter@computer.org
[2] Georgia Institute of Technology, Atlanta, GA 30332, USA
[3] University of Tennessee–Knoxville, Knoxville, TN 37996, USA

Abstract. As detailed in recent reports, HPC architectures will continue to change over the next decade in an effort to improve energy efficiency, reliability, and performance. At this time of significant disruption, it is critically important to understand specific application requirements, so that these architectural changes can include features that satisfy the requirements of contemporary extreme-scale scientific applications. To address this need, we have developed a methodology supported by a toolkit that allows us to investigate detailed computation, memory, and communication behaviors of applications at varying levels of resolution. Using this methodology, we performed a broad-based, detailed characterization of 12 contemporary scalable scientific applications and benchmarks. Our analysis reveals numerous behaviors that sometimes contradict conventional wisdom about scientific applications. For example, the results reveal that only one of our applications executes more floating-point instructions than other types of instructions. In another example, we found that communication topologies are very regular, even for applications that, at first glance, should be highly irregular. These observations emphasize the necessity of measurement-driven analysis of real applications, and help prioritize features that should be included in future architectures.

1 Introduction

As detailed by several reports [1,2], HPC architectures will continue to change over the next decade in response to efforts to improve energy efficiency, reliability, and performance. At this time of significant disruption, it is critically

Support for this work was provided by U.S. Department of Energy, Office of Science, Advanced Scientific Computing Research. The work was performed at the Oak Ridge National Laboratory, which is managed by UT-Battelle, LLC under Contract No. DE-AC05-00OR22725 to the U.S. Government. Accordingly, the U.S. Government retains a non-exclusive, royalty-free license to publish or reproduce the published form of this contribution, or allow others to do so, for U.S. Government purposes.

© Springer International Publishing Switzerland 2014
S. Jarvis et al. (Eds.): PMBS 2013 Workshops, LNCS 8551, pp. 3–24, 2014.
DOI: 10.1007/978-3-319-10214-6_1

important to understand the requirements of contemporary extreme-scale scientific applications, so that these architectural changes can include features that satisfy these requirements. The proper mapping of these features to these future architectures will ultimately result in the best return on investment in these future systems. For example, in just the past few years, we have seen various new capabilities in contemporary processors and networks (e.g., integrated GPU and CPU, integrated random number generator, transactional memory, fine-grained power management, MPI collective offload, etc.) that have a significant impact on application performance.

In contrast to workload characterization performed in the last twenty years, today's characterizations must be more broad and yet more detailed in order to inform the design of these new architectures. Identifying architecture independent characteristics of applications is challenging, and generating these characteristics using a uniform, crosscutting methodology is vital to prioritization and efficiency.

In this paper, we present a methodology for examining important computation and communication behaviors for a representative set of real-world extreme-scale applications. Our initial toolkit, presented here, allows us to consistently and uniformly measure various behaviors in these applications: instruction mixes, memory access patterns and capacity, point-to-point messaging frequency and payload size, collective frequency, operation, and payload size, and communication topology.

For our applications, we have selected a substantial number of important U.S. Department of Energy (DOE) applications. Also, we have identified several new proxy applications, which are being developed by DOE Co-design centers, and we investigate these "proxy apps" with the same tools in order to identify differences between proxy apps and the applications they are meant to represent. The applications, proxy apps, and benchmarks we studied are summarized in Tab. 2.

With these measurements, we identify a number of observations (in Sect. 5), which we believe can inform decisions about future architectures.

1.1   Key Metrics and Methods

We identified several key metrics (Tab. 1) and methods for measuring those metrics for our study. We focus on processor instructions, memory behavior, and communication using the Message Passing Interface [3] (MPI), which is used by most of our applications. Later sections describe each metric and methodology in detail.

1.2   Related Work

A considerable amount of previous work [4–9] has characterized scientific applications using a variety of metrics and methodologies. This previous work provided detailed information about scientific applications, which typically focused

Table 1. Key metrics and methods

Category	Metrics
Computation	
Instruction mix	Instruction categories and counts
SIMD mix, width	SIMD counts and vector widths
Memory bandwidth	Achieved R/W memory bandwidth per socket
Reuse Distance	Temporal data locality
Communication	
Point-to-Point	Frequency, volume, type, topology
Collective	Frequency, volume, type, operator

on a specific metric, like communication. These existing studies are not sufficient going forward, however. With continued development of applications and algorithms, we need to continuously revisit these questions. And, as mentioned earlier, the new architectural decisions facing HPC are forcing us to answer new questions.

On another front, with the growing importance of benchmarks and proxy applications, we want to clearly distinguish these smaller programs from the more complex existing (or future) applications they are meant to represent. In particular, we want to identify the metrics that they represent well, and, perhaps more importantly, the metrics that they do *not* represent.

1.3 Assumptions and Caveats

Any characterization study comes with a set of assumptions and caveats. In this section, we outline some of these topics. First, although it would be preferred to have an idealized architecture for performing these measurements, running these full applications on a simulator or emulator at scale would be impractical. Instead, we identified a single architecture and software system on which we preformed all of our experiments to ensure consistency and understanding of application measurements. In particular, because processor instructions and semantics differ across platforms, it was very important to use the same processor and compilation system to conduct this analysis. We describe this platform in Sect. 1.4. Second, since our focus is scalable scientific applications, we included measurements of communication behavior and the runtime software, namely MPI, in our analysis. Third, these applications, particularly the proxy apps, are changing rapidly. Our toolkit is built to regenerate this analysis frequently, expecting such rapid changes. In this work, we present a snapshot of the behaviors for a specific version of each application. Finally, many of these applications and benchmarks can be applied to a wide range of problems in terms of both algorithms and data sizes. In our experiments, we selected problem sizes that were representative of typical application experiments; however, for a small set of our measurements, such as reuse distance, we had to reduce the problem size in order to complete the measurements in a practical amount of time. We identify those constraints in our discussion of the results.

1.4   Experimental Platform

For our application characterizations, we used the Georgia Institute of Technology's Keeneland Initial Delivery System [10] (KID). KID uses the scalable node architecture of the HP Proliant SL-390G7. Each node has two Intel Westmere host CPUs, 24GB of main memory, a Mellanox Quad Data Rate (QDR) InfiniBand HCA, and a local disk. The system has 120 nodes with 240 CPUs.

At the time of our experiments, the KID software environment was based on the CentOS 5.5 Linux distribution. In addition to the CentOS distribution's default software development environment based around the GNU Compiler Collection (GCC), the Intel 2011 and PGI 12 compilers are available to users of the system. To support efficient use of the system's CPUs , math libraries such as the Intel Math Kernel Library (MKL) are also available.

2   Instruction Mix

A program's *instruction mix* captures the number and type of the instructions the program executes when applied to a given input. To collect application instruction mixes from fully optimized x86-64 executable files (also called binaries), our toolkit uses a performance modeling framework called MIAMI. MIAMI uses a PIN [24]-based front-end to recover the application control flow graph (CFG) and record the execution frequency of select control flow graph edges during program execution. After the program finishes, MIAMI recovers the execution frequency of all CFG basic blocks, builds the loop nesting structure, and uses XED [25] to decode the instructions of each executed basic block. We decode the x86 instructions into generic operations that resemble RISC instructions. Thus, arithmetic instructions with memory operands are decoded into multiple micro-ops: one for the actual arithmetic operation, plus one additional micro-op for each memory read and write operation performed by the x86 instruction. Each micro-op has associated attributes such as bit width, data type (integer or floating-point), unit type (scalar or vector), and vector length where applicable.

In our methodology, we aggregate these micro-ops into a few coarser categories as seen in Tab. 3. Load and store operations are all classified as either *MemOps* if they operate on scalar values, or *MemSIMD* if they operate with vector data. Arithmetic operations are classified as floating-point vs. integer, and also as scalar vs. SIMD, resulting in four exclusive categories. The *Moves* category includes scalar and vector register copy operations, as well as data conversions from one data type to another or between different precisions of the same data type. All conditional and unconditional branches, as well as direct and indirect jumps, are classified as *BrOps*. Finally, the *Misc* category includes all other types of instructions, such as traps, pop count, memory fence and other synchronization operations.

Table 2. Applications and kernels

Application	Area	Description	Input Problems
Benchmarks and Proxy Applications			
HPCC [11]	Benchmark	Collection of kernels to test system-wide and node-level performance	Two nodes (24 MPI tasks), sized to use approximately 50% of memory
AMG [12]	Multigrid Solver	Parallel solver for linear systems on unstructured grids	Built-in Laplace problem on unstructured domain with anisotropy.
Nekbone	Fluid Dynamics	Mini-application of Nek5000, customized to solve basic conjugate gradient solver	Conjugate gradient solver for linear or block geometry
MOCFE [13]	Neutron Transport	Simulates deterministic neutron transport equation parallelized across energy groups, angles, and mesh	Ten energy groups, eight angles, and weakly scaled mesh
LULESH [14]	Hydrodynamics	High deformation event modeling code via Lagragian shock hydrodynamics	Sedov blast wave problem in three spatial dimensions
Applications			
S3D [15,16]	Combustion	Direct numerical solver for the full compressible Navier-Stokes, total energy, species, and mass continuity equations	Amplitude pressure wave with ethylene-air chemistry on weakly scaled domain
SPASM [17]	Materials	Short-range molecular dynamics	Cu tensile test with the embedded atom method
GTC [18]	Fusion	Particle-in-cell code for studying microturbulence in magnetically confined plasmas	16 toroidal planes, number of domains for plane decomposition varied, 5 particles/cell/domain
ddcMD [19]	Molecular Dynamics	Classical molecular dynamics via flexible domain decomposition strategy	Molten metal re-solidification, 256 MPI processes
LAMMPS [20]	Molecular Dynamics	Large-scale Atomic/Molecular Massively Parallel Simulator	LJ - atomic fluid with Lennard-Jones potential; EAM - Cu with EAM potential; RHODO - rhodopsin protein with long range forces
Nek5000 [21]	Fluid Dynamics	A computational fluid dynamics solver based on the spectral element method	3D MHD
POP [22]	Climate	Ocean circulation model part of the Community Climate System Model [23]	192x128x20 domain with balanced clinic distribution over 8 MPI processes

Collecting instruction mixes from application binaries has both advantages and disadvantages. Working at the binary level reveals the precise instruction stream that gets executed on the machine after all the compiler optimizations are applied. In addition, classifying the semantics of low level machine instructions is less error prone than trying to understand the resulting instruction mix of a high level source code construct. Compilers often need to generate many auxiliary machine instructions to perform a simple source code operation such as an array access. On the other hand, compiler choice and compiler optimizations may affect the reported instruction mixes. In particular, the quality of the register allocator has a direct effect on the number of memory operations in the instruction stream. Other scalar optimizations influence the number of auxiliary instructions that end up in the final application binary.

In our methodology, we strive to be consistent in how we profile applications, making sure that we used the same compiler and optimization flags in all cases. This consistency allows us to more directly compare the instruction mixes from the applications under study.

Table 3. Instruction category descriptions

Category	Description
MemOps	Scalar load and store operations
MemSIMD	SIMD vector load and store operations
Moves	Integer and floating-point register copies; data type and precision conversions
FpOps	Scalar floating-point arithmetic
FpSIMD	Vector floating-point arithmetic
IntOps	Scalar integer arithmetic
IntSIMD	Vector integer arithmetic
BrOps	Conditional and unconditional branches; direct and indirect jumps
Misc	Other miscellaneous operations, including pop count, memory fence, atomic operations, privileged operations

SIMD. Many commodity microprocessors used in today's supercomputers include support for Single Instruction Multiple Data (SIMD) instructions. When executed, an SIMD instruction performs the same operation on several data values simultaneously to produce multiple results. In contrast, a non-SIMD instruction produces at most a single value. On processors that support SIMD instructions, using such instructions is desirable because it increases the amount of data parallelism possible using a given number of instructions. From another perspective, using SIMD instructions places less demand on the memory subsystem for instruction fetches and data loads and stores compared to a sequence of non-SIMD instructions that perform the same sequence of operations. SIMD instructions were introduced for commodity microprocessors in the latter half of the 1990s [26,27] and promoted as support for accelerated graphics and gaming. However, many operations used for graphics and gaming are also useful in scientific computing, making modern SIMD instruction set extensions such as the

Streaming SIMD Extensions 4 (SSE4) [28] an attractive target for developers of scientific applications.

We use an instruction's extension as reported by XED to classify instructions as vector or scalar operations. Some modern compilers commonly generate SSE instructions even for scalar arithmetic, because the SIMD execution path is faster than the x87 pipelines on current x86 architectures. To make the instruction mix metric less dependent on the compiler, we classify SIMD instructions that operate on a single data element as scalar. Therefore, our reported SIMD counts correspond to true vector instructions that operate on multiple data, and the SIMD counts may be lower than a classification based exclusively on instruction extensions.

Table 4. Instruction mix (percentage of all instructions, NOPs excluded)

Target	MemOps%	MemSIMD%	FpOps%	FpSIMD%	IntOps%	IntSIMD%	Moves%	BrOps%	Misc%
HPCC:HPL	0.9	19.2	0.1	60.2	3.1	0.0	15.7	0.8	0.0
HPCC:MPIFFT	24.1	5.7	11.3	11.3	22.5	0.1	18.5	6.4	0.0
HPCC:MPIRandomAccess	28.2	3.3	0.0	0.0	41.1	1.8	10.9	14.6	0.1
HPCC:PTRANS	27.5	1.1	6.7	0.9	36.4	1.1	20.3	6.0	0.0
Graph 500	24.7	0.1	0.0	0.0	37.6	0.0	22.5	15.1	0.0
AMG (setup)	17.3	0.1	0.4	0.0	53.0	0.0	3.1	26.1	0.0
AMG (solve)	29.8	1.3	15.7	0.6	21.3	0.0	20.4	10.9	0.0
MOCFE	31.2	10.1	1.0	6.7	28.8	0.1	10.8	10.9	0.1
Nekbone(1024Weak)	31.3	5.1	0.3	21.2	12.1	0.1	25.3	4.7	0.0
LULESH	31.1	2.2	29.7	4.6	2.2	0.0	28.9	1.2	0.0
S3D	19.1	14.0	3.3	18.3	19.9	2.1	14.4	7.7	1.0
SPASM	31.7	0.4	21.9	0.4	13.5	0.2	24.1	7.8	0.0
GTC	32.7	0.0	7.6	0.3	38.3	0.0	4.4	16.6	0.0
ddcMD	28.6	0.2	34.9	0.3	7.1	0.0	26.7	2.3	0.0
LAMMPS_EAM	36.4	0.0	28.8	0.0	8.6	0.3	20.6	5.2	0.0
LAMMPS_LJ	33.7	0.1	22.6	0.0	10.4	0.0	27.6	5.6	0.0
LAMMPS_RHODO	35.1	0.5	18.5	1.0	14.4	0.2	22.5	7.8	0.0
Nek5000 (MHD)	29.6	2.6	2.4	9.1	23.3	0.1	25.7	7.2	0.1
POP	18.6	15.1	8.4	14.2	20.3	1.2	14.8	7.5	0.0

Results. For this study, we classify SIMD instructions into three categories: memory, integer, and floating-point as seen in Tab. 3. Note that SIMD register copy operations are not reported separately. Instead, they are aggregated together with their scalar counterparts in the *Moves* category.

Table 4 shows the instruction mix captured from benchmarks, proxy apps, and full applications. A few commonalities and distinctions are noteworthy. First, HPL is strikingly different from every other benchmark, proxy app, and full

Table 5. Distribution of data sizes for Memory/Move/Arithmetic Instructions. A/B/C/D/E format represents percentage of instructions working on 8/16/32/64/128 bit width data, respectively. (*In FpOps for HPCC:MPIFFT, E in the A/B/C/D/E format indicates 80 bits.*)

Target	MemOps					Moves					IntOps					IntSIMD					FpOps					FpSIMD				
	8	16	32	64	128	8	16	32	64	128	8	16	32	64	128	8	16	32	64	128	8	16	32	64	128	8	16	32	64	128
HPCC:HPL	0	0	1	3	96	0	0	2	0	97	0	0	17	83	0	0	0	100	0	0	0	0	0	100	0	0	0	1	99	0
HPCC:MPIFFT	2	2	9	69	19	0	0	13	36	44	0	0	26	74	0	0	0	86	14	0	0	0	0	95	5*	0	0	5	95	0
HPCC:MPI-RA	3	2	14	71	11	1	0	32	66	1	0	0	15	85	0	0	0	100	0	0	0	0	0	100	0	0	0	0	0	0
HPCC:PTRANS	1	1	55	40	4	0	0	54	30	16	0	0	75	25	0	0	0	100	0	0	0	0	0	100	0	0	0	40	60	0
Graph 500	0	0	32	68	0	0	0	16	84	0	0	0	10	90	0	0	0	100	0	0	0	0	0	0	0	0	0	0	0	0
AMG (setup)	0	0	61	38	1	0	0	23	67	10	0	0	53	47	0	0	0	100	0	0	0	0	0	100	0	0	0	66	34	0
AMG (solve)	0	0	34	62	4	0	0	6	54	40	0	0	4	96	0	0	0	99	1	0	0	0	0	100	0	0	0	0	100	0
Nekbone	1	1	6	79	14	0	0	1	35	64	0	0	25	75	0	0	0	100	0	0	0	0	0	100	0	0	0	0	100	0
LULESH	0	0	3	90	7	0	0	12	41	47	0	0	48	52	0	0	0	0	100	0	0	0	0	100	0	0	0	41	59	0
S3D	0	0	5	52	42	0	0	29	54	17	0	0	28	72	0	0	0	79	21	0	0	0	0	100	0	0	0	3	97	0
GTC	0	0	36	64	1	0	0	2	17	81	0	0	4	95	0	0	0	100	0	0	0	0	88	12	0	0	0	77	23	0
ddcMD	0	0	4	95	1	0	0	11	48	41	0	0	28	72	0	0	0	68	32	0	0	0	0	100	0	0	0	45	55	0
LAMMPS.EAM	0	0	15	84	0	0	0	10	36	53	0	0	60	40	0	0	0	100	0	0	0	0	0	100	0	0	0	0	0	0
LAMMPS.LJ	0	0	11	88	0	0	0	12	40	48	0	0	62	38	0	0	0	100	0	0	0	0	0	100	0	0	0	0	0	0
LAMMPS.RH	1	1	14	84	1	0	0	14	36	50	0	0	52	48	0	0	0	95	5	0	0	0	0	100	0	0	0	13	87	0
NEK5000 (MHD)	1	0	14	77	8	0	0	10	35	55	0	0	42	58	0	0	0	100	0	0	0	0	0	100	0	0	0	0	100	0
POP	1	0	8	47	45	0	0	10	35	55	0	0	19	81	0	0	0	100	0	0	0	0	0	100	0	0	0	16	84	0

application. It is composed of over 60% floating-point operations; this is nearly double the next highest code (35% in ddcMD). It has the lowest number of branch operations (less than 1%) as well; most codes are many times higher. Virtually every one of its memory and floating-point operations are vectorized, which is unique among our test codes, and it has the lowest fraction (20%) of instructions devoted to memory operations. With respect to instruction mix, HPL has little in common with the "real" computational science applications we studied.

A comparison of instruction mixes can also provide interesting insights into how well a proxy app represents its full application. For instance, consider the Nekbone proxy app intended to represent some characteristics of the Nek5000 application. Though similar in some ways, we also see clear differences: the fraction of floating-point instructions in Nekbone is about double that of Nek5000, and the fraction of integer instructions is about half that of Nek5000. The different solvers in LAMMPS also exhibited some dissimilarities, such as a higher floating-point instruction mix for EAM and a higher integer mix for RHODO, but the similarities across these LAMMPS benchmarks outweighs their differences. For AMG, we separate the setup phase from the solution phase, as the setup phase tended to run longer than the solution phase for the benchmark problems we used. We saw a vast difference in the instruction mixes between these phases, with a much greater integer instruction mix during setup, and many more floating-point instructions during the solution.

Looking at trends across all of our test cases, memory operation mix is — except for HPL — quite similar across the codes. Most comprise 30% to 35% memory instructions, though the fraction of those that are SIMD varies from none to at most half.

The fraction of integer instructions is surprisingly high across a number of applications. A few standout examples in the applications are in GTC and the setup phase of AMG, at 38% and 53%, respectively. In benchmarks, HPCC's MPI-RandomAccess and PTRANS and Graph500 are high as well, around 40% integer instructions. Excluding LULESH (2.2%), the remaining codes are between 7% to 29% integer instructions. Interestingly, though integer instruction count is more than we expected, no code has any significant fraction of vectorized integer instructions; most between 0% and 0.2%, and S3D is the highest at 2%.

Table 5 shows the distribution of memory/move/arithmetic instructions according to their working data sizes, which can provide additional insight about the workloads, especially for designing more specialized hardware. The results in the table indicate that most of memory/arithmetic instructions work on either 32 or 64 bits, as expected.

3   Memory Behavior

3.1   Memory Bandwidth

All memory systems have a limited data transfer speed due to the limited capacity of hardware queues in the processor and the memory controller, the finite number of buffers and ports in memory DIMMs, as well as the limited width and frequency of memory buses. Due to improvements in computational through-put such as speculative execution and hardware prefetching, applications often become bottlenecked by the transfer capacity of the memory system. This effect is exacerbated as the number of cores on a single chip increases, since those cores compete for limited memory resources.

It is important to understand how applications exercise the memory system. One metric that provides insight is the consumed memory bandwidth, which for many applications is a measure of achieved throughput. Memory bandwidth is defined as the ratio between the amount of data transferred to and from memory, and the time it takes to execute the application.

Achieved memory bandwidth is a performance metric dependent on both the application and the underlying architecture. We use hardware performance counters to measure the number of read and write transactions to memory. Modern micro-processors expose hardware performance events at the memory controller level. These events count read memory requests caused by both data accesses missing in the cache and prefetch requests initiated by the hardware prefetcher, as well as write transactions due to modified cache lines being written back to memory.

In our methodology, we use PAPI [29]-based calipers that record the number of read and write memory transactions as well as the wall clock time it takes to execute the code between the calipers. We compute separate bandwidth results for memory reads and writes.

Results. Each microprocessor in our experimental platform has its own inte-grated memory controller. As a result, we are interested primarily in the achieved memory bandwidths per socket. Figure 1 presents the read and write memory bandwidths per socket we measured for our test applications. The figure also includes the sustained peak machine bandwidth for one socket, measured for different ratios of read and write memory transactions. To measure these peak bandwidths, we wrote a micro-benchmark that accesses a large block of memory and modifies part of the memory. By varying the amount of memory modi-fied, our micro-benchmark achieves different ratios of memory writes to memory reads. Note that with a write-allocate cache policy, our micro-benchmark can generate write and read memory transactions in a ratio of at most 1:1.

The data in Fig. 1 shows that POP is running very close to the test machine's peak memory bandwidth. Therefore, POP is memory bandwidth limited and would not benefit from an increase in core concurrency without similar increases in available bandwidth. At the other end of the spectrum, LULESH and GTC achieve only a small fraction of the machine's memory bandwidth. Because LULESH does not have MPI support, it was executed only in serial mode, achiev-ing about 2GB/s of combined read and write memory bandwidth per core. GTC, however, does use MPI, and still exhibited a low memory bandwidth even when four GTC processes were run on each socket. The low GTC memory bandwidth results indicate that GTC is likely memory latency limited.

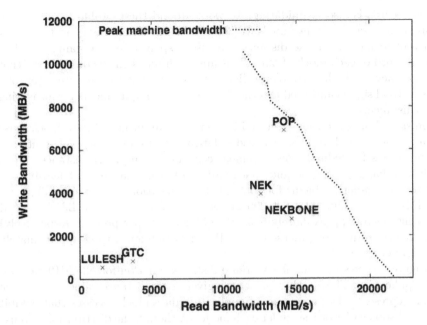

Fig. 1. Measured application bandwidths and sustained peak machine bandwidth per socket

Nek5000 and Nekbone are in between these two extremes. They achieve a significant fraction of the sustained machine bandwidth, with some room for core concurrency scaling. We also note that Nek5000 generates a higher ratio of write memory transactions than its proxy, Nekbone.

3.2   Reuse Distance

Reuse distance is defined as the number of distinctive data elements accessed between two consecutive references to the same element. We use reuse distance as a metric to quantify the pattern of data reuse or program locality. Reuse distance is independent of architecture, because it measures the volume of the intervening data accesses between two accesses. Reuse distance largely determines cache performance. For a fully associative cache under Least Recently Used replacement, reuse distance can accurately measure the number of cache hits or misses, given cache configurations. Reuse distance also allows direct comparison of data behavior across applications. As the memory hierarchy becomes deeper and more adaptive, it is increasingly important to quantify reuse distance to optimize application performance.

Measuring reuse distance is challenging due to its high cost in terms of time and space. For each memory access, we need to check previous memory access records to count distinctive data elements, which is often time consuming. For a program accessing a large amount of data, the space required to save previous access records is also intimidating. To work around these problems, we use an approximate reuse distance analysis [30] with a Pin-based binary instrumentation tool to measure reuse distance. We use a splay tree to organize the last access record of each block of data. This approach relies on the observation that the accuracy of the last couple of digits of a reuse distance rarely matter [30]. This method significantly reduces the time and space requirements for measuring reuse distance.

Results. Using the tool described in Sect. 3.2, we measured data block reuse distance for 12 applications. We used a data block size of 64 bytes. Despite our optimizations for reducing measurement cost, measuring reuse distance empirically still has a high time and space cost. To make measurement feasible, we had to use smaller problems for some of the applications we studied. Thus, for LAMMPS, we simulated 1,600,000 atoms per process with the LJ and EAM problems (using approximately 575 MB and 498 MB per process, respectively) and 128,000 atoms per process for the RHODO problem (using approximately 474 MB per process).

Figure 2 shows the cumulative reuse distance function for one MPI task for each application. The X axis represents a given reuse distance value x, while the Y axis represents the percentage of application data block accesses that exhibit a reuse distance of x or less under each model. Although the distribution of reuse distance for a specific application is strongly correlated to the input problem size, Fig. 2 shows that the reuse difference (and hence program locality) differs greatly

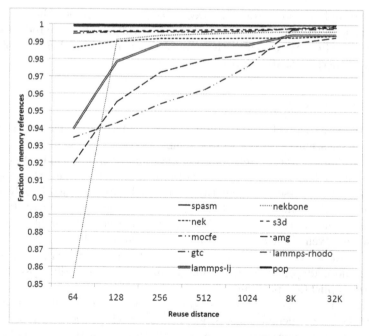

Fig. 2. Cumulative distribution functions (CDF) of reuse distance

between applications. In addition, reuse distance curves often have one or more knees and plateaus, which correspond to different working sets [31]. In many cases, the shape of a specific plot (knees and plateaus) is similar across different inputs [32]. Thus, although we used a single input per program in this study for most programs, our measurements suggest the applications, proxy apps, and benchmarks exhibit a wide diversity of working sets.

Figure 2 shows a substantial difference between Nekbone and Nek5000 with respect to reuse distance. In particular, 98% of Nek5000 memory references have a reuse distance of less than 64, while the corresponding number for Nekbone is only 85%. Upon further investigation, we found that Nekbone's run time is dominated by the conjugate gradient method (CG) and this method does not have good data locality. On the other hand, Nek5000 employs various numerical algorithms, including CG. Some of these algorithms have much better data locality than CG, which explains the higher concentration of reuse distances of less than 64 for Nek5000.

In Fig. 2, each CDF curve exhibits only a few plateaus/knees, showing that the reuse distance is highly concentrated in a few ranges. For example, AMG, Nekbone, and LAMMPS-LJ have 3, 2, and 3 plateaus/knees, respectively. This is consistent with earlier studies of reuse distance [31,32]. In addition, for SPASM, MOCFE, GTC, and POP, more than 99% memory references have reuse distances less than 64. The high concentration of reuse distance in a few ranges suggests that if a cache's size is just large enough to hold a few concentrated ranges, the cache performance will be almost the same as that of a larger cache. However, because of the differences in the concentrated ranges across applications, a dynamic cache with a few configurable effective cache sizes may be desirable for systems with a varied workload.

4   Communication

The efficiency and scalability of communication and synchronization operations is a critical determinant of the overall performance of most parallel programs. In this study, we focus on programs that use MPI for communication and synchronization, for two basic reasons. First, most scalable scientific applications use MPI including the applications we study here. Second, MPI defines an interface that allows straightforward capture of an application's messaging characteristics, so there are many tools available for measuring a program's MPI behavior.

In our methodology, the MPI data transfer operations we consider fall into two categories: *point-to-point* (P2P), in which a single sending MPI task transfers data to a single receiving MPI task, and *collective*, in which a group of processes participate in an operation such as a data broadcast or an all-to-all data exchange.

Table 6. Basic communication characteristics. (P2P and Coll % are the percentage of invocations of each class of MPI subroutines.)

Application	P2P %	Coll %	P2P Subroutines	Coll Subroutines	Comments
AMG	99.7	0.3	Recv, Isend, Irecv	Allreduce, Bcast, Allgather, Scan	In setup, even P2P messages are extremely small (<128 bytes).
Nekbone (linear)	39.8	60.2	Isend, Irecv	Allreduce	P2P or Allreduce gather-scatter implementation chosen dynamically
Nekbone (3D)	88.6	11.4	Isend, Irecv		
MOCFE	44.1	55.9	Isend, Irecv	Allreduce, Reduce	
S3D	99.7	0.3	Isend, Irecv, Send	Allreduce, Bcast	3D Nearest Neighbor on Reg. Grid, periodic BC
SPASM	100.0	negl	SendRecv	Allreduce, Barrier	3D Nearest Neighbor on Reg. Grid, periodic BC
GTC	78.9	21.1	SendRecv	Allreduce	1D Nearest Neighbor along toroid domain
ddcMD	90.0	10.0	Isend, Irecv, Send, Recv	Allreduce, Bcast, Gather, Scatter	Unstructured, flexible domain decomposition
LAMMPS-EAM	99.0	1.0			Large P2P messages (>500KB), small collective messages (<64 Bytes); RHODO adds non-neighbor P2P comm. for long-range forces
LAMMPS-LJ	100.0	0.0	Send, Irecv	Allreduce	
LAMMPS-RHODO	97.7	2.3			
Nek5000	96.6	3.4	Isend, Irecv, Send, Recv	Bcast, Allreduce, Barrier	2D/3D nearest-neighbor communication patterns on an unstructured grid
POP	54.4	45.6	Isend, Irecv	Allreduce	2D Nearest Neighbor

Table 7. P2P communication characteristics. Buffer size columns show histogram bin upper limit

Application	Topology	n	Buffer Size Min	Max	Med.
AMG	Unstructured in 2D extruded to 3D	256	2^3	2^{22}	2^7
Nekbone	Linear	128	2^9	2^9	2^9
Nekbone	3D geometry	128	2^6	2^{22}	2^{14}
MOCFE	3 Dim of Parallelism – Mesh, Energy Group, & Angle	256	2^{13}	2^{14}	2^{14}
S3D	3D Nearest Neighbor	256	2^5	2^{16}	2^{15}
SPASM	3D Nearest Neighbor	256	2^3	2^{13}	2^6
GTC	1D Nearest Neighbor along the toroid domain	256	2^4	2^{19}	2^{18}
ddcMD	3D unstructured	256	2^3	2^{17}	2^{15}
LAMMPS-EAM	3D Nearest Neighbor	96	2^3	2^{22}	2^{20}
LAMMPS-LJ	3D Nearest Neighbor	96	2^{21}	2^{21}	2^{21}
LAMMPS-RHODO	Mainly 3D Nearest Neighbor	96	2^3	2^{22}	2^{17}
Nek5000	2D/3D nearest-neighbor	128	2^3	2^{20}	2^{10}
POP	2D Nearest Neighbor	64	2^9	2^{12}	2^9

In this study, we examined the communication behavior of our test applications running on the KID system's Infiniband interconnection network. Table 6 summarizes the communication behavior of the applications we studied. In the table, the columns indicating percentage of point-to-point and collective communication operations show the percentage of the total MPI operation count.

To collect data about application communication behavior and performance, we use mpiP version 3.3. Normally mpiP presents summary statistics about a program's MPI behavior, but we modified mpiP to also collect data about the number of point-to-point operations performed between each pair of program processes and the volume of data transferred in those operations. Our modified mpiP outputs this data in the form of adjacency matrices. Visualizing such matrices is a concise and effective way to communicate the topology of a program's point-to-point communication behavior. For example, visualizing the adjacency matrix for an application whose tasks communicate only with their nearest neighbors in a Cartesian topology (e.g., a 3D stencil operation) produces a distinctive, repeating pattern near the matrix diagonal. With some practice, common communication patterns can be recognized in these visualizations. We also modified mpiP to generate histograms of the data sizes used in point-to-point and collective operations. These histograms give an indication of the type of demands a program places on a system's interconnection network, such as whether a program performs a large number of collective operations involving small messages.

4.1 Point-to-Point Communication

Figure 3 shows average point-to-point communication volume per iteration for three benchmark problems used in our study. In each case, the data shown was captured during the first ten iterations of the program's main loop. These figures display the communication data as a matrix, such that the block at location (s, d) is colored according to the volume of data sent from MPI rank s to MPI rank d.

Figure 3a shows the average communication volume for the LAMMPS EAM benchmark running on 96 processes. The repeated pattern in the figure reflects a three-dimensional nearest-neighbor communication pattern. Figure 3b also suggests a three-dimensional nearest-neighbor communication pattern, but unlike the pattern for the EAM benchmark the pattern suggests that sub-groups of processes participate in communication topology that is fully-connected within each sub-group. Also, there is a significant amount of point-to-point communication between MPI tasks that are not neighbors in the spatial decomposition. This is to be expected, because unlike the EAM benchmark, the Rhodo benchmark includes long range forces in its computation of potential. These two matrices

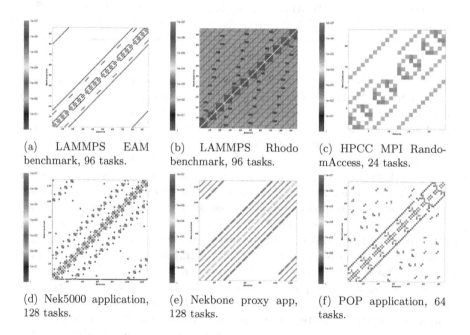

(a)   LAMMPS   EAM benchmark, 96 tasks.

(b)   LAMMPS   Rhodo benchmark, 96 tasks.

(c) HPCC MPI RandomAccess, 24 tasks.

(d) Nek5000 application, 128 tasks.

(e) Nekbone proxy app, 128 tasks.

(f) POP application, 64 tasks.

Fig. 3. Average volume of point-to-point communication. Color scale is consistent across all plots.

also illustrate how much the communication pattern of the same program can vary depending on the problem input.

Figure 3c presents the average point-to-point communication volume per iteration for the HPCC MPI RandomAccess phase. Because the RandomAccess benchmark performs updates to memory locations selected randomly with a uniform distribution across all processes involved in the benchmark, one expects to see that each MPI task communicated approximately the same amount to each of the other MPI tasks, giving a matrix that is all one color except on the diagonal (since a process need not use MPI operations for updates within itself). Thus, the communication pattern shown in the figure, a nearest neighbor pattern, is counter-intuitive. In fact, the figure is correct and results from the use of an algorithm optimization that organizes the available MPI tasks into a virtual hypercube topology and routes messages along this topology.

Figure 3d and 3e highlight the differences in point-to-point communication patterns between a full application, Nek5000, and a proxy app intended to mimic that application's behavior, Nekbone. The proxy app's communication pattern is much more regular than that of the full application. Note that this difference does not necessarily mean the proxy app is not a valid stand-in for the full application, but it does suggest that the proxy is not a good representative *with respect to communication behavior* for the input set we used.

Finally, Fig. 3f shows the average point-to-point communication volume for the well-studied POP application. This figure suggests POP's primary point-to-point communication pattern is nearest neighbor, but that some processes also communicate with processes that aren't necessarily neighbors. This non-neighbor communication appears somewhat random, and is likely a result of the way that the earth's oceans are mapped to the available MPI tasks.

4.2 Collective Communication

The programs we studied exhibited substantial variety in their collective communication behavior. The programs varied in the number and size distribution of the messages they sent using collective operations, but most that used collectives did so using small message sizes. For example, our three LAMMPS benchmark problems either did not use collectives at all during the main computation phase (LJ benchmark), or sent very little data per operation (EAM and RHODO, which performed collectives using messages with fewer than 64 bytes). Likewise, the "global" phases of the HPCC benchmark exhibited more varied behavior. Both MPIRandomAccess and MPIFFT exhibited a bimodal distribution, with some small collective operations (fewer than 32 bytes) but also larger collective operations (MPIRandomAccess issued over 250,000 collective operations that sent 256KB per process, while MPIFFT issued operations using 256MB per process). In both cases, the operations involving a larger amount of data were all-to-all operations. Like LAMMPS, the collective operations in PTRANS all involved small amounts of data per operation. Our modified version of mpiP reported no collective data transfer operations used within the HPL phase of the benchmark suite. Inspection of the HPCC source code shows that HPL *does* use collective operations, but it uses its own implementation based on MPI point-to-point operations instead of the MPI collective operations. Because mpiP only collects data about calls to MPI functions, our current methodology cannot detect these data transfers as logically collective operations.

5   Observations

In this section, we make a number of observations from this evidence for future architectures. First, we consider instruction mix.

1. None of the applications makes use of integer SIMD instructions, even though some of the applications do a reasonable amount of integer calculation.
2. About half of tested applications have more integer operations (IntOps + IntSIMD) than floating-point operations (FpOps + FpSIMD).
3. All applications except for LULESH have non-negligible amount of integer computations.
4. MemSIMD is rare, only occurring in S3D, POP, and MOCFE. And in those three cases, it is still lower (by percentage) than non-SIMD mem ops.
5. For all apps except ddcMD, the number of memory operations (MemOps + MemSIMD) are greater than the number of floating-point operations (FpOps + FpSIMD).
6. When FpSIMD is high, the number of branches is always low.

Second, we review the memory behavior of our applications. Not surprisingly, memory behavior has a dramatic impact on performance, but it is also more difficult to measure.

1. POP runs at close to peak machine bandwidth and generates a higher ratio of write memory transactions than the other applications in this study.
2. GTC achieves a very low memory bandwidth utilization, indicating a poor memory access pattern.
3. The reuse distance is highly concentrated in a few ranges, indicating the opportunity for cache architecture improvements.

Third, communication is one of the most important behaviors in determining overall performance for scalable scientific applications.

1. All of the distributed memory applications use the `Allreduce` collective operation with small data payloads (i.e., one double precision number). This analysis reconfirms an earlier observations [9], and has been used to motivate hardware support for collective offload engines in the interconnect.
2. In general, the applications and benchmarks exhibited either a uni-modal collective communication distribution with very small payloads, or a bimodal distribution with both small payloads and very large payloads. Often the large amounts of data sent were used in `Alltoall` operations, such that each process sent a smaller amount of data to each other process, but the aggregate amount of data sent was large.

3. The communication operations for several of the applications we studied were nearly all point-to-point (P2P) operations (by count). This preference for P2P operations appears to be driven mainly by the need for scalability; collective operations, even when implemented with optimal algorithms, can serve as a scalability limitation. Nevertheless, most applications require at least a few collective operations.

4. As expected, the basic P2P communication behavior of the applications that explicitly simulate a physical system is a nearest neighbor communication pattern. The applications differ significantly, however, in how much data is transmitted through those P2P operations, and whether they exhibit an element of non-neighbor communication.

5. The runtime communication selection in Nek5000 and Nekbone reconfirms that a well-optimized collective communication library generally performs better than the P2P-based counterpart.

Finally, aside from specific architecture metrics, we also compare some of the proxy applications against real applications. Benchmarks and proxy applications are very valuable because these kernels provide hardware and software architects with comprehensible code segments that can be simulated and easily rewritten in alternative programming languages. However, because these benchmarks and proxy applications are precisely simplified versions of their real-world counterparts, they also can have different behaviors.

1. Not surprisingly, HPL is a significant outlier from all the applications we tested: practically all (79.4%) of its instructions are memory and floating-point SIMD operations. HPL has more that twice the number of floating-point operations than the other applications, proxy apps, and benchmarks we studied.

2. The proxy app (e.g., Nekbone) and the corresponding full application (e.g., Nek5000) can have different reuse distance distributions. It is important to investigate the full application to understand data locality.

3. Proxy applications and benchmarks tend to have higher rates of SIMD instructions because complex memory access patterns have been removed from compute-intensive loops, and the compiler can optimize and identify SIMD optimizations with higher clarity.

4. Finally, the communication topologies that we measured show that some of the proxy apps do not necessarily represent the communication behavior of the application they are intended to model.

6 Summary

We have presented an empirical analysis of several important scalable scientific applications, benchmarks, and proxy applications. Using a methodology supported by a toolkit of performance tools that allows us to study detailed computation, memory, and communication behavior at varying levels of resolution, we confirmed many of our expectations but also found a number of surprises. In this time of rapid architectural change for the sake of balancing energy efficiency and reliability against realized performance, the quantitative measurements provided by applying our methodology are critical for finding the right balance point.

References

1. Dongarra, J., Beckman, P., Moore, T., Aerts, P., Aloisio, G., Andre, J.C., Barkai, D., Berthou, J.Y., Boku, T., Braunschweig, B., Cappello, F., Chapman, B., Chi, X., Choudhary, A., Dosanjh, S., Dunning, T., Fiore, S., Geist, A., Gropp, B., Harrison, R., Hereld, M., Heroux, M., Hoisie, A., Hotta, K., Jin, Z., Ishikawa, Y., Johnson, F., Kale, S., Kenway, R., Keyes, D., Kramer, B., Labarta, J., Lichnewsky, A., Lippert, T., Lucas, B., Maccabe, B., Matsuoka, S., Messina, P., Michielse, P., Mohr, B., Mueller, M.S., Nagel, W.E., Nakashima, H., Papka, M.E., Reed, D., Sato, M., Seidel, E., Shalf, J., Skinner, D., Snir, M., Sterling, T., Stevens, R., Streitz, F., Sugar, B., Sumimoto, S., Tang, W., Taylor, J., Thakur, R., Trefethen, A., Valero, M., van der Steen, A., Vetter, J., Williams, P., Wisniewski, R., Yelick, K.: The international exascale software project roadmap. International Journal of High Performance Computing Applications **25**(1), 3–60 (2011)
2. Kogge, P., Bergman, K., Borkar, S., Campbell, D., Carlson, W., Dally, W., Denneau, M., Franzon, P., Harrod, W., Hill, K., Hiller, J., Karp, S., Keckler, S., Klein, D., Lucas, R., Richards, M., Scarpelli, A., Scott, S., Snavely, A., Sterling, T., Williams, R.S., Yelick, K.: Exascale computing study: Technology challenges in achieving exascale systems. Technical report, DARPA Information Processing Techniques Office (2008)
3. Snir, M., Gropp, W.D., Otto, S., Huss-Lederman, S., Walker, D., Dongarra, J., Lumsdaine, A., Lusk, E., Nitzberg, B., Saphir, W. (eds.): MPI-the complete reference (2-volume set) 2nd edn. Scientific and Engineering Computation. MIT Press, Cambridge (1998)
4. Asanovic, K., Bodik, R., Catanzaro, B., Gebis, J., Husbands, P., Keutzer, K., Patterson, D., Plishker, W., Shalf, J., Williams, S.: The landscape of parallel computing research: A view from berkeley. Technical Report UCB/EECS-2006-183, EECS Department, University of California, Berkeley (2006)
5. Vetter, J.S., Yoo, A.: An empirical performance evaluation of scalable scientific applications. In: SC 2002, Baltimore, MD, USA. IEEE (2002)
6. Shalf, J., Kamil, S., Oliker, L., Skinner, D.: Analyzing ultra-scale application communication requirements for a reconfigurable hybrid interconnect. In: Proceedings of the 2005 ACM/IEEE Conference on Supercomputing, p. 17. IEEE Computer Society (2005)
7. Brightwell, R., Underwood, K.D.: An analysis of the impact of mpi overlap and independent progress. In: Proceedings of the 18th Annual International Conference on Supercomputing, Malo, France, pp. 298–305. ACM (2004)
8. Riesen, R.: Communication patterns. In: 20th International Parallel and Distributed Processing Symposium (IPDPS), 8 p. (2006)
9. Vetter, J.S., Mueller, F.: Communication characteristics of large-scale scientific applications for contemporary cluster architectures. In: International Parallel and Distributed Processing Symposium (IPDPS), Ft. Lauderdale, Florida (2002)
10. Vetter, J.S., Glassbrook, R., Dongarra, J., Schwan, K., Loftis, B., McNally, S., Meredith, J., Rogers, J., Roth, P., Spafford, K., Yalamanchili, S.: Keeneland: Bringing heterogeneous GPU computing to the computational science community. IEEE Computing in Science and Engineering **13**(5), 90–95 (2011)

11. Dongarra, J.J., Luszczek, P.: Introduction to the hpcchallenge benchmark suite. Technical Report ICL-UT-05-01, Innovative Computing Laboratory, University of Tennessee-Knoxville (2005)
12. Brown, P.N., Falgout, R.D., Jones, J.E.: Semicoarsening multigrid on distributed memory machines. SIAM Journal on Scientific Computing 21(5), 1823–1834 (2000)
13. Smith, M.A., Marin-Lafleche, A., Yang, W.S., Kaushik, D., Siegel, A.: Method of characteristics development targeting the high performance Blue Gene/P computer at argonne national laboratory. In: Proceedings of the International Conference on Mathematics and Computational Methods Applied to Nuclear Science and Engineering (MC 2011). American Nuclear Society (2011)
14. Karlin, I., Bhatele, A., Chamberlain, B.L., Cohen, J., Devito, Z., Gokhale, M., Haque, R., Hornung, R., Keasler, J., Laney, D., Luke, E., Lloyd, S., McGraw, J., Neely, R., Richards, D., Schulz, M., Still, C.H., Wang, F., Wong, D.: Lulesh programming model and performance ports overview. Technical Report LLNL-TR-608824, Lawrence Livermore National Laboratory (December 2012)
15. Chen, J.H., Choudhary, A., de Supinski, B., DeVries, M., Hawkes, E.R., Klasky, S., Liao, W.K., Ma, K.L., Mellor-Crummey, J., Podhorszki, N., Sankaran, R., Shende, S., Yoo, C.S.: Terascale direct numerical simulations of turbulent combustion using S3D. Computational Science and Discovery 2(1) (2009)
16. Spafford, K.L., Meredith, J.S., Vetter, J.S., Chen, J., Grout, R., Sankaran, R.: Accelerating S3D: A GPGPU case study. In: HeteroPar 2009: Proceedings of the Seventh International Workshop on Algorithms, Models, and Tools for Parallel Computing on Heterogeneous Platforms (2009)
17. Germann, T.C., Kadau, K.: Trillion-atom molecular dynamics becomes a reality. International Journal of Modern Physics C 19(09), 1315–1319 (2008)
18. Lee, W.W.: Gyrokinetic approach in particle simulation. Physics of Fluids 26, 556–562 (1983)
19. Richards, D.F., Glosli, J.N., Chan, B., Dorr, M.R., Draeger, E.W., Fattebert, J.L., Krauss, W.D., Spelce, T., Streitz, F.H., Surh, M.P., Gunnels, J.A.: Beyond homogeneous decomposition: Scaling long-range forces on massively parallel systems. In: Proceedings of the Conference on High Performance Computing, Networking, Storage and Analysis, SC 2009. ACM, New York (2009)
20. Plimpton, S.: Fast parallel algorithms for short-range molecular dynamics. Journal of Computational Physics 117, 1–19 (1995)
21. Fischer, P., Lottes, J., Kerkemeier, S.: Nek5000 website (2008)
22. Smith, R.D., Dukowicz, J.K., Malone, R.C.: Parallel ocean general circulation modeling. Physica D 60(1–4), 38–61 (1992)
23. Collins, W.D., Blackmon, M.L., Bonan, G.B., Hack, J.J., Henderson, T.B., Kielh, J.T., Large, W.G., McKenna, D.S., Bitz, C.M., Bretherton, C.S., Carton, J.A., Chang, P., Doney, S.C., Santer, B.D., Smith, R.D.: The Community Climate System Model version 3 (CCSM3). Journal of Climate 19(11), 2122–2143 (2006)
24. Luk, C.K., Cohn, R., Muth, R., Patil, H., Klauser, A., Lowney, G., Wallace, S., Reddi, V.J., Hazelwood, K.: Pin: building customized program analysis tools with dynamic instrumentation. In: Proceedings of the 2005 ACM SIGPLAN Conference on Programming Language Design and Implementation, PLDI 2005, pp. 190–200. ACM, New York (2005)
25. Intel Corporation: XED, http://software.intel.com/sites/landingpage/pintool/docs/53271/Xed/html
26. Intel Corporation: Intel Architecture software developer's manual, vol. 1: basic architecture (1999)

27. Advanced Micro Devices Inc: 3DNow! technology manual (2000)
28. Intel Corporation: Intel SSE4 programming reference (April 2007)
29. Browne, S., Dongarra, J., Garner, N., London, K., Mucci, P.: A portable programming interface for performance evaluation on modern processors. The International Journal of High Performance Computing Applications **14**, 189–204 (2000)
30. Ding, C., Zhong, Y.: Predicting whole-program locality through reuse distance analysis. In: ACM SIGPLAN Conference on Programming Language Design and Implementation (2003)
31. Schuff, D.L., Parsons, B.S., Pai, V.S.: Multicore-aware reuse distance analysis. In: Workshop on Performance Modeling, Evaluation, and Optimization of Ubiquitous Computing and Networked Systems (2010)
32. Ding, C., Zhong, Y.: Reuse distance analysis. Technical Report UR-CS-TR-741, Computer Science Department, University of Rochester (2001)

Performance Evaluation of the Intel Sandy Bridge Based NASA Pleiades Using Scientific and Engineering Applications

Subhash Saini[✉], Johnny Chang, and Haoqiang Jin

NASA Advanced Supercomputing Division
NASA Ames Research Center
Moffett Field, CA 94035-1000, USA
{subhash.saini,johnny.chang,haoqiang.jin}@nasa.gov

Abstract. We present a performance evaluation of Pleiades based on the Intel Xeon E5-2670 processor, a fourth-generation eight-core Sandy Bridge architecture, and compare it with the previous third generation Nehalem architecture. Several architectural features have been incorporated in Sandy Bridge: (a) four memory channels as opposed to three in Nehalem; (b) memory speed increased from 1333 MHz to 1600 MHz; (c) ring to connect on-chip L3 cache with cores, system agent, memory controller, and QPI agent and I/O controller to increase the scalability; (d) new AVX unit with wider vector registers of 256 bit; (e) integration of PCI-Express 3.0 controllers into the I/O subsystem on chip; (f) new Turbo Boost version 2.0 where base frequency of processor increased from 2.6 to 3.2 GHz; and (g) QPI link rate from 6.4 to 8 GT/s and two QPI links to second socket. We critically evaluate these new features using several low-level benchmarks, and four full-scale scientific and engineering applications.

1 Introduction

The Intel Nehalem, a third generation architecture (Xeon 5600 series) introduced in 2009, offers some important initial steps toward ameliorating the memory bandwidth problem [1, 2]. The Intel X5600 launched in 2010 is the Westmere series and it is a 32 nm die shrink of Nehalem. The Nehalem architecture has overcome problems associated with the sharing of the front-side bus (FSB) in previous processor generations by integrating an on-chip memory controller and by connecting the two processors through the Intel QuickPath Interconnect (QPI) and to the input/output (I/O) hub. The result is more than three times greater sustained-memory bandwidth per core than the previous-generation dual-socket architecture. It also introduced hyper-threading (HT) technology (or simultaneous multi-threading, "SMT") and Intel Turbo Boost technology 1.0 ("Turbo mode") that automatically allow processor cores to run faster than the base operating frequency if the processor is operating below rated power, temperature, and current specification limits [3].

However, third generation Nehalem architecture still has performance and scalability bottlenecks due to scalability of L3 cache bandwidth, I/O, limited memory bandwidth, low performance of Turbo Boost, and low HT performance due to inadequate

© Springer International Publishing Switzerland 2014
S. Jarvis et al. (Eds.): PMBS 2013 Workshops, LNCS 8551, pp. 25–51, 2014.
DOI: 10.1007/978-3-319-10214-6_2

memory bandwidth per thread, low bandwidth between two processors on a node, etc. In 2012, Intel introduced a fourth-generation eight-core architecture Intel Xeon processor E5-2670 ("Sandy Bridge") that introduced new architectural features and extensions and mechanisms, which has significantly improved overall performance [4]. This processor is also used in large-scale heterogeneous systems such as Stampede with co-processor Intel Xeon Phi based on the Many Integrated Core (code-named Knight's Corner) architecture and Yellowstone [1], [5], [6]. New and extended features of Sandy Bridge architecture are:

a) A ring to connect on-chip L3 cache with cores, system agent, memory controller, and QPI agent and I/O controller to increase the scalability. L3 cache per core has been increased from 2 MB to 2.5 MB.

b) New micro-ops (L0) cache that caches instructions as they are decoded. The cache is direct mapped and can store 1.5 K micro-ops.

c) New Intel Advanced Vector Extensions (AVX) unit with wider vector registers of 256 bit in Sandy Bridge instead of 128 bit in Westmere, thereby doubling the floating-point performance.

d) Integration of PCI-Express 3.0 controllers into the I/O subsystem on chip. PCIe lanes have been increased from 36 to 40. Earlier QPI was used to connect to I/O hub.

e) New Turbo Boost version 2.0 where frequency boost of processor is up to 600 MHz instead of up to 400 MHz.

f) Two QPI links connecting first processor to second processor instead of one link. QPI link rate increases from 6.4 to 8 GT/s.

g) Two loads plus one store per cycle instead of one load plus one store, thereby doubling load bandwidth.

h) Four memory DDR3 channels as opposed to three in Westmere.

i) Memory speed increased from 1333 MHz in Westmere to 1600 MHz in Sandy Bridge.

The potential performance improvement of Sandy Bridge architecture over Nehalem architecture (Nehalem and Westmere processors) is attributed due to increasing three memory channels to four, increasing memory speed from 1333 MHz to 1600 MHz, and new technology/architecture such as ring connecting cores, L3 cache (2.5 MB vs. 2 MB per core), QPI agent, memory controller and I/O controller, and system agent.

In the past, several researchers have evaluated the performance of high performance computing systems [14-20]. To the best of our knowledge, this is the first paper to conduct a:

a) Critical and extensive performance evaluation and characterization of an SGI ICE X cluster based on the Intel Xeon E5-2670, hereafter called "Sandy Bridge", using High Performance Computing Challenge (HPCC) suite, memory latency and bandwidth benchmarks, NAS Parallel Benchmarks (NPB), and four real-world production-quality scientific and engineering applications (Overflow,

MITgcm, USM3D, and CART3D) taken from the existing workload of NASA and U.S. aerospace industry [7-13]

b) Detailed comparison of SGI ICE X cluster based on the Intel Xeon E5-2670 connected by 4x FDR IB with an SGI ICE 8400EX based on the Intel Xeon 5670, connected by 4x QDR IB-connected hypercube topology (hereafter called "Westmere") using network latency and bandwidth benchmarks of HPCC suite [7].

c) Detailed performance comparison of AVX and SSE4.2 instructions for Sandy Bridge using NPB and four full-scale applications.

d) Performance evaluation of Turbo Boost 2.0 for Sandy Bridge and its comparison with Turbo Boost 1.0 for Westmere using NPB and four full-scale applications.

e) Performance evaluation of hyper-threading (HT) (or simultaneous multi-threading, "SMT") for Sandy Bridge and Westmere using NPB and four full-scale applications.

f) Measurement of the latency and memory load bandwidth of L1 cache, L2 cache, L3 cache and main memory for Sandy Bridge and Westmere.

The remainder of the paper is organized as follows: Section 2 provides details of the Pleiades-Sandy Bridge and Pleiades-Westmere systems; in Section 3 we briefly describe the benchmarks and applications used in the current study; in Section 4 we present our results comparing the performance of the two systems; and in Section 5 we present our conclusions.

2   Computing Platforms

We used NASA's Pleiades supercomputer, an SGI Altix ICE system located at NASA Ames Research Center. Pleiades comprises 11,776 nodes interconnected with an InfiniBand (IB) network in a hypercube topology [1]. The nodes are based on four different Xeon processors from Intel: Harpertown, Nehalem-EP, Westmere-EP and Sandy Bridge. In this study, we used only the Westmere-EP and Sandy Bridge based nodes.

2.1   Pleiades Sandy Bridge

As shown in Figure 1, the Sandy Bridge-based node has two Xeon E5-2670 processors, each with eight cores. Each processor is clocked at 2.6 GHz, with a peak performance of 166.4 Gflop/s. The total peak performance of the node is therefore 332.8 Gflop/s. Each core has 1.5K μ ops, 64 KB of L1 cache (32 KB data and 32 KB instruction) and 256 KB of L2 cache. All eight cores share 20 MB of last level cache (LLC), also called L3 cache. The on-chip memory controller supports four DDR3 channels running at 1600 MHz, with a peak-memory bandwidth per processor of 51.2 GB/s (and twice that per node). Each processor has two QPI links to connect with the second processor of a node to form a non-uniform-memory access (NUMA) architecture. The QPI link runs at 8 GT/s ("T" for transfer), at which rate 2 bytes can be transferred in each direction, for an aggregate of 32 GB/s. Each link runs at 16 GB/s in each direction simultaneously [1].

Following are the new and extended architectural features of Sandy Bridge.

New Features

L0 (μ-ops) Cache: In Sandy Bridge, there is a μ-ops cache that caches instructions as they are decoded. The cache is direct mapped and can store 1.5 K μ-ops. The μ-ops cache is included in the L1(I) cache. The size of the actual L1(I) and L1(D) caches has not changed, remaining at 32 KB each (for total of 64 KB).

Last Level Cache (LLC) / L3 Cache: In Westmere, all cores have their own private path to the L3 cache. Sandy Bridge has a bi-directional 32-byte ring interconnect that connects the 8 cores, the L3-cache, the QPI agent and the integrated memory controller. The ring replaces the individual wires from each core to the L3-cache. The bus is made up of four independent rings: a data ring, request ring, acknowledge ring, and snoop ring. The QPI link agent, cores, L3 cache segments, DDR3 memory controller, and an I/O controller all have stops on this ring bus. The L3 cache is divided into eight slices/blocks, which are connected to the eight cores, and the system agent through a ring interconnect. The red boxes in Fig. 1 are ring stations. Each core can address the entire cache. Each slice gets its own stop station and each slice/block has a full cache pipeline. In Westmere, there is a single cache pipeline and queue that all cores forward requests to, whereas in Sandy Bridge, cache pipeline is distributed per cache slice.

AVX: Intel Advanced Vector Extensions (AVX) is a new set of x86 instruction-set extensions of SSE4.2 [22]. It increases the width of the registers from 128 bits to 256 bits. Each register can hold eight single-precision floating-point values or four double-precision floating-point values that can be operated on in parallel using SIMD (single-instruction, multiple-data) instructions. AVX also adds three-register instructions (e.g., z=x+y), whereas previous instructions could only use two registers (x=x+y). Square root and reciprocals vectorize with 128 bit-wide (SSE4.2) but do not vectorize with AVX. In AVX, alignment of data is to 32 bytes boundary, whereas in SSE4.2, it is 16 bytes boundary.

QPI 2.0: In Nehalem/Westmere, one QPI 1.0 link connects the two processors/sockets of the node to form a non-uniform-memory access (NUMA) architecture to do point-to-point communication; the other connects to the IO hub [4]. The QPI link runs at 6.4GT/s, at which rate 2 bytes can be transferred in each direction, for a rate of 12.8 GB/s in each direction per QPI link and a total 25.6 GB/s bidirectional rate per link. In Sandy Bridge, two QPIs at 8.0 GT/s connect the two processors/sockets of the node and deliver 16 GB/s in each direction with a total of 32 GB/s bidirectional. In Westmere, the total inter-processor bandwidth is 51.6 GB/s, whereas in Sandy Bridge, it is 128 GB/s, an increase of 148%.

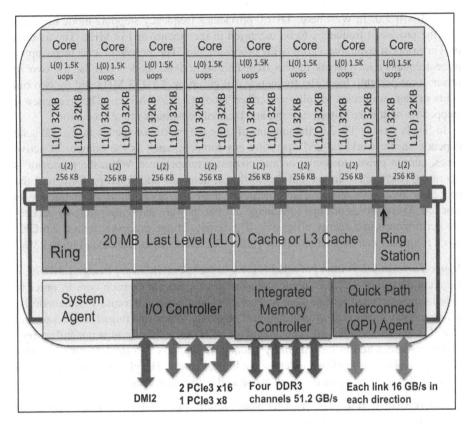

Fig. 1. Schematic diagram of a Sandy Bridge processor

Memory Subsystem: The improvements to Sandy Bridge's floating-point performance by AVX instruction increase the demands on the load/store units. In Nehalem/Westmere, there are three load and store ports: load, store address, and store data for L1(D) cache. The memory unit can service two memory requests per cycle, i.e., 16 bytes load and 16 bytes store, for a total of 32 bytes per cycle. In Sandy Bridge, the load and store address ports are now symmetric so each port can service a load or store address to L1(D) cache. By adding a second load/store port, Sandy Bridge can handle two loads plus one store per cycle automatically. The memory unit can service three memory requests per cycle, two 16 bytes load and a 16-byte store, for a total of 48 bytes per cycle.

Extended Features

Several existing features such as Turbo Boost, HT, the number of memory channels, and the speed of the memory bus of Nehalem architectures (Nehalem-EP, Westmere-EP, etc.) have been significantly enhanced and extended in Sandy Bridge architecture, as described below.

Turbo-Boost 2.0: In Westmere, TB 1.0 provides a frequency-stepping mode that enables the processor frequency to be increased in increments of 133 MHz. The amount of Turbo boost available varies with processor bin. The processor can turbo up to three frequency increments in less than half-subscribed mode—that is, for two or fewer cores per chip busy, the frequency can go up by 3 x 133 MHz and by two bin splits in half-subscribed to fully-subscribed mode (2 x 133 MHz). The frequency is stepped up within the power, current, and thermal constraints of the processor.

In Sandy Bridge TB 2.0, the amount of time the processor spends in the TB state depends on the workload and operating environment, such as the number of active cores, current power consumption and processor temperature. When the processor is operating below these limits and the workload demands additional performance, the processor frequency dynamically increases until the upper limit of frequency is reached. There are algorithms to manage current, power, and temperature to maximize performance and energy efficiency. The Sandy Bridge processor with a 2.6 GHz clock frequency can boost its frequency up to 3.2 GHz, i.e., an increase of up to 23%.

Hyper-Threading 2.0: Intel provided HT 1.0 in Nehalem. In Sandy Bridge E5-2670, it is enhanced to HT 2.0. HT enables two threads to execute on each core in order to hide latencies related to data access. These two threads can execute simultaneously, filling unused stages in the functional unit pipelines. When one thread stalls, a second thread is allowed to proceed. The advantage of HT is its ability to better utilize processor resources and to hide memory latency. It supports two threads per core, presenting the abstraction of two independent logical cores. The physical core contains a mixture of resources, some of which are shared between threads:

(a) *replicated resources* (register state, return stack buffer, and the instruction queue);
(b) *partitioned resources* (load buffer, store buffer, and reorder buffer);
(c) *shared resources* (L1, L2, and L3 cache); and
(d) *shared resources unaware of the presence of threads* (execution units).

Memory Speed: Memory speed increased from 1333 MHz in Westmere to 1600 MHz in Sandy Bridge, an increase of bandwidth by 20%.

Memory Channels: The number of memory channels increased from 3 in Westmere to 4 in Sandy Bridge, an increase in bandwidth by 33%.

Networks Interconnects (FDR and QDR)

The Sandy Bridge nodes are connected to the two fabrics (ib0 and ib1) of the Pleiades InfiniBand (IB) network via the dual-port, four-link fourteen data rate (4x FDR) IB Mezzanine card on each node, as well as via the Mellanox FDR IB switches in the SGI ICE X IB Premium Blade. The FDR runs at 14 Gbits/s per lane. With four links, the total bandwidth is 56 Gbits/s (7 GB/s). On each node, the IB Mezzanine card sits on a sister board next to the motherboard, which contains the two-processor sockets.

There are 18 nodes per Individual Rack Unit (IRU). These 18 nodes are connected to two Mellanox FDR IB switches in an SGI ICE X IB Premium Blade to join the ib0 fabric. Another set of connections between the 18 nodes and a second Premium Blade is established for ib1. However, Westmere nodes are connected via four link quad data rate (4x QDR) IB running at 40 Gbits/s or 5 GB/s. Peak bandwidth of 4x FDR IB is 1.75 times that of 4x QDR (56 Gbits/s vs. 32 Gbits/s).

Table I presents the characteristics of Sandy Bridge and Westmere.

Table 1. Characteristics of Sandy Bridge and Westmere

Characteristic	Pleiades-Sandy Bridge	Pleiades-Westmere
Processor:		
Processor architecture	Sandy Bridge	Nehalem
Processor type	Intel Sandy Bridge-EP (Xeon E5-2670)	Intel Westmere-EP (Xeon X5670)
Base frequency (GHz)	2.60	2.93
Turbo Boost Version	V2.0, up to 600 MHz	V1.0, up to 400 MHz
Turbo frequency (GHz)	3.2	3.33
Floating/clock/core	8	4
Perf. per core (Gflop/s)	20.8	11.7
Number of cores	8	6
Peak performance	166.4	70.3
L0 (micro-op) Cache	1.5K micro-ops	None
L1 cache size	32 KB (I)+32 KB(D)	32 KB (I)+32 KB(D)
L2 cache size	256 KB/core	256 KB/core
L3 cache size (MB)	20 shared	12 shared
L3 cache network	Ring	Individual links
Memory type	4 channels DDR3 - 2 DIMMS per channel	3 channels DDR3 - 2 DIMMS per channel
Memory speed (MHz)	1600	1333
HyperThreads / core	2	2
I/O controller	On chip	Off chip
PCI Lanes	40 Integrated PCIe 3.0	36 Integrated PCIe 2.0
PCIe 3.0 Speed	8 GT/s	none
Node:		
Number of processors	2	2
Main memory (GB)	32	24
No. of Hype Threads	32	24
Inter socket QPI links	2	1
QPI frequency (GT/s)	8.0	6.4
New instruction	AVX	AES-NI

Table 1. (*Continued*)

Number of QPIs	2	1
Performance ./node (Gflop/s)	332.8	140.6
Interconnects		
Interconnect type	4x FDR IB	4x QDR IB
Peak network performance Gbits/s	56	32
Network topology	Hypercube	Hypercube
Compiler, Libraries, operating system and File System:		
Compiler	Intel 12.1	Intel 12.1
MPI library	MPT 2.06	MPT 2.06
Math library	Intel MKL 10.1	Intel MKL 10.1
Type of file system	Lustre	Lustre
Operating system	SLES11SP1	SLES11SP1
System Name	SGI ICE X	SGI ICE 8400EX

3   Benchmarks and Applications

In this section we present a brief description of the benchmarks and applications used in this study.

3.1   HPC Challenge Benchmarks (HPCC)

The HPCC benchmarks are intended to test a variety of attributes that can provide insight into the performance of high-end computing systems [7]. These benchmarks examine not only processor characteristics but also the memory subsystem and system interconnects.

3.2   Memory Subsystem Latency and Bandwidth

A deep understanding of the performance of the hierarchical memory system of Sandy Bridge is crucial to understanding application performance. We measured the latency and bandwidth for L1, L2, L3 caches and main memory for both Sandy Bridge and Westmere [8].

3.3   NAS Parallel Benchmarks (NPB)

The NPB suite contains eight benchmarks comprising five kernels (CG, FT, EP, MG, and IS) and three compact applications (BT, LU, and SP) [9]. We used NPB MPI version 3.3, Class C in our study. BT, LU, and SP are typical of full production-quality science and engineering applications.

3.4   Science and Engineering Applications

For this study, we used four production-quality full applications representative of NASA's workload.

OVERFLOW-2 is a general-purpose Navier-Stokes solver for CFD problems [10]. The code uses finite differences in space with implicit time stepping. It uses overset-structured grids to accommodate arbitrarily complex moving geometries. The dataset used is a wing-body-nacelle-pylon geometry (DLRF6) with 23 zones and 36 million grid points. The input dataset is 1.6 GB in size, and the solution file is 2 GB.

CART3D is a high-fidelity, inviscid CFD application that solves the Euler equations of fluid dynamics [11]. It includes a solver called Flowcart, which uses a second-order, cell-centered, finite volume upwind spatial discretization scheme, in conjunction with a multi-grid accelerated Runge-Kutta method for steady-state cases. In this study, we used the geometry of the Space Shuttle Launch Vehicle (SSLV) for the simulations. The SSLV uses 24 million cells for computation, and the input dataset is 1.8 GB. The application requires 16 GB of memory to run.

USM3D is a 3-D unstructured tetrahedral, cell-centered, finite volume Euler and Navier-Stokes flow solver [12]. Spatial discretization is accomplished using an analytical reconstruction process for computing solution gradients within tetrahedral cells. The solution is advanced in time to a steady-state condition by an implicit Euler time-stepping scheme. The test case used 10 million tetrahedral meshes, requiring about 16 GB of memory and 10 GB of disk space.

MITgcm (MIT General Circulation Model) is a global ocean simulation model for solving the equations of fluid motion using the hydrostatic approximation [13]. The test case uses 50 million grid points and requires 32 GB of system memory and 20 GB of disk to run. It writes 8 GB of data using Fortran I/O. The test case is a ¼ degree global ocean simulation with a simulated elapsed time of two days.

4   Results

In this section we present our results for low-level benchmarks, HPCC suite, memory subsystem latency and bandwidth benchmarks, NPB, and four full applications (Overflow, Cart3D, USM3D, and MITgcm).

4.1   Memory Latency and Bandwidth

In this section we present the memory latency and memory load bandwidth of Sandy Bridge and Westmere. Figure 2 shows the memory latency of two systems. It exhibits step function pattern with four steps; each step corresponds to L1 cache, L2 cache, L3 cache and main memory. L1 cache latency is 1.2 ns for both Sandy Bridge and Westmere. L2 cache latency is 3.5 ns and 3 ns for Sandy Bridge and Westmere respectively. L3 cache latency is 6.5 ns for both Sandy Bridge and Westmere. Main memory latency is 28 ns and 24 ns for Sandy Bridge and Westmere respectively. L2 cache latency and main memory latency is higher on Sandy Bridge than that on Westmere.

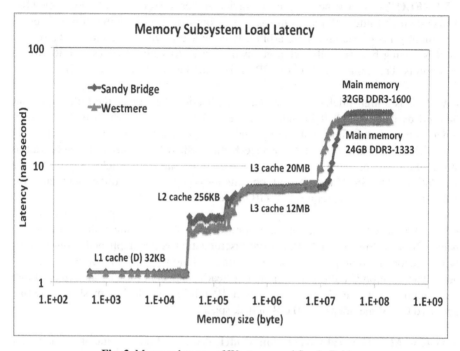

Fig. 2. Memory latency of Westmere and Sandy Bridge

Figure 3 shows the memory load bandwidth of L1 cache, L2 cache, L3 cache and main memory for the two systems. Read and write bandwidth is higher on Sandy Bridge than on Westmere except for L3 cache, where it higher on Westmere. The reason for higher read bandwidth is due to the fact that Sandy Bridge has two memory loads compared to one memory load in Westmere.

4.2   HPC Challenge Benchmarks (HPCC)

In this section we present results for HPCC Version 1.4.1 benchmarks for two systems [7]. We discuss the intra-node and inter-node performance separately.

Intra-Node HPCC Performance: In this section we present the intra-node HPCC results for Westmere and Sandy Bridge. In Figure 4 we show the performance of a subset of HPCC suite benchmarks. The performance gains by Sandy Bridge are 66%, 64%, 65%, 66%, 80%, and 141% for G-FFTE, EP-STREAM, G-Random Access, G-PTRANS, EP-DGEMM, and G-HPL, respectively, over Westmere. The performance of Sandy Bridge is superior to that of Westemere due to faster memory speed, extra memory controller, larger L3 cache, higher Gflop/s per core, etc.

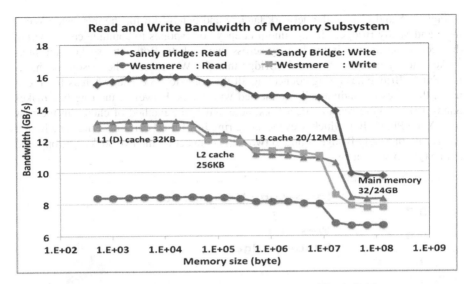

Fig. 3. Memory load bandwidth of Westmere and Sandy Bridge

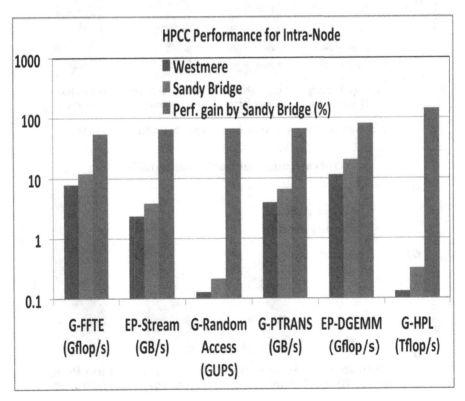

Fig. 4. Performance of HPCC on Westmere and Sandy Bridge nodes

Figures 5 and 6 show the network latency and bandwidth for the intra-node West-mere and Sandy Bridge. The minimum latency corresponds to communication within the socket and the maximum latency across two sockets. Both intra-socket and inter-socket latency is higher for Sandy Bridge than for Westmere. The reason for this is that Sandy Bridge has a ring connecting all the cores to L3 cache, whereas for West-mere, the cores are individually connected with wires. However, the ring bus makes Sandy Bridge more scalable than Westmere and is the method of choice in the new Intel Xeon Phi (MIC), which uses the same ring bus for 60 cores on a die. The higher bandwidth of Sandy Bridge is due to two QPIs connecting the two sockets as opposed to one QPI in Westmere.

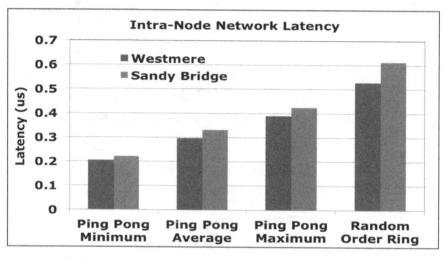

Fig. 5. Network latency of Westmere and Sandy Bridge within nodes

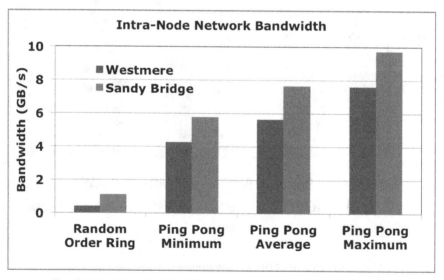

Fig. 6. Network bandwidth of Westmere and Sandy Bridge within nodes

Inter-Node HPCC Performance: In this section we present inter-node HPCC results for the two systems [7]. In Figure 7, we plot performance of the compute-intensive embarrassingly parallel (EP) DGEMM (matrix-matrix multiplication) for the two systems. The theoretical one-core peak for Sandy Bridge is 20.8 Gflop/s, and for Westmere it is 11.7 Gflop/s. When using Turbo mode on Westmere, the processor core frequency can be increased by up to three 133 MHz increments, raising its peak to 13.32 Gflop/s. The performance gain by Sandy Bridge is 20% to 30% for numbers of cores ranging from 16 to 512 due to the fact that it has higher compute performance per core and has a 20% faster memory speed (1600 MHz vs. 1333 MHz).

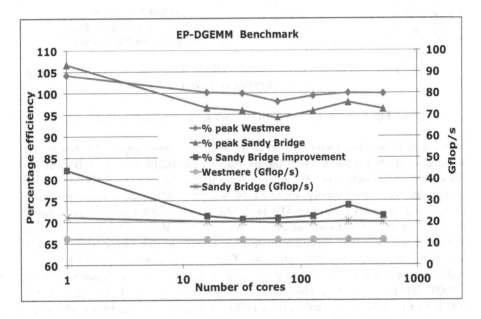

Fig. 7. Performance of EP-DGEMM on Westmere and Sandy Bridge

In Figure 8, we plot performance of the compute-intensive global high-performance LINPACK (G-HPL) benchmark. For both Sandy Bridge and Westmere we give the efficiency for their base frequencies of 2.6 GHz and 2.93 GHz, respectively. The efficiency of Westmere is higher than that of Sandy Bridge and decreases gradually from 16 to 512 cores. In addition, the efficiency of Westmere is higher than that of Sandy Bridge in the entire range of cores except for 16 and 512 cores. The performance gain by Sandy Bridge in terms of floating-point operations is 68% to 87% better than that on Westmere due to better memory bandwidth per core and better Gflop/s performance per core.

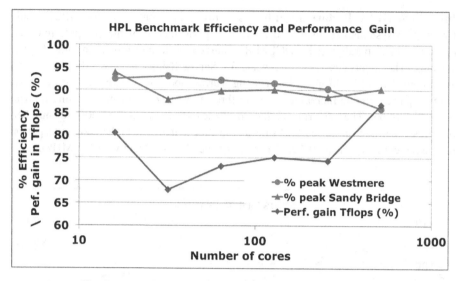

Fig. 8. Performance of G-HPL on Westmere and Sandy Bridge

In Figure 9, we show memory bandwidth for each system using the EP-Stream Tri-ad benchmark. For a single core, the measured bandwidths were 14 GB/s and 9.6 GB/s for Sandy Bridge and Westmere, respectively, i.e., 45.8% higher for Sandy Bridge due to faster memory speed (1600 vs. 1333 MHz; 20% faster on Sandy Bridge) and larger L3 cache (2.5 MB vs. 2 MB per core; 25% larger cache on Sandy Bridge). For 16 cores, these values decreased to 3.8 GB/s and 2.6 GB/s due to memory contention. The aggregate node level bandwidth for Sandy Bridge in fully subscribed mode was then 3.8 x 16 = 60.8 GB/s, which translates into 59 percent of peak-memory bandwidth (102.4 GB/s per node = 2 processors x 4 channels x 8 bytes x 1600 MHz per processor). The faster memory bus enables Sandy Bridge to deliver both higher peak-memory bandwidth and efficiency, producing significant advantages for memory-intensive codes.

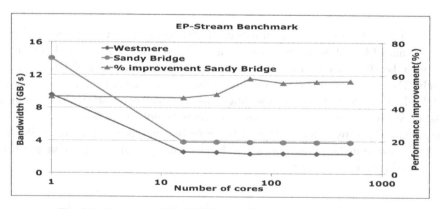

Fig. 9. Performance of EP-STREAM on Westmere and Sandy Bridge

In Figure 10, we show the minimum, average and maximum Ping-Pong latency for Westmere and Sandy Bridge. The minimum latency on both systems is around 0.25 μs, this corresponding to latency within a processor/socket. The maximum latency on both systems is around 2 μs, except for 16 cores where latency for Sandy Bridge is 74% lower than that on Westmere. This is because for Westmere, one needs two nodes (12 cores each), whereas one needs only one Sandy Bridge node (16 cores). The average latency of Sandy Bridge is lower than Westmere by 12% to 24%, except for 16 cores where it is better by 60%.

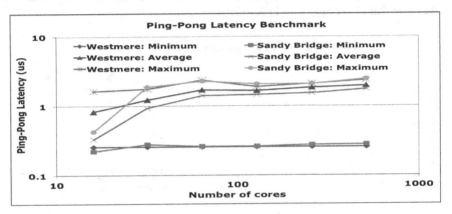

Fig. 10. Ping-Pong Latency on Westmere and Sandy Bridge

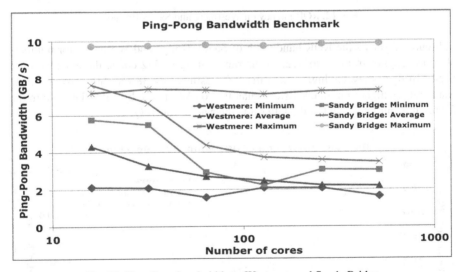

Fig. 11. Ping-Pong bandwidth on Westmere and Sandy Bridge

Figure 11 shows the minimum, average and maximum ping-pong bandwidth for Westmere and Sandy Bridge. The maximum bandwidth is within 16 cores on one Sandy Bridge node and two Westmere nodes. The maximum bandwidths are 9.8 GB/s and 7.2 GB/s for Sandy Bridge and Westmere, respectively. The reason for this is that for 16 cores, Sandy Bridge has two sockets with 8 cores each connected via 2 QPI with 8 GT/s, whereas Westmere has 2 sockets with 6 cores each connected via one QPI of 5 GT/s and it is via QDR to another node. For a large number of cores, bandwidth is again higher in Sandy Bridge nodes than Westmere nodes, as the former is connected by FDR and latter by QDR.

Figure 12 shows the Random Order Ring (ROR) latency for Sandy Bridge and Westmere. For 16 cores, latency for Sandy Bridge is lower than that of Westmere because in the former it is intra-node latency, whereas in the latter it is inter -node latency. For numbers of cores ranging from 32 to 512, latency for Sandy Bridge is higher than that of Westmere by 11% to 70%.

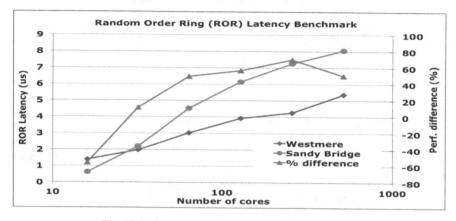

Fig. 12. ROR latency on Westmere and Sandy Bridge

Figure 13 shows the ROR bandwidth of Sandy Bridge and Westmere for numbers of cores ranging from 16 to 512. In the range of 32 to 512 cores, the bandwidth on Sandy Bridge is always higher than that of Westmere by 38% to 80%. At 16 cores, bandwidth is higher on Sandy Bridge than that on Westmere by 155% because in the former it is intra node and in the latter it is inter node via IB QDR.

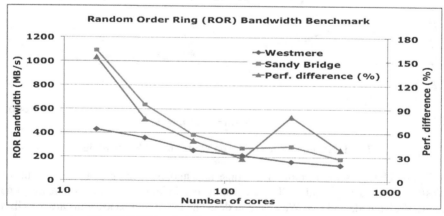

Fig. 13. ROR bandwidth on Westmere and Sandy Bridge

In Figure 14, we plot performance of the Random Access benchmark as Giga Updates per second (GUP/s) for 16 to 512 cores for the two systems. In the entire range of cores we studied, the performance was much better on Sandy Bridge than on Westmere. Up to 32 cores, the performance on Sandy Bridge is higher than that on Westmere by 17%. The superior performance on Sandy Bridge is due to the FDR IB and higher memory bandwidth. Scaling is very good on Sandy Bridge and Westmere because of the almost constant bisection bandwidth for 512 cores of the hypercube topology used in these two systems.

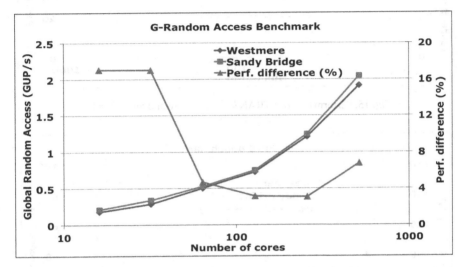

Fig. 14. GUP benchmark on Westmere and Sandy Bridge

In Figure 15, we plot the performance of the PTRANS benchmark for the two systems. The benchmark performance primarily depends on the network and to a lesser extent on memory bandwidth. At 512 cores, it was 74 GB/s for Sandy Bridge and 51.3 GB/s on Westmere. The performance was better by 44% on Sandy Bridge than on Westmere due to the use of FDR IB. Scaling of the benchmark was very good on both systems because of the constant bisection bandwidth for the relatively small number of cores (up to 512) on these two systems.

In Figure 16, we plot the performance of the G-FFT benchmark on Sandy Bridge and Westmere. The benchmark's performance depends on a combination of flops, memory, and network bandwidth. The FDR IB and higher sustained-memory bandwidth enable Sandy Bridge to outperform Westmere. Scaling was better on Sandy Bridge than on Westmere. At 512 cores, performance was 166.2 and 123.4 Gflop/s on Sandy Bridge and Westmere, respectively. We note that the performance on Sandy Bridge is especially high at 16, 64, and 256 cores. The reason for this is that for Sandy Bridge, these numbers correspond to whole number of 1, 4 and 16 nodes, whereas for Westmere, they correspond to 2, 6 and 22 nodes. FFT involves all-to-all communication, which takes much longer in the case of Westmere due to poor network (QDR IB vs. FDR IB).

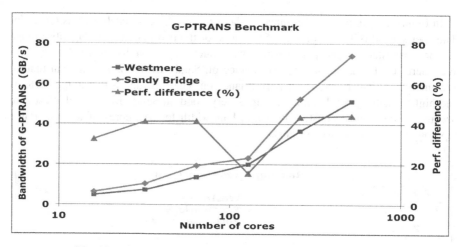

Fig. 15. Performance of PTRANS on Westmere and Sandy Bridge

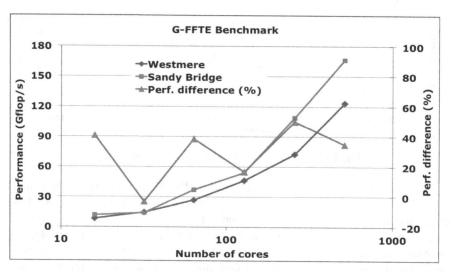

Fig. 16. Performance of G-FFTE on Westmere and Sandy Bridge

4.3   Science and Engineering Applications

In this subsection, we focus on the comparative performance of four full applications (Overflow, Cart3D, USM3D, and MITgcm) on the two systems [10-13]. The time for all the four applications is for the main loop, i.e., compute and communication time, and does not include I/O time.

Figures 17-20 provide the performance and scalability of the four full-scale applications used in this study. Each figure shows the scaling performance on the Sandy Bridge and Westmere systems along with the percentage performance gain on Sandy Bridge.

Overflow: Figure 17 shows time per step for 16 cores to 512 cores for Overflow. The performance of Overflow on Sandy Bridge is much better than on the Westmere system across the entire range of cores. The Overflow performance on Sandy Bridge is higher by 29% to 46% for cores ranging from 16 to 512 cores. Overflow is a memory-intensive application, and therefore performance was better on Sandy Bridge than on Westmere because memory bandwidth per core of the former is better (3.8 vs. 2.6 GB/s), an advantage of 46%. About 20% of the performance gain of Overflow on Sandy Bridge is from faster memory speed (1600 MHz vs. 1333 MHz). In addition, Sandy Bridge has an advantage, especially for large numbers of cores, as its L3 cache is 2.5 MB per core compared with 2 MB per core of L3 for Westmere, which translates into a gain of 25%.

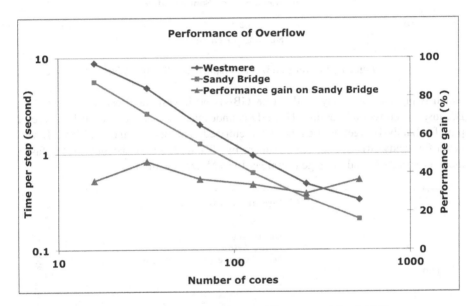

Fig. 17. Time per step for Overflow on Westmere and Sandy Bridge

Cart3D: Figure 18 shows the time to run Cart3D for 16 cores to 512 cores on the two systems. The performance of Cart3D was higher on Sandy Bridge than on Westmere by about 20% due to faster memory speed (1600 MHz vs. 1333 MHz). Using Intel Performance Monitor Unit (PMU) we found that Cart3D is only 1% vectorized so it does not benefit from 256-bit long vector pipeline of Sandy Bridge [21].

USM3D: Figure 19 shows the USM3D cycle time per step for a range of cores. USM3D is an unstructured mesh-based application that solves a sparse matrix by the Gauss-Seidel method and uses indirect addressing. The L2/L3 caches are poorly utilized, and almost the entire data has to come from main memory. Using PMU, we found that 72% of the data comes from the main memory [21]. Being memory-intensive, its performance depends exclusively on the memory bandwidth,

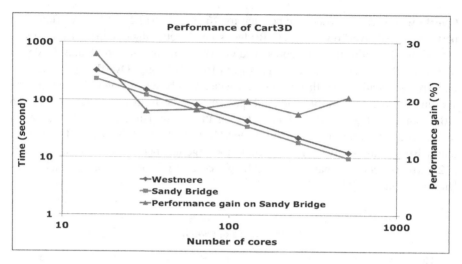

Fig. 18. Time for Cart3D on Westmere and Sandy Bridge

which is highest for Sandy Bridge (3.8 GB/s) and lowest for Westmere (2.6 GB/s). Because of indirect addressing, USM3D cannot make use of the 256-bit long vector pipe for Sandy Bridge, as it cannot be vectorized. The performance of USM3D was better on Sandy Bridge than on Westmere by 20% to 25%, consistent with the faster memory speed of Sandy Bridge (1600 vs. 1333 MHz), a gain of 20%.

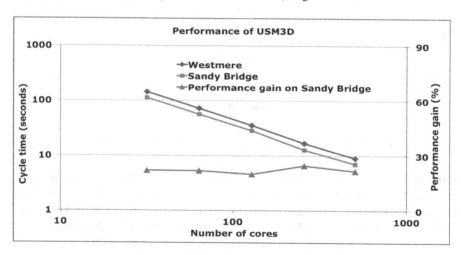

Fig. 19. Time for USM3D on Westmere and Sandy Bridge

MITgcm: Figure 20 shows the time to run the climate modeling application MITgcm [13]. This code is memory-bound and network bound. Since Sandy Bridge provides the higher memory bandwidth (3.8 GB/s vs 2.6 GB/s) and better network (FDR IB vs QDR IB), MITgcm performs much better on this system than on Westmere by about 40%.

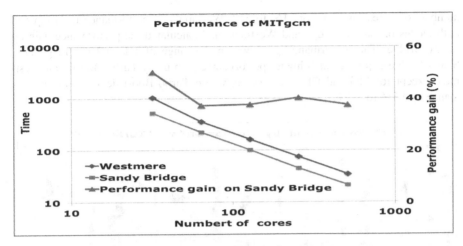

Fig. 20. Time for MITgcm on Westmere and Sandy Bridge

Figure 21 shows a summary of the performance gain by Sandy Bridge over Westmere for four applications: Overflow, Cart3D, USM3D and MITgcm. Using PMU, we found that USM3D and Cart3D have a low vectorization of 20% and 1% respectively and thus cannot make use of the 256-bit long vector pipe [21]. However, both the applications are memory bound; therefore, they benefit from faster memory speed (1600 MHz vs. 1333 MHz; 20% faster on Sandy Bridge) and exhibit performance gains of 17% to 20%. On the other hand, the other two applications, Overflow and MITgcm, have 64% and 50% vectorization, respectively, and are also memory-bound, so their performance gain is much higher (20% to 50%).

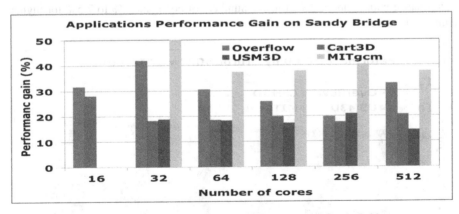

Fig. 21. Applications performance on Westmere and Sandy Bridge

Performance Impact of Turbo Boost

In this subsection, we compare results for the MPI version of the NPB with Turbo Boost on and off. Figure 22 shows the measured performance gain of Turbo Boost on Sandy Bridge over Westmere. We ran six NPBs (MG, SP, CG, FT, LU, and BT) for numbers of cores ranging from 16 to 512. We tabulated performance in Gflop/s in both modes on Sandy Bridge and Westmere and calculated the performance gain by Sandy Bridge. The performance gain was in the range of 1% to 10%. In general, Sandy Bridge enjoys a much higher performance gain using Turbo Boost than Westmere except for MG and FT at 512 cores, where Turbo Boost degrades the performance by 1.7% to 3.2%.

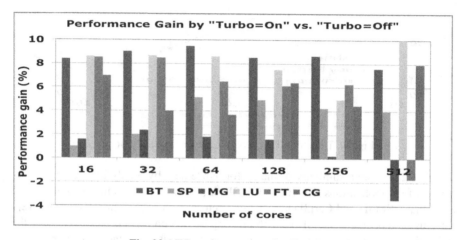

Fig. 22. NPB performance on Sandy Bridge

Figure 23 shows the performance gain in Turbo mode for Sandy Bridge for the applications Overflow, Cart3D, USM3D and MITgcm. The performance gain due to Turbo mode by Overflow and Cart3D is 8% to 10%. For MITgcm and USM3D, the performance gain is about 3% at lower numbers of cores and 6% to 7.5% for higher number of cores.

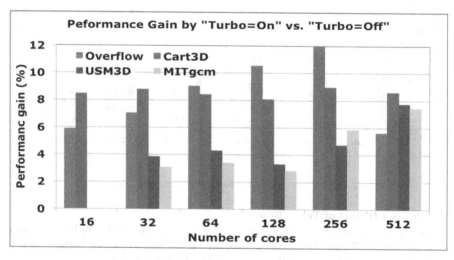

Fig. 23. Applications performance on Sandy Bridge

Performance Impact of AVX

Figure 24 shows the performance gain of AVX in Sandy Bridge for the Class C size of six NPB benchmarks [22]. The largest difference between the AVX and SSE4.2 is for the compute intensive benchmarks (e.g.,BT and LU) and the least gain is by memory-bound benchmarks (e.g., MG and SP). We see for BT the benchmark AVX version versus SSE 4.2 version gives 6-10% improvement, whereas it is 6% for EP, 2-4% for FT, 7-12% for LU, 2-4% for MG, and 1-5% for SP. CG is the only benchmark whose performance degrades in AVX mode. CG uses a sparse BLAS-2 (sparse matrix times vector) and involves indirect addressing, and as such, it cannot be vectorized so unable to use the vector pipeline.

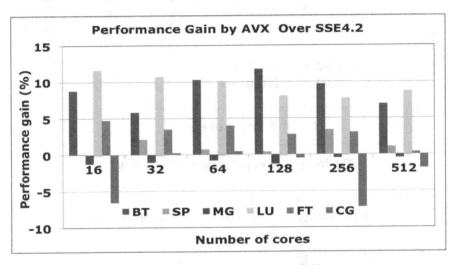

Fig. 24. NPB performance on Sandy Bridge

Figure 25 shows the performance gain in AVX in Sandy Bridge for the four applications. The performance gain for these applications is almost insignificant and ranges from +2% to -3%. Cart3D shows higher performance in AVX mode.However, memory bound applications such as Overflow, MITgcm, and USM3D don't benefit from AVX; in fact, their performance degrades.

Impact of Hyper-Threading

In Figures 26 and 27, we show the performance gain from HT by Overflow, Cart3D, USM3D and MITgcm on Sandy Bridge and Westmere. With HT, the node can handle twice as many processes (32/24) as without HT (16/12). With more processes per node, there is greater communication overhead. In other words, more processes compete for the same host channel adapter (HCA) on the node. On the other hand, additional processes (or threads) can steal cycles in cases of communications imbalance or memory access stalls. The result is better overall performance for main memory bound applications. For example, USM3D, where 70% of the data comes from main memory because of indirect addressing, can't reuse the L2/L3 cache and

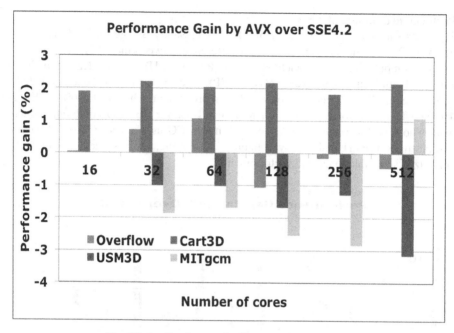

Fig. 25. Applications performance on Sandy Bridge

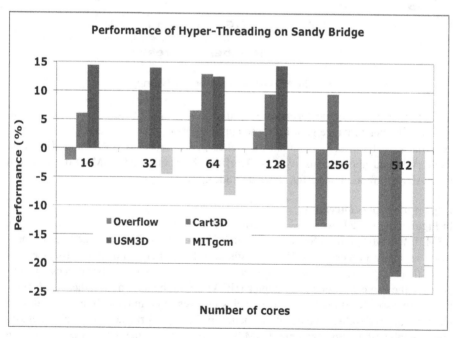

Fig. 26. Applications performance gain from HT on Sandy Bridge

thus gets an opportunity to hide the memory latency. Cart3D also benefits from HT as the code is 99% scalar and has more opportunities to schedule the instructions in the pipeline. Overflow and MITgcm are 64% and 51% vectorized, respectively, so they do not benefit from HT as there is saturation of floating point units. The reason why Overflow does not benefit from HT is because it is very cache-sensitive. Running in HT mode reduces the amount of L3 cache available to each process, so data has to be fetched from main memory instead of from L3 cache, causing HT performance to suffer [3]. On Sandy Bridge, the performance gain by HT for USM3D and Cart3D is almost two times that on Westmere.

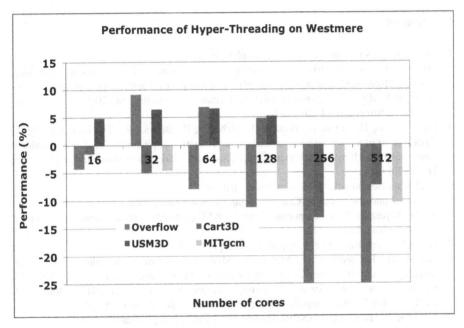

Fig. 27. Applications performance gain from HT on Westmere

5   Conclusions

In this paper, we conducted a comprehensive performance evaluation and analysis of the Pleiades-Sandy Bridge computing platform, using low-level benchmarks, the NPB, and four NASA applications. Our key findings are as follows:

- The revamped Turbo Boost 2.0 overclocking mechanism on Sandy Bridge is more efficient than the prior implementation TB 1.0 on Westmere. The impact of Turbo Boost in Sandy Bridge is almost doubled relative to Westmere (9% vs. 4%).
- The advantage of AVX over SSE4.2 instructions is insignificant, ranging from +2% to -3%.

- The performance of Hyper-Threading technology on Sandy Bridge is much better than that on Westmere and is helpful in some cases, but for HPC applications this is not universal. The impact of Hyper-Threading on Sandy Bridge is almost doubled that on Westmere for USM3D and Cart3D (10% vs. 4%).
- The memory bandwidth of Sandy Bridge is about 40% higher than that of Westmere.
- The performance of 4x FDR IB is 40% better than that of 4x QDR IB.
- The overall performance of Sandy Bridge is about 20% to 40% better than that of Westmere for the NASA workload.

References

1. http://www.nas.nasa.gov/hecc/resources/pleiades.html
2. Saini, S., Naraikin, A., Biswas, R., Barkai, D., Sandstrom, T.: Early performance evaluation of a "Nehalem" cluster using scientific and engineering applications. In: Proceedings of the ACM/IEEE Conference on High Performance Computing, SC 2009, Portland, Oregon, USA, November 14-20 (2009)
3. Saini, S., Jin, H., Hood, R., Barker, D., Mehrotra, P., Biswas, R.: The impact of hyper-threading on processor resource utilization in production applications. In: 8th International Conference on High Performance Computing, HiPC 2011, Bengaluru, India, December 18-21 (2011)
4. Intel Xeon Benchmark - Intel.com, www.intel.com/Xeon
5. Texas Advanced Computing Center – *Stampede*, www.tacc.utexas.edu/stampede
6. NCAR-Wyoming Supercomputing Center (NWSC), https://www2.cisl.ucar.edu/resources/yellowstone/hardware
7. HPC Challenge Benchmarks, http://icl.cs.utk.edu/hpcc/
8. Schöne, R., Hackenberg, D., Molka, D.: Memory performance at reduced CPU clock speeds: an analysis of current x86_64 processors. In: Proceedings of the 2012 USENIX Conference on Power-Aware Computing and Systems (HotPower 2012), Hollywood, USA, October 7 (2012), http://dl.acm.org/citation.cfm?id=2387869.2387878
9. NAS Parallel Benchmarks (NPB), http://www.nas.nasa.gov/publications/npb.html
10. OVERFLOW, http://aaac.larc.nasa.gov/~buning/
11. Mavriplis, D.J., Aftosmis, M.J., Berger, M.: High Resolution Aerospace Applications using the NASA Columbia Supercomputer. In: Proc. ACM/IEEE, SC 2005, Seattle, WA (2005)
12. USM3D, http://tetruss.larc.nasa.gov/usm3d/
13. M.I.T General Circulation Model (MITgcm), http://mitgcm.org/
14. Saini, S., Talcott, D., Jespersen, D., Djomehri, J., Jin, H., Biswas, R.: Scientific application-based performance comparison of SGI Altix 4700, IBM POWER5+, and SGI ICE 8200 supercomputers. In: High Performance Computing, Networking, Storage and Analysis, SC 2008, Austin, Texas, November 15-21 (2008)
15. Morozov, V., Kumaran, K., Vishwanath, V., Meng, J., Papka, M.E.: Early Experience on the Blue Gene/Q Supercomputing System. In: IEEE IPDPS, Boston, May 20-23 (2013)
16. Barker, K., Davis, K., Hoisie, A., Kerbyson, D.J., Lang, M., Pakin, S., Sancho, J.C.: Entering the Petaflop Era: The Architecture and Performance of Roadrunner. In: Proceedings of IEEE/ACM Supercomputing, SC 2008, Austin, TX (November 2008)

17. Barker, K., Hoisie, A., Kerbyson, D.: An Early Performance Analysis of POWER7-IH HPC Systems. In: SC 2011, Seattle, November 12-18 (2011)
18. Kerbyson, D.J., Barker, K.J., Vishnu, A., Hoisie, A: Comparing the Performance of Blue Gene/Q with Leading Cray XE6 and InfiniBand Systems. In: ICPADS 2012, pp. 556–563 (2012)
19. Alam, S., Barrett, R., Bast, M., Fahey, M., Kuehn, J., McCurdy, C., Rogers, J., Roth, P., Sankaran, R., Vetter, J., Worley, P., Yu, W.: Early Evaluation of IBM BlueGene/P. In: Proceedings of the ACM/IEEE International Conference for High Performance Computing, Networking, Storage and Analysis, SC 2008, Austin, TX, November 15-21 (2008)
20. Alam, S.R., Barrett, R.F., Fahey, M.R., Kuehn, J.A., Messer, O.E., Mills, R.T., Roth, P.C., Vetter, J.S., Worley, P.H.: An Evaluation of the ORNL Cray XT3. International Journal for High Performance Computer Applications 22, 52–80 (2008)
21. *PMU* Performance Monitoring PerfMon | *Intel®* Developer Zone software.intel.com/en-us/tags/18842
22. Intel® Architecture Instruction Set Extensions Programming Reference, 319433-014 (August 2012) http://software.intel.com/en-us/avx

Analysis of Cray XC30 Performance Using Trinity-NERSC-8 Benchmarks and Comparison with Cray XE6 and IBM BG/Q

M.J. Cordery[1]([✉]), Brian Austin[1], H.J. Wassermann[1], C.S. Daley[1],
N.J. Wright[1], S.D. Hammond[2], and D. Doerfler[2]

[1] NERSC, Lawrence Berkeley National Laboratory, Berkeley, CA, USA
{mjcordery,baustin,hjwasserman,csdaley,njwright}@lbl.gov
[2] Center for Computing Research, Sandia National Laboratories Albuquerque,
Albuquerque, NM, USA
{sdhammo,dwdoerf}@sandia.gov

Abstract. In this paper, we examine the performance of a suite of applications on three different architectures: Edison, a Cray XC30 with Intel Ivy Bridge processors; Hopper and Cielo, both Cray XE6's with AMD Magny–Cours processors; and Mira, an IBM BlueGene/Q with PowerPC A2 processors. The applications chosen are a subset of the applications used in a joint procurement effort between Lawrence Berkeley National Laboratory, Los Alamos National Laboratory and Sandia National Laboratories. Strong scaling results are presented, using both MPI-only and MPI+OpenMP execution models.

Keywords: Benchmarking · HPC · Performance

1 Introduction

The classic parallel programming model, MPI, faces several new challenges on petaflop computing platforms, which are dominated by multicore-per-node architectures [1,2]. These challenges include reduced memory capacity per core, reduced memory and network bandwidth per core, and the inefficiency of using two-sided messages to handle a large amount of fine-grain communication. These challenges will only be exacerbated as the field of high performance computing moves forward into the exa-scale era wherein application developers will no longer be able to achieve significant performance and scalability gains with an MPI-only programming model. As on-node parallelism increases, effective use of future technologies will require exposing more fine-grained data parallelism, better management of data placement and data movement, exploiting longer vector units, and exploring task-based parallelism and communication reducing algorithms. To this end, several laboratories within the Department of Energy (DOE) are collaborating on the FastForward project to research both new technologies and new execution models. While this program advances, DOE laboratories are working with their scientists and code development teams to address these issues.

© Springer International Publishing Switzerland 2014
S. Jarvis et al. (Eds.): PMBS 2013 Workshops, LNCS 8551, pp. 52–72, 2014.
DOI: 10.1007/978-3-319-10214-6_3

This collaborative effort also extends to the realm of system procurement where, in a debut effort, Lawrence Berkeley Laboratory (LBL), Los Alamos National Laboratory (LANL) and Sandia National Laboratories (SNL) (the later two comprising ACES, the Alliance for Computing at Extreme Scales), have entered a partnership to jointly procure two systems. While one of the goals of this partnership is to drive favorable economies of scale, a substantial benefit is the opportunity for various DOE labs to better understand each other's system requirements and workload characteristics. This understanding will yield future architectures that cover the broadest range of scientific computing needs and are not defined by and targeted at any specific workload. As part of this pro-curement, each of the involved laboratories contributed a selection of benchmark codes that represent an important part of their workload. The primary aim of this paper is to evaluate the performance characteristics of this new suite of benchmarks on state-of-the art platforms, especially at high concurrencies. Fur-thermore we are interested in how well different execution models perform on different architectures, especially the comparison between the classical MPI-only execution model and a hybrid model using many relatively lightweight threads. To this end, we present results showing how each benchmark strong scales on three different architectures: Edison, a Cray XC30 at NERSC; Hopper, a Cray XE6 (also at NERSC); and Mira and Vulcan, both IBM Blue Gene/Q machines at Argonne National Laboratory and Lawrence Livermore National Laboratory, respectively. We compare and contrast the performance of the selected bench-marks on each machine when using an MPI-only execution model and, at the other extreme, how each scales when using the maximum number of OpenMP threads possible on a node (or, in the case of Hopper and Edison, the maximum number of threads possible in a NUMA domain). Short of an exhaustive study, this will give us some sense of the range of performance possible for intermediate mixes of MPI tasks and OpenMP threads. It is also of interest to us how this new suite of benchmarks aligns with previous metrics of system performance, in this case NERSC's Sustained System Performance (SSP) metric.

In summary, the principle contributions of this paper are

- On a node-per-node basis, the Cray XC-30 offers a significant performance advantage over both the Cray XE6 and IBM's BlueGene/Q, by 1.8-3.8x and 1.8-9.4x respectively, over a range of node counts. Based on a metric of performance per watt, however, the Cray XE6 and the BlueGene/Q are more equivalent.
- For the benchmarks used in this paper, over the range of nodes considered, hybrid MPI+OpenMP applications currently run slower than MPI applica-tions across all platforms. The principle reason for this appears to be that the OpenMP implementations of the applications are not as efficient as the MPI ones at expressing parallelism.
- The benchmarks used, which represent the workloads at leading DOE super-computing centers, have low computational intensity and their performance is primarily limited by memory bandwidth.

The paper is organized as follows: Section 2 describes the experimental platforms. Section 3 presents a description of the benchmark applications used as well as their general strategies for both MPI and OpenMP parallelism. Performance results of the benchmark applications and microbenchmarks are presented in Section 4. Related work is presented in Section 5. Finally, we summarize our conclusions and future work in Section 6.

2 Test Platform Descriptions

2.1 BlueGene/Q: Mira and Vulcan

BlueGene/Q is the third revision to IBM's high-performance BlueGene architecture. Each BG/Q node consists of embedded PowerPC cores clocked at 1.6GHz which include a 256-bit SIMD (QPX) vector processing unit. Each core is dual-issue, 4-way multithreaded, and has a 16KB L1 data cache. In order to run at the dual-issue rate, at least two threads must be running per core. Each BG/Q processor chip contains 18 cores (with 16 being available to the user, one to handle OS tasks, and a spare core to increase chip yields) connected with a crossbar to a 32MB L2 and the network interface. The two memory controllers per chip can provide a sustained bandwidth of up to 28 GB/s to 16GB of DRAM. Nodes are connected in a high-bandwidth 5D torus. In this paper, we use both the Mira machine located at Argonne National Laboratory (49,152 nodes) and Vulcan, an open-science relative of Sequoia, installed at the Lawrence Livermore National Laboratory (24,576 nodes). Although the machines vary in size, the operating system and compiler implementation are identical and so we treat them as equivalent for the purposes of benchmarking the BlueGene/Q architecture.

2.2 Cray XE6: Hopper

Hopper is a Cray XE6 machine deployed at NERSC. The XE6 is based on commodity AMD processors connected via HyperTransport to a custom interconnect. Each processor includes six 2.1GHz AMD Opteron cores with each core having a 128-bit SIMD (SSE3) vector floating-point unit, and 64KB L1 and 512KB L2 caches. Cores are connected to a 6MB L3 cache (1MB reserved as a probe filter) and two DDR3-1333 memory controllers. There are four processor chips per node. The interconnect is a Cray custom-designed "Gemini" architecture. Each Gemini chip is connected to two nodes, and the Gemini chips are connected together in a 3D-torus with dimensions 17x8x24.

2.3 Cray XC30: Edison

Edison is a Cray XC30 (Cascade) supercomputer recently installed at NERSC. The XC30 architecture is based on commodity Intel processors connected via PCI Express 3.0 to a custom interconnect. Each processor is a 12-core, 2.4 GHz Intel E-series Xeon (Ivy Bridge). The core includes a 256-bit SIMD (AVX) vector

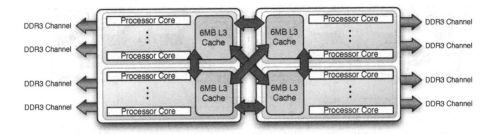

Fig. 1. Node Architecture of Hopper

floating-point unit and 32KB L1 and 256KB L2 caches. Each processor-core permits up to two-way hyperthreading and is connected to the four DDR3-1866 memory controllers and 20MB L3 cache via an arbitrated ring-bus. Nodes of Edison feature two processor sockets and are grouped into quad-node blades for connection to a dragonfly topology interconnect via a Cray Aries NIC. In total, the machine contains 5200 compute nodes, providing over 120,000 compute cores.

3   Benchmarks Descriptions and Problem Definitions

In the emerging many-core era, it will become impractical for applications to run with an MPI-only programming model. The rapidly increasing number of cores per node and the relatively slow growth of associated memory and memory bandwidth means that each MPI task will not only be able to access smaller amounts of memory and memory bandwidth than today, but will also encounter more contention for on- and off-node network resources. For these reasons, there is increasing pressure to move applications to hybrid execution models where, say, MPI is used for decomposing problems across nodes at a coarse level and a lightweight threaded API is used to perform finer-grained compute work (and possibly handle communications) on a node. To this end, we are interested in the ability of the applications presented below to scale with an increasing number of threads and how that performance compares to an MPI-only programming model.

For each application, we present a set of strong scaling results using an MPI-only execution model and an MPI+OpenMP model. In the former, we increase only the number of MPI ranks and in the latter we increase the number of MPI ranks but only use one MPI rank per socket, filling the remainder of the compute cores on each socket with OpenMP threads. In each case, we completely fill each node on each machine with either tasks or tasks and threads (though we do not examine hyper-threading on Edison) and then compare results on a node-per-node basis and examine what tradeoffs or limitations might exist.

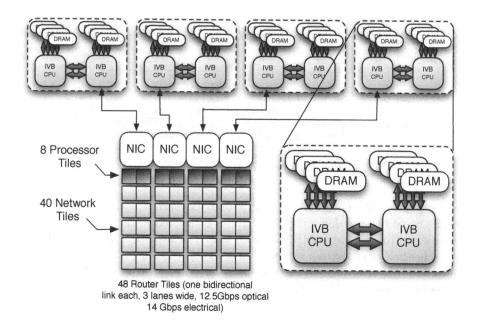

8 Processor
Tiles

40 Network
Tiles

NIC NIC NIC NIC

48 Router Tiles (one bidirectional
link each, 3 lanes wide, 12.5Gbps optical
14 Gbps electrical)

Fig. 2. Cray XC30 Node Architecture

In summary, for the three test platforms our execution modes are:

– **Mira/Vulcan**
  - 16 MPI tasks per node, 4 OpenMP threads per core
  - 1 MPI task per node, 64 OpenMP threads
– **Hopper**
  - 24 MPI tasks per node
  - 4 MPI tasks per node, 6 OpenMP threads per NUMA domain (24 OpenMP threads in total)
– **Edison**
  - 24 MPI tasks per node
  - 2 MPI tasks per node, 12 OpenMP threads per NUMA domain (24 OpenMP threads in total)

Each of the benchmark problems (except FLASH) is a smaller version of the large problems defined for the NERSC8/Trinity procurement. Each problem was weak-scaled down by two to four times in order to provide a sufficiently interesting range of data points for the compute capabilities of the test platforms. Each of the benchmark codes and problem definitions is now briefly described.

3.1 MILC

MILC (MIMD Lattice Computation) is a widely used, computationally intense application designed to compute gauge fields as described by the theory of quantum chromodynamics (QCD). The computational grid is a four-dimensional space-time grid (x, y, z, t) with quark fields, defined as 3x3 complex vectors, at the grid points and gluon variables, defined as 3x3 unitary matrices, defined at the 'links' between grid points [3]. The most computationally intense part of the program is the conjugate gradient solver which determines how the motion of the quarks is affected by the gluons [3]. The four dimensional lattice is decomposed so that the sub-grid assigned to each MPI task has the minimum possible surface-to-volume ratio. Following Gottlieb and Tamhankar [4], the code has fine-grain parallelism implemented with OpenMP directives, mostly on loops over all grid points in the lattice. Communications in MILC are largely dominated by point-to-point transfers associated with the 4D halo exchanges and global reductions associated with the conjugate gradient solver. MILC has been an important part of previous NERSC procurements as it is representative of NERSC's high energy physics workload and because the stencil computation and conjugate gradient solver stress both the memory and interconnect bandwidths, respectively.

The four dimensional space-time grid (x, y, z, t) used for this paper has dimensions 64x64x64x192. At the base concurrency of 12288 MPI tasks, this yields an 8x8x8x8 grid for each MPI task.

3.2 GTC

GTC is a 3-dimensional code used to study microturbulence in magnetically confined toroidal fusion plasmas via the Particle-In-Cell (PIC) method [5]. GTC is used for fusion energy research and thus represents an important part of NERSC's workload. It solves the gyro-averaged Vlasov equation in real space using global gyrokinetic techniques and an electrostatic approximation. The Vlasov equation describes the evolution of a system of particles under the effects of self-consistent electromagnetic fields. The unknown is the flux, $f(t, x, v)$, which is a function of time t , position x, and velocity v, and represents the distribution of particles (electrons and ions) in phase space. This model assumes a collision-less plasma; i.e., the particles interact with one another only through a self-consistent field and thus the algorithm scales as N instead of N^2, where N is the number of particles. The version of GTC used here uses a fixed 1-D spatial decomposition with 64 domains in the toroidal direction and P particle domains within a toroidal domain for a total of 64*P MPI tasks. Fine-grained parallelism is implemented by using OpenMP over the particles in a particle domain and some grid related work within a toroidal domain. Communications in GTC are largely dominated by MPI allreduces that merge each task's copy of the field and MPI send/receives that move particles between domains. Furthermore, because of the gather/scatter particle operations in GTC, the code is known to be particularly sensitive to memory latency [5], though it is also sensitive to memory bandwidth.

It is not possible to strong scale GTC without fundamentally changing the problem because the number of MPI tasks is fixed by the number of particle domains (see above). Increasing the MPI concurrency would also increase the number of particles being simulated. Hence, rather than examining strong scaling through MPI, we examine the strong scaling through OpenMP threads, i.e. we fix the MPI concurrency and increase the number of nodes used by increasing the number of OpenMP threads per node. The base problem size is defined for 4800 MPI tasks (75 particle domains) with 32,359 particles per MPI task.

3.3 FLASH

FLASH is a publicly available, multi-physics code with core capabilities which include Adaptive Mesh Refinement (AMR) and explicit solvers for hydrody-namics and magneto-hydrodynamics [6,7]. It has been used to simulate X-ray bursts, Type Ia supernovae, Core Collapse supernovae, galaxy cluster formation and laser-driven High Energy Density Physics (HEDP) experiments. It is paral-lelized by dividing the underlying mesh into blocks (patches) and assigning the blocks to different MPI tasks. Each block contains a halo of guard cells which are updated after each solver time-advancement. The solvers are multithreaded using conditionally compiled OpenMP directives around either loops over blocks or loops over grid points.

In this paper we run the Sedov test case, which is a pure hydrodynamics problem involving the self-similar evolution of a spherical blast wave from an initial pressure perturbation. The application is configured to use the unsplit hydrodynamics solver and a uniform resolution grid containing 1152^3 grid points. We use a uniform mesh and not the adaptive mesh provided by Paramesh because Paramesh is not multithreaded and so the MPI vs MPI+OpenMP comparison would be less interesting. The uniform mesh provides one block per MPI task and so the OpenMP directives over grid points are conditionally compiled into the application. Note that the uniform mesh is an important capability which is appropriate in simulations with relatively smooth fluid flow, such as simulations of weakly-compressible homogeneous isotropic turbulence [8].

3.4 Finite Element (MiniFE)

Many of the engineering applications in use at Sandia and other HPC computing sites require the implicit solution of a nonlinear system of equations. As these systems increase in size and complexity, the runtime becomes dominated by the performance of basic mathematical operations employed by the solver rou-tines - these typically feature some combination of dot-products, vector scaling or AXPBY operations and sparse-matrix-vector products.

The MiniFE mini-app [9], part of the Mantevo suite [10], is an implementation of a finite-element generation, assembly and solve for an unstructured problem. Although the solver employed in MiniFE - a simple conjugate gradient solver - is more simplistic than those used for production applications, the kernels that contribute to the CG solver provide many of the characteristics of those used in production applications and, in a number of studies, have been shown to provide reasonable runtime and behavioral correlation [11].

3.5   Unstructured Mesh Transport (UMT)

UMT is a proxy application from the NNSA's ASC program, written and maintained by LLNL, which performs the solution of a time- and energy-dependent discrete ordinate radiation problem in three dimensions on an spatially unstructured grid. The algorithm employs deterministic S_n methods to model the transfer of thermal protons in a three dimensional domain. Parallelism within the UMT code is provided by decomposing the unstructured spatial grid onto MPI tasks and using OpenMP threads to implement fine-grained parallel processing over angles during the transport phase.

4   Performance Results

4.1   STREAM

To measure the memory bandwidth performance, which can significantly impact many scientific codes, we ran the STREAM benchmark on each of the test platforms. For each platform, we configured the test to utilize 60% of the on–node memory. For Hopper and Edison, we ran separate copies of STREAM on each of the NUMA domains and used enough OpenMP threads to fill each domain. For Mira, we only ran one instance of the benchmark and ran with 64 OpenMP threads. The reported STREAM Triad results are as follows: Hopper - 53.9 GB/s, Edison - 103.3 GB/s, Mira - 28.6 GB/s per node.

Knowing the relative magnitude of the memory bandwidth between machines can be useful when comparing the performance of codes that are memory bandwidth sensitive. In Figure 3, we show roofline models of the three test platforms using the measured STREAM values and the known peak gigaflops/s/core rate defined by each platform's CPU clock speed and peak flops/clock. The roofline model [12] is a convenient visual means of identifying if a code is compute bound or memory bandwidth bound and can be used to guide optimization efforts. If a code makes good use of spatial and temporal locality in its memory references, the memory subsystem should be able to keep the vector units of the CPU full and thus the code should operate at near the peak floating point rate (compute bound). If not, a code's performance will be limited by the memory bandwidth (memory bandwidth bound). In the roofline model, these two variables, floating point performance and memory bandwidth, are assumed to be related through operational intensity, i.e. the number of floating point operations per byte of DRAM traffic. Thus, the roofline of a platform is defined by the following formula

$$PeakGFlops/s = MIN($$
$$PeakFloatingPointPerformance,$$
$$PeakMemoryBandwidth * OperationalIntensity)$$

The roofline for each compute platform is divided into two segments. The horizontal segment represents the upper floating-point limit imposed by the architecture. The sloped portion of the roofline represents the upper limit of performance imposed by the peak memory bandwidth of the system.

If we now measure the compute intensity and gigaflops/s rate of a code we can plot them in the figure. Codes which tend to fall on the horizontal portion of the roofline for a platform are considered to be compute bound as their performance is limited by the number of floating point operations that a CPU can execute each clock cycle. Codes which fall on the sloping part of the roofline are considered to be limited by memory bandwidth. Code performance may fall beneath the roofline if its performance is limited by the other features of the architecture or if it is composed of kernels with different computational intensities.

Figure 3 shows the measured performance of each of the Trinity/NERSC8 applications when running each application's 'large' test case on Hopper using an MPI-only execution model. The operational intensity for each code was measured using Cray's Craypat performance analysis tool and the gflops/s rates were determined using the floating point counts reported from IPM performance analysis tool and the run time values returned by each application. The results in this figure point out that the applications in the procurement, and those studied in more detail in this paper, are limited in performance by the rate that the memory subsystem can feed the processor. Simply adding more floating point capability will not increase performance. The other observation is that all of the benchmarks have relatively low computational intensity (<1), though it must be stressed that that the data points shown are for the entire code and not for any individual kernel which may show higher performance. Because of this, it will be difficult for any of these applications to attain a platform's peak floating point performance. This fact may have an impact on both machine inter-comparisons and the selection of systems for procurement. In the former case, architectures become compared based largely on their peak memory bandwidth and not the inherent computational advantages available on each processor. In the latter case, application developers and system procurement teams may find it easier to choose machines with higher peak memory bandwidth rather than refactoring their applications, or researching new algorithms, to better use the CPU. As CPUs increase in core count and complexity these issues may become increasingly prominent.

4.2   NERSC-6 Applications on Hopper and Edison

While the majority of this paper focuses on performance analysis of codes selected from the Trinity-NERSC8 benchmark suite, we also present results for the NERSC-6 application benchmarks [13] to facilitate comparison to previous benchmarking work on other computational platforms. Like the Trinity-NERSC8 suite, the NERSC-6 benchmarks were selected to span an appropriate cross-section of scientific domains and algorithms. The Community Atmospheric Model (CAM) is a significant component of the climate science workload; it uses 3-dimensional finite volume methods to simulate dynamical (e.g. fluid flow) and physical (e.g. precipitation) processes in the atmosphere. GAMESS implements a broad range of *ab initio* models of quantum chemistry. IMPACT-T is a relativistic particle-in-cell code used to simulate accelerator physics. MAE-STRO is an astrophysics code that uses algebraic multigrid methods to simulate

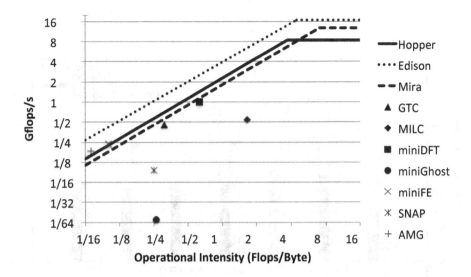

Fig. 3. Roofline model of test systems and NERSC8/Trinity benchmarks. The lines in the plot show the roofline for each test system which is obtained from the peak floating point performance per core and the measured memory bandwidth from the STREAM benchmark. Each symbol marks the actual results obtained on Hopper for test cases that run on order 1000 nodes.

pre-ignition phases of Type Ia supernovae. PARATEC is a plane-wave density functional theory code used for materials science; its functionality and performance characteristics are quite similar to MiniDFT, which has supplanted it in the Trinity-NERSC8 benchmark suite. GTC and MILC are included in both benchmark suites and were described in Section 3. Detailed descriptions of the NERSC-6 codes and inputs are available in [13].

One feature that distinguishes Edison's Ivy Bridge processors from Hopper's Magny–Cours processors is the availability of Hyperthreading Technology. When hyperthreading is enabled, each physical core presents itself to the OS as two logical cores. The logical cores share some resources of the physical core (such as cache, memory bandwidth and FPUs), but have independent architectural states. Hyperthreading has the potential to increase resource utilization if an application cannot exhaust a critical shared resource with a single instruction stream. Thus, on Edison jobs can be run in a single-stream mode (with one process per physical core) or dual-stream mode (with two processes per physical core). The sharing of resources generally causes dual-stream jobs to run roughly half as fast as single-stream jobs with the same MPI concurrency, but a net increase in throughput may be achieved if the dual-stream job uses half as many nodes for less than twice the single-stream walltime.

Figure 4 compares the performance of the NERSC-6 benchmarks on Hopper and Edison. Edison's single-stream performance is 1.9-2.6 times faster than

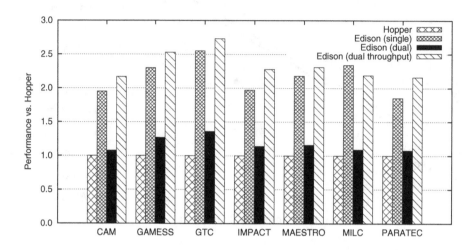

Fig. 4. NERSC-6 Application speedup relative to Hopper. Each benchmark was run on Hopper and on Edison in single- and dual-stream modes. The dual-stream throughput accounts for reduced node counts needed in dual-stream mode.

Hopper. The dual-stream performance is predictably about 50% less than single-stream, however dual-stream 'throughput performance' (which is identically 2x the dual-stream performance) is up to 2.75 greater than Hopper, and marginally better than the Edison single-stream performance for all codes except MILC. Edison's NERSC-6 SSP is 253 TF/s, nearly double Hopper's 137 TF/s.

4.3   Application Performance On Test Platforms

MILC. The strong scaling performance results for MILC are shown in Figure 5. The base configuration for these experiments was 12288 MPI tasks (512 nodes on Hopper/Edison and 192 nodes on Mira). Note that, for Mira, the node count is lower as we placed 64 MPI tasks on a node since MILC's memory usage for this problem can easily fit within the 16GB per node available.

Across the range of nodes where they overlap, the MPI-only runs on Edison are 2.2-3.8 times faster than on Hopper whereas they are 1.9-3.8 times faster than on Mira. The hybrid models on Edison compared to Hopper show a similar speedup as the MPI-only runs, but the hybrid runs on Edison are 6.8-9.4 times faster than on Mira.

For all three platforms, the hybrid model is slower than the MPI-only model. If we look in ranges where the parallel efficiency is still reasonably good, the hybrid models on Hopper are 2-3x slower than the MPI-only version, on Edison they are about 2x slower, and on Mira they are about 3.5x slower. Looked at another way, on both Hopper and Edison, the hybrid models need approximately twice the concurrency to equal the same performance as an MPI-only model. On Mira, the hybrid model needs nearly four times the concurrency. On the x86 architectures at least, this indicates that there are many serial sections remaining in the code.

As for scaling, the MPI-only/hybrid code on Hopper shows a 2.5x/3.9x speed up over an 8x increase in concurrency whereas on Edison there is a 4.2x/6.5x speedup. On Mira, the same versions show a 22.3x/24.5x speedup over a 64x increase in concurrency. One interesting feature is the bend in Mira's MPI-only scaling curve at 3072 nodes which is possibly due to a change in MPI protocols. This is supported by the fact that the hybrid model on Mira does not show this behavior - message sizes (which are presumed to trigger the protocol switch) are significantly larger for the hybrid code.

While it appears that the Hopper and Edison MPI-only models both become slower than their hybrid counterparts between 1024 and 2048 nodes, this effect is the result of a loss of scaling due to increased MPI traffic at higher MPI concurrencies. If we look at the compute time (wall clock - communication time) then this cross-over disappears and the hybrid compute times are slower than the MPI-only compute times across the range of nodes shown. The compute time only efficiency curves highlight the fact that while all of the models scale well out to 2048 nodes, they decline markedly after that point, presumably because they've reached the point where the serial portions of the OpenMP code start to become important.

The parallel efficiency figure is interesting that, while MILC on Edison shows some evidence of superlinear speedup for both the hybrid and MPI-only models, neither Hopper nor Mira do. The lack of superlinearity in the latter two platforms may simply be due to cache size differences. While MPI-only models of MILC often show superlinearity because of their typical memory footprint on a node, the hybrid version shows more. This is presumably because the working set per core of the hybrid code is smaller than in the MPI only version of the code.

GTC. The performance results for the OpenMP strong scaling experiment for GTC are shown in Figure 6. For Hopper, we ran with 1,2,3 and 6 threads per NUMA domain, for Edison we ran with 1,2,3,4,6, and 12 threads per NUMA domain, and for Mira, we ran with 4, 8, 16, 32 and 64 threads per node. On Hopper, GTC speeds up 4.1x using six threads, on Edison it sees a 9.2x speedup over twelve threads, and on Mira it sees an 8.72x speed up when going from four threads per node to 64 (a factor of 16).

The differences in the performance between the three different platforms may, to first order, be explained by differences in clock speed and memory bandwidth. On a node per node basis, Edison is approximately 2-2.6x faster than Hopper, increasing with node count, and Mira is 2.6-2.8x slower than Hopper, with Edison being approximately 7-7.8x faster than Mira. To look at it in a different way, to

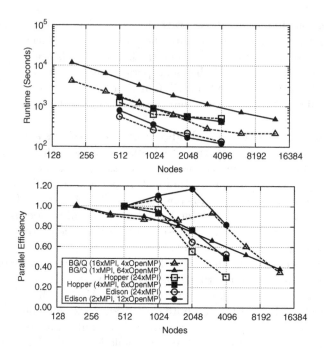

Fig. 5. MILC Performance

run as fast as the 200 node case on Edison, Hopper requires three times as many nodes and Mira requires over nine times as many nodes.

To first order, the differences in the parallel efficiency curves can be understood by removing the MPI communication times from the run times and then recalculating the parallel efficiency. Following that procedure, all three platforms follow nearly the same parallel efficiency curve, with Edison's curve being only marginally affected by this correction. At larger numbers of nodes, the overall performance of GTC becomes limited by the growing influence of MPI collective (allreduce) communications. However, this appears to be less of a factor on Edison as evidenced by it's better scaling.

FLASH. The FLASH experiments are run with a uniform resolution grid of 1152^3 cells and use 512 to 4096 nodes on all 3 platforms with additional experiments on Mira which use up to 32,768 nodes. In 1 MPI rank per core configurations, this gives a workload per MPI rank which is representative of a typical production FLASH simulation with Paramesh on Mira. In such a simulation, each MPI rank typically updates 10 to 20 blocks, each consisting of 16^3 cells. For comparison, in the 512 node experiment on Hopper, each MPI rank is assigned approximately the same number of cells as 30 16^3 blocks. Our strong scaling study is important because it spans the full range of typical production simulations corresponding to 30, 15, 8 and 4 16^3 blocks per MPI rank. In all experiments we obtain the FLASH run time from the "evolution" time stamp in

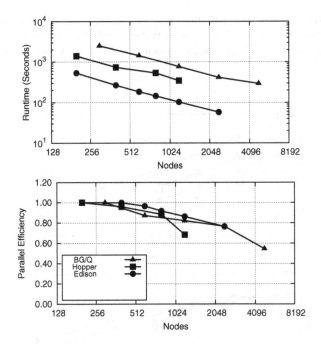

Fig. 6. GTC Performance

the FLASH log file. This is appropriate because initialization time is small and becomes negligible in production simulations which consist of multiple 12-hour runs chained together.

The performance results in Figure 7 show that at a given node count the fastest time to solution is obtained on Edison in 1 MPI rank per core configuration. We see that it takes approximately a factor of 8x more nodes on Mira to improve upon a given Edison time. The parallel efficiency of FLASH tails off at higher node count mainly because the unsplit hydrodynamics solver in FLASH replicates certain guard cell computations. We find that the biggest strong scaling loss comes from the computation of Riemann state values for *all* cell interfaces within a single block. Work could be saved by communicating the guard cell Riemann state values instead of replicating this computation. The communication vs. computation trade-off should be investigated because the replicated work is actually more than the necessary local work in FLASH simulations with Paramesh and blocks of 16^3 cells.

In all cases, the 1 MPI rank per core experiments are faster than the 1 MPI rank per NUMA domain experiments. One notable observation is that the Hopper platform shows the smallest difference between the MPI per core and MPI per NUMA domain performance. This is partially because there are only 6 OpenMP threads per MPI rank instead of 12 (Edison) or 64 (Mira) and so the impact of serial code sections is smaller. Hopper also spends less time in MPI in the per NUMA domain experiments than in the per core experiments. This is the opposite to what we observe on both Edison and Mira and perhaps indicates contention in the network is slowing down the MPI rank per core guard cell exchange on Hopper.

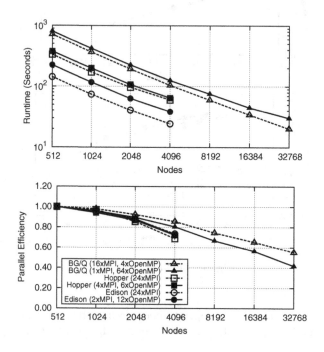

Fig. 7. FLASH Performance

MiniFE. The results for MiniFE are for a strong scaled study with data points at 512, 1024, 2048 and 4096 nodes for each platform. The input parameters were chosen to use nominally 4 TB of aggregate memory capacity, 8 GB, 4 GB, 2 GB and 1 GB per node respectively, in order to be sufficiently larger than the last level cache and hence fully utilize the memory hierarchy. The metric chosen for this study is overall solve time for the conjugate gradient solver. The CG solver contains three distinct operations, a DOT product, a WAXPY operation, and a sparse matrix vector (SpMV) product. All three operations have been parallelized with OpenMP. The SpMV product takes the majority of time in the calculation, approximately 80% for the Hopper cases at 512 nodes. The amount of time spent in MPI communication is not negligible and there can be effects as scale increases on less balanced architectures.

The timing and parallel efficiency results for MiniFE are shown in Figure 8. In general MiniFE performs similarly for the two mixes of MPI and OpenMP on the respective platforms. There are some deviations at 4096 nodes, but they are not significant. MiniFE scales well on both the BG/Q and Edison platforms, near 90% or better parallel efficiency. On the Hopper platform, scaling is somewhat erratic. This behavior has been observed with MiniFe in other studies of the Cray XE6 architecture, with the primary contributor being the DOT product operation. This behavior is repeatable and has been demonstrated on multiple instantiations of the architecture. It is believed to be an artifact of the non-uniform communication performance of the Gemini 3D torus and how the problem is laid out on the machine. Although this is usually not a major performance issue, this study observed significant performance degradation at 4096 nodes, where parallel efficiency drops to less than 70%. The authors surmise that if run at 8192 nodes, parallel efficiency would improve to the 90+% range seen at 2048 nodes. In summary, Edison provides the best overall time to solution. Both Hopper and the BG/Q platform require approximately four times as many nodes to achieve similar performance.

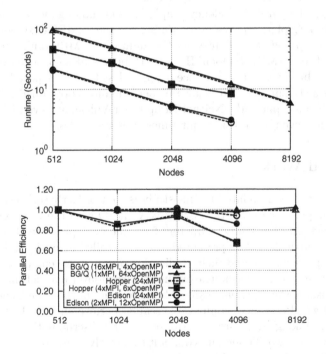

Fig. 8. MiniFE Performance

UMT. The results for UMT are for a strong scaled study with data points at 512, 1024, 2048 and 4096 nodes for each platform. The input parameters were chosen to use nominally 4 TB of aggregate memory capacity, 8 GB, 4 GB,

2 GB and 1 GB per node respectively, in order to be sufficiently larger than the last level cache and hence fully utilize the memory hierarchy. The metric chosen was cumulative work time. For UMT much of the work for each MPI rank does not contain OpenMP directives, the only section of the code that has OpenMP is the step which loops over all the angles of the transport problem. Although this is a major computational part of the solve phase, if a node has weak single core performance, cases with minimal MPI parallelism may inherently have lower performance. However, the results below show that there can be exceptions.

The timing and parallel efficiency results for UMT are shown in Figure 9. For the BG/Q and Edison platforms, the cases which use more MPI parallelism perform significantly better than the respective cases with higher OpenMP parallelism, as surmised above. However, for the Hopper platform the two cases show essentially equal performance across all scales. Further analysis shows that the 24xMPI case does indeed spend approximately 20% less time in the computational sections of the code, but spends approximately 70% more time in the MPI routines than the 4xMPI/6xOpenMP case. So for this problem, on this platform, the total solve time is roughly equal.

Looking at the parallel efficiency graph, Edison shows good scaling for both cases. The BG/Q platform has good scaling for the 1xMPI/64xOpenMP case, but scaling drops off significantly as the number of MPI ranks per node is increased in the 16xMPI/4xOpenMP case. Hopper scales consistently between the two cases, but overall performance drops to less than 40% parallel efficiency at 4096 nodes. In summary, best overall performance is obtained with Edison using 24 MPI ranks per node. Neither Hopper nor Vulcan achieve the same level of performance, even when using four times as many nodes.

5   Related Work

The work most directly related to this study is that of Kerbyson et al. [14] who compared the performance of the IBM Blue Gene/Q with the Cray XE6 and an Infiniband system. That study is different from the work presented herein in several ways: in particular, they presented a more detailed analysis of the network interconnect performance and their application performance comparison focused on weak-scaling of codes without examining thread-level parallelism. Like Kerbyson, we observe the excellent scaling characteristics of the Blue Gene/Q interconnect, but we also observe comparable scaling performance in the Cray XC30 interconnect, making this system attribute less of a discriminating performance factor between the two. Though it is difficult to directly compare weak and strong scaling results of different problems over different node counts, we observe that both GTC and MILC on the Cray XE6 had roughly similar speedups over the Blue Gene/Q as those observed in [14].

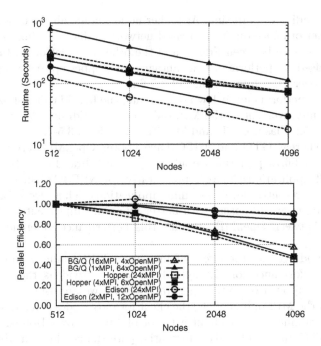

Fig. 9. UMT Performance

6 Summary and Conclusions

As we have seen in this study, it is possible to see significant performance gains on
modern architectures with larger faster caches and better memory bandwidth. In
terms of raw performance acquired through improvements in memory bandwidth
and an improved interconnect, the Cray XC30 is a significant step forward from
its predecessor, the Cray XE6. For the MPI-only codes, for the smallest node
counts and where parallel efficiency is still good, the range of speedup from
Hopper to Edison is about 2x which is expected based on clock speeds and
memory bandwidth figures. Comparing Edison to Mira is a bit more interesting
as on a per core basis we expect an Edison core to be 5.4x the speed of a Mira
hardware core. Comparing on a node level, and correcting for node counts, we
expect an Edison node to have 8x the performance of a Mira node (single thread
per core). In this case Mira performs more admirably with MiniFE and Flash
running on Edison only 4.2 and 4.3x faster, respectively. Both MILC and UMT
perform even better showing speedups on Edison relative to Mira of about 2-
2.5x. For the case of MILC, the improved performance on Mira is possibly the
result of the latter's 5D torus network being more amenable to MILC's 4D halo
exchanges and Mira's ability to hide memory latency, which is also an important
performance limiter for MILC. The UMT code also shows a speedup on Edison
of 2.6x, implying that it is able to exploit at least two hardware threads on
Mira effectively and may also be able to exploit hardware threading to hide the

latency of its indirect addressing. At higher node counts, all the codes showed a decrease in performance due to increased network traffic resulting in increasing gaps in performance between Edison and the other two platforms. In this case, Edison increased it's performance advantage over Hopper up to a range of about 2.5-3.8x and over Mira from a range of 3.5-6x.

Comparing performance at low node counts, the hybrid codes show a similar performance improvement to the MPI-only codes on Edison relative to Hopper of about 1.8-2.5x. Flash, UMT, and MiniFE all perform 3.5-4x better on Edison than Mira, whereas GTC and MILC have poorer OpenMP performance and Edison has a 6.2-6.7x performance advantage over Mira. The latter two codes are older full applications, more representative of NERSC's current workload than the more recently developed mini-applications. Thus, we expect that if we migrate to newer code bases with better OpenMP implementations and less serialization between OpenMP sections, this performance difference would be reduced.

At high node counts the effect of increasing MPI traffic, again, decreases application performance for the hybrid models and widens the performance advantage of Edison. However, in general, because we are using far fewer MPI tasks than in the MPI-only models, the effect for most codes is relatively modest with Edison gaining at most about a factor of 1.0-1.5x over Hopper and Mira. Still, both GTC and MILC take substantial performance hits on Mira at high node counts with Edison's advantage increasing to 7.8x and 9.4x, respectively, thus adding network overhead to already marginal OpenMP performance.

Through this study, we can see the advantages of Edison's improved memory bandwidth and interconnect on performance both on individual application performance and on NERSC's system performance metric, the SSP. Comparing the XC30 system to the BG/Q system is more difficult. While the Cray provides roughly 4x greater application performance per core (as shown in Section 4) the IBM system may be more attractive on an efficiency or total energy cost basis. BG/Q nodes require less electrical power than the XC30: Edison uses about 280 W/node when running LINPACK, and Mira uses about 80 W/node. Thus, at peak utilization, one Edison node uses 3.5x the power of a Mira node, which places the two systems on near-equal footing when compared by a performance per Watt metric.

Finally, we also observed that all of the benchmarks used in this study have low computational intensity, making them sensitive to memory bandwidth performance. Figure 3 clearly shows that all of the codes used in this study are significantly limited by the memory bandwidth of each platform, and overall the results principally track the differences in memory bandwidth between the machines. All would benefit greatly from code optimizations to increase their computational intensity, regardless of any increases in memory bandwidth performance. A telling feature of this study is that while a few purpose-written mini-applications (e.g. MiniFE) may exhibit nearly co-equal performance between MPI and hybrid versions, the hybrid version of most applications is slower, in some cases markedly so. It is clear that application developers will need to invest substantial time and effort into either refactoring their codes for the many-core era or selecting new algorithms to improve threaded performance. These changes must be made with one eye toward reducing serialization and communications, and another toward increasing data reuse in order to reduce memory traffic. In fact, this work has already begun for several of these codes [15,16]. The hybrid results presented here simply reflect a slightly older code base.

Acknowledgments. All authors from Lawrence Berkeley National Laboratory were supported by the Office of Advanced Scientific Computing Research in the Department of Energy Office of Science under contract number DE-AC02-05CH11231. This research used resources of the National Energy Research Scientific Computing Center (NERSC), which is supported by the Office of Science of the U.S. Department of Energy under Contract No. DE-AC02-05CH11231.

Sandia National Laboratories is a multi-program laboratory managed and operated by Sandia Corporation, a wholly owned subsidiary of Lockheed Martin Corporation, for the U.S. Department of Energy's National Nuclear Security Administration (NNSA) under contract DE-AC04-94AL85000.

This research used resources of the Argonne Leadership Computing Facility at Argonne National Laboratory, which is supported by the Office of Science of the U.S. Department of Energy under contract DE-AC02-06CH11357.

References

1. Geist, G.A.: Sustained petascale: The next MPI challenge. In: Cappello, F., Herault, T., Dongarra, J. (eds.) PVM/MPI 2007. LNCS, vol. 4757, pp. 3–4. Springer, Heidelberg (2007)
2. Challenges for the message passing interface in the petaflops era, www.cs.uiuc.edu/homes/wgropp/bib/talks/tdata/2007/mpifuture-uiuc.pdf
3. Bauer, B., Gottlieb, S., Hoefler, T.: Performance modeling and comparative analysis of the MILC Lattice QCD application su3_rmd. In: Proc. CCGRID 2012: IEEE/ACM International Symposium on Cluster, Cloud, and Grid Computing (2012)
4. Gottlieb, S., Tamhankar, S.: Benchmarking MILC with OpenMP and MPI. Nucl. Phys. Proc. Suppl. **94**, 841–845 (2001)
5. Ethier, S., Tang, W.M., Lin, Z.: Gyrokinetic particle-in-cell simulations of plasma microturbulence on advanced computing platforms. Journal of Physics: Conference Series **16**, 1–15 (2006)
6. Fryxell, B., Olson, K., Ricker, P., Timmes, F.X., Zingale, M., Lamb, D.Q., MacNeice, P., Rosner, R., Truran, J.W., Tufo, H.: FLASH: An Adaptive Mesh Hydrodynamics Code for Modeling Astrophysical Thermonuclear Flashes. The Astrophysical Journal Supplement Series **131**(1), 273 (2000)
7. The Flash Center for Computational Science, University of Chicago. FLASH User's Guide. Version 4.0 (September 2012), http://flash.uchicago.edu/site/flashcode/user_support/flash4_ug.pdf
8. Antypas, K., Calder, A., Dubey, A., Fisher, R.T., Ganapathy, M.K., Gallagher, B., Reid, L.B., Riley, K., Sheeler, D.J., Taylor, N.: Scientific Applications on the Massively Parallel BG/L Machine. In: PDPTA, vol. 2006, pp. 292–298 (2006)

9. Heroux, M.A., et al.: Improving Performance via Mini-applications. Technical Report SAND2009-5574, Sandia National Laboratories (September 2009), https://software.sandia.gov/mantevo/

10. Heroux, M.A.: Mantevo project web page, https://software.sandia.gov/mantevo/

11. Barrett, R.F., Crozier, P.S., Doerfler, D.W., Hammond, S.D., Heroux, M.A., Thornquist, H.K. Trucano, T.G., Vaughan, C.T.: Summary of work for asc 12 milestone 4465: Characterize the role of the mini-application in predicting key performance characteristics of real applications. Sandia National Laboratories, Tech. Rep. SAND, 4667 (2012)

12. Williams, S.W., Waterman, A., Patterson, D.A.: Roofline: An insightful visual performance model for floating-point programs and multicore architectures. Technical Report UCB/EECS-2008-134, EECS Department, University of California, Berkeley (October 2008)

13. Antypas, K., Shalf, J., Wasserman, H.: NERSC-6 Workload Analysis and Benchmark Selection Process. Technical Report LBNL 10143, Lawrence Berkeley National Laboratory (2008)

14. Kerbyson, D.J., Barker, K.J., Vishnu, A., Hoisie, A.: Comparing the performance of Blue Gene/Q with leading Cray XE6 and InfiniBand systems. In: Proceedings of the 2012 IEEE 18th International Conference on Parallel and Distributed Systems, ICPADS 2012, pp. 556–563. IEEE Computer Society, Washington, DC (2012)

15. Oliker, L.: Personal communication (2013)

16. Joó, B., Kalamkar, D.D., Vaidyanathan, K., Smelyanskiy, M., Pamnany, K., Lee, V.W., Dubey, P., Watson III, W.: Lattice QCD on intel®xeon phi^{TM} coprocessors. In: Kunkel, J.M., Ludwig, T., Meuer, H.W. (eds.) ISC 2013. LNCS, vol. 7905, pp. 40–54. Springer, Heidelberg (2013)

Analysis of Data Reuse in Task-Parallel Runtimes

Miquel Pericàs[1]([⊠]), Abdelhalim Amer[2],
Kenjiro Taura[3], and Satoshi Matsuoka[1,2]

[1] Global Scientific Information and Computing Center,
Tokyo Institute of Technology, Tokyo, Japan
pericas.m.aa@m.titech.ac.jp, matsu@is.titech.ac.jp
[2] Department of Mathematical and Computing Sciences,
Tokyo Institute of Technology, Tokyo, Japan
amer@matsulab.is.titech.ac.jp
[3] Graduate School of Information Science and Technology,
The University of Tokyo, Tokyo, Japan
tau@eidos.ic.i.u-tokyo.ac.jp

Abstract. This paper proposes a methodology to study the data reuse quality of task-parallel runtimes. We introduce an coarse-grain version of the reuse distance method called *Kernel* Reuse Distance (KRD). The metric is a low-overhead alternative designed to analyze data reuse at the socket level while minimizing perturbation to the parallel schedule. Using the KRD metric we show that reuse depends considerably on the system configuration (sockets, cores) and on the runtime scheduler. Furthermore, we correlate KRD with hardware metrics such as cache misses and work time inflation. Overall we found that KRD can be used effectively to assess data reuse in parallel applications. The study also revealed that several current runtimes suffer from severe bottlenecks at scale which often dominate performance.

1 Introduction and Background

Tasking has become an established technique to program multicore systems. This programming scheme supports many variations of parallel control, including nested, recursive and irregular parallelism. Task-parallel models, such as OpenMP [1], Threading Building Blocks [2] or Cilk [3], allow the developer to annotate functions or code blocks for asynchronous task execution and add synchronization points to process the children tasks' outputs. An underlying runtime tracks dependencies among tasks and *schedules* ready tasks to physical cores.

1.1 Scalability of Runtimes

Although the functionality of a runtime for homogeneous multicore systems may seem simple, developing efficient and scalable implementations is challenging. Design decisions can adversely affect execution time:

© Springer International Publishing Switzerland 2014
S. Jarvis et al. (Eds.): PMBS 2013 Workshops, LNCS 8551, pp. 73–87, 2014.
DOI: 10.1007/978-3-319-10214-6_4

Runtime Overheads. Operations such as task creation, synchronization or scheduling introduce *non-work* cycles that can considerably increase execution time. Runtime pressure grows with the number of workers and with finer task granularities. Contention can easily occur at scale. Runtimes should be as lightweight as possible to avoid such bottlenecks.

Scheduling Constraints. Runtimes may place restrictions on task scheduling to simplify implementation or to set bounds on resource consumption. For example, some runtimes never migrate tasks once they have started. Some runtimes also limit the depth of nesting to avoid unlimited stack growth. Such constraints limit dynamic parallelism which manifests as non-work overheads in the form of processor idle time.

Resource Sharing. Scheduling policies, such as *work-first* [4] or its dual *help-first*, and *work stealing* [5] techniques, determine the execution order of tasks. The resulting schedule defines the order of work *kernels* and their sharing of resources. A task order that ignores data locality issues can increase cache misses and generate work time inflation (WTI) [6].

In this work we use the term *non-work overheads* for any kind of processor activity that is not directly related to the program's main functionality, which is carried out by *work kernels* and the control necessary to setup their execution. The non-work overheads include runtime execution and *parallel idleness* [7]. Tasks may include several kernels, but the kernels themselves do not generate any new tasks. OVR_N and WTI_N (*Non-work Overheads* and *Work Time Inflation* at N cores) are two measurable scaling factors that describe the increase of execution time on N cores (T_N) relative to the *ideal* parallel execution time ($\frac{T_1}{N}$). WTI_N quantifies the increase of the total work time at N cores ($Work_N$) relative to the work time of the serial execution ($Work_1$). OVR_N quantifies the increase in the total running time of all threads ($T_N \times N$) relative to the total time during which threads are performing work ($Work_N$):

$$T_N = \frac{T_1}{N} \times WTI_N \times OVR_N \tag{1}$$

$$WTI_N = \frac{Work_N}{Work_1} \tag{2}$$

$$OVR_N = \frac{T_N \times N}{Work_N} \tag{3}$$

Using this formulation, the speed-up on N cores becomes:

$$\text{Speed-Up}_N = \frac{T_1}{T_N} = \frac{N}{WTI_N \times OVR_N} \tag{4}$$

1.2   Performance Tools

Application developers are often unaware of such issues and are then surprised by the bad performance of their applications as they scale to many cores. Quality tools are needed to detect these problems. Profilers and tracers provide insight into *non-work overheads* [7–10] by quantifying load imbalance and runtime activity overhead. *Scheduling constraints* are more difficult to analyze, since they relate to algorithmic decisions inside the runtimes. Similarly, *caching problems* caused by scheduling decisions may be hard to identify. Low data locality exploitation in users' code, on the other hand, is a well known topic addressed by several tools [11–13].

This paper focuses on the problem of understanding caching problems introduced by the runtime scheduler in task-parallel applications. To analyze the impact of schedulers on data reuse we propose a methodology based on the concept of the reuse distance [14]. By analyzing the reuse distance observed at each last level cache, the metric allows to make a system-level assessment on the reuse performance of different runtimes.

1.3   Contributions

This paper makes the following contributions: 1) We describe the implementation of the Kernel Reuse Distance (KRD), a metric based on to the reuse distance targeting the analysis of temporal locality in task-parallel applications. 2) Using KRD we evaluate the temporal locality of two benchmarks using four schedulers. Our analysis reveals that differences in reuse increase with the number of cores and sockets. 3) We study the correlation between the KRD metric and hardware metrics such as cache misses and work time inflation. As part of this research we also observed that, at scale, performance and work time inflation are often dominated by runtime bottlenecks.

This paper is organized as follows: Section 2 sets the scenario by analyzing the scalability of two benchmark applications. Section 3 describes the KRD metric and its implementation. The metric is applied in Section 4 to observe how temporal locality is influenced by runtime schedulers and to study its correlation with performance metrics. We conclude in Sections 5 and 6 by discussing weaknesses of the approach and by summarizing the main conclusions.

2   Case Study: Matrix Multiplication and the Fast Multipole Method

The development of KRD is motivated with a scalability study of two codes: Matrix Multiplication (*MATMUL*) and the Fast Multipole Method (*FMM*).

2.1   Benchmarks

The *MATMUL* code is a SIMD-optimized divide-and-conquer implementation which includes a task parallel implementation based on Cilk-like **spawn** and sync constructs [4]. The code recursively bisects the matrices until all three sub-matrices A, B and C fit in the L1 cache. For the experiment we use input matrices of size 4096×4096, which translates into 64MB per matrix (single precision). On our test environment (described below) the granularity of each task (kernel) is about 17 microseconds.

The *Fast Multipole Method* is based on the exaFMM-dev code developed by Rio Yokota [15]. The *FMM* algorithm contains multiple steps. We focus only on the dominant phase: the dual tree traversal, which includes the two main kernels: M2L (multipole-to-local) and P2P (particle-to-particle). We run one *FMM* timestep on 1 million particles organized as a plummer distribution. The multipole expansion coefficient is set to 5 and the number of particles per leaf box is 32. The tree traversal phase is also parallelized by a divide and conquer approach [16], and uses the same Cilk-like constructs as *MATMUL*. The *FMM* kernels are quite small, with each call to M2L only 500 nanoseconds. To avoid excessive overhead the recursion stops when less than 300 bodies remain under the current subtree, yielding multiple kernels per task. On our test system, the average size of one task is 3.25 microseconds.

2.2 Experimental Infrastructure

We benchmark the codes on a 4-socket x86-64 server featuring 4× Intel Xeon E7-4807 (Westmere-EX) processors, each with 6 cores clocked at 1.86GHz. The cores have a 32KB L1 data cache (8-way set associative) and a 256KB L2 cache (8-way). The six cores share a 18MB last level cache (L3) with 16 ways. Hyperthreading is not used. When scaling to multiple cores, we first allocate all the cores in one socket and then fill the cores from a different socket. All codes were compiled using gcc version 4.7. The research platform runs a Linux distribution with kernel version 2.6.32.

The Cilk-like constructs are translated into API calls for three runtimes, identified as follows:

MTH : MassiveThreads [17,18] is a lightweight task-parallel library that features a work-first scheduler, per-core LIFO task queues, and a random work stealer similar to the MIT-Cilk design.

TBB : Threading Building Blocks [2,19] is a C++ template library for task parallelism with a help-first approach, per-core LIFO task queues and random work stealer. Although TBB supports thread affinities [20], we do not use this feature in order to compare the same code. We use version tbb41_20130116oss.

QTH : Qthread [21–23] is a lightweight threading package that implements a help-first scheduler. Qthread adds a new level to the task queues' hierarchy called *shepherds*. Shepherds can be assigned per socket to create a shared LIFO task queue among the workers (i.e. cores) of the socket. The goal is to improve the use of the shared cache. We refer to this configuration as QThread/Socket. We also test a configuration with one shepherd per core, we which identify as

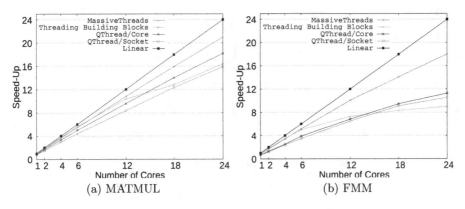

(a) MATMUL

(b) FMM

Fig. 1. Speed-ups

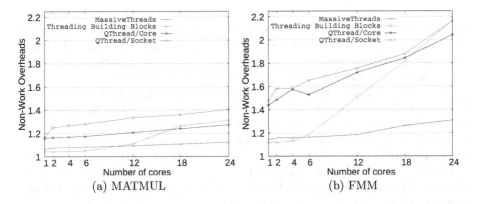

(a) MATMUL

(b) FMM

Fig. 2. Non-Work Overheads

QThread/Core. Qthread also has a bulk work-stealer. By default it attempts to steal 50% of the victim's workload. The Qthread version we use is 1.9.

2.3 Scalability Analysis

The applications were manually instrumented with our own profiling library, which we describe later. This library measures execution times, work time inflation and non-work overheads. Figures 1, 2 and 3 show the speed-ups and non-work overheads (OVR_N) for the two applications and four schedulers when scaling from 1 to 24 cores. We also show the product of the speed-up and over-head normalized by the number of cores. Using the earlier equation we derive (Speed-Up$_N \times \text{OVR}_N/N$) = $1/\text{WTI}_N$. The product is thus a measure of the speed-down caused by work time inflation.

The figures show that scalability of these applications is highly dependent on the runtime. Using MassiveThreads, speed-ups of up to 21× and 18× are

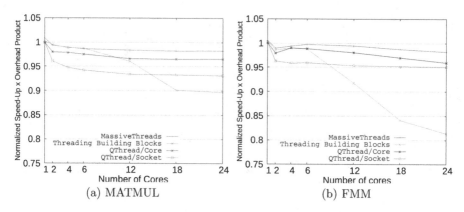

Fig. 3. Speed-up Overhead Product

achieved for *MATMUL* and *FMM* at 24 cores, respectively. TBB displays very good scaling until the first socket is filled, but performance degrades at higher core counts. Qthreads performance is already degraded in the single socket scenario. However, it scales better than TBB for multiple sockets.

These results are highly correlated with the non-work overheads. Massive-Threads is the only runtime that does not suffer from a large increase, with 30% overhead in the worst case. The other runtimes suffer about 2-4× higher overheads at high core counts. Both *MATMUL* and *FMM* have small task sizes, which MassiveThreads is designed to handle efficiently. Qthread's single core overheads demonstrate that it is more heavy and suffers under fine-grained parallelism. However, scaling to higher cores reveals just a smooth degradation. TBB's overheads are lower than MassiveThreads for a single socket but increase fast for multiple sockets. The `QTH/Socket` overheads are consistently larger than those of `QTH/Core`. `QTH/Socket` features a per-socket shared LIFO task queue which is accessed by all workers in a shepherd. The frequency of accesses to the queue is proportional to the number of workers sharing it and inversely proportional to the average task size. For small task sizes and large number of workers this method is likely to suffer from contention.

The third plot shows the *Speed-Up* × *Non-work Overhead* product normalized by the number of cores. In the ideal case this metric should yield 1.0. A value below 1.0 indicates work time inflation. The plots show that work time inflation is an important issue, contributing a further performance reduction of up to 20% in the worst case (*FMM* with TBB). Since kernels never block, WTI can only be attributed to destructive resource sharing. This effect is mainly observed as an increased number of cache misses and/or increased memory access latencies. Two factors can cause this: 1) When the memory subsystem or system interconnect is overloaded, average memory access latency increases. In addition, runtime bottlenecks -such as excessive contention on a global lock- can steal bus cycles from the memory subsystem which further contribute to increase latencies.

2) A change in the work time can also be caused by data locality variations. Different kernel schedules, for example, impact temporal locality and cache misses.

Measuring how much of work time inflation is caused by the runtime and how much is due to locality is difficult because of the small kernel sizes and because of the high overheads of accessing hardware performance monitors using the Linux `perf` subsystem [24]. To identify work time inflation due to temporal locality issues we look for a scenario with minimal non-work overheads. For the case of *MATMUL*, MassiveThreads and TBB have overheads around or below 1.1× until 12 cores (2 sockets). Figure 3 (a) shows a work time difference of about 2% between MTH and TBB at 12 cores that must be related to different task orders. At 24 cores this difference is around 8%. The KRD metric defined in the next section can provide additional insight regarding the origin of additional cache misses.

3   Kernel Reuse Distance

To characterize the effects of task ordering on temporal locality we start with the reuse distance metric [14]. The reuse distance has traditionally been used as a measure of cache performance [25]. It processes traces of memory accesses and counts the number of unique addresses between two accesses to the same element. This count is also called the *stack distance.*

When analyzing task-parallel applications it is important to minimize perturbation to the runtime task schedule. Heavyweight instrumentation to generate address traces may impact the execution and result in a parallel schedule that is not representative. To reduce overheads we extend the method to collect data accesses only in bulk at kernel execution times. For each data structure that is an input or output to a kernel, an identifier (usually its base address), a timestamp, and its size in bytes are recorded. We rely on manual instrumentation to perform these actions.

A trace of data accesses is recorded separately for each core. To analyze the reuse on a per-node[1] basis we process a *merged trace* containing all the kernel inputs and outputs accessed by the cores sharing the same last level cache. The trace is synchronized using the timestamps. Using this *merged trace*, the stack distances are computed and the histogram is generated. When a system contains multiple nodes, we summarize the contribution of each by generating per-node histograms and then reporting their summation.

Altogether, this set of modifications on top of the reuse distance is called the Kernel Reuse Distance metric (KRD). KRD is is a low-overhead and architecture independent method that provides an intuitive measure of data reuse. Its correlation to hardware metrics such as cache misses and performance is analyzed later. Figure 4 shows a diagram explaining the methodology in a single socket environment with two cores. Two workers are running, one on each core, and generating a series of kernel data accesses. To analyze the last level cache and

---

[1] In this work we use *node* as shorthand for *NUMA node.*

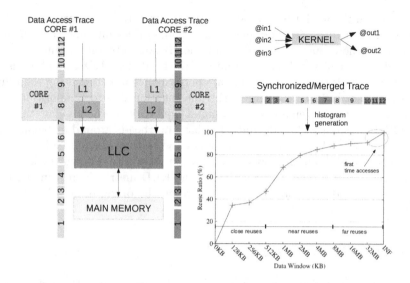

Fig. 4. Generation of the KRD metric for a single socket with two cores

memory access, the traces are merged and the reuse histogram is generated. The histogram shows the ratio of data reuses that occur within a certain data window, shown on the x-axis. All elements have a first access. This event is included in the last data point labeled as INF (infinity). In the multiple nodes scenario, work steal activity across nodes introduces additional *cold* accesses. By looking at the number of accesses that contribute to the INF category, one can observe the effects of inter-node work steals.

For visualization purposes, we subdivide the histogram into *close*, *near*, and *far* reuses. This choice is arbitrary but will help later in describing the plots. As a rule of thumb, we use close reuses for those that fall within L2 cache size, near reuses for those within last level cache (LLC) size, and far reuses for those beyond the size of the LLC.

3.1 Implementation Details

We implemented KRD as a set of tools that can compute the histograms from traces generated by our own low overhead profiling and tracing facility called LoI (low-overhead instrumentation). LoI is designed to analyze task-parallel applications with fine grained kernels. LoI attempts to be as lightweight as possible in order to not influence the task parallel schedule. The library associates timestamps to events, and either aggregates execution times for individual kernels or generates timestamped traces. Timestamps are obtained by using the x86 TSC facility [26]. For both applications the tracing facility increases execution time less than 5% in the worst case.

4   Experimental Evaluation

This section describes two experiments. We begin by generating KRD profiles for *MATMUL* and *FMM* to display how reuse changes with the runtime scheduler. Next we analyze the correlation between the KRD metric and hardware performance counters.

4.1   KRD Correlation with Runtime Schedulers

Figures 5–7 show the KRD plots for the two benchmarks using the four tested runtime schedulers on three hardware configurations: single core, one fully-populated socket and four sockets.

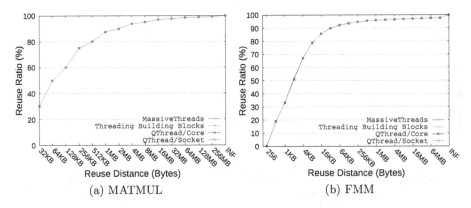

(a) MATMUL   (b) FMM

Fig. 5. Kernel Reuse Distance plots for a single core

The *single core* histograms show that in the absence of work steals, different schedulers have little impact on the temporal reuse of recursive divide and conquer task-parallel codes. In fact, for *MATMUL*, the KRDs of both work-first and help-first policies are identical. This is not surprising as the recursive bisecting of the matrices and corresponding task generation are symmetric. Work-first and help-first execute the leaf kernels in reverse order, but this has no effect on the reuse distance. For *FMM* the decomposition is not completely symmetric because of a property of the algorithm which allows to discard one of the branches based on a condition (mutual interactions). However, differences between schedulers are still barely noticeable.

Differences start to emerge when one socket is fully populated (6 threads), particularly on *MATMUL*. `QThread/Socket` stands out, having the highest reuse ratio at almost all distances. This good performance results from `QThread/Socket`'s usage of a global LIFO queue shared by all the workers. In this design, workers tend to execute tasks that have been recently generated by other workers. Since programs are commonly optimized for data reuse on the serial path,

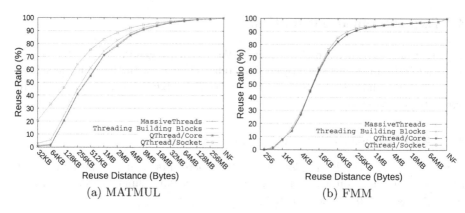

Fig. 6. Kernel Reuse Distance plots for one socket (6 cores)

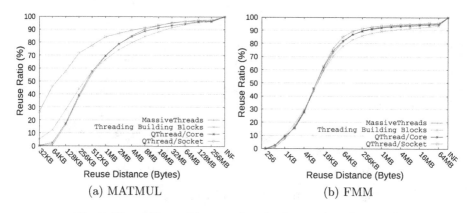

Fig. 7. Kernel Reuse Distance plots for four sockets (24 cores)

this policy improves cache sharing [23]. TBB also shows improved reuse compared to MTH and QTH/Core when executing *MATMUL*. This is probably a side-effect of the TBB scheduling restrictions [19]. MTH and QTH/Core, on the other hand, implement just a fully distributed random work stealer. It has the worst reuse performance, but offers the advantage of simplicity. The differences between schedulers are considerably smaller in the case of *FMM*. QTH/Socket is still better for close reuses, but the difference is only 3% at most. Other schedulers show almost no differences. The similarity between histograms is likely a result of *FMM*'s tree traversal algorithm, which conditionally executes two kernels that operate on independent data. Furthermore, the non-homogeneous input (*plummer* distribution) generates an irregular kernel pattern that is harder for schedulers to optimize.

The histograms for the 4-socket scenario are similar to the 1-socket case. QTH/Socket again shows the best reuse performance, but this time it is closely

Table 1. Hardware Metrics and WTI for 2-socket scenario

Runtime	Exec. Time	LLC Misses	Kernel Time & Inflation
MTH	1.642 sec	1.829×10^6	17441ns (1.0250×)
TBB	1.742 sec	2.807×10^6	17898ns (1.0519×)
QTH/Core	1.859 sec	2.339×10^6	17767ns (1.0441×)
QTH/Socket	2.111 sec	1.987×10^6	18401ns (1.0814×)

followed by MTH for far reuses. Surprisingly, in this multi-socket scenario, TBB has the worst reuse performance for far reuses, trailing the other schedulers at a noticeable distance. Compared to the single-socket plots, one important fact revealed by the four-socket KRD histograms is the larger amount of cold accesses. This is expected, as separate sockets have disjoint caches which need to be warmed up separately. KRD can be used to understand how many first time accesses occurred, which indirectly correlates to the size of the working set observed at each socket. QThread/Socket shows the lowest ratio of cold accesses while TBB shows the highest amount. A larger number of cold accesses means that the scheduler is distributing tasks that share the same working set across different nodes. TBB implements several restrictions in its scheduling algorithm that limit which tasks can be stolen and disallows the migration of tasks that have already started [19]. These limitations might be forcing TBB into a suboptimal work partitioning.

The fact that the KRD histograms can be correlated with different schedulers is an encouraging result. Next we address the question whether these plots can be correlated with actual performance.

4.2   KRD Correlation with Hardware Metrics

In the second experiment, we attempt to correlate the results of the KRD metric with last level cache misses and work time inflation. To do so we select a scenario with low runtime overheads to minimize possible perturbation. For *MATMUL* using 2 sockets (12 cores), MTH and TBB present non-work inflation of about 1.1×, while the QTH/Core overhead is about 1.2×. The KRD plot of far reuses (i.e. beyond 18MB) for this configuration is reported in Figure 8. Table 1 reports hardware performance counters and time measurements collected as averages of five runs. The kernel times are average over all kernel executions ($\sim 1 \times 10^6$) and have been collected by reading the x86 timestamp counter at each kernel call (RDTSC). The LLC misses column reports the per-core LAST_LEVEL_CACHE_MISSES metric from Intel's Architectural PerfMon [26], as reported by PAPI [27].

We first compare MTH and TBB, which have similar overheads. The KRD plot in Figure 8 shows that for all distances beyond 16 MB, MTH has a higher percentage of reuses than TBB. The LLC size of the Westmere-EX chip is 18 MB, which makes it worth to analyze of the data point at 32 MB. For MTH, 3.57% of the kernel references access data with a reuse distance beyond 32 MB, while

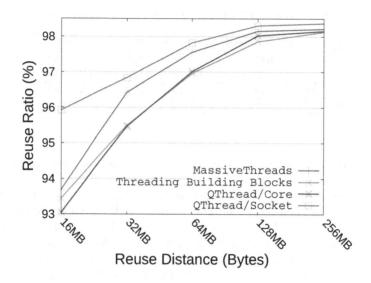

Fig. 8. Far reuses for *MATMUL* in the 2-socket, 12 core scenario

for TBB the number of far reuses is 4.5%. This 25% difference correlates to a 53% increase in LLC misses and to a work time inflation of 2.7% compared to MassiveThreads.

For QTH/Core, the KRD plots show that it has higher number of far reuses than MTH but less than TBB for distances of more than 32MB. The number of LLC misses and the work time inflation are between those of TBB and MTH. This relation is also clearly observed at high distances (e.g. 128MB) and also for cold misses. It suggests that these data points might be good indicators for cache misses and WTI.

The KRD plot also shows that QTH/Socket has overall the smallest amount of far reuses (3.15% at 32MB). However, its number of cache misses is higher than MassiveThreads, and its work time inflation is the highest of all four schedulers. QTH/Socket has comparatively high overheads (1.33×). A closer analysis using perf record revealed that the *MATMUL* benchmark spends about 25% in two Qthread functions (qt_scheduler_get_thread and qt_hash_lock), both of which include memory bus locking activity. Bus locking increases memory access latencies, and is a probable explanation for the observed work time inflation.

The 2.7% difference between MTH and TBB may seem very small, but is also expected since the studied algorithm (*MATMUL*) is not particularly memory intensive. At 4 sockets TBB has about 10% higher work time inflation compared to MTH. In the case of *FMM*, the relative inflation reaches 45% for the memory bound M2L kernel on 4 sockets. Depending on the algorithm work time inflation can become an important issue.

5   Discussion

Although KRD shows correlation with work inflation and cache misses, it should be used mainly as an intuitive model. The KRD metric contains many simplifications that are the result of the constraints set by our original goal: to qualitatively measure temporal reuse in task-parallel programs. The requirement of minimal overhead is an important consideration which enables only a coarse-grained, manually-instrumented tracking of data accesses. The model does not consider other accesses such as stack accesses, based on the assumption that kernel (heap) data accesses dominate cache performance.

KRD does also not attempt to measure spatial locality among individual accesses. Our original goal was to analyze the effects of different schedulers on data reuse. Different schedules might, however, benefit more or less from prefetchers. If such an effect is large, then extending KRD with a metric to quantify spatial locality [28] might be a worthy addition.

One limitation of the current model is that it does not provide enough information to model the effects of cache coherence protocols [29,30]. When one core writes a data structure allocated in the last level cache of a different socket, this will conceptually result in a cache-to-cache *transfer*. The KRD metric currently uses only the notion of intra-socket data accesses. It can report increases in cold misses due to work stealing operations, but it cannot model misses due to cache line invalidations. As part of our future work we plan to extend KRD by classifying accesses into reads and writes. This will allow a simple modeling of the effects of cache coherence.

Finally we would like to note that, while the KRD model has been developed with task-parallel runtimes in mind, it is actually quite generic as it does not instrument tasks, but the kernels inside tasks. This allow it to be applied to study any kind of shared memory parallel framework.

6   Conclusions

In this work we have attempted to provide some insight on the impact of task-parallel schedulers on temporal locality and its effect on performance. We developed a coarse-grained version of the reuse distance metric to study reuse in task parallel executions. Based on our analysis of two benchmarks and four runtime schedulers we observed that schedulers can have considerable impact on the reuse distance, and that the reuse quality depends considerably on the system configuration. Furthermore we observed correlation between the KRD metric and hardware metrics such as last level cache misses and average kernel execution time. However, we also observed that runtime contention can be dominant in high core count scenarios, thus minimizing overheads should take precedence over locality optimizations.

Acknowledgments. This work has been supported by a JSPS postdoctoral fellowship (P-12044). We would like to thank the anonymous reviewers for their valuable feedback.

References

1. OpenMP ARB: Openmp specification (July 2013), http://www.openmp.org/mp-documents/OpenMP4.0.0.pdf
2. Intel Corporation: Threading building blocks, https://www.threadingbuilding-blocks.org/
3. MIT Csail Supertech Research Group: The cilk project, http://supertech.csail.mit.edu/cilk/
4. Frigo, M., Leiserson, C.E., Randall, K.H.: The Implementation of the Cilk-5 Multithreaded Language. In: Proceedings of SIGPLAN 1998 (June 1998)
5. Mohr, E., Kranz, D.A., Halstead, R.H.: Lazy Task Creation: A technique for Increasing the Granularity of Parallel Programs. IEEE Transactions on Parallel and Distributed Systems 2(3) (July 1991)
6. Olivier, S.L., de Supinski, B.R., Schulz, M., Prins, J.F.: Characterizing and Mitigating Work Time Inflation in Task Parallel Programs. In: Proceedings of SC 2012 (November 2012)
7. Tallent, N.R., Mellor-Crummey, J.M.: Effective Performance Measurement and Analysis of Multithreaded Applications. In: Proceedings of PPoPP 2009 (February 2009)
8. Knüpfer, A., Brunst, H., Doleschal, J., Jurenz, M., Lieber, M., Mickler, H., Müller, M.S., Nagel, W.E.: The Vampir Performance Analysis Tool-Set, pp. 139–155. Springer, Heidelberg (2008)
9. Barcelona Supercomputing Center: Extrae User Guide Manual (May 2013)
10. Virtual Institute - High Productivity Supercomputing: SCORE-P User Manual (2013)
11. McCurdy, C., Vetter, J.: Memphis: Finding and Fixing NUMA-related Performance Problems on Multi-core Platforms. In: Proceedings of ISPASS 2010 (March 2010)
12. Liu, X., Mellor-Crummey, J.: Pinpointing Data Locality Problems Using Data-centric Analysis. In: Proceedings of CGO 2011 (April 2011)
13. Intel Corporation: Intel VTune Amplifier XE 2013 (2013), http://software.intel.com/en-us/intel-vtune-amplifier-xe
14. Mattson, R., Gecsei, J., Slutz, D., Traiger, I.: Evaluation techniques for storage hierarchies. IBM Systems Journal 9(2), 78–117 (1970)
15. Yokota, R.: exafmm-dev, https://bitbucket.org/rioyokota/exafmm-dev
16. Taura, K., Yokota, R., Maruyama, N.: A Task Parallelism Meets Fast Multipole Methods. In: Proceedings of the SCALA 2012 Workshop (November 2012)
17. The MassiveThreads Team: Massivethreads: A lightweight thread library for high productivity languages, http://code.google.com/p/massivethreads/
18. Nakashima, J., Nakatani, S., Taura, K.: Design and implementation of a customizable work stealing scheduler. In: Proceedings of the 3rd International Workshop on Runtime and Operating Systems for Supercomputers, ROSS 2013, pp. 9:1–9:8 (2013)
19. Intel Corporation: TBB: Scheduling algorithm, http://www.threadingbuilding-blocks.org/docs/help/reference/task_scheduler/scheduling_algorithm.htm
20. Acar, U.A., Blelloch, G.E., Blumofe, R.D.: The Data Locality of Work Stealing. In: Proceedings of SPAA 2000 (2000)
21. The Qthread Team: The qthread library, http://www.cs.sandia.gov/qthreads/
22. Wheeler, K., Murphy, R., Thain, D.: Qthreads: An API for programming with millions of lightweight threads. In: IEEE International Symposium on Parallel and Distributed Processing, pp. 1–8 (2008)

23. Olivier, S.L., Porterfield, A.K., Wheeler, K.B., Prins, J.F.: Scheduling Task Parallelism on Multi-Socket Multicore Systems. In: Proceedings of ROSS 2011, pp. 49–56 (2011)
24. Weaver, V.M.: Linux perf_event Features and Overhead. In: Proceedings of the 2013 FastPath Workshop (2013)
25. Beyls, K., D'Hollander, E.H.: Reuse distance as a metric for cache behavior. In: Proceedings of the IASTED Conference on Parallel and Distributed Computing and Systems, pp. 617–662 (2001)
26. Intel Corporation: Intel 64 and ia-32 architectures software developer's manual volume 3b, http://www.intel.com/content/www/us/en/processors/architectures-software-developer-manuals.html
27. PAPI Team: Performance application programming interface, http://icl.cs.utk.edu/papi/
28. Weinberg, J., McCracken, M.O., Strohmaier, E., Snavely, A.: Quantifying Locality In The Memory Access Patterns of HPC Applications. In: Proceedings of the 2005 ACM/IEEE Conference on Supercomputing (November 2005)
29. Intel Corporation: An Introduction to the Intel QuickPath Interconnect (2009)
30. Hackenberg, D., Molka, D., Nagel, W.E.: Comparing Cache Architectures and Coherency Protocols on x86–64 Multicore SMP Systems. In: Proceedings of MICRO 2009 (December 2009)

Performance Modeling
and Simulation

Using Simulation to Evaluate the Performance of Resilience Strategies at Scale

Scott Levy[1(✉)], Bryan Topp[1], Kurt B. Ferreira[2], Dorian Arnold[1],
Torsten Hoefler[3], and Patrick Widener[2]

[1] Department of Computer Science, University of New Mexico, Albuquerque, USA
{slevy,betopp,darnold}@cs.unm.edu
[2] Scalable System Software, Sandia National Laboratories, Albuquerque, USA
{kbferre,pwidene}@sandia.gov
[3] Computer Science Department, ETH Zürich, Zürich, Switzerland
htor@inf.ethz.ch

Abstract. Fault-tolerance has been identified as a major challenge for
future extreme-scale systems. Current predictions suggest that, as systems grow in size, failures will occur more frequently. Because increases in
failure frequency reduce the performance and scalability of these systems,
significant effort has been devoted to developing and refining resilience
mechanisms to mitigate the impact of failures. However, effective evaluation of these mechanisms has been challenging. Current systems are
smaller and have significantly different architectural features (e.g., interconnect, persistent storage) than we expect to see in next-generation
systems. To overcome these challenges, we propose the use of simulation. Simulation has been shown to be an effective tool for investigating
performance characteristics of applications on future systems. In this
work, we: identify the set of system characteristics that are necessary for
accurate performance prediction of resilience mechanisms for HPC systems and applications; demonstrate how these system characteristics can
be incorporated into an existing large-scale simulator; and evaluate the
predictive performance of our modified simulator. We also describe how
we were able to optimize the simulator for large temporal and spatial
scales—allowing the simulator to run 4x faster and use over 100x less
memory.

1 Introduction

Fault-tolerance has been identified as a major challenge for exascale-class systems. As systems grow in scale and complexity, failures become increasingly
likely; impacting performance and scalability. Current predictions suggest that
for next-generation systems the mean time between failures could fall to hours,

Sandia National Laboratories is a multi-program laboratory managed and operated
by Sandia Corporation, a wholly owned subsidiary of Lockheed Martin Corporation,
for the U.S. Department of Energy's National Nuclear Security Administration under
contract DE-AC04-94AL85000.

© Springer International Publishing Switzerland 2014
S. Jarvis et al. (Eds.): PMBS 2013 Workshops, LNCS 8551, pp. 91–114, 2014.
DOI: 10.1007/978-3-319-10214-6_5

or even minutes [1]. As failure rates increase, more time is spent preparing for and recovering from failures and less time is spent doing (useful) application work. Given these dire predictions and the dynamics of fault-tolerance techniques, significant effort has been and is being devoted to investigations aimed at improving system resilience and related mechanisms.

Effective evaluation of fault-tolerance strategies on extreme-scale systems has been difficult for several reasons. Most significantly, researchers often need to study machines that either: are larger than those that are currently available; or have hypothetical architectures or configurations. As a result, existing systems are not sufficient to evaluate the performance impact of fault tolerance techniques on next-generation extreme-scale systems. Tests performed on these systems cannot accurately account for the impact of scale and may not be able capture the impact of architectural features (e.g. interconnect technologies) whose performance varies dramatically from current systems. Second, the largest and most advanced current machines generally are not accessible to most researchers. Third, analytic techniques for predicting performance in future systems are lacking. While good models for coordinated checkpointing exist [2,3], we lack analytical tools for predicting the performance impact of many other fault tolerance mechanisms (for example, message-logging [4], communication-induced checkpointing [5] and hierarchical checkpointing [6]).

The broader objective of this project is to study general fault-tolerance techniques and their impacts on application performance. However, for the work presented in this paper, we focused on *checkpoint/restart*. Checkpoint/restart (or *rollback recovery*) is the technique most commonly used on today's systems. During normal operation, checkpoint/restart protocols [7] periodically record the state and address space of all application processes to stable storage devices. When a process fails, a new incarnation of the failed process is *recovered* from the most recent checkpoint – therefore limiting lost work. For distributed applications, coordinated checkpointing pauses all processes to record a globally consistent snapshot of the application's state. Uncoordinated checkpointing protocols avoid synchronization overheads and I/O contention by allowing each process to checkpoint independently. Uncoordinated checkpointing protocols also avoid rolling back non-failed processes. While there have been a number of studies which show that the overheads of checkpoint/restart could be prohibitively expensive for future extreme-scale systems [8–10], there has been a great effort in the research community to optimize these rollback/recovery protocols to ensure they remain viable [4,9,11–17].

Researchers have shown that simulation is an effective tool for investigating the performance characteristics of applications on current and hypothetical future systems [9,18–20]. In this paper, we focus on efficient simulation of the impact of coordinated and uncoordinated checkpoint/restart protocols on application performance. Our approach is motivated by two observations: (1) simulation can be very computationally expensive, and simulation efficiency is maximized by considering only the features of the computing environment that are relevant to the performance impact of checkpoint/restart; and (2) the coarse-grained operation of checkpoint/restart (on the order of minutes to hours) allows us to forego the overheads and complexities of cycle-accurate simulation. Based on these observations, we hypothesize that like operating system noise [21, 22], resilience mechanisms (e.g., writing checkpoints, restarting after a failure or redoing lost work) can be modeled as CPU detours. A CPU detour is a number of CPU cycles that are used for something other than the application.

In this work, we provide a principled approach to simulating checkpoint/restart based fault-tolerance for large-scale HPC systems in a failure-prone environment. Based on this approach, we also present an efficient and accurate framework for simulating the performance impact of coordinated and uncoordinated checkpoint/restart protocols for existing and hypothetical extreme-scale systems and applications. Specific contributions of the work include:

- A survey of system, application, and resilience characteristics required for accurate and efficient simulation of extreme-scale workloads in a failure-prone environment;
- A prototype checkpoint/restart simulation framework, based on functional and performance-oriented extensions to LogGOPSim [20] which decrease memory consumption by over 100x and runtime by 4x;
- A validation of our hypothesis that resilience overheads can be modeled as CPU detours; and
- An evaluation of the predictive performance of our simulation approach showing an error of less than 3% against an analytic model for checkpointing in a failure-free environment.

The organization of this paper is as follows: in the next section, we discuss the relevant system, application, failure and resilience characteristics that must be considered by our framework. Additionally, this section offers more background on checkpoint/restart protocols and shows how they factor into our considerations. Section 3 provides an overview of LogGOPSim, the simulator that serves as the basis of our prototype. In Section 4, we describe the functional and performance-oriented extensions we made to LogGOPSim to improve its ability to simulate coordinated and uncoordinated checkpoint protocols at our desired time and space scales. In Section 5, we evaluate the impact of our performance optimizations and validate the accuracy of the extended simulator for checkpoint/restart. We then discuss related works in Section 6, and finally, we summarize the impact our current contributions and plans for future work in Section 7.

2   Considerations for Resilience at Scale

Toward the goal of efficient, large-scale simulations that allow us to evaluate resilience techniques, we must identify the relevant hardware and software characteristics that impact simulation performance. We now describe our principled approach to identifying these characteristics: we consider system features, application behavior, fault-tolerance mechanisms and the impact of failures.

2.1 Hardware Characteristics

Our objective is to develop a simulation framework that will enable us to evaluate resilience techniques on current and future systems. The simulator must be able to accurately and efficiently model the impact of faults and fault tolerance on application performance given the: (a) temporal scale, (b) spatial scale and (c) architectural features of next-generation extreme-scale systems.

Temporal Scale. Faults and fault tolerance mechanisms typically operate at large time-scales (for example, minutes, hours or even weeks). As we stated in the introduction, projected mean-time-to-interrupt (MTTI) on the first exascale machines are on the order of hours. Additionally, many of the target applications are long running, and the behaviors of the applications as well as the systems are expected to be dynamic. As a result, simulating resilience requires a simulator that can model relatively long periods of application execution.

Spatial Scale. The largest current HPC systems are comprised of tens of thousands of nodes. If current predictions hold, an exascale system may be nearly an order of magnitude larger. Our simulator must be capable of modeling the behavior of systems that are much larger than any that are currently available.

Architectural Features. The first exascale system is not projected to appear until sometime after 2020 [23]. In the intervening span of years, we expect advances in interconnect and persistent storage technologies. Our simulator should also allow us to evaluate the impact of these advances on resilience mechanisms.

2.2 Application Characteristics

Our simulator must be capable of accounting for the performance aspects of the applications behavior. Prior research and experience has shown that it may be sufficient to do this at the course granularity of the target application's computation, specifically: its *communication graph*, a description of how processes communicate with each other; its *computation time*, the time between communication events; and its *dependencies*, a partial ordering of all communication and computation events. In the next section, we show how these characteristics interplay with resilience mechanisms.

2.3 Impact of Checkpoint/Restart Mechanisms

In checkpoint/restart protocols [24], the application or system saves snapshots of application state, *checkpoints*, to persistent storage. In coordinated checkpointing, all processes checkpoint at the same time (in order to mark a consistent global state), and in the event of a process failure, all processes must revert to their most recent checkpoint. While coordinated checkpoint/restart is the predominant approach, it suffers several limitations including increased overhead with system size and global process perturbations during checkpoint and recovery phases. Uncoordinated checkpoint/restart protocols, in which processes can checkpoint and recover independently, address these limitations – though they introduce new ones. In addition to these coarse protocols, many optimizations have been proposed including: diskless [25–27], hierarchical [6, 28] communication-induced [29] and incremental checkpointing [14, 30]. Despite the proliferation of resilience mechanisms, we lack effective methods for evaluating the true costs of each of these approaches on exascale systems [31].

Given the large temporal and spatial scales of the simulated systems that we wish to consider, effective simulation demands that we eliminate unnecessary detail. Existing work on modeling and simulation of coordinated checkpointing provides a guidepost on the required components and level of details [2, 3, 32].

In a failure-free environment, we can accurately model the impact of coordinated checkpointing by considering: the *checkpoint time*, amount of time that checkpointing activities prevent the application from executing; the *checkpoint interval*, time between consecutive checkpoints; and the *work time*, amount of time that the application would execute in the absence of checkpointing activities. Checkpoint time may require further refinement to include a process *coordination* phase, a *checkpoint calculation* phase during which time the checkpoint data is computed, the *checkpoint commit* time to write the checkpoint to stable storage and a *resumption* phase to continue normal application execution.

For approaches like uncoordinated checkpointing that lack explicit coordination, we also need to consider the application characteristics like communication patterns described previously. Consider a simple uncoordinated checkpointing strategy where each process generates checkpoints strictly according to local policies. Communication dependencies may cause checkpointing activities in one process to perturb the behavior and performance of other processes. For example, if the recipient of a message is busy generating a checkpoint then reception of the message may be delayed until the checkpoint is complete. Further, all actions that are dependent on the reception of the message will also be delayed. Additionally, many asynchronous resilience techniques use message logging [24] to mitigate recovery costs. Accounting for this activity also requires that we incorporate information about communication patterns into our simulation.

2.4   Impact of Failures

Meaningful evaluation of resilience mechanisms necessarily includes the introduction of failures. Initially, we consider only fail-stop failures. To accurately simulate the impact of the occurrence of failures on application performance, at a minimum, we need to consider: (a) failure characterization; (b) restart time; and (c) recovery description.

Failure Characterization. To evaluate the impact of faults in the context of a resilience mechanism, we require a description of how failures occur in the simulated system. Although this could be expressed in many ways, the most common and succinct description of failure occurrences is a probability distribution.

Restart Time. When a failure occurs, some time elapses before any computation can be undertaken on the failed node. To account for this fact, we need to know the time between the occurrence of a failure and the moment when the failed node can resume computation. This includes time to restart failed nodes and processes and to read checkpoints from persistent storage, but does not include any time for recovery. For example, in the case of coordinated checkpointing, the end of the restart interval coincides with the beginning of rework (i.e., redoing work lost due to the failure).

Recovery Model. When the failed node has restarted and is able to resume computation, there is typically some amount of work that needs to be redone before the system can again make meaningful forward progress. For example, in coordinated checkpointing, all of the computation between the last valid checkpoint and the occurrence of the failure needs to be redone. Typically, each resilience mechanisms presents a different method for recovering from a failure. Therefore, to accurately account for the cost of recovering from a failure, we need a model for each resilience mechanism that allows us to determine the amount of time that will elapse before the application resumes forward progress.

3   LogGOPSim

In this section, we describe LogGOPSim [20,33], the simulator we extend to meet the requirements prescribed by the considerations in Section 2. We choose LogGOPSim because it is shown to be accurate, freely available and fast enough to support large-scale simulations while already capturing many of the application and hardware characteristics we require (as we discuss). As described in Section 4, functionally, we simply needed to extend it to account for checkpoint/restart and failure recovery.

3.1   Simulating Application Characteristics

LogGOPSim is an application simulator based on the LogP model [34]. LogP and its variants have a long history of accurately predicting the performance of large-scale parallel applications and algorithms. The simulation framework consists of three major components: a trace collector (liballprof), a schedule generator (SchedGen), and an optimized discrete-event simulator (LogGOPSim).

The trace collector records the actual MPI communication of the target application. The schedule generator uses the MPI traces to generate a schedule that captures the required characteristics of control- and dataflow of the application

Table 1. Summary of the parameters needed for accurate simulation of HPC applications in a failure-prone system

Required to Model	Parameter Name	Parameter Description
All Checkpointing	COORDINATION TIME	time for processes to coordinate the taking of a checkpoint
	CHECKPOINT COMPUTATION	time to compute a checkpoint
	CHECKPOINT COMMIT TIME	time to write a checkpoint to stable storage
	CHECKPOINT INTERVAL	time between consecutive checkpoints
	WORK TIME	time-to-solution without failures or resilience mechanisms
Uncoordinated Checkpointing	COMMUNICATION GRAPH	details of inter-process communication
	COMPUTATION EVENTS	failure-free computation pattern of the application
	DEPENDENCIES	partial ordering of communication and computation events
Failure Occurrences	FAILURE CHARACTERIZATION	rate and distribution of failures
	RESTART TIME	time to read a checkpoint from stable storage after a failure
	RECOVERY MODEL	a model of the time required before forward progress can resume

while preserving the happens-before relationship of events within the application. The discrete-event simulator reads the generated schedule, performs a full LogGOPS simulation and reports the completion time of each process.

This validated simulation framework was developed to simulate applications at scale, and has the ability to extrapolate from traces collected on smaller scale systems. This allows for the simulation of platforms larger than those currently in existence while keeping the same communication characteristics (equivalent to weak-scaling of the application). Although the extrapolated trace may not precisely represent the communication pattern on the larger system, the impact of this inaccuracy has been shown to be small [20] if extrapolation factors are bounded. This framework has been used to evaluate the performance of collective communications [35] and the impact of OS noise [22] on large-scale applications. A detailed study of the simulation framework and its functionality is presented in [20].

3.2   Simulating Hardware Characteristics

Because LogGOPSim was initially developed to model application performance in large-scale systems [22], it allows us to model systems with the characteristics described in the preceding section. First, it provides the simulation scale necessary for evaluating checkpointing techniques. For a single collective operation, LogGOPSim can simulate up to 10,000,000 processes. For more general workloads, it is capable of simulating more than 64,000 processes.

Second, with some minor modifications, LogGOPSim is also capable of simulating the necessary temporal scale. The initial implementation of LogGOPSim was intended for comparatively short simulations. As a result, the temporal scope of the simulations that can be executed by the unmodified simulator is significantly limited by the size of the simulating system's memory. To achieve the temporal scale that we needed with reasonable quantities of system memory, we made some simple modifications to LogGOPSim. These modifications are discussed more fully in a subsequent section.

Third, LogGOPSim also allows us to model the impact of emerging interconnect technologies. Working within the LogGOPS model, we can simulate the impact of many changes in network behavior on resilience techniques by modifying the model's parameters. In addition, as we discuss more fully below, our model of resilience mechanisms allows us to evaluate how improvements to persistent storage systems (e.g., the widespread availability of local SSDs) will affect the performance of resilience mechanisms.

4   Extending LogGOPSim for Large Scale Resilience Research

4.1   Simulating Failures and Resilience

The key insight that allows us to use LogGOPSim is that resilience mechanisms (e.g., writing checkpoints, restarting after a failure, redoing lost work) can be modeled as CPU *detours*. A CPU detour is a number of CPU cycles that are used for something other than advancing the application's computation, similar to OS noise [21,22]. One key difference between OS noise and these resilience detours is that resilience "noise" events may need to be replayed synchronously with the application communication/computation pattern rather than asynchronously as is typical of OS noise.

We model resilience in LogGOPSim using a new library, libsolipsis, that generates CPU detours based on a specified resilience mechanism and the application's communication pattern. Similar to liballprof, the library links to the application using the MPI profiling interface, intercepting all MPI calls. The output of this library is a per-process detour file that can be provided as input to LogGOPSim. The detour file contains the timestamp and the duration of each of the resilience mechanism detours. The duration of detours, T_{detour}, that represent checkpoints are computed using the following expression.

$$T_{detour} = T_{coord} + T_{ckpt} + T_{commit}$$

where

$$T_{coord} = \text{time to coordinate the taking of a checkpoint}$$
$$T_{ckpt} = \text{time to compute a checkpoint}$$
$$T_{commit} = \text{time to commit the checkpoint to stable storage}$$

We also generate detours to represent the impact of node failure and optimistic message logging. In the case of failure, the duration of the detour includes the restart and rework time on the failed node; `libsolipsis` computes the rework time by calculating the amount of simulated time that has elapsed since the previous checkpoint. For optimistic message logging, `libsolipsis` determines the time required to write the message to the log given the bandwidth to stable storage.

For the purposes of this work, we focus on the libraries' ability to emulate performance of two popular resilience mechanisms: coordinated checkpointing and asynchronous checkpointing with message logging [7].

We focus on these on these two methods because coordinated checkpoint/restart is currently the most popular approach and asynchronous checkpointing has been proposed as a low-overhead checkpoint option for future extreme-scale systems.

For asynchronous checkpointing with message logging, our library generates detour files that contain the timestamp and the duration of the local checkpoints. Because no coordination is required, $T_{coord} = 0$. Also, for simplicity, we currently assume that $T_{ckpt} = 0$. For pessimistic message logging [7], we modify the CPU overhead parameter (o in the LogGOPS model) for send operations (o_s) to account for the log write to stable storage. The `LogGOPSim` simulator uses a single detour file to simulate the local checkpoints in the system; to model the asynchronous nature of these checkpoints, each node starts at a different location in the file.

For coordinated checkpoint/restart, the library generates a detour file that contains the timestamp and the duration of each checkpoint taken by the application. For this work, we have assumed bulk-synchronous parallel (BSP) applications. Because applications of this type are largely self-synchronizing, we set $T_{coord} = 0$. And again, for simplicity, we are currently assuming that $T_{ckpt} = 0$. When the simulation is run, we use the "`--noise-cosched`" option of the `LogGOPSim` simulator. This option ensures that the detour file is co-scheduled on all processors, thereby simulating coordinated checkpoint/restart. We also force each process to start at the beginning of the detour file to ensure proper timing of checkpoints.

To simulate failure, the library generates failure times for each node from a random distribution based on a per-node mean time between failure (MTBF). When a failure is generated, the library adds a detour event that includes the the time required to restart from the last checkpoint and the time required for rework (i.e., the time since the last checkpoint). The `LogGOPSim` simulator will ensure that all communication in the trace file that depends on the failed node will be delayed until the node has "recovered".

4.2   Optimizing LogGOPSim for Scale

To simulate periods of execution long enough to be meaningful for fault tolerance (i.e., application wallclock times long enough that application failures are expected) while keeping traces manageable, we extended LogGOPSim to support automatic execution trace extrapolation. Because LogGOPSim was originally designed to simulate single collective operations and short application traces it assumed a comparatively small input dataset. In our use cases, the extent to which the existing LogGOPSim could scale up the length of simulated execution and the number of simulated nodes was severely limited by the amount of available memory.

LogGOPSim, as originally published, requires a pre-processing step which performs the extrapolation to generate communication data for all simulated nodes. The simulator binary then attempts to map this file into virtual memory and use it directly as input data about simulated events. The size of this file is proportional to both the length of the simulated execution and the number of simulated nodes. As a result, simulating long running applications or large-scale systems requires very large data sets. Additionally, when collecting data at varying scales, a user would be required to re-run the entire toolchain from the trace data to the simulator with different parameters.

We re-wrote the input handling portion of LogGOPSim to include two critical changes. First, the modified simulator performs extrapolation in main memory as needed, rather than as a pre-processing step on disk. The traces generated from profiling an MPI application are used directly as input, and are proportional in size to the original profiled node count, rather than the extrapolated node count. Second, the simulator works on a small sliding window of input data, rather than mapping it in all at once. The code loads and extrapolates data from the traces at fine granularity, loading only a small portion of the trace file at a time. Because of these changes, the simulator's memory usage, shown in Fig. 1, remains constant independent of input trace size. In other words, the same amount of memory would be required to simulate a minute, hour, day, week or month of application execution time!

In theory, an operating system should be able to perform this type of efficient memory allocation when using a system call such as mmap. However, on the Linux 2.6.32 systems that we used, windowing the input data at the application level allowed for much greater scales before the system started to thrash.

5   Evaluating Our LogGOPSim Extensions

5.1   Correctness of the Extensions

We have verified with a careful comparison of the sequences of simulation events generated by each of the two simulators that our modified LogGOPSim produces exactly the same sequence and timing of simulated events as the original LogGOPSim. Moreover, the two simulators produce identical simulated runtimes.

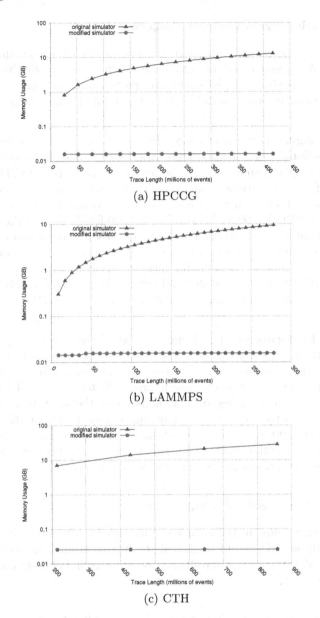

(a) HPCCG

(b) LAMMPS

(c) CTH

Fig. 1. Comparison of the memory consumption required to simulate a system running one of three applications using the original LogGOPSim simulator and our modified version as a function of input trace length. Our windowing protocol decouples memory usage from trace length. As a result, with a fixed memory budget, our modifications allows us to simulate much longer periods of applcation execution than was possible with the original simulator.

5.2   Evaluating Performance Enhancements

In this section, we evaluate the performance impact of our modifications to LogGOPSim. We consider two important metrics to evaluate our changes, maximum memory requirement and simulation performance in events/second, and then finally examine overall wallclock time for simulating the same problem.

Memory Usage. With our changes, the amount of disk space needed is no longer proportional to the node extrapolation factor, and the amount of RAM needed is no longer proportional to the length of the trace data. This enables simulation of long executions of many nodes: for the traces used here, memory usage decreased dramatically as shown in Fig. 2. Memory usage dropped by a factor of 20 for HPCCG, 60 for LAMMPS, and 900 for CTH, with the magnitude of the drop related to an applications communication pattern and the greatest distance between the initiation of a non-blocking operation and waiting for its completion. This increase of available memory allowed us to simulate over 12 minutes of HPCCG at 256K nodes and over 7 minutes of LAMMPS at 256K nodes in a short amount of time, as shown in Figures 2(a) and 2(b), respectively.

Simulation Performance. Fig. 3 and Fig. 4 show the increase in performance for our simulation framework. We show this increase both in terms of event per second of the simulator (Fig. 3) and the wall clock time to perform the simulation (Fig. 4). We see from these figures, a factor of 2.5 to 4X increase in performance from our modifications. We believe that the substation performance benefits stem from the smaller cache footprint of our implementation. We note that simulation performance decreases slightly as the number of simulated nodes increases. We are working on characterizing this decrease. However, we conclude that the achieved performance is sufficient for our purposes.

5.3   Validating Checkpoint Simulation

In this section, we present the data we collected to validate our simulator. We use both analytic models and small-scale testing to ensure that our simulator accurately models the impact of resilience mechanisms in failure-free and failure-prone environments.

Failure-Free Analytic Model of Coordinated Checkpointing. We begin with a simple analytic model for coordinated checkpointing. Equation 1 models application performance in terms of its wall clock time-to-solution, T_w, in a failure-free environment.

$$T_w = T_s + \frac{T_s}{\tau} \times \delta \qquad (1)$$

where T_w is the wall clock time, T_s is the solve time of the application without any resilience mechanism, τ is the checkpoint interval [2], and δ is the checkpoint

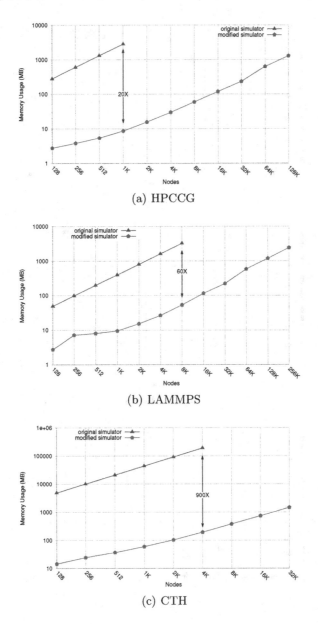

(a) HPCCG

(b) LAMMPS

(c) CTH

Fig. 2. Comparison of the memory consumption required to simulate a system running one of three applications using the original `LogGOPSim` simulator and our modified version. With a fixed memory budget, our modifications allows us to simulate systems that are significantly larger than could be simulated with the original simulator. The memory consumption decrease varies by communication pattern and varies from 20X for HPCCG to 900X for CTH.

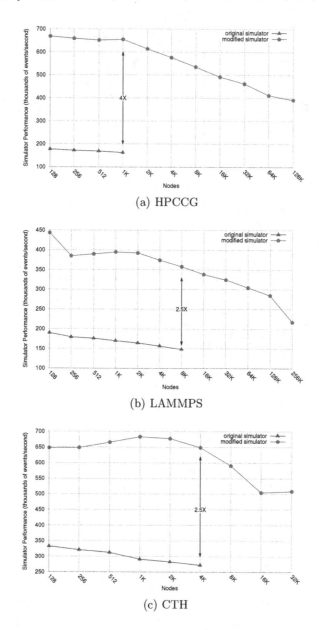

Fig. 3. Comparison of simulator performance, measured in events/second, when simulating a system running one of three applications using the original LogGOPSim simulator and using our improved version. Due to the memory requirements of the original simulator, we were unable to obtain results for simulations of large-scale systems using the original simulator. The simulation performance increase varies by application communication pattern and varies from 2.5X for LAMMPS and CTH to 4X for HPCCG.

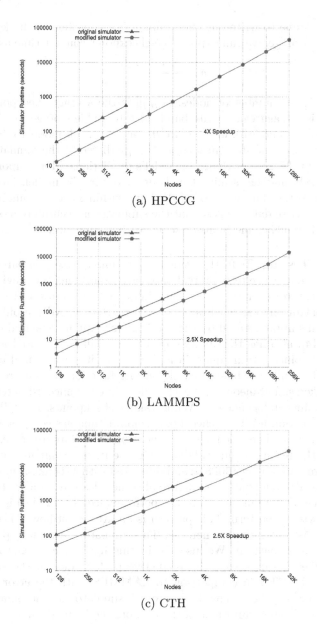

(a) HPCCG

(b) LAMMPS

(c) CTH

Fig. 4. Comparison of simulator runtime, measured in seconds (lower is better), for the original LogGOPSim simulating systems running three different applications using simulator and using our improved version. Due to the memory requirements of the original simulator, we were unable to obtain results for simulations using the original simulator for large-scale systems. Similar to Fig. 3, the simulation wallclock speedup varies by application; from 2.5X for LAMMPS and CTH to 4X for HPCCG.

commit time (time to write one checkpoint). For coordinated checkpointing to shared stable storage, we can express the checkpoint commit time as:

$$\delta = \frac{N * ||c_{avg}||}{\beta} \qquad (2)$$

where N is the number of nodes, $||c_{avg}||$ is the average checkpoint size per node, and β is the aggregate write bandwidth to stable storage.

In Figures 5(a) and 5(b), we compare the output of this model to the output of our simulator. The times-to-solution for CTH predicted by the simulator are very accurate, about 3% greater than the model's predictions. More importantly, the simulator closely matches scaling trends predicted by the model. Moreover, the simulated times-to-solution for LAMMPS are within 1% of the analytic model. On the whole, these data suggest that the simulator is accurately modeling how the impact of resilience mechanisms scales with system size.

Small-Scale Testing. To further validate our simulator, we compared it against the results of small-scale tests on real hardware. The simulator provides us with fine-grained control over the checkpoint interval and duration. To mimic this degree of control on real hardware, we constructed an MPI profiling library, libchkpt. This library, based on the the libhashckpt incremental checkpointing library [14], also has the ability to take both full coordinated and uncoordinated checkpointing techniques, in additional to its incremental coordinated techniques. The full coordinated checkpointing functionality ensures all checkpoints are taken simultaneously on each node, while the uncoordinated approach takes checkpoints independently. While taking checkpoints, the CPU is taken from the application until the checkpoint commit time has completed.

For our purposes here, we focus on validating the failure-free case. Fig. 6 and Fig. 7 show the results of this validation. These figures compare the total wall clock time simulated by LogGOPSim and measured with libchkpt running on our test platform. For reference, each figure also includes the total wall clock time in the absence of any failures. Note the performance of CTH in Fig. 6 exhibits a distinct sawtooth pattern. This pattern is an artifact of how CTH scales the computation as nodes counts increase. The simulator accurately predicts this complex sawtooth pattern. We also see in this figure the simulators error in prediction. We also note that the predictive performance of the simulator is less accurate for CTH in comparison to LAMMPS, with the error in time to solution bounded by 20%. This is due to the simulator not accounting for OS noise on the node and limitations of the network model used. In our testing, OS interference is not being generated to simplify analysis, though the simulator allows for such accounting. This OS interfere has been shown to greatly influence impact CTH performance [21]. Also, though the LogGOPSim simulator is capable of sophisticated network models, in this work we use a simple network model which does not account for network contention. As CTH does a fair amount of bulk data transfer, network contention can be an issue.

Overall, these figures show that LogGOPSim closely tracks the results measured with libchkpt. For all the configurations that we examined, the absolute

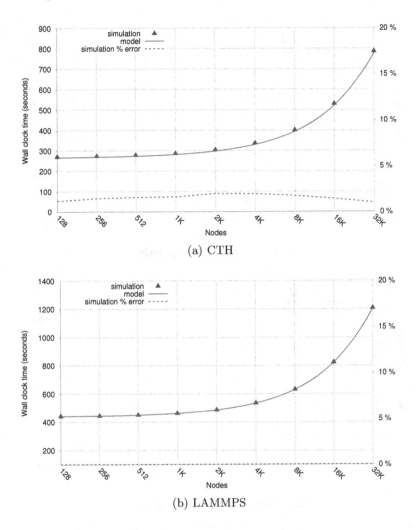

Fig. 5. Validation of the simulator against the simple analytic model described in Equation 1 for coordinated checkpointing to stable storage in a failure-free environment for CTH and LAMMPS. The model and the simulator use identical values for the T_s (for each application), τ, and δ. The simulation error is less than 3% for CTH and less than 1% for LAMMPS across the tested node count range.

wall clock time simulated by `LogGOPSim` is within 20% of the measured values. More importantly, `LogGOPSim` closely mimics the trends we observe with `libchkpt` even as performance deviates from performance on actual hardware.

6   Related Work

Although fault tolerance for HPC has been a very active area of research, few tools exist that allow us to project behavior beyond small-scale systems. As

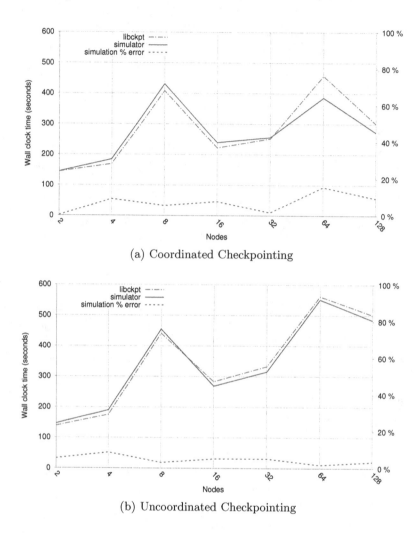

(a) Coordinated Checkpointing

(b) Uncoordinated Checkpointing

Fig. 6. Performance of `LogGOPSim` simulation against a coordinated and uncoordinated checkpointing library for CTH. The simulator and `libchkpt` use identical values for T_w (failure free performance), τ (checkpoint interval), and δ (checkpoint commit time). The simulation error in this figure is less than 20%, with this differences attributed to platform features not being simulated. For example, interference from the OS is not being generated in this case to simplify analysis. This OS interfere has been shown to greatly influence impact CTH performance [21].

we discussed above, simulating fault tolerance techniques requires an appropriate level of detail about the communication of the target application. Without an accurate representation of application communication, we cannot accurately simulate some fault tolerance techniques (e.g., asynchronous checkpointing). Too much detail unnecessarily reduces simulator performance. The application sim-

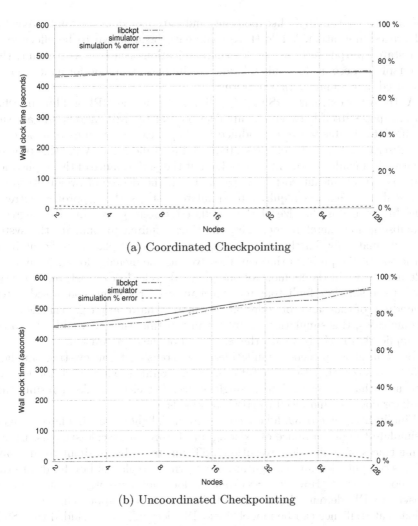

Fig. 7. Performance of `LogGOPSim` simulation against an coordinated and uncoordinated checkpointing library for LAMMPS. The simulator and `libchkpt` use identical values for T_w (failure free performance), τ (checkpoint interval), and δ (checkpoint commit time). The simulation error in this figure is shown to be less than 5% in the range tested.

ulators for fault tolerance that do exist tend to fall to either extreme; either they are not communication-accurate or they simulate communication in much greater detail than believed necessary.

In [32], Riesen et al. present a simulator that can model the impact of node failure on application performance in the context of traditional coordinated checkpoint/restart. This simulator can also account for process replication. Tikotekar et al. take a similar approach in [36]. They present a simulator that models coordinated checkpointing and can also simulate fault prediction and process migration. While these tools have been shown to be effective for their stated purposes, they are not communication-accurate. As a result, they are unable to account for fault tolerance techniques whose performance may be influenced by communication patterns.

At the other extreme is xSim [37]. xSim builds on the MPI profiling interface and interposes itself between the application and the MPI library. As a result, the simulator is able to run unmodified HPC applications. Scaling is achieved by oversubscribing the nodes of the system used for validation. While this provides us with a tremendous amount of detail about the performance of the application, it imposes a significant cost. Due to limits on the degree of oversubscription, large-scale systems are required to simulate systems that approach extreme-scale. Moreover, as the size of the simulated system grows and the degree of oversubscription therefore increases, the time required to simulate the system grows dramatically. Lastly, this oversubscription could place significant limits on the size of the problem that can be solved as the memory for each simulated node must exist in the memory of one physical node. In contrast, our approach allows us to simulate fault tolerance mechanisms for systems comprised of tens or hundreds of thousands of nodes on very modest hardware (e.g., a single node). In some cases, this simulation completes in less time than it would take to run the application itself, but with the less detail of the computation.

Boteanu et al. present a fault tolerance extension to an existing simulator in [38]. However, they target a datacenter environment where each job is a discrete unit that is assigned to a single processing element. As a result, their simulator does not map well to HPC workloads.

Finally, SST/macro [39, 40] is a coarse-grained, lightweight simulator designed to simulate the performance of existing and future large-scale systems. By collecting traces of application execution, SST/macro is able to simulate the application's computation and computation patterns at scales and on hardware that does not yet exist. However, SST/macro does not currently account for the impact of CPU detours. Because the foundation of our approach is the observation that resilience can be modeled as CPU detours, we concluded that SST/macro was not a suitable starting point for our investigation.

7   Conclusion and Future Work

We presented in this work, a new and promising approach to simulation at scale of fault-tolerance mechanisms based on the checkpoint/restart model. We identified a set of platform, application, and resilience characteristics required for accurate and efficient simulation; described a prototype framework based on extensions to a validated and freely-available application simulator implementing the LogP model; shown how resilience processing overheads can be effectively modeled as CPU detours; and demonstrated empirically that our approach accurately predicts, with an error of less than 3%, the impact of resilience mechanisms. Our modifications to the LogGOPSim simulator greatly decreased its memory consumption by a factor of 100 or greater and runtime by a factor of 4. This performance increase allows us to evaluate potential resilience solutions at meaningful application and temporal scales, while also enabling the modeling of future interconnection and storage technologies.

The design space for evaluating resilience methods in large-scale HPC applications is young and still evolving. While our simulation framework has expanded that space in new and useful ways, several areas for future work remain. Among these, we intend to extend the framework to provide failure injection for large-scale simulation. Additional failure types should also be modeled, e.g. corruption of application memory or network traffic. We understand that this may mean re-evaluating the granularity of our simulation to ensure proper and effective simulation. We are also investigating mechanisms to integrate both coarse- and fine-grained simulation for failures. This will allow us to use coarse-grained simulation in areas where failures do not occur, and fine-grained simulation when failures or other interesting events do occur. We also plan to address support for additional resilience mechanisms such as hierarchical checkpointing, replication-based approaches, process migration and cloning, as well as integration with ongoing standards efforts like the current fault tolerance proposal put forth in the MPI Forum [41]. Finally, we plan to further investigate performance limitations of our current simulation framework, including analyzing the benefit of parallelizing the simulator.

References

1. Bergman, K., et al.: Exascale computing study: Technology challenges in achieving exascale systems (September 2008), http://www.science.energy.gov/ascr/Research/CS/DARPAexascale-hardware(2008).pdf
2. Daly, J.T.: A higher order estimate of the optimum checkpoint interval for restart dumps. Future Gener. Comput. Syst. **22**(3), 303–312 (2006)
3. Bouguerra, M.-S., Gautier, T., Trystram, D., Vincent, J.-M.: A flexible checkpoint/restart model in distributed systems. In: Wyrzykowski, R., Dongarra, J., Karczewski, K., Wasniewski, J. (eds.) PPAM 2009, Part I. LNCS, vol. 6067, pp. 206–215. Springer, Heidelberg (2010)
4. Guermouche, A., Ropars, T., Brunet, E., Snir, M., Cappello, F.: Uncoordinated checkpointing without domino effect for send-deterministic MPI applications. In: International Parallel Distributed Processing Symposium (IPDPS), pp. 989–1000 (May 2011)
5. Alvisi, L., Elnozahy, E., Rao, S., Husain, S., de Mel, A.: An analysis of communication induced checkpointing. In: Twenty-Ninth Annual International Symposium on Fault-Tolerant Computing, Digest of Papers, pp. 242–249 (1999)
6. Monnet, S., Morin, C., Badrinath, R.: A hierarchical checkpointing protocol for parallel applications in cluster federations. In: Proceedings of the 18th International Parallel and Distributed Processing Symposium, p. 211. IEEE (2004)
7. Elnozahy, E.N.M., Alvisi, L., Wang, Y.-M., Johnson, D.B.: A survey of rollback-recovery protocols in message-passing systems. ACM Comput. Surv. **34**(3), 375–408 (2002)

8. Oldfield, R.A., Arunagiri, S., Teller, P.J., Seelam, S., Varela, M.R., Riesen, R., Roth, P.C.: Modeling the impact of checkpoints on next-generation systems. In: 24th IEEE Conference on Mass Storage Systems and Technologies, pp. 30–46 (September 2007)

9. Ferreira, K., Riesen, R., Bridges, P., Arnold, D., Stearley, J., Laros III, J.H., Oldfield, R., Pedretti, K., Brightwell, R.: Evaluating the viability of process replication reliability for exascale systems. In: Lathrop, S., Costa, J., Kramer, W. (eds.) SC. ACM (November 2011)

10. Schroeder, B., Gibson, G.A.: A large-scale study of failures in high-performance computing systems. In: International Conference on Dependable Systems and Networks (DSN) (June 2006)

11. Kannan, S., Gavrilovska, A., Schwan, K., Milojicic, D.: Optimizing checkpoints using NVM as virtual memory. In: Proceedings of the International Parallel and Distributed Processing Symposium, IPDPS 2013. ACM, New York (2013)

12. Dong, X., Muralimanohar, N., Jouppi, N., Kaufmann, R., Xie, Y.: Leveraging 3D PCRAM technologies to reduce checkpoint overhead for future exascale systems. In: Proceedings of the Conference on High Performance Computing Networking, Storage and Analysis, SC 2009, pp. 57:1–57:12. ACM, New York (2009)

13. Bronevetsky, G., Marques, D., Pingali, K., McKee, S., Rugina, R.: Compiler-enhanced incremental checkpointing for openmp applications. In: IEEE International Symposium on Parallel & Distributed Processing, pp. 1–12 (2009)

14. Ferreira, Kurt B., Riesen, Rolf, Brighwell, Ron, Bridges, Patrick, Arnold, Dorian: libhashckpt: hash-based incremental checkpointing using GPU's. In: Cotronis, Yiannis, Danalis, Anthony, Nikolopoulos, Dimitrios S., Dongarra, Jack (eds.) EuroMPI 2011. LNCS, vol. 6960, pp. 272–281. Springer, Heidelberg (2011)

15. Moody, A., Bronevetsky, G., Mohror, K., de Supinski, B.R.: Design, modeling, and evaluation of a scalable multi-level checkpointing system. In: ACM/IEEE International Conference for High Performance Computing, Networking, Storage and Analysis (SC 2010), pp. 1–11 (2010), http://dx.doi.org/10.1109/SC.2010.18

16. Ibtesham, D., Arnold, D., Bridges, P.G., Ferreira, K.B., Brightwell, R.: On the viability of compression for reducing the overheads of checkpoint/restart-based fault tolerance. In: 2012 41st International Conference on Parallel Processing, pp. 148–157 (2012)

17. Guermouche, A., Ropars, T., Snir, M., Cappello, F.: HydEE: Failure containment without event logging for large scale send-deterministic mpi applications. In: IPDPS, pp. 1216–1227. IEEE Computer Society (2012)

18. Mubarak, M., Carothers, C.D., Ross, R., Carns, P.: Modeling a million-node dragonfly network using massively parallel discrete-event simulation. In: 2012 SC Companion: High Performance Computing, Networking, Storage and Analysis (SCC), pp. 366–376. IEEE (2012)

19. Zheng, G., Wilmarth, T., Jagadishprasad, P., Kalé, L.V.: Simulation-based performance prediction for large parallel machines. International Journal of Parallel Programming 33(2–3), 183–207 (2005)

20. Hoefler, T., Schneider, T., Lumsdaine, A.: LogGOPSim - Simulating Large-Scale Applications in the LogGOPS Model. In: Proceedings of the 19th ACM International Symposium on High Performance Distributed Computing, pp. 597–604. ACM (June 2010)

21. Ferreira, K.B., Bridges, P., Brightwell, R.: Characterizing application sensitivity to os interference using kernel-level noise injection. In: Proceedings of the 2008 ACM/IEEE Conference on Supercomputing, p. 19. IEEE Press (2008)

22. Hoefler, T., Schneider, T., Lumsdaine, A.: Characterizing the Influence of System Noise on Large-Scale Applications by Simulation. In: International Conference for High Performance Computing, Networking, Storage and Analysis (SC 2010) (November 2010)
23. Simon, Horst D.: Barriers to exascale computing. In: Daydé, Michel, Marques, Osni, Nakajima, Kengo (eds.) VECPAR. LNCS, vol. 7851, pp. 1–3. Springer, Heidelberg (2013)
24. Elnozahy, E.N., Alvisi, L., Wang, Y.-M., Johnson, D.B.: A survey of rollback-recovery protocols in message-passing systems. ACM Computing Surveys 34(3), 375–408 (2002)
25. Plank, J.S., Li, K., Puening, M.A.: Diskless checkpointing. IEEE Transactions on Parallel and Distributed Systems 9(10), 972–986 (1998)
26. Plank, J.S., Kim, Y.B., Dongarra, J.J.: Algorithm-based diskless checkpointing for fault tolerant matrix operations. In: Twenty-Fifth International Symposium on Fault-Tolerant Computing, Digest of Papers, Pasadena, CA, USA, pp. 351–360. IEEE Comput. Soc. Press, Los Alamitos (1995)
27. Silva, L.M., Silva, J.G.: An experimental study about diskless checkpointing. In: 24th EUROMICRO Conference, Vasteras, Sweden, pp. 395–402. IEEE Computer Society Press (August 1998)
28. Monnet, S., Morin, C., Badrinath, R.: Hybrid checkpointing for parallel applications in cluster federations. In: IEEE International Symposium on Cluster Computing and the Grid, CCGrid 2004, pp. 773–782. IEEE (2004)
29. Alvisi, L., Elnozahy, E., Rao, S., Husain, S.A., De Mel, A.: An analysis of communication induced checkpointing. In: Twenty-Ninth Annual International Symposium on Fault-Tolerant Computing. Digest of Papers, pp. 242–249. IEEE (1999)
30. Gioiosa, R., Sancho, J.C., Jiang, S., Petrini, F., Davis, K.: Transparent, incremental checkpointing at kernel level: a foundation for fault tolerance for parallel computers. In: Proceedings of the 2005 ACM/IEEE Conference on Supercomputing, p. 9. IEEE Computer Society (2005)
31. Widener, P., Ferreira, K., Levy, S., Bridges, P.G., Arnold, D., Brightwell, R.: Asking the right questions: benchmarking fault-tolerant extreme-scale systems. In:Proc. 6th Workshop on Resiliency in High Performance Computing, Aachen,Germany (August 2013), in conjunction with Euro-Par 2013
32. Riesen, R., Ferreira, K., Stearley, J., Oldfield, R., Laros III, J.H., Pedretti, K., Brightwell, R., et al.: Redundant computing for exascale systems. Technical report SAND2010-8709. Sandia National Laboratories (2010)
33. Hoefler, T.: LogGOPSim - A LogGOPS (LogP, LogGP, LogGPS) Simulator and Simulation Framework (April 10, 2013), http://www.unixer.de/research/LogGOPSim/
34. Culler, D., Karp, R., Patterson, D., Sahay, A., Schauser, K.E., Santos, E., Subramonian, R., von Eicken, T.: LogP: towards a realistic model of parallel computation. SIGPLAN Not. 28(7), 1–12 (1993)
35. Hoefler, T., Siebert, C., Lumsdaine, A.: Group Operation Assembly Language - a flexible way to express collective communication. In: ICPP-2009 - The 38th International Conference on Parallel Processing. IEEE (September 2009)
36. Tikotekar, A., Vallée, G., Naughton, T., Scott, S.L., Leangsuksun, C.: Evaluation of fault-tolerant policies using simulation. In: 2007 IEEE International Conference on Cluster Computing, pp. 303–311. IEEE (2007)
37. Bohm, S., Engelmann, C.: xSim: The extreme-scale simulator. In: 2011 International Conference on High Performance Computing and Simulation (HPCS), pp. 280–286. IEEE (2011)

38. Boteanu, A., Dobre, C., Pop, F., Cristea, V.: Simulator for fault tolerance in large scale distributed systems. In: 2010 IEEE International Conference on Intelligent Computer Communication and Processing (ICCP), pp. 443–450. IEEE (2010)
39. Janssen, C.L., Adalsteinsson, H., Cranford, S., Kenny, J.P., Pinar, A., Evensky, D.A., Mayo, J.: A simulator for large-scale parallel computer architectures. International Journal of Distributed Systems and Technologies (IJDST) 1(2), 57–73 (2010)
40. Sst: The structural simulation toolkit (2011), http://sst.sandia.gov/about_sstmacro.html
41. Bland, W., Bouteiller, A., Herault, T., Hursey, J., Bosilca, G., Dongarra, J.J.: An evaluation of user-level failure mitigation support in MPI. In: Träff, J.L., Benkner, S., Dongarra, J.J. (eds.) EuroMPI 2012. LNCS, vol. 7490, pp. 193–203. Springer, Heidelberg (2012)

Characterizing the Impact of Prefetching on Scientific Application Performance

Collin McCurdy[1], Gabriel Marin[2]([✉]), and Jeffrey S. Vetter[1,3]

[1] Oak Ridge National Laboratory, Oak Ridge, TN 37831, USA
{cmccurdy,vetter}@ornl.gov
[2] University of Tennessee, Knoxville, TN 37996, USA
gmarin@utk.edu
[3] Georgia Institute of Technology, Atlanta, GA, USA

Abstract. In order to better understand the impact of hardware and software data prefetching on scientific application performance, this paper introduces two analysis techniques, one *micro-architecture*-centric and the other *application*-centric. We use these techniques to analyze representative full-scale production applications from five important Exascale target areas. We find that despite a great diversity in prefetching effectiveness across and even within applications, there is a strong correlation between regions where prefetching is most needed, due to high levels of memory traffic, and where it is most effective. We also observe that the application-centric analysis can explain many of the differences in prefetching effectiveness observed across the studied applications.

Keywords: Performance evaluation · Data streaming · Prefetching

1 Introduction

Due to power and scaling limitations, the available DRAM per processing core is projected to shrink dramatically (up to a factor 33) by the time systems reach Exascale [1]. While innovations in NVRAM technology (Memristors [2], STT-RAM [3], PCRAM [4]) offer the hope of more dense and thus more bountiful memory, it would likely come at the expense of latency.

Memory parallelism reduces the impact of latency. Data prefetching, that is identifying data that will be needed and moving it closer to the processing unit so that it is available when required by a running application, can increase memory parallelism and is therefore potentially extremely important in this new environment. However, prefetching always carries the danger that ineffective prefetches will degrade performance: data that is either not used, or will not be used in a timely fashion, can remove useful data from caches near the processing unit where it is needed.

Surprisingly, this extremely important, yet potentially dangerous, mechanism is largely hidden from users. Software prefetching instructions are generally

© Springer International Publishing Switzerland 2014
S. Jarvis et al. (Eds.): PMBS 2013 Workshops, LNCS 8551, pp. 115–135, 2014.
DOI: 10.1007/978-3-319-10214-6_6

inserted by compiler, and prefetching structures are *micro*-architectural features in hardware.

In order to better understand the impact of data prefetching on scientific application performance, this paper introduces two analysis techniques.

The first technique is *micro-architecture*-centric: we use mechanisms that allow disabling of hardware prefetching in a particular hardware implementation (AMD 10H [5]), along with hardware performance counters that accurately measure prefetching events, to systematically probe the space in an existing design, isolating the effects of multiple levels of hardware prefetchers on applications.

The second technique is *application*-centric: we have designed a tool that abstractly simulates hardware mechanisms for stream detection *for an arbitrary number of streams*, allowing us to determine the number of streams active at any one time in an application.

We have used these techniques to analyze representative full-scale production applications from five important Exascale target areas: fusion energy (GTC), climate (CAM-HOMME), molecular dynamics (LAMMPS), materials science (NEK), and combustion (S3D). We have further identified the dominant loop nests in each application, enabling a deeper understanding of underlying reasons for performance.

Overall, despite a great diversity in prefetching effectiveness (as measured by performance improvement over no prefetching) across and even within applications, we see a strong correlation between regions where prefetching is most needed (due to high levels of memory traffic) and where it is most effective.

Additionally, we find:

- While hardware prefetching always improves application performance in the applications we studied, compiler-inserted software prefetches improve performance substantially in some applications, but degrade performance substantially in other applications.
- While a hardware prefetcher at later levels of the memory hierarchy (such as the memory controller) can boost *serial* performance significantly, contention for the shared resource can substantially reduce effectiveness in a parallel context.
- Prefetching substantially increases already high levels of memory parallelism, *even in applications that prominently feature irregular data accesses*.

2   Related Work

There is a great deal of work in the literature regarding both hardware and software prefetching.

Work regarding hardware prefetching tends to focus on new ideas for prefetching structures and implementations. The ideas are implemented in simulators and evaluated using benchmarks, or portions of benchmarks, meant to represent full applications [6–9].

Literature on software prefetching focuses primarily on algorithms for determining where compilers should automatically insert prefetch instructions, again evaluated using benchmarks though often running on actual hardware [10–12].

There is little work in the literature evaluating the impact of *existing* microarchitectural and compiler prefetching implementations on full-scale application performance.

As regards our methodology, while there is plenty of discussion on the World Wide Web about mechanisms for disabling prefetching, and even small studies that benchmark performance of embedded systems kernels with and without prefetching hardware enabled [13], to our knowledge this is the first description of work that systematically enables and disables multiple levels of prefetching mechanisms to isolate their impact on full-scale application performance.

Previous work has used simulators [14] and models [15] to understand the performance limits of prefetching. A description of our approach for characterizing the number of inherent streams in an application, technique developed as part of this study, has been expanded and published separately in [16].

3   Prefetching Hardware and Software

Prefetching is a very effective technique for hiding memory latency and increasing application performance. Prefetching works by eagerly loading into the cache data that is expected to be needed in the near future. To be most effective, the data must be fetched sufficiently far in advance that its loading is completed by the time the micro-processor needs it. At least as important, prefetching must predict correctly the data that must be fetched in advance. Incorrect predictions increase demand on the memory subsystem, possibly evicting useful data from caches, and increase bandwidth use.

Prefetching comes in two main flavors: software prefetching and hardware prefetching. Software prefetching is the more common type of prefetching. Compilers generally, but also programmers, insert explicit prefetch instructions in the code to fetch data that will be needed in the near future. Prefetch instructions are similar to load instructions, except that they do not create a dependence on the loaded data. In addition, temporal hints can be associated with prefetch instruction to indicate the cache level where data should be loaded.

Hardware prefetching works without any support from the compiler or the programmer. Prefetchers based on Jouppi's stream buffers [17] are nowadays commonly found in modern micro-processors. The hardware detects easy to recognize access patterns, such as strided memory accesses, and speculatively fetches the memory addresses predicted to be accessed in the near future. While a compiler may perform more expensive analysis on the program code and can understand more complex memory access patterns, the hardware can observe the stream of dynamic addresses which may be regular even if the access pattern cannot be statically predicted. Thus, each one of the two approaches can perform better in different situations.

In rare cases, software prefetching can hurt performance due to increased issue demand on the load/store units. The hardware prefetcher works outside the core, and thus it does not affect issue bandwidth. However, both prefetch approaches can increase memory bandwidth demand. In the following section we look more closely at the two hardware prefetchers of the AMD 10H micro-architecture, and we perform an empirical evaluation of their performance.

3.1   AMD Hardware Prefetchers

While the topic of hardware prefetching has been extensively studied in litera-ture, few details have been disclosed about the actual implementations used by AMD microprocessors. We know that the AMD Shanghai and the AMD Istan-bul micro-architectures incorporate two levels of hardware prefetching. The first prefetcher is associated with the data cache level and is replicated across all the cores of a microprocessor. We call this the DC prefetcher. The DC prefetcher analyzes the stream of memory addresses generated by data cache misses and attempts to predict addresses that will be accessed by the CPU core in the near future. If a predicted memory location is not already in the data cache, the prefetcher fetches that data from L2, L3 or from DRAM. Because the prefetched data is brought into the data cache, the prefetcher operates at cache line size granularity.

The second prefetcher, the MC prefetcher, is associated with the memory controller. It operates on the stream of memory addresses produced by accesses that miss in the last level of cache and that originate from any of the cores connected to that memory controller. The MC prefetcher fetches data into a separate prefetch buffer to avoid conflicts with data loaded into the CPU caches.

The prefetchers operate by recognizing strided memory accesses. When a prefetcher recognizes an address stream, it stores the stream information into an internal data structure, and fetches the location that is predicted to be accessed next. Such streaming prefetchers can track multiple data streams at the same time, and the prefetch distance, how many predicted accesses ahead to prefetch, can be adjusted based on the observed behavior.

The prefetchers' performance is affected by several design choices: 1) the *maximum stride* represents the largest streaming stride that can be detected by the hardware; 2) the *stream table size* determines how many distinct streams can be tracked concurrently; 3) the *associativity of the stream table* determines the probability of getting conflicts in the stream table; 4) the *prefetch distance*, how many lines in advance to prefetch, determines if the prefetched data is fully loaded into the cache by the time the application needs it.

Based on data published by AMD [18], the DC prefetcher can fetch data up to 3 lines in advance, while the MC prefetcher fetches data up to 5 lines in advance. We analyze the other characteristics empirically. To understand the prefetch-ers' characteristics, we developed a micro-benchmark to observe the effects on performance while we probe part of the design space. The micro-benchmark executes streaming memory accesses with a configurable behavior. Command line arguments control the number of concurrent streams, the stride between consecutive accesses to the same stream, the total size of the memory block used by the benchmark, the number of memory access to be performed, and

Table 1. Event sets used in the study. Note that there is some duplication of events between sets, allowing sanity checks. Additionally, each event set implicitly includes CYCLES (as read from the Time Stamp Counter register via the rdtsc instruction).

SET	Event 1	Event 2	Event 3	Event 4
BASE	cycles	inst	sse_ops	L1_acc
L1	L1_acc	L1_miss	L1_frL2	L1_frNB
L2	L2_req_DC	L2_miss	L2_fill	L2_evict
L2REQ	L2_req	L2_req_DC	L2_req_PF	L2_req_SNP
L3	L3_req	L3_miss	L3_fill	L3_evict
MC	MemCtl	MemCtlWr	MemCtlRd	MemCtlPf
NODE	Rd_Req0	Rd_Req1	DRAM_Req0	DRAM_Req1
TLB	L2TLB_hit	TLB_miss	L2_req_TLB	L2m_TLB
PF	L2_req_PF	L2m_pf	MemCtlPf	sw_pf_ALL
SWPF	sw_pf_LS	sw_pf_NTA	ineff_L1	ineff_L2

Table 2. Benchmark configurations used in the empirical evaluation

Configuration Name	Mem Size (in MB)	# of Streams	Stream Size (in pages)	Stride (in lines)
MaxStride	96	1	8*k+1	-8 to +8
Align 1	32	1 – 24	16*k+1	1
Align 2	32	1 – 24	16*k+2	1
Align 4	32	1 – 24	16*k+4	1
Align 8	32	1 – 24	16*k+8	1
Align 16	32	1 – 24	16*k+0	1
Parallel	32	1 – 24	8*k+1	1

the data alignment between different streams. In addition, the micro-benchmark uses pointer chasing for all its memory accesses to prevent the compiler from inserting prefetch instructions. We used hardware counters to measure the sets of performance events L2REQ and MC shown in Table 1, while running the micro-benchmark with different configuration parameters.

3.2   Empirical Evaluation of the AMD 10H Prefetchers

Table 2 presents a summary of the parameters used for the experiments in this study. While most parameters are self explanatory, we discuss briefly the values chosen for some of them.

All the streams operate on a contiguous block of memory of size given by the *Mem Size* parameter. This memory block is divided into a number of equally sized chunks, corresponding to the number of streams. The micro-benchmark executes memory accesses from each stream in a round-robin fashion. The total memory block size and the number of streams determine an address alignment among the streams. While we were trying to understand the sizes of the different hardware tables by varying the number of concurrent streams in our micro-benchmark, we were seeing a lot of unexplained performance variation in our measurements. Hence, we concluded that some of the hardware data structures must have limited associativity and what we were observing were access conflicts.

To understand these effects, we added the *Stream Size* parameter to control the alignment between two consecutive streams. Based on empirical observations and due to reasons that will be explained in Section 3.2, we try to control the stream alignments at page granularity. We added three parameters to control this alignment. A page factor specifies that the stream size is a multiple of the given number of pages. Thus, $16 * k$ specifies that the stream size is a multiple of 16 pages. Second, a page term specifies how many additional pages are added to the stream size. A stream size of $16 * k + 1$ means that the streams are a multiple of 16 memory pages, and then one more page is added. Using these two parameters we can enforce the page alignment between two streams. For example, a stream size of $16 * k + 2$ specifies that the streams are two page aligned, but they are not 4-page, 8-page or 16-page aligned.

However, even with these alignments we were still observing noise in our measurements, noise that was caused by the 2-way associativity of the L1 cache. The AMD Shanghai and Istanbul micro-architectures have 64KB, 2-way set-associative L1 data caches. Thus, each cache way is 32KB, or 8 pages. By trying to align the streams at 2, 4, 8 and 16 pages, accesses to all streams were hitting in one or a handful of cache sets causing the prefetched data to be evicted before it was used. We were also observing conflict effects on the running times when both prefetchers were disabled. To fix this issue, we added a third parameter which specifies a number of cache lines to be added to the size of each stream. This parameter is not included in Table 2, but it was set to 1 for all experiments. By staggering the streams by one cache line, we ensure that consecutive accesses to different streams hit in different L1 sets, while only affecting the desired stream page alignment for accesses near page boundaries.

We often use the terms *prefetch* or *prefetching effectiveness* during this empirical evaluation, to quantify the performance of the hardware prefetchers. Our micro-benchmark generates only clean strided accesses. For this section, we define *prefetching effectiveness* to mean the fraction of data accesses to the next memory level that are initiated by the hardware prefetcher. Thus, for the DC prefetcher, the prefetching effectiveness is computed as

$$DC_{effectiveness} = L2\_req\_PF/L2\_req\_DC,$$

where $L2\_req\_PF$ represents the number of requests to L2 initiated by the DC hardware prefetcher, and $L2\_req\_DC$ represents the number of L2 requests originating from the data cache. Note that the latter event includes both requests to L2 caused by L1 cache misses and requests initiated by the DC prefetcher.

Similarly, the MC prefetching effectiveness is computed as

$$MC_{effectiveness} = MemCtlPf/MemCtlRd,$$

where the *MemCtlPf* event counts the number of memory requests initiated by the memory controller prefetcher, and *MemCtlRd* counts the total number

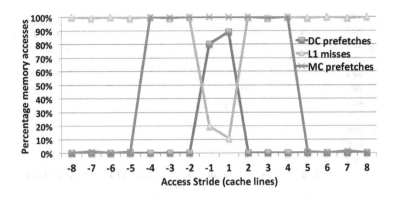

Fig. 1. Prefetch effectiveness as a function of access stride

of memory read requests. These events are listed in Table 1, and are measured using the hardware performance counters present on the AMD 10H architecture.

In Section 5, we evaluate the performance of the hardware prefetchers by measuring their impact on the running time of five full-scale production applications.

Maximum Stride. To understand the maximum streaming stride recognized by the two AMD prefetchers, we collected hardware counter events using configuration *MaxStride* shown in Table 2, while enabling one prefetcher at a time. Figure 1 plots the prefetching effectiveness computed for each of the two hardware prefetchers as we varied the memory access stride between -8 and +8 cache lines. We also plot the number of L1 cache misses normalized to the total number of L2 requests originating from the data cache. As explained in Section 3.1, the MC prefetcher brings prefetched data into a buffer located at the memory controller level. Thus, a successful prefetch does not lower the observed number of L3 misses, but only their latencies.

The data clearly shows that the DC prefetcher recognizes only streams with a stride of one cache line, while the MC prefetcher recognizes streams with a stride of up to four cache lines. The two prefetchers recognize both forward and backward streaming accesses. We also notice that the DC prefetcher does not initiate all the data requests to L2 even for our simple, synthetic access pattern. Streams recognized by the DC prefetcher live only inside one page. A stream is discarded on a page boundary and a new stream must be recognized inside the new page. It takes three strided accesses to recognize an address stream. Thus, a number of accesses to each page are not prefetched.

Table Size and Associativity. Because prefetch streams live only inside one memory page, and based on empirical observations from our initial experiments that suggested the occurrence of some type of resource conflict based on the page index of the streams, we believe that the DC prefetcher has at least one

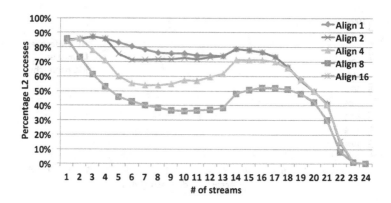

Fig. 2. DC prefetcher effectiveness as a function of stream count and page alignment

low associativity hardware structure that is indexed by the low bits of the page number. To verify these observations, we performed a set of experiments where we forced the streams to be separated by different powers of two numbers of pages. We used configurations *Align 1* to *Align 16* from Table 2 to understand the size of the hardware structures in the two prefetchers, and to determine if there are any associativity effects.

Figure 2 shows the DC prefetcher's effectiveness for different numbers of concurrent streams, from 1 to 24, and for different page alignments among streams. Each curve corresponds to the streams being separated by a multiple of the specified number of pages, but not by a multiple of a larger power of two, see also the discussion at the start of Section 3.2. We can make several observations based on these empirical results. Looking at the data points corresponding to x values of 1 to 8 streams for the different stream alignments, we observe a pattern that suggests the presence of a low associativity hardware structure.

Let the curve labeled *Align 1* be the baseline configuration. When stream locations are aligned by a multiple of 2 pages, the prefetcher performs as well as the baseline configuration up to a number of 4 streams. After that, its effectiveness decreases. When streams are aligned by 4 pages, the prefetcher performs at the baseline level up to 2 streams, while for 8- and 16-page aligned streams, the prefetcher's performance decreases for any number of streams larger than 1. These observations suggest the presence of a direct mapped, 8 entries structure in the DC prefetcher, which is indexed by the page number. However, the DC prefetcher continues to perform reasonably well up to 16-20 streams, which indicates that the 8-entries hardware structure is not the main limiting factor. Its direct-mapping, however, affects the prefetcher's effectiveness, especially for page alignments of 4-pages and larger powers of two.

Figure 3 presents the data collected for the MC prefetcher. Unlike the DC prefetcher, the MC prefetcher does not seem to be affected by the streams' page alignment. We should note, however, that our alignment is enforced on virtual addresses, and the MC prefetcher operates on a stream of physical addresses.

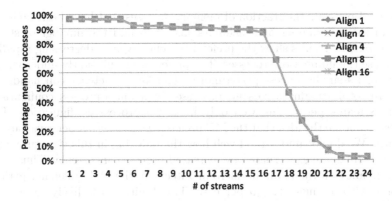

Fig. 3. MC prefetcher effectiveness as a function of stream count and page alignment

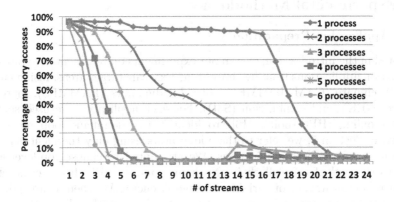

Fig. 4. Parallel MC prefetch effectiveness

Even so, the MC prefetcher seems to have a more consistent behavior, with only a slight decrease in effectiveness for more than five concurrent streams. The prefetcher's performance drops more sharply after 16 streams, suggesting the presence of a 16-entries hardware structure. However, the fact that its effectiveness drops somewhat gradually, may still indicate that a hardware structure is set-associative.

Parallel Performance. While the DC prefetcher is private to each core, the MC prefetcher operates on the stream of physical addresses generated by all the cores. In this section, we analyze briefly the MC prefetcher's effectiveness as we increase the number of processes generating memory accesses. To evaluate the parallel effectiveness of the MC prefetcher, we loaded different numbers of concurrent instances of the micro-benchmark running configuration *Parallel* from Table 2, from one to six concurrent instances.

Figure 4 presents the fraction of memory accesses that have been prefetched as we varied the number of benchmark instances and the number of streams per process. The results show the prefetcher's effectiveness decreasing rapidly as we increase the number of processes. The prefetcher significantly underperforms relative to its single process performance. The MC prefetcher can handle well only 8-10 total streams across all processes in a multi-process configuration, with 10 streams performing well only in a two process configuration. These numbers reinforce the idea that the MC prefetcher has a set-associative hardware structure. We do not understand well how the indexing in this structure works, but the conflicts are exacerbated by increased process concurrency. Thus, at full core occupancy on the Istanbul micro-architecture, the MC prefetcher performs well only with a single stream per core. This limitation is likely to adversely affect the scaling of applications from one to six cores.

4   Experimental Methodology

4.1   Application Preparation

As noted in the introduction, we ran our experiments on representative full-scale production applications from five important Exascale target areas: fusion energy (GTC), climate (CAM-HOMME), molecular dynamics (LAMMPS), materials science (NEK), and combustion (S3D). For each application we used sample-based profiling (HPCToolkit [19]) to identify five dominant loop nests. For brevity, in Section 5, we refer to these loop nests using only the identifiers *loop* 1 − 5 for each of these applications. We attempted to choose top-level loops close to the end of the call chain. No loops contain MPI library calls, eliminating potential impact of variable message latencies. We then 'calipered', i.e., marked the beginning and the end, the chosen loops with calls to the API of another tool (Memphis [20]), which collects performance counter data with very low overhead, allowing precise attribution of counted events to loops.

4.2   Hardware Experiments

On AMD hardware, bits in model-specific registers (MSRs) determine whether the hardware prefetching structures described in Section 3.1 are operational. We have implemented a user space tool that accesses the MSRs to enable or disable the hardware prefetch mechanisms on demand.

We enable and disable software prefetching through the use of PGI compiler (version 12.3 [21]) flags, creating two executables, one with prefetching instructions inserted and one without. PGI's '-fastsse' level of optimization, often used by application teams when running on high performance computing systems, automatically inserts prefetch instructions where it deems suitable. We use the '-Mnoprefetch' flag to disable prefetching. We have made no attempt to otherwise control the compiler's decisions about prefetching.

Of the eight possible combinations (MC on or off, DC on or off, and SW on or off), we chose to measure six:

- N: No prefetching, hardware or software, enabled.
- S: Only software prefetching enabled.
- M: Only memory controller prefetcher (MC) enabled.
- D: Only data cache prefetcher (DC) enabled.
- H: Both hardware prefetchers, MC and DC, enabled.
- HS: All prefetching mechanisms, hardware and software, enabled.

For each of the six combinations, we ran each application ten times, one for each event set described in Table 1, once in serial mode and once in parallel (MPI). The parallel runs used all available cores in a single socket. We pinned processes to cores, in both serial and parallel runs, using the 'rankfile' mechanism provided by the OpenMPI [22] implementation.

Finally, we performed the full experiment on two AMD 10H platforms: a Shanghai implementation with four cores per socket, and an Istanbul implementation with six cores per socket.

4.3   Stream Simulator Experiments

To help us understand the observed prefetching performance on the full-scale production applications, we wrote a tool to abstractly understand the number of concurrent streams in an application [16]. The tool, written on top of PIN [23], works on unmodified and fully-optimized x86-64 binaries. In fact, for the software simulation runs of the full applications, we used the same executables as for the hardware measurements.

On each memory access, the simulator detects if the access is part of a stream or not. If the access is part of a stream, it also computes the number of concurrent streams active at that time. Optionally, memory accesses can be filtered by a configurable cache simulator. In this case, only cache misses are further classified as streams or not. For our full application results in Section 5, we performed two simulation runs: 1) one simulation corresponding to the DC prefetcher detects streams with a stride of +/- 1 cache lines, and accesses are filtered by a 64KB, 2-way set-associative cache; 2) a second simulation corresponding to the MC prefetcher detects streams with a stride of up to four cache lines, and accesses are filtered by a 6MB, 48-way set-associative cache.

We stress tested the tool by analyzing memory access patterns generated by different synthetic micro-benchmarks, and the tool correctly identified streaming behavior in each case. Figure 5 shows a simple validation of the stream simulation algorithm for the micro-benchmark presented in Section 3.2 with up to 12 concurrent streams. The figure presents the distribution of stream counts detected by the tool for several runs of the micro-benchmark using different stream counts.

Each bar in the figure represents one execution of the micro-benchmark, using one, two, three, four, five, and twelve concurrent streams, respectively. The entries in the graph's legend show the different categories in which a memory access can be classified, representing how many parallel streams are active at that time. If a memory access is not part of any stream, it is classified instead

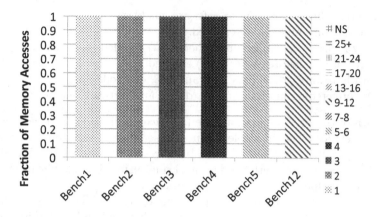

Fig. 5. Stream count simulation for micro-benchmark runs with different numbers of streams

as *NS* (Not a Stream). On the *y* axis we stack the normalized counts of memory accesses that fall into each of the categories listed in the legend. The stacks must sum up to 1 in each case.

The main loop of the micro-benchmark executes perfectly strided accesses. The simulation tool correctly detects this behavior and the actual number of streams in each benchmark execution. While these tests are very simple, they give us an opportunity to explain how the stream simulation data is presented in the Results section.

5   Experimental Results

5.1   Serial Results

Figures 6 to 10 collect results from serial runs. Figure 6 demonstrates the overall performance improvements of prefetching mechanisms, in isolation and working cooperatively, over no prefetching (N).

Hardware prefetching (H) always helps, improving performance by as much as 27% for *GTC*. Though in all applications other than *LAMMPS*, the DC prefetcher alone is responsible for a large fraction of the gain, the two hardware prefetchers are always more effective in tandem than alone, providing up to a 5% improvement over the best individual result (again in *GTC*). On the other hand, while software prefetching (S) alone helps *GTC*, *NEK*, and *S3D* by up to 5%, it degrades *LAMMPS* performance slightly, and *CAM* performance significantly (7%).

Memory Traffic. Figure 7 summarizes the memory requirements of the applications when prefetching is turned off, overall (in the 'step' bin) and by each representative loop nest, as measured in memory controller transactions

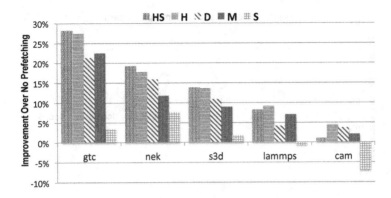

Fig. 6. Performance improvement over no prefetching (N) (($cycles - N\_cycles)/N\_cycles$) for the following combinations of prefetching strategies: software only (S), memory-controller prefetcher only (M), data-cache prefetcher only (D), both hardware prefetchers (H), both hardware prefetches with software (HS)

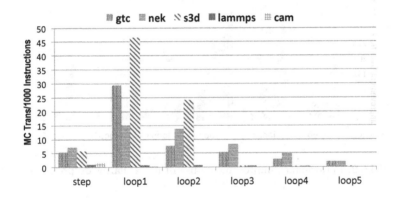

Fig. 7. Memory Controller Transactions w/o prefetching

per thousand instructions. Note that the loop nests are ordered high-to-low by memory requirement, and that the ordering is preserved in the remaining figures.

While the *GTC* and *NEK* loop nests demonstrate a fairly uniform and relatively high memory requirement, reflected in the overall 'step' numbers, *S3D*'s overall need, also high, is attributable to the extreme traffic generated by only two loop nests. In contrast, the working sets of *LAMMPS* and *CAM* appear to fit comfortably in cache, resulting in exceedingly low traffic to memory.

Figures 9 and 10 isolate the performance improvements of the DC and MC prefetchers respectively. Note the correlation between the loop nests with the highest memory requirements and those that see the greatest benefit from prefetching. The same result holds at the application step level.

Finally, Fig. 8 isolates the impact of software prefetching. In most cases (*CAM* and *LAMMPS*), performance degradation corresponds to low memory traffic,

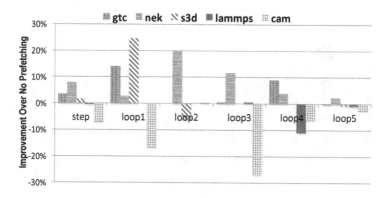

Fig. 8. Performance improvements from software prefetching

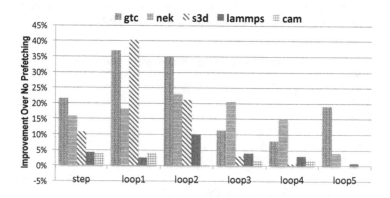

Fig. 9. Performance improvements from the DC hardware prefetcher

likely due to replacement of important data close to the processor with unneeded data from memory. This conclusion is supported by significantly higher memory traffic for these loop nests when software prefetching is enabled (not shown). The one exception is the second loop nest in *S3D*, in which the compiler-generated prefetches clearly get in the way of heavy demand traffic.

Memory Parallelism. Figure 11 demonstrates the inherent memory paral-lelism (i.e., with no prefetching enabled) for the three memory-intensive applica-tions, and the additional memory parallelism provided by the dcache prefetcher. We arrive at these numbers by dividing total DRAM accesses by the results of counters that measure *non-overlapped* requests to DRAM.

We start by noting that the base memory-parallelism is quite high for *NEK* and *S3D*, over 4 and close to 8 respectively for a full step. Parallelism is lower for *GTC*, due to a large number of indirect array accesses that serialize many memory references. Nevertheless, the DC prefetcher substantially increases

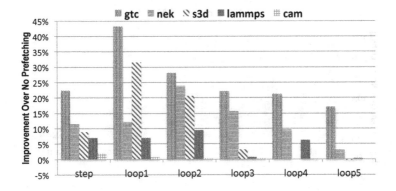

Fig. 10. Performance improvements from the MC hardware prefetcher

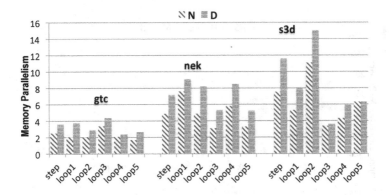

Fig. 11. Inherent memory parallelism (N) and increase due to DC prefetcher (D)

parallelism for all applications, by more than 50% overall. Again, in general the effect is greater for loops with higher memory requirements.

5.2 Parallel Results

Figures 12 and 13 presents results for parallel runs using all available cores on Shanghai (12) and Istanbul platforms (13). On Shanghai, while the DC prefetcher performance is quite stable between serial and parallel runs, the improvement due to the MC prefetcher alone for *GTC*, *NEK* and *S3D* declines markedly.

In all cases, the loss in productivity leads to a significant decrease in the performance boost due to hardware prefetching (H) from serial to parallel runs, accounting for a full 5% decrease for *GTC*. Based on analysis of loop level results, we find that the decrease in M productivity is due to a combination of contention for stream resources in the prefetching mechanism, and memory bandwidth constraints.

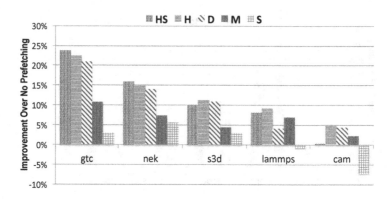

Fig. 12. Performance improvement over no prefetching (N) for parallel (MPI) runs with 4 processes per socket (Shanghai)

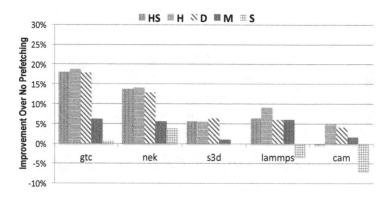

Fig. 13. Performance improvement over no prefetching (N) for parallel (MPI) runs with 6 processes per socket (Istanbul)

GTC. The hardware prefetchers produce significantly lower performance improvements during the parallel runs for three loop nests in GTC: *loop 1* (-18%), *loop 4* (-15%), and *loop 3* (-9%). In all cases, drops in MC performance gains substantially outweigh drops in DC prefetcher gains.

While *loop 1* has significant memory bandwidth requirements, with per-core memory bandwidth dropping from 3.2 GB/s in serial mode to 2 GB/s in parallel, the other two have more modest requirements and do not suffer a significant drop. However, both suffer from a marked drop in prefetch efficiency, as measured by the percentage of memory accesses due to prefetches: prefetch efficiency drops from 95% to 9% for *loop 4* , and from 98% to 21% for *loop 3*.

Interestingly, constructive interference from extra memory references due to the addition of DC prefetcher in H and HS runs slightly improves the MC prefetch efficiency for both *loop 4* and *loop 3*. However, for *loop 1*, the addition of DC

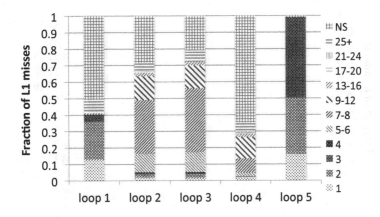

Fig. 14. L1 miss stream coverage for GTC. Each bar on the x axis corresponds to one loop nest. On the y axis we have the percentage of cache misses that fall into each category listed in the graph's legend, depending on the number of concurrent streams active at that time.

prefetcher requests introduces *destructive* interference in the parallel case, reducing efficiency from 97% to 68%.

Stream simulation results, presented in Figs. 14 and 15, explain both the benefit of MC in the serial case, and the decrease in its benefit in the parallel case. Figure 14 demonstrates that most DC misses in *loop 1* and *loop 4* are not streaming accesses, and the majority of references in *loops 2 and 3* require more than seven streams.

As noted earlier, *GTC* features a large number of indirect accesses. The substantial reduction in non-streaming accesses observed in Fig. 15 demonstrates that the L3 cache acts as a filter, removing irregular reference patterns that confuse the DC prefetcher, and leaving a small number of regular streams for the MC prefetcher. Furthermore, the simulation tool reveals that *loop 1* features a stride-4 reference pattern, due to the memory layout of the inner dimension of two dominant array variables, which cannot be detected by the DC prefetcher. Figure 15 also shows that the first four loop nests in GTC require 5 to 8 streams per process at the memory controller level, and Fig. 4 showed us that the MC prefetcher becomes much less effective in a multi-process configuration at higher levels of streaming concurrency.

S3D and NEK. Two loop nests in *S3D* and one in *NEK* exhibit similar behavior with respect to MC prefetcher performance. Figures 16 and 17 present stream simulation results for *S3D*. In contrast with *GTC*, Fig. 16 shows that the streams in both *S3D* loops should easily be covered by the DC prefetcher. However, since the L3 miss rate is extremely high for these loops, the MC prefetcher sees very nearly the same streams. Though the number of streams at the MC for the two loops is quite low, two and three concurrent streams, respectively, we still see a

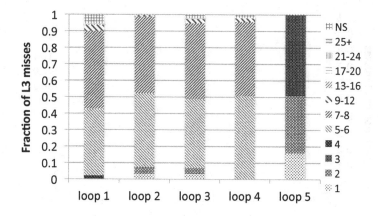

Fig. 15. L3 miss stream coverage for GTC

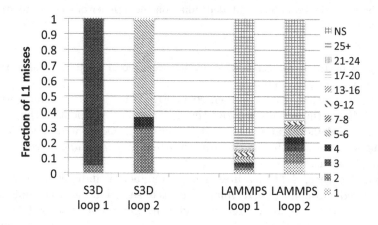

Fig. 16. L1 miss stream coverage for S3D and LAMMPS

substantial reduction in prefetch efficiency in the hardware results, particularly for the second loop nest, likely due to associativity conflicts.

LAMMPS. Finally, *LAMMPS* is unique in that the MC prefetcher improves performance of the dominant loop nest (*loop 1*), and the contribution is not diminished during a parallel run. The stream simulation results in Figs. 16 and 17 again explain the reason for this behavior. Based on the Fig. 16 results, the *loop 1* accesses that the DC prefetcher sees are for the most part not streamable. However, the filtered accesses that the MC sees easily fit into a single stream, in other words the accesses come from a single program array. The program-level explanation for this behavior is that the loop nest computes interactions between atoms and while access to the atoms is highly irregular, access to the

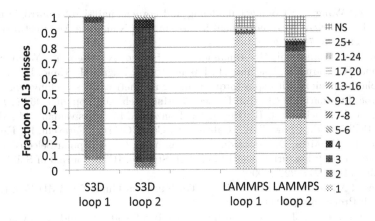

Fig. 17. L3 miss stream coverage for S3D and LAMMPS

neighbor list is regular. While accesses to the atom data exhibits reuse in L3, the interaction list is linearly traversed with no temporal reuse inside the loop.

6   Conclusion

In order to better understand the impact of data prefetching on scientific application performance, this paper has introduced two techniques, one *micro-architecture*-centric and the other *application*-centric, to analyze the prefetching performance of five important Exascale target applications.

We have found that despite a great diversity in prefetching effectiveness, there is a strong correlation between regions where prefetching is most needed (due to high levels of memory traffic) and where it is most effective. Further, we found that while hardware prefetching always improved application performance in the applications we studied, compiler-inserted software prefetches degraded performance for two applications with extremely low memory requirements.

We also found that a hardware prefetcher at later levels of the memory hierarchy can boost *serial* performance significantly, but contention for the shared resource can substantially reduce effectiveness in a parallel context. Finally we found that prefetching substantially increases already high levels of memory parallelism, *even in applications that prominently feature irregular data accesses.*

References

1. Ashby, S., Beckman, P., Chen, J., Colella, P., Collins, B., Crawford, D., Dongarra, J., Kothe, D., Lusk, R., Messina, P., Mezzacappa, T., Moin, P., Norman, M., Rosner, R., Sarkar, V., Siegel, A., Streitz, F., White, A., Wright, M.: The opportunities and challenges of exascale computing. Technical report, U.S. Department of Energy (2010)

2. Chen, Y., Wang, X.: Compact modeling and corner analysis of spintronic memristor. In: IEEE/ACM International Symposium on Nanoscale Architectures 2009 (Nanoarch), pp. 7–12 (2009)
3. Hosomi, M., Yamagishi, H., Yamamoto, T., Bessho, K., Higo, Y., Yamane, K., Yamada, H., Shoji, M., Hachino, H., Fukumoto, C., Nagao, H., Kano, H.: A novel nonvolatile memory with spin torque transfer magnetization switching: spin-ram. In: Proc. International Electron Device Meeting Tech. Dig., pp. 459–462 (2005)
4. Bedeschi, F., Fackenthal, R., Resta, C., Donze, E.M., Jagasivamani, M., Buda, E.C., Pellizzer, F., Chow, D.W., Cabrini, A., Calvi, G.M.A., Faravelli, R., Fantini, A., Torelli, G., Mills, D., Gastaldi, R., Casagrande, G.: A Bipolar-Selected Phase Change Memory Featuring Multi-Level Cell Storage. IEEE Journal of Solid-State Circuits **44**(1), 217–227 (2009)
5. Advanced Micro Devices Inc: Software Optimization Guide for AMD Family 10h and 12h Processors (2011)
6. Chen, T.F., Baer, J.L.: A performance study of software and hardware data prefetching schemes. In: Proceedings of the 21st Annual International Symposium on Computer Architecture, ISCA 1994, pp. 223–232. IEEE Computer Society Press, Los Alamitos (1994)
7. Srinath, S., Mutlu, O., Kim, H., Patt, Y.N.: Feedback directed prefetching: Improving the performance and bandwidth-efficiency of hardware prefetchers. In: Proceedings of the 2007 IEEE 13th International Symposium on High Performance Computer Architecture, HPCA 2007, pp. 63–74. IEEE Computer Society, Washington, DC (2007)
8. Ebrahimi, E., Mutlu, O., Lee, C.J., Patt, Y.N.: Coordinated control of multiple prefetchers in multi-core systems. In: Proceedings of the 42nd Annual IEEE/ACM International Symposium on Microarchitecture, MICRO 42, pp. 316–326. ACM, New York (2009)
9. Ebrahimi, E., Lee, C.J., Mutlu, O., Patt, Y.N.: Prefetch-aware shared resource management for multi-core systems. In: Proceedings of the 38th Annual International Symposium on Computer Architecture, ISCA 2011, pp. 141–152. ACM, New York (2011)
10. Callahan, D., Kennedy, K., Porterfield, A.: Software prefetching. In: Proceedings of the Fourth International Conference on Architectural Support for Programming Languages and Operating Systems, ASPLOS-IV, pp. 40–52. ACM, New York (1991)
11. Santhanam, V., Gornish, E.H., Hsu, W.C.: Data prefetching on the hp pa-8000. In: Proceedings of the 24th Annual International Symposium on Computer Architecture, ISCA 1997, pp. 264–273. ACM, New York (1997)
12. Luk, C.K., Mowry, T.C.: Automatic compiler-inserted prefetching for pointer-based applications. IEEE Trans. Comput. **48**(2), 134–141 (1999)
13. Intel Corporation: Optimizing embedded system performance-impact of data prefetching on a medical imaging application (2006)
14. Puzak, T.R., Hartstein, A., Emma, P.G., Srinivasan, V.: When prefetching improves/degrades performance. In: Proceedings of the 2nd Conference on Computing Frontiers, CF 2005, pp. 342–352. ACM, New York (2005)
15. Liu, F., Solihin, Y.: Studying the impact of hardware prefetching and bandwidth partitioning in chip-multiprocessors. SIGMETRICS Perform. Eval. Rev. **39**(1), 37–48 (2011)

16. Marin, G., McCurdy, C., Vetter, J.S.: Diagnosis and optimization of application prefetching performance. In: Proceedings of the 27th International ACM Conference on International Conference on Supercomputing, ICS 2013, pp. 303–312. ACM, New York (2013)
17. Jouppi, N.P.: Improving direct-mapped cache performance by the addition of a small fully-associative cache and prefetch buffers. In: Proceedings of the 17th Annual International Symposium on Computer Architecture, ISCA 1990, pp. 364–373. ACM, New York (1990)
18. Advanced Micro Devices Inc: BIOS and Kernel Developer's Guide (BKDG) For AMD Family 10h Processors (2010)
19. Adhianto, L., Banerjee, S., Fagan, M., Krentel, M., Marin, G., Mellor-Crummey, J., Tallent, N.R.: HPCToolkit: Tools for performance analysis of optimized parallel programs. Concurrency and Computation: Practice and Experience **22**(6), 685–701 (2010)
20. McCurdy, C., Vetter, J.: Memphis: Finding and fixing numa-related performance problems on multi-core platforms. In: Proc. of the 2010 IEEE Intl. Symp. on Performance Analysis of Systems Software, pp. 87–96 (March 2010)
21. Portland Group International Inc: PGI Compiler User's Guide (2012)
22. Gabriel, E., et al.: Open MPI: goals, concept, and design of a next generation MPI implementation. In: Kranzlmüller, D., Kacsuk, P., Dongarra, J. (eds.) EuroPVM/MPI 2004. LNCS, vol. 3241, pp. 97–104. Springer, Heidelberg (2004)
23. Luk, C.K., Cohn, R., Muth, R., Patil, H., Klauser, A., Lowney, G., Wallace, S., Reddi, V.J., Hazelwood, K.: Pin: building customized program analysis tools with dynamic instrumentation. In: Proceedings of the 2005 ACM SIGPLAN Conference on Programming Language Design and Implementation, PLDI 2005, pp. 190–200. ACM, New York (2005)

Performance Modeling of Gyrokinetic Toroidal Simulations for a Many-Tasking Runtime System

Matthew Anderson[✉], Maciej Brodowicz, Abhishek Kulkarni, and Thomas Sterling

School of Informatics and Computing, Center for Research in Extreme Scale Technologies, Indiana University, Bloomington, Indiana
{andersmw,mbrodowi,adkulkar,tron}@crest.iu.edu
http://www.crest.iu.edu

Abstract. Conventional programming practices on multicore processors in high performance computing architectures are not universally effective in terms of efficiency and scalability for many algorithms in scientific computing. One possible solution for improving efficiency and scalability in applications on this class of machines is the use of a many-tasking runtime system employing many lightweight, concurrent threads. Yet a priori estimation of the potential performance and scalability impact of such runtime systems on existing applications developed around the bulk synchronous parallel (BSP) model is not well understood. In this work, we present a case study of a BSP particle-in-cell benchmark code which has been ported to a many-tasking runtime system. The 3-D Gyrokinetic Toroidal code (GTC) is examined in its original MPI form and compared with a port to the High Performance ParalleX 3 (HPX-3) runtime system. Phase overlap, oversubscription behavior, and work rebalancing in the implementation are explored. Results for GTC using the SST/macro simulator complement the implementation results. Finally, an analytic performance model for GTC is presented in order to guide future implementation efforts.

Keywords: Performance modeling · ParalleX · Many-tasking runtime systems

1 Introduction

The level of thread parallelism provided by the multicore processors pervasive in present-day high performance computing systems has increased the relative prominence of the concept of many-tasking: implementing an application using many lightweight concurrent threads for a wide variety of application components. Many-tasking enables several key execution concepts crucial for improving performance and scalability, including: task oversubscription, or the overdecomposition of a problem resulting in multiple tasks competing for a single computational resource; overlapping of computational phases, including overlapping communication and computation phases in order to hide network latency; and intelligent task scheduling, resulting in implicit load balancing controlled by the task scheduler. These benefits have been documented across a wide variety of software libraries and runtime systems, including more

© Springer International Publishing Switzerland 2014
S. Jarvis et al. (Eds.): PMBS 2013 Workshops, LNCS 8551, pp. 136–157, 2014.
DOI: 10.1007/978-3-319-10214-6_7

recently using MPI [25], OpenMP [11], Charm++ [27], Unified Parallel C (UPC) [12], MPI+OpenMP [6], MPI+UPC [10], Intel Threading Building Blocks (TBB) [32,34], High Performance ParalleX (HPX) [9,26], Cilk plus [1], Chapel [7], XKaapi [15], Coarray Fortran 2.0 [40], and Qthreads [38]. For several decades, the qualitative characteristics of many-tasking have been set forth in the Actors model [20], Multilisp [35], Fortress [2], and X10 [8].

While the many-tasking capabilities of runtime systems and libraries continue to improve, scientific applications overwhelmingly employ the bulk synchronous parallel (BSP) model [24,36]. Porting an application designed around the BSP model to a many-tasking execution model can involve significant development time and algorithm redesign costs while the performance benefits of such a transition are hard to quantify before performing the port. Specific case studies and discrete event simulators can assist in identifying and quantifying such performance benefits. This work provides a specific case study as well as a discrete event simulator built for the ParalleX execution model [14] to assist in quantifying expected performance improvements resulting from transitioning an application from the BSP model to a many-tasking execution model.

In the case study presented here, we examine the effects of transitioning the 3D Gyrokinetic Toroidal Code (GTC) [13] from a BSP model to the ParalleX execution model as implemented by the HPX-3 runtime system. HPX-3 is an experimental, ParalleX-compliant runtime system developed in C++ at the Louisiana State University. It features lightweight (user space) multithreading, advanced synchronization primitives called Local Control Objects (LCOs), parcel based communication that extends the concept of active messages, and Active Global Address Space (AGAS). All computational objects created by an HPX program are assigned unique identifiers by AGAS and are free to migrate between compute nodes; HPX provides mechanisms that can transparently access both local and remote objects using the same interface. This approach facilitates building of parallel, asynchronous, message-driven applications that are capable of migrating work to data when beneficial to overall performance.

GTC uses the particle-in-cell method [37] for plasma simulations and forms part of the NERSC-6 suite of benchmarks [4]. There are numerous performance studies on the MPI version of GTC [39,40] across a wide array of architectures making it an ideal candidate for this case study. The metrics explored here include performance, communication characteristics, and the overlap of phases both in cases with an ideal load balance and a moderate load imbalance.

Complementing the GTC implementation effort in HPX-3 are two additional performance modeling efforts: one using coarse grained simulation of GTC with the SST/macro simulator [19] and the second using an analytic performance model of GTC for ParalleX. Overall, this work makes the following new contributions:

– It provides both a simple legacy migration path for a BSP style code to run in a many-tasking runtime system with minimal modifications and a performance comparison between the different modalities of computation. The legacy migration path consists only of enforcing thread safety and replacing MPI calls with task model equivalents.

- It examines the phase overlap and implicit load balancing capabilities of a many-tasking runtime system executing a code designed for BSP and quantifies the benefits derived from these capabilities.
- It provides a performance simulator for comparing performance, communication, and phase overlap characteristics for a BSP style code in a many-tasking runtime system.
- It provides an analytic performance model of GTC using the ParalleX execution model.

This work is divided into six parts. Work related to this study and where this study fits into the broader discussion about many-tasking execution models is discussed in Section 2. Section 3 introduces the GTC code as well as the methodology behind the GTC port to HPX-3. It presents the implementation results exploring performance, communication, and phase overlap. Section 4 introduces the skeleton GTC code and its use within SST/macro for gauging the impact of key runtime system overheads on performance. Section 5 presents an analytic performance model based on ParalleX and developed for GTC. Section 6 presents our conclusions.

2 Related Work

There are several recent efforts to explore how an application changes when transitioning from MPI to a new runtime system or programming model. The Livermore Unstructured Lagrange Explicit Shock Hydrodynamics (LULESH) applications was recently examined using a wide range of conventional and emerging programming models, including MPI, OpenMP, MPI+OpenMP, CUDA, Charm++, Chapel, Liszt, and Loci [28]. The numerous application implementations contain a wide range of source code line counts and implementation choices specific to each programming model in order to systematically explore productivity benefits of each. They found that several emerging programming models showed significant productivity benefits over conventional approaches as measured by the number of lines of code needed to produce the parallel implementation of LULESH. However, they also found that several models required significant additional development just to match the performance of the MPI version.

Several other studies have compared and contrasted performance using microbenchmarks with a focus on execution overhead, such as in Appeltauer et al. [5] using context-oriented languages and in Gilmanov et al. [16] using task models. Olivier et al. [33] discusses comparisons of task models using an imbalanced task graph as the proxy application. However, no study exists which examines the performance characteristics of a full application designed for BSP but run in a many-tasking runtime system where the only change to the original code is thread safety enforcement and the replacement of MPI calls with task model equivalents. Performance simulators for task models along with their comparisons to BSP are also missing from the literature.

Madduri et al. explore the impact of multicore-specific optimizations for gyrokinetic toroidal simulations and report up to 2x speedup using hybrid MPI-OpenMP and MPI-OpenMP-CUDA GTC versions [30]. Performance improvements by overlapping computation and communication for GTC using OpenMP tasking have also been demonstrated previously [29].

There are multiple performance modeling efforts either using coarse grained simulation or analytic performance models. Hoefler et al. [22] enumerate how analytic performance models can guide systematic performance tuning. Hendry [17] analyzed and reported on the MPI based GTC skeleton code for the SST/macro coarse grained simulator with a focus on reducing power consumption while maintaining performance. Analytic performance models for MPI collectives were explored by Angskun et al. [3] while Mathis et al. [31] created a performance model for particle transport.

3   A Case Study: GTC

Using the default input parameters for GTC, we examine the code scaling, phase, and performance characteristics in this section. The default parameter case evolves 3.2 million particles using the particle-in-cell approach inside a toroidal mesh with 3.6 million gridpoints for 150 steps with four point gyro-averaging on the mesh. Figure 1 provides a visualization at a timestep in the simulation showing particles location and speed in the mesh.

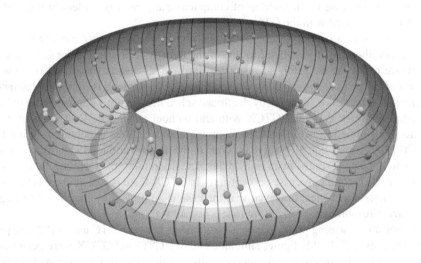

Fig. 1. A timestep in the GTC simulation showing tracking of select particles in the toroidal mesh. The color indicates the speed of the particle while the lines dividing the torus indicate the domain decomposition across processors or threads for this simulation.

The GTC algorithm utilizes six basic types of communication operations: allreduce, broadcast, split communicator, gather, reduce, and send/receive. In order to port GTC to HPX-3, nonblocking implementations of each of these operations were created using

HPX-3. The port from MPI to HPX-3 consists of replacing all MPI calls with their HPX-3 equivalents, after making the original GTC code thread safe so that it can be used with a multithreaded runtime system like HPX-3. The GTC version ported to HPX-3 is identified as GTCX. Output from GTC and GTCX were verified to be identical out to 15 significant digits for 8 separate analysis fields. Simulations were conducted on a 16 node cluster of Intel Xeon E5-2670 2.60 GHz processors providing 16 cores per node with InfiniBand interconnect between nodes. Each node is equiped with 32 GB of 1600 MHz RDIMMS.

While GTC and GTCX are nearly identical in terms of the codebase, their computational phase characteristics are not. GTCX is capable of overlapping computational phases by overdecomposing the problem into more lightweight concurrent threads than execution resources (cores). This overdecomposition of the problem enables the overlap of computation and communication phases in an effort to hide network latency when used in conjunction with the nonblocking HPX-3 equivalents of MPI collectives. The computational phases for GTC on 64 cores is illustrated in Figures 2-3. In Figure 2, the number of MPI processes running GTC was equivalent to the number of computational resources. In Figure 3, however, the number of HPX-3 threads running GTCX was a factor of two greater than the number of resources. The phases of computation are color coded; however, in the HPX-3 case in Figure 3, context switching is usually how waiting for communication is manifested since the communication calls are nonblocking. A noticeable increase in the overlap of computational phases is evident in the GTCX simulation compared with the GTC simulation.

The increase in overlap of computational phases becomes more evident by introducing a synthetic load imbalance to one of the threads or processes. For GTC, a load imbalance results in the idling of resources until the slowest process catches up with the rest of the processes in its computation. For GTCX, the load is implicitly balanced among the resources on the node by the thread scheduler. Figure 4 compares the phases of computation for GTC and GTCX with and without a synthetic load imbalance. In Figure 4, a synthetic load imbalance involving computing the ϕ potential during the GTC/GTCX Poisson equation solve is added to the process or thread identified as zero. This load imbalance results in an immediate increase in time spent waiting for communication in GTC for all processes except zero. In GTCX there is also an increase in time spent in context switches; however, that increase is amortized by the thread manager maximizing resource usage resulting in less overall waiting.

Direct strong scaling performance measurements between GTC and GTCX are presented in Figure 5. In this figure, simulations using GTC and GTCX were performed five times prior to averaging and reporting the results. The results also include performance results from a version of the GTC code manually implemented to use non blocking collectives from MPICH2 but without oversubscription. The GTC and GTCX performance is nearly identical on very few codes while GTCX suffers a considerable decrease in performance at 16 cores and higher, matching the GTC performance only at 128 cores where the GTC code has already stopped scaling. The GTCX implementation continues to scale beyond 128 cores and produces the fastest result at 256 cores. As will be explored in detail later in Section 3, the use of blocking collectives contributes to some of the performance degradation observed in GTC. The MPI version of GTC which uses non blocking collectives provides an intermediate comparison point

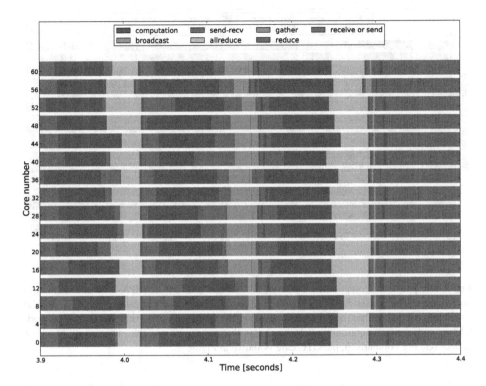

Fig. 2. The phases of computation for a portion of a second in a GTC (MPI based) simulation on 64 cores. The phases for every fourth processor are plotted in the vertical axis for GTC. There is no oversubscription in this case; blocking MPI collectives ensure the computational phases do not overlap signficantly. For comparison with GTCX (HPX-3 based), see Figure 3 where the computational phases for the operations corresponding to those here are plotted.

between standard GTC and GTCX where blocking collectives are removed but no over-subscription is present.

With the exception of a few cases, GTCX generally lags GTC performance in spite of the increase computational phase overlap and network latency hiding capability of GTCX. However, it also continues to scale even when the GTC code has stopped scaling. The overheads associated with thread creation ($2\,\mu s$) and context switching ($1.2\,\mu s$) as well as a large overhead in the network layer contributes to mitigating many of the performance benefits in GTCX resulting from an increase in overlapping computational phases. The legacy migration path used to create the GTCX code from GTC involves minimal code modification and no code restructuring in order to achieve more efficient performance for a many-tasking execution model. Restructuring GTC for a specific programming model has resulted in significant performance gains for GTC before (e.g. see [30]). However, for many legacy applications, restructuring an application code base

Computation and communication phases in GTCX on 64 cores

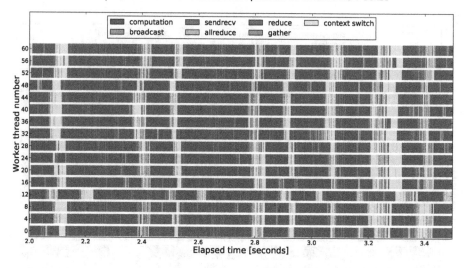

Fig. 3. The phases of computation a portion of a second in a GTCX (HPX-3 based) simulation on 64 cores. The phases for every fourth core are plotted in the vertical axis for GTCX. The simulation oversubscribes the computational resources by a factor of two in order to hide network latency and overlap more computational phases than otherwise possible when using blocking collectives. For comparison, the GTC case is shown in Figure 2.

for use in a new programming model is not a viable option while the legacy migration path explored here could easily be achieved at the compiler level.

Overlapping computational phases, hiding network latency, and removing global barriers in computation give key performance benefits which can improve scalability in applications provided the runtime system overheads can be kept in check. Understanding how these overheads can affect application performance is crucial for making design decisions and extracting more parallelism in a simulation. While runtime system overheads cannot be easily changed in an implementation in order to empirically observe their impact on overall application performance, overheads can be changed and experimented with using a discrete event simulator. The following section explores this behavior in the context of the SST/macro simulator.

4   GTCX in SST/Macro

To explore the scalability characteristics beyond the bounds of available physical machines we used SST/macro simulator [19] developed at Sandia National Laboratory. SST/macro is a coarse-grain simulator, which offers a good balance of simulation speed, accuracy of results, scaling of the model to arbitrary number of nodes, and support of emulation on alternative architectures. As such, it is ideal for realistic modeling of applications at scale, studying the effects of network parameters and topology on

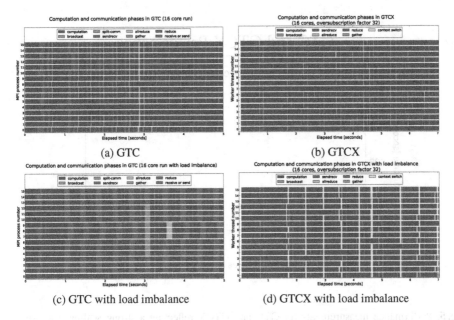

(a) GTC

(b) GTCX

(c) GTC with load imbalance

(d) GTCX with load imbalance

Fig. 4. Computational phase diagrams for GTC and GTCX with and without a synthetic load imbalance on 16 cores are presented here. For GTC, a load imbalance results in the idling of resources until the slowest process catches up with the rest of the processes in its computation as seen by comparing (a) and (c). There is also an increase in idled resources for GTCX in the presence of a load imbalance; however, the difference between (b) and (d) for GTCX is not as substantial as that for GTC due to the ability to overlap computational phases and implicitly load balance.

performance, and software prototyping of new algorithms and library designs. SST/-macro accomplishes this through skeletonization of the modeled applications which is a process of creating simplified code that approximately reproduces the behavior of the original application, but without having to produce the same computational results. From the network perspective, skeletons preserve the control flow of communication code, resulting in as much as order of magnitude potential speedup. Currently, the conversion process of the original application code to an equivalent skeleton is manual, although compiler assisted utilities are being developed at Indiana University. The simulation runs as a single process (shared address space), with component application processes emulated by user level threads.

SST/macro is capable of modeling with significantly more diverse range of parameters than most of the commonly available tools used to predict the performance of MPI applications based on execution traces, such as LogGOPSim [23]. For example, compute node parameters include core affinities, memory contention along with NUMA effects, and NIC contention. Network switch models support packet arbitration, adaptive routing, and buffering parameters. The network topologies are represented accurately and may support message traffic as flows, packets, or packetized flows. Moreover, trace gathering may substantially stress the I/O subsystem due to volume

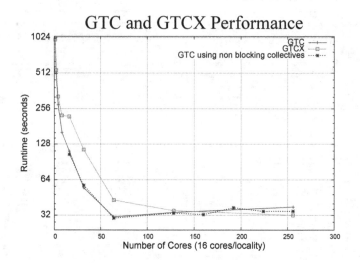

Fig. 5. Performance measurements for GTC and GTCX reflecting a strong scaling test. Also shown is a version of GTC implemented using non blocking collectives but without oversubscription. GTCX performance varies significantly based on the number of lightweight threads used to decompose the problem. The GTCX results presented here reflect the use of the empirically discovered optimal number of lightweight threads for decomposition. While GTCX is able to overlap more computational phases than GTC, it also suffers from higher overheads in the form of thread creation and context switches resulting in slightly worse performance than GTC from 16 to 128 cores.

of stored data; this frequently interferes with network operation if the storage devices are attached to the same interconnect. SST/macro is free of these issues.

The GTCX implementation explored in Section 3 illustrated key characteristics distinguishing the many-tasking behavior of ParalleX from the MPI behavior of the Communicating Sequential Processes (CSP) exection model. These include computational phase overlap, overdecomposition, network latency hiding, implicit load balancing, and intelligent task scheduling. However, the GTCX implementation performance in Section 3 was generally at par or worse than the MPI implementation due to the large overheads introduced by the runtime system implementation. The SST/macro toolkit, in contrast to a full runtime system implementation, is able to represent the parallel machine using models to estimate processing and network components and thereby modify the size of the overheads. Recently, HPX-3 semantics were added to SST/-macro in order to model application performance using that runtime system at different overhead levels [18]. This section explores GTCX, the HPX-3 implementation of GTC, using the SST/macro simulator with different runtime system overheads on the Hopper supercomputer (Cray XE6, Opteron 6172 12 cores at 2.10 GHz).

As a tool for co-design, SST/macro is frequently used for coarse grained rather than cycle accurate simulation. SST/macro is also often used in conjunction with a skeleton code, where all computation has been removed from an application except for

Context switch overhead impact on GTCX

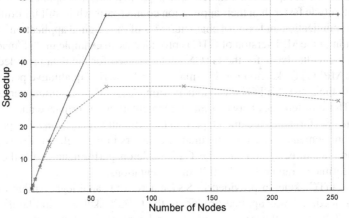

Fig. 6. Comparison of strong scaling for GTCX with two different context switch overheads. The smaller context switch overhead is .1μs while the larger is 10 ms. Results using empirically determined near-optimal oversubscription factors are plotted.

GTC and GTCX using SST/macro

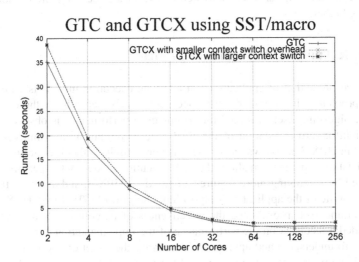

Fig. 7. Predicted performance comparison for GTC and GTCX using SST/macro. For GTCX, two different context switch overheads are examined. No oversubscription was applied to GTCX; consequently GTCX and GTC closely mirror each other in performance.

communication and control. This enables the skeleton to be used for fast prototyping and making other design decisions. Actual non-control computations in the skeleton code are replaced with counters in order to record the computational cost without actually performing the computation entailed. Consequently, skeleton applications can run orders of magnitude faster than their application counterparts while still faithfully modeling the communication and control characteristics of the original application. A skeleton application of the MPI version of GTC is provided as an example in SST/macro; this skeleton served as the basis for the GTCX skeleton used for the data provided in this section. The MPI GTC skeleton for SST/macro, while sharing qualitative performance behavior with the actual MPI GTC implementation, does differ in runtime performance prediction. These differences between the implementation performance and the skeleton's predicted performance are due, in part, to the difficulty of replacing computational loops in the implementation with computation counters in the skeleton. Consequently, in this section we directly compare the GTC skeleton performance with the GTCX skeleton performance rather than the full implementations.

Using the GTC skeleton provided in SST/macro, the same legacy migration path described in Section 3 was applied producing the GTCX skeleton. Unlike the implementation in 3, however, the thread overheads and context switching overheads can be changed as a parameter in SST/macro in order to model the performance impact of these overheads. Figure 6 shows GTCX strong scaling behavior for context switch overheads differing by 5 orders of magnitude from .1μs to 10 ms. Figure 7 compares the predicted performance between GTC and GTCX in SST/macro without the benefit of oversubscription. Not surprisingly, without oversubscription in GTCX, the results from GTC and GTCX are very similar. Context switching overheads become more pronounced at 64 cores or higher.

5   GTCX Analytic Performance Model

Performance prediction of applications in alternate execution models is an emerging research problem. The overall performance gain largely depends on the characteristics of the algorithm itself. Limited improvement in performance is observed already by a straightforward translation of the BSP-style communication primitives to their equivalent in HPX-3, as shown earlier. This is due entirely to the finer-grained concurrency and dataflow parallelism allowed by the execution model. Better performance can be achieved by leveraging more features admitted by HPX-3, and at times, through a complete rewrite of the application's algorithm. Our port of GTC to the HPX-3 many-tasking runtime system evaluated the effectiveness of its core parallelism constructs and provided a feedback on the performance of the implementation at relatively modest scales. To understand and appropriately quantify the effect of overlapping computation with communication through oversubscription and dataflow parallelism, in this section, we introduce an analytic performance model of the gyrokinetic toroidal simulation (GTC) code.

Analytic models that calculate the long-time running cost of parallel applications have to strike a trade-off between accuracy and overall cost. The model described in this section captures the essential computation and communication characteristics of the six

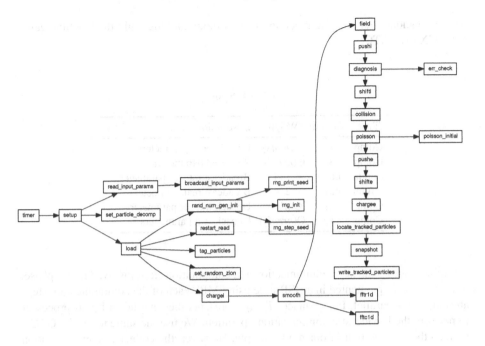

Fig. 8. Static Call Graph of GTC

key phases in the application. Through parameter sweeps of the overheads involved, and varying the degree of overlap, bounds for performance benefits of an alternate execution model are obtained.

GTC employs the Particle-in-Cell formalism to model the plasma interactions. The PIC algorithm involves six main phases executed at each time step. The static call-graph of the core GTC algorithm is shown in Figure 8.

The total runtime of GTC for a given sample input depends several parameters such as the number of particle domains (*npartdom*), the 1D toroidal decomposition (*ntoroidal*), the size of the grid, the number of particles per cell etc. For a given input and simulation parameters, the total runtime cost is the sum of the initialization and the execution time of the six phases for *n* timesteps as given in Eqn. 1.

$$T_{total} = T_{setup} + \sum_{i=1}^{n} \left(T_{charge} + T_{poisson} + T_{field} + T_{smooth} + T_{push} + T_{shift} \right) \quad (1)$$

5.1 Setup

In this phase, the GTC simulation is set up by reading the input parameters. Both integer and real parameters are read separately from an input file by the main process. These parameters are packed and broadcasted to all other processes where they are subsequently unpacked and assigned locally. Relative to other phases, the time taken by this phase is rather negligible and bounded by constant factor. We expand on this phase only to elucidate our analytic modeling methodology and highlight the key time gains in GTCX over GTC.

Table 1. Setup

Type	Action	Weight	Description
Comp	s_1	$\Theta(nints)$	Read integer parameters
Comp	s_2	$\Theta(nreals)$	Read real parameters
Comm	bcast	144	Broadcast integer parameters
Comm	bcast	224	Broadcast real parameters
Comp	k_1	$\Theta(nints)$	Unpack integer parameters
Comp	k_2	$\Theta(nreals)$	Unpack real parameters

Table 1 shows the key communication and computation steps involved in this phase. Since GTC is implemented in a BSP style using MPI, each of the communication steps are inherently parallel. For instance, T_{bcast} represents the time taken by all processes to perform the broadcast communication operation. We use the same terms for GTCX to keep the presentation of our model simple. However, the collective communication operations can themselves be decomposed into their constituent point-to-point operations as shown below.

The time taken by the main process for this phase is given by

$$T_{setup} = s_1 + s_2 + T_{send}(144) + T_{send}(224)$$

and the time at all of the other processes is

$$T_{setup} = T_{recv}(144) + T_{recv}(224) + k_1 + k_2$$

Here, $T_{send}(x)$ and $T_{recv}(x)$ is the time taken to send and receive x bytes respectively. The computation time between the communication operations is measured empirically by profiling the application. Since we are primarily interested in comparative analysis (between GTC and GTCX), using one of the many analytic communication models to represent the communication costs is also a viable approach.

For instance, in the Hockney communication model [21], the time to send or receive a message of size m is given by $T_m = \alpha + \beta m$. Using this, a linear broadcast of n messages of size m to P processes can be computed as follows:

$$T_{bcast} = n(P - 1) \cdot \left(m \cdot (\alpha + \beta m)\right)$$

Assuming no network congestion and full bisection-bandwidth, this approximates the time to perform broadcast at all processes.

Since there are no data dependences between the broadcast of the integer and real parameters, GTCX can execute them concurrently in separate HPX-3 tasks, such that the computation and communication is overlapped. Even when using a single task in HPX-3, we have Eqn. 2.

$$T_{setup} = s_1 + T_{bcast}(144) + \max\left(s_2 + T_{bcast}(224), T_{bcast}(144) + k_1\right) + T_{bcast}(224) + k_2 \tag{2}$$

Here, the packing (and sending) of the real parameters (s_2 and $T_{bcast}(224)$) is overlapped with the unpacking (and receiving) of the integer parameters (k_1 and $T_{bcast}(144)$).

By having two lightweight threads (one to send the integer parameters, and the other to send the real parameters) run concurrently, both the tasks can be effectively overlapped, as in Eqn. 3.

$$T_{setup} = \max\left(s_1 + T_{bcast}(144), s_2 + T_{bcast}(224)\right) + \max\left(k_1, k_2\right) \tag{3}$$

The degree of overlap is bounded by δ subject to factors such as the number of system threads in HPX-3 and the progress of communication with respect to computation.

5.2 Charge

In this phase, the charge from the particle data is deposited onto the grid using a particle-grid interpolation step. The computation operations in this phase, as shown in Table 2 are asymptotically bounded above the number of particles in each process. The load-balance of the computation step, thus, largely depends on the particle distributions. The steps c_1, c_2 iterate through the particle array and update grid locations in memory corresponding to the four-point ring representing the charged particles. The effective time taken by these steps depends on the arithmetic intensity of each step and non-deterministic architectural factors such as cache behavior etc. These can either be ignored completely, or measured empirically for a given run.

Table 2. Charge

Type	Action	Weight	Description
Comp	c_1	$\Omega(mi)$	Particle-grid interpolation
Comp	c_2	$\Omega(mgrid \cdot mzeta)$	Set density
Comm	allreduce	$mgrid \cdot (mzeta + 1)$	Deposit charge density on the grid
Comp	c_3	$\Omega(mpsi)$	Poloidal end cell
Comm	sendrecv	$mgrid$	Send density array to left and receive from right
Comp	c_4	$\Omega(mpsi \cdot mzeta \cdot mtheta_i)$	Flux surface average and normalization
Comm	allreduce	$mpsi + 1$	Global sum of phi00

The time taken by this step, Eqn. 4, is the global sum of the computation steps, an allreduce communication step to deposit charge density on the grid and the computation of the global sum of ϕ.

$$T_{charge} = c_1 + c_2 + T_{allreduce}(mgrid \cdot (mzeta + 1)) + c_3$$
$$+ T_{sendrecv}(mgrid) + c_4 + T'_{allreduce}(mpsi + 1) \qquad (4)$$

In GTCX, the loop to iterate through the array in c_2 is fused with the point-to-point communication operations in $T_{allreduce}$ so that they are interleaved and executed concurrently. Thus, the time to compute the global sum at all processes ($T_{allreduce}$) is offset by the time to iterate through the array to be reduced (c_2) by a constant factor δ. The time taken for the complete charge step for GTCX is given by

$$T_{charge} = c_1 + \max\left(c_2, T_{allreduce}\right) + c_3 + T_{sendrecv}(mgrid) + \max\left(c_4, T'_{allreduce}\right)$$
$$= c_1 + c_2 + \delta + c_3 + T_{sendrecv}(mgrid) + c_4 + \delta' \qquad (5)$$

where $T_{allreduce} = c_2 + \delta$, $T'_{allreduce} = c_4 + \delta'$

Note that, here, we assume that there is a strong synchronization step (barrier) between phases. The degree of overlap between computation and communication (δ and δ') depend on the subscription factor in GTCX. They cannot be zero due to the data dependence between the operations, and the finite time to execute them.

Table 3. Poisson

Type	Action	Weight	Description
Comp	p_1	$\Omega(mzeta \cdot mgrid \cdot mring)$	Initialization
Comm	allgather	$\frac{mzeta}{npartdom}$	Gather full array ϕ on PEs
Comp	p_2	$\Omega(mzeta \cdot mgrid)$	Assign full array ϕ
Comp	p_3	$\Omega(mzeta \cdot mpsi)$	In equilibrium unit

5.3 Poisson

The gyrokinetic Poisson equation is solved on the grid in this phase. The compute phases are asymptotically bounded above by the grid size ($\Omega(mgrid)$). The only communication step in the reference codes (GTC and GTCX) is an allgather collective operation. The other steps are shown in Table 3.

In case of GTC, the time taken to execute this phase depends on the available processor parallelism. It is given by Eqn. 6.

$$T_{poisson} = p_1 + T_{allgather}(\cdot) + p_2 + p_3 \qquad (6)$$

For GTCX, the performance gain due to oversubscription and dataflow parallelism is bounded by the factor δ. With true dataflow parallelism obtained by loop fusion and the conversion of sub-arrays into futures, the allgather communication step is effectively executed concurrently with both p_1 and p_2. The marked end times of the allgather and p_2 steps are determined by:

$$T_{poisson} = \max\left(p_1, T_{allgather}, p_2\right) + p_3$$
$$= p_1 + \delta + p_3 \qquad (7)$$

where $T_{allgather} = p_1 + \delta_1$, $p_2 = T_{allgather} + \delta_2$, $\delta = \delta_1 + \delta_2$

5.4 Field

This phase computes the electric field on the grid. As the previous phase (Poisson), it scales with the number of the poloidal grid points. The data redistribution involves array shifts and thus, the communication pattern is captured by MPI's `sendrecv` function calls. In GTCX, the send and receive operations are decoupled and hence can be scheduled closer to the actual data sinks and sources in the dataflow graph.

Table 4. Field

Type	Action	Weight	Description
Comp	f_1	$\Omega(mzeta \cdot mgrid \cdot mpsi)$	Finite difference for e-field
Comm	sendrecv	$mgrid$	Send ϕ to right and receive from left
Comm	sendrecv	$mgrid$	Send ϕ to left and receive from right
Comp	f_2	$\Omega(mzeta \cdot mgrid)$	Unpack ϕ boundary and calculate E_zeta
Comm	sendrecv	$3 \cdot mgrid$	Send E to right and receive from left
Comp	f_3	$\Omega(mgrid + mzeta \cdot (mpsi + 1))$	Unpack end points

The operations to shift the ϕ array and compute the electric field E are referred in Table 4. The time taken in GTC to perform the field phase for a given simulation step is approximated by

$$T_{field} = f_1 + 2 \cdot T_{sendrecv}(mgrid) + f_2 + T'_{sendrecv}(3 \cdot mgrid) + f_3 \qquad (8)$$

The array shift of ϕ is overlapped with the computation of finite difference for the electric field. After the ϕ boundaries are unpacked, the calculuation of the electric field is fused with its communication operations. These optimizations result in a time reduction given by Eqn 9

$$T_{field} = \max\left(f_1, T_{sendrecv}(mgrid), T_{sendrecv}(mgrid)\right) + f_2 + \delta \qquad (9)$$

where $T'_{sendrecv} = f_2 + \delta_1, \quad f_3 = T'_{sendrecv} + \delta_2, \quad \delta = \delta_1 + \delta_2$

5.5 Smooth

In this phase, the potential and charge density undergo radial smoothing. The computation kernels s_1, s_2 and s_3 perform grid-accesses relative to the grid size (mgrid). As shown in Table 5, a 2D-matrix is transposed using scatter and gather collective operations.

Eqns 10 and 11 can be used to approximate the times required to execute this phase in GTC and GTCX respectively.

$$T_{smooth} = s_1 + 2 \cdot T_{sendrecv}(mgrid) + s_2 + T_{sendrecv}(mgrid) + \sum_{i=1}^{ntoroidal} \left(s_3 + T_{gather}\right)$$

$$+ \sum_{i=1}^{ntoroidal} \left(s_4 + T_{scatter}\right) + s_5 + T'_{sendrecv}(mgrid) + T_{gather}(\cdot) \qquad (10)$$

Table 5. Smooth

Type	Action	Weight	Description
Comp	s_1	$\Omega(mzeta \cdot (mgrid + mpsi))$	-
Comm	sendrecv	$mgrid$	Parallel Smoothing: send ϕ to right and receive from left
Comm	sendrecv	$mgrid$	Parallel Smoothing: send ϕ to left and receive from right
Comp	s_2	$\Omega(mgrid \cdot mzeta)$	-
Comm	sendrecv	$mgrid$	Toroidal BC: send ϕ to left and receive from right
Comp	s_3	$\Omega(mzeta \cdot (mgrid + mpsi))$	-
Comm	gather	$mtdiag \cdot mz \cdot (idiag2 - idiag1 + 1)$	Transpose a 2D-matrix from $(ntoroidal, mzeta \cdot mzbig)$ to $(1, mzetamax \cdot mzbig)$
Comp	s_4	$\Omega(ntoroidal \cdot mz)$	-
Comm	scatter	$mtdiag \cdot mz \cdot (idiag2 - idiag1 + 1)$	Transpose a 2D-matrix from $(ntoroidal, mzeta \cdot mzbig)$ to $(1, mzetamax \cdot mzbig)$
Comp	s_5	$\Omega(mgrid)$	Interpolate field
Comm	sendrecv	$mgrid$	Toroidal BC: send ϕ to right and receive from left
Comm	gather	$\frac{2 \cdot mtdiag}{ntoroidal} \cdot nummode$	Dominant (n, m) mode history data

The optimizations due to overlapping of computation with the send and receive operations are similar to those described in the "field" phase. The transposition of the 2D-matrix involves gather and scatter operations equal to the number of toroidal domains.

$$T_{smooth} = \max\left(s_1, T_{sendrecv}(mgrid), T_{sendrecv}(mgrid)\right) + \max\left(s_2, T_{sendrecv}(mgrid)\right)$$

$$+ \sum_{i=1}^{ntoroidal} \left(s_3 + \delta_1 + s_4 + \delta_2\right) + s_5 + \delta_3 + T_{gather}(\cdot) \qquad (11)$$

where $T_{gather} = s_3 + \delta_1, \quad T_{scatter} = s_4 + \delta_2, \quad T'_{sendrecv} = s_5 + \delta_3$

5.6   Push

In this phase, the particles are advanced using the field array computed in the previous phases. Since, this phase is dependent on the size of the particle arrays at each processor, the particle distribution among the processors determines the execution time of the computation steps that are bounded below by $\Omega(mi)$.

Table 6 lists the computation and communication steps involved in this phase. Despite having a higher arithmetic intensity, the communication operations in this phase are relatively expensive, making it a critical phase in the algorithm. The grid data accesses made by tasks $\{p_1, \ldots, p_4\}$ are irregular and results in bad cache behavior without any data reorganization.

$$T_{push} = p_1 + T_{allreduce}(8) + T_{allreduce}(4) + p_2 + 2 \cdot T_{allreduce}(2 \cdot mflux)$$

$$+ p_3 + T_{allreduce}(\cdot) + p_4 + T_{reduce}(\cdot) \qquad (12)$$

Table 6. Push

Type	Action	Weight	Description
Comp	p_1	$\Omega(mi)$	Runge-Kutta method
Comm	allreduce	8	Calculate total sum of weights
Comm	allreduce	4	Calculate total number of particles
Comp	p_2	$\Omega(mi)$	Out of boundary particle
Comm	allreduce	$2 \cdot mflux$	Restore temperature profile
Comp	p_3	$\Omega(mflux + mi)$	-
Comm	allreduce	$mpsi + 1$	Heat flux psi
Comm	allreduce	$2 \cdot mflux$	Compute marker,energy,particle
Comp	p_4	$\Omega(mpsi(mzeta + 1))$	Field energy
Comm	reduce	3	Total field energy from all toroidal domains

The time taken to execute this phase in GTC (Eqn 12) and that to execute in GTCX (Eqn 13) are shown.

$$T_{push} = \max\left(p_1, T_{allreduce}(8), T_{allreduce}(4)\right)$$
$$+ \max\left(p_2 + \delta_1, p_3 + \delta_2\right) + T_{allreduce}(2 \cdot mflux) + p_4 + T_{reduce}(\cdot) \qquad (13)$$

where $\quad T_{allreduce}(2 \cdot mflux) = p_2 + \delta_1, \quad T_{allreduce}(mpsi + 1) = p_3 + \delta_2$

5.7 Shift

The shift phase actually moves particles between toroidal domains. This involves communication of the number of particles to be shifted, the packing and shifting of particles to neighboring toroidal domains (using MPI's `sendrecv` operation), and unpacking of particles. The particles are moved in the $\pm zeta$ direction only one domain at a time.

The time required for GTC (T_{shift}) is simply the sum of the times required for the communication and computation steps shown in Table 7.

$$T_{shift} = s_1 + T_{allreduce}(4) + s_2 + 2 \cdot T_{sendrecv}(8) + 2 \cdot T_{sendrecv}(msend, mrecv) + s_3 \quad (14)$$

Table 7. Shift

Type	Action	Weight	Description
Comp	s_1	$\Omega(mi)$	-
Comm	allreduce	4	Total number of particles to be shifted
Comp	s_2	$40 \cdot \Theta(1)$	Pack particles and fill holes
Comm	sendrecv	8	Send number of particles to move right
Comm	sendrecv	$msendright, mrecvleft$	Send particle to right and receive from left
Comm	sendrecv	8	Send number of particles to move left
Comm	sendrecv	$msendleft, mrecvright$	Send particle to left and receive from right
Comp	s_3	$20 \cdot \Theta(1)$	Unpack particles

As shown in Eqn 15, the computation step s_1 cannot be overlapped with the first allreduce operation. Since the time to send the number of particles to shift is negligible, it is not accounted by the overlapping of the time to move the particle data.

$$T_{shift} = s_1 + T_{allreduce}(4) + 2 \cdot T_{sendrecv}(msend, mrecv) + s_3 \qquad (15)$$

where
$$T_{sendrecv}(msend, mrecv) = T_{sendrecv}(8) + \delta$$
$$T_{sendrecv}(8) \ll T_{sendrecv}(msend, mrecv)$$

5.8   Model Validation

To quantify the performance benefits of removing global barriers and overlapping computation steps in GTCX, we evaluated our model with the parameters shown in Table 8.

Figure 9 shows a strong-scaling plot of GTC against GTCX for an assumed, fixed degree of overlap (δ) for each of the phases. The execution times for the computation and communication steps of GTC were determined empirically by the output data of an actual run. The model errors were found to be within 15% of the execution time.

Table 8. Parameters used for validating the model

Parameter	Value	Parameter	Value
nints	36	micell	2
nreals	28	ntoroidal	1 to 256
mzetamax	64	npartdom	1
mpsi	90	nsteps	150
mthetamax	640	numberpe	1 to 256
mgrid	32449	mi	64718 to 258872

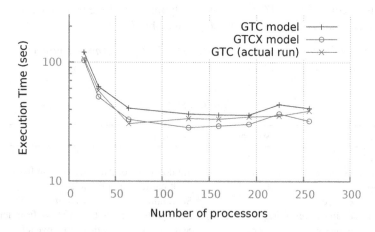

Fig. 9. Comparative analysis of the GTC and GTCX performance model

6 Conclusions

Implementing GTC in HPX-3 and SST/macro for HPX-3 has highlighted some key characteristics of many-tasking runtime systems while at the same time exposing some performance deficiencies. The removal of global barriers, the increase in overlapping phases of computation, and the presence of implicit load balancing all helped to extract more parallelism in GTCX while the increased overhead due to oversubscription and context switching mitigated the impact of those improvements. The legacy migration application path for GTCX enabled overlapping computational phases and intelligent scheduling of threads but did not take advantage of any code re-writes or data restructuring that would have more directly benefited from a many-tasking execution model. The GTCX and GTC code performance generally resembled each other both in the full implementation and in SST/macro with only small performance and scaling gains registered in GTCX at the area where GTC had already stopped scaling. Comparative analysis based on the performance model enabled us to quantify the benefits due to overlapping computation phases.

Acknowledgments. We would like to thank Gilbert Hendry and Hartmut Kaiser for their technical assistance.

References

1. http://cilkplus.org/ (2012)
2. Allen, E., Chase, D., Hallett, J., Luchangco, V., Maessen, J.-W., Ryu, S., Steele Jr., G.L., Tobin-Hochstadt, S.: The Fortress language specification, version 1.0 (March 2008)
3. Angskun, T., Bosilca, G., Fagg, G.E., Gabriel, E., Dongarra, J.J.: Performance analysis of mpi collective operations. In: Proceedings of the 19th IEEE International Parallel and Distributed Processing Symposium (IPDP 2005) - Workshop 15 (2005)
4. Antypas, K., Shalf, J., Wasserman, H.: Nersc-6 workload analysis and benchmark selection process. Technical Report LBNL 1014E, National Energy Research Scientific Computing Center Division Ernest Orlando Lawrence Berkeley National Laboratory (August 2008)
5. Appeltaue, M., Hirschfeld, R., Haupt, M., Lincke, J., Perscheid, M.: A comparison of context-oriented programming languages. In: International Workshop on Context-Oriented Programming, COP 2009, pp. 6:1–6:6. ACM, New York (2009)
6. Cappello, F., Etiemble, D.: Mpi versus mpi+openmp on the ibm sp for the nas benchmarks. In: ACM/IEEE 2000 Conference on Supercomputing, p. 12 (2000)
7. Chamberlain, B., Callahan, D., Zima, H.: Parallel programmability and the Chapel language. Int. J. High Perform. Comput. Appl. **21**(3), 291–312 (2007)
8. Charles, P., Grothoff, C., Saraswat, V., Donawa, C., Kielstra, A., Ebcioglu, K., von Praun, C., Sarkar, V.: X10: an object-oriented approach to non-uniform cluster computing. SIGPLAN Not. **40**, 519–538 (2005)
9. Dekate, C., Anderson, M., Brodowicz, M., Kaiser, H., Adelstein-Lelbach, B., Sterling, T.: Improving the scalability of parallel N-body applications with an event-driven constraint-based execution model. International Journal of High Performance Computing Applications **26**(3), 319–332 (2012)
10. Dinan, J., Balaji, E., Lusk, E., Sadayappan, P., Thakur, R.: Hybrid parallel programming with mpi and unified parallel c. In: Proceedings of the 7th ACM International Conference on Computing Frontiers, CF 2010, pp. 177–186. ACM, New York (2010)

11. Duran, A., Teruel, X., Ferrer, R., Martorell, X., Ayguade, E.: Barcelona OpenMP tasks suite: A set of benchmarks targeting the exploitation of task parallelism in OpenMP. In: Proceedings of the 2009 International Conference on Parallel Processing, ICPP 2009, pp. 124–131. IEEE Computer Society, Washington, DC (2009)

12. El-Ghazawi, T., Cantonnet, F., Yao, Y.: Evaluations of UPC on the Cray X1. In: CUG 2005 Proceedings, New York, NY, USA, p. 10 (2005)

13. Ethier, S., Tang, W.M., Lin, Z.: Gyrokinetic particle-in-cell simulations of plasma microturbulence on advanced computing platforms. Journal of Physics: Conference Series **16**(1), 1 (2005)

14. Gao, G. Sterling, T., Stevens, R. Hereld, M., Zhu, W.: Parallex: A study of a new parallel computation model. In: IEEE International Parallel and Distributed Processing Symposium, IPDPS 2007, pp. 1–6 (2007)

15. Gautier, T., Lima, J.V.F., Maillard, N., Raffin, B.: Xkaapi: A runtime system for data-flow task programming on heterogeneous architectures. In: Proc. of the 27th IEEE International Parallel and Distributed Processing Symposium (IPDPS) (2013)

16. Gilmanov, T., Anderson, M., Brodowicz, M., Sterling, T.: Application characteristics of many-tasking execution models. In: Proc. of the 2013 International Conference on Parallel and Distributed Processing Techniques and Applications (PDPTA) (2013)

17. Hendry, G.: Decreasing Network Power with On-Off Links Informed by Scientific Applications. In: The Ninth Workshop on High-Performance, Power Aware Computing (May 2013)

18. Hendry, G., Rodrigues, A.: Simulator for exascale co-design, http://sst.sandia.gov/publications.html

19. Hendry, G., Rodrigues, A.: Sst: A simulator for exascale co-design. In: Proc. of the ASCR/ASC Exascale Research Conference (2012)

20. Hewitt, C., Baker, H.G.: Actors and continuous functionals. Technical report, Cambridge, MA, USA (1978)

21. Hockney, R.W.: The communication challenge for mpp: Intel paragon and meiko cs-2. Parallel Comput. **20**(3), 389–398 (1994)

22. Hoefler, T., Gropp, W., Snir, M., Kramer, W.: Performance Modeling for Systematic Performance Tuning. In: International Conference for High Performance Computing, Networking, Storage and Analysis (SC 2011), SotP Session (November 2011)

23. Hoefler, T., Schneider, T., Lumsdaine, A.: LogGOPSim - simulating large-scale applications in the LogGOPS model. In: Proceedings of the 19th ACM International Symposium on High Performance Distributed Computing, pp. 597–604. ACM (June 2010)

24. HPC University and the Ohio Supercomputer Center. Report on high performance computing training and education survey, http://www.teragridforum.org/mediawiki/images/5/5d/HPCSurveyResults.FINAL.pdf

25. Iancu, C., Hofmeyr, S., Blagojevic, F., Zheng, Y.: Oversubscription on multicore processors. In: 2010 IEEE International Symposium on Parallel Distributed Processing (IPDPS), pp. 1–11 (April 2010)

26. Kaiser, H., Brodowicz, M., Sterling, T.: ParalleX an advanced parallel execution model for scaling-impaired applications. In: International Conference on Parallel Processing Workshops, ICPPW 2009, pp. 394–401 (September 2009)

27. Kale, L.V., Krishnan, S.: Charm++: Parallel Programming with Message-Driven Objects. In: Wilson, G.V., Lu, P. (eds.) Parallel Programming Using C++, pp. 175–213. MIT Press (1996)

28. Karlin, I., Bhatele, A., Keasler, J., Chamberlain, B.L., Cohen, J., DeVito, Z., Haque, R., Laney, D., Luke, E., Wang, F., Richards, D. Schulz, M., Still, C.H.: Exploring traditional and emerging parallel programming models using a proxy application. In: Proc. of the 27th IEEE International Parallel and Distributed Processing Symposium (IPDPS) (2013)

29. Koniges, A., Preissl, R., Kim, J., Eder, D., Fisher, A., Masters, N., Mlaker, V., Ethier, S., Wang, W., Head-Gordon, M., Wichmann, N.: Application Acceleration on Current and Future Cray Platforms. In: CUG 2010, the Cray User Group Meeting (May 2010)
30. Madduri, K., Ibrahim, K.Z., Williams, S., Im, E.-J., Ethier, S., Shalf, J., Oliker, L.: Gyrokinetic toroidal simulations on leading multi- and manycore hpc systems. In: Proceedings of 2011 International Conference for High Performance Computing, Networking, Storage and Analysis, SC 2011, pp. 23:1–23:12. ACM, New York (2011)
31. Mathis, M.M., Kerbyson, D.J., Hoisie, A.: A performance model of non-deterministic particle transport on large-scale systems. Future Gener. Comput. Syst. **22**(3), 324–335 (2006)
32. McCool, M.D., Robison, A.D., Reinders, J.: Structured parallel programming patterns for efficient computation (2012)
33. Olivier, S., Prins, J.F.: Comparison of OpenMP 3.0 and other task parallel frameworks on unbalanced task graphs. International Journal of Parallel Programming **38**(5–6), 341–360 (2010)
34. Reinders, J.: Intel Threading Building Blocks: Outfitting C++ for Multi-Core Processor Parallelism, 1st edn. O'Reilly Media (July 2007)
35. Robert, J., Halstead, H.: Multilisp: a language for concurrent symbolic computation. ACM Trans. Program. Lang. Syst. **7**(4), 501–538 (1985)
36. Stitt, T., Robinson, T.: A survey on training and education needs for petascale computing, http://www.prace-project.eu/IMG/pdf/D3-3-1_document_final.pdf
37. Tskhakaya, D.: The particle-in-cell method. In: Fehske, H., Schneider, R., Weie, A. (eds.) Computational Many-Particle Physics. Lecture Notes in Physics, vol. 739, pp. 161–189. Springer, Heidelberg (2008)
38. Wheeler, K., Murphy, R., Thain, D.: Qthreads: An API for Programming with Millions of Lightweight Threads. In: International Parallel and Distributed Processing Symposium. IEEE Press (2008)
39. Wu, X., Taylor, V.: Performance modeling of hybrid mpi/openmp scientific applications on large-scale multicore cluster systems. In: 2011 IEEE 14th International Conference on Computational Science and Engineering (CSE), pp. 181–190 (2011)
40. Yang, C., Murthy, K., Mellor-Crummey, J.: Managing asynchronous operations in coarray fortran 2.0. In: Proc. of the 27th IEEE International Parallel and Distributed Processing Symposium (IPDPS) (2013)

Toward Better Simulation of MPI Applications on Ethernet/TCP Networks

Paul Bédaride[1], Augustin Degomme[2], Stéphane Genaud[3], Arnaud Legrand[2], George S. Markomanolis[4], Martin Quinson[1], Mark Stillwell[5](✉), Frédéric Suter[6], and Brice Videau[2]

[1] Loria/INRIA/University of Nancy, Nancy, France
{paul.bedaride,martin.quinson}@loria.fr
[2] CNRS/INRIA/University of Grenoble, Grenoble, France
{augustin.degomme,arnaud.legrand,brice.videau}@imag.fr
[3] University of Strasbourg, Strasbourg, France
genaud@unistra.fr
[4] INRIA, LIP, ENS Lyon, Lyon, France
gmarko01@ens-lyon.fr
[5] School of Engineering, Cranfield University, Bedford, UK
m.stillwell@cranfield.ac.uk
[6] IN2P3 Computing Center, CNRS, Lyon-Villeurbanne, France
fsuter@cc.in2p3.fr

Abstract. Simulation and modeling for performance prediction and profiling is essential for developing and maintaining HPC code that is expected to scale for next-generation exascale systems, and correctly modeling network behavior is essential for creating realistic simulations. In this article we describe an implementation of a flow-based hybrid network model that accounts for factors such as network topology and contention, which are commonly ignored by other approaches. We focus on large-scale, Ethernet-connected systems, as these currently compose 37.8 % of the TOP500 index, and this share is expected to increase as higher-speed 10 and 100GbE become more available. The European Mont-Blanc project, which studies exascale computing by developing prototype systems with low-power embedded devices, uses Ethernet-based interconnect. Our model is implemented within SMPI, an open-source MPI implementation that connects real applications to the SimGrid simulation framework. SMPI provides implementations of collective communications based on current versions of both OpenMPI and MPICH. SMPI and SimGrid also provide methods for easing the simulation of large-scale systems, including shadow execution, memory folding, and support for both online and offline (i.e., post-mortem) simulation. We validate our proposed model by comparing traces produced by SMPI with those from real world experiments, as well as with those obtained using other established network models. Our study shows that SMPI has a consistently better predictive power than classical LogP-based models for a wide range of scenarios including both established HPC benchmarks and real applications.

© Springer International Publishing Switzerland 2014
S. Jarvis et al. (Eds.): PMBS 2013 Workshops, LNCS 8551, pp. 158–181, 2014.
DOI: 10.1007/978-3-319-10214-6_8

1 Introduction

In the High Performance Computing (HPC) field, accurately predicting the execution time of parallel applications is of utmost importance to assess their scalability, and this is particularly true for applications slated for deployment on next-generation exascale systems. While much effort has been put towards understanding the high-level behavior of these applications based on abstract communication primitives, real-world implementations often provide a number of confounding factors that may break basic assumptions and undermine the applicability of these higher level models. For example, implementations of the MPI standard can select different protocols and transmission mechanisms (e.g., eager vs. rendez-vous) depending on message size and network capabilities. Simple delay-based models also do not account for network realities such as network topology and contention. In this work we demonstrate how even relatively minor deviations in low-level implementation can adversely affect the ability of simulations to predict real-world performance, and propose a new network model that extends previous approaches to better account for topology and contention in high-speed TCP networks. We focus on large-scale, Ethernet-connected systems, which currently compose 37.8% of the TOP500 index [1]. This share is only expected to increase as higher-speed 10 and 100GbE become more available. The European Mont-Blanc project studies exascale computing by developing prototype systems with low-power embedded devices and Ethernet-based Interconnect [2].

Packet-level simulation has long been considered the "gold standard" for modeling network communication, and is available for use in a number of simulation frameworks [3,4]. However, there are a number of reasons to consider alternatives when simulating parallel applications. First, such applications are likely to generate large amounts of network traffic, and packet-level simulation has high overheads, resulting in simulations that may take significantly longer to run than the corresponding physical experiments. Second, implementing packet-level simulations that accurately model real world behavior requires correctly accounting for a vast array of factors [5]. In practice, there is little difference between an inaccurate model and an accurate model of the wrong system.

When packet-level simulation becomes too costly or intractable, the most common approach is to resort to simpler delay models that ignore the network complexity. Among these models, the most famous are those of the LogP family [6–9]. The LogP model was originally proposed by Culler et al. [6] as a realistic model of parallel machines for algorithm design. It was claimed as more realistic than more abstract models such as PRAM or BSP. This model captures key characteristics of real communication platforms while remaining amenable to complexity analysis. Unfortunately, while this model may reflect the behavior of specialized HPC networks from the early 1990s, it ignores potentially confounding factors present in modern-day systems.

Flow-based models are a reasonable alternative to both simple analytic models and expensive and difficult-to-instantiate packet-level simulation. In a flow based model, network traffic is treated as a steady state fluid flow through interconnected pipes of varying lengths and sizes (representing delay and bandwidth). Flow-based models are computationally tractable while being able to account for factors such as network heterogeneity. We seek to capture the advantages of a flow-based approach by extending existing validated models of point-to-point communication to better account for network topology and message contention. Recent work suggests that well-tuned flow-based simulation may be able to provide reasonably accurate results for less effort than packet-based simulation, and at much lower cost [10].

Our model is implemented within SMPI [11], an open-source MPI implementation that connects real-world applications to the SimGrid [12] simulation framework. With SMPI, standard MPI applications written in C or FORTRAN can be compiled and run in a simulated network environment, and traces documenting computation and communication events can be captured without incurring errors from tracing overheads or improper synchronization of clocks as in physical experiments. SMPI has recently been extended so that the low-level implementations of MPI collective operations more accurately reflect current production versions of both OpenMPI and MPICH. SMPI and SimGrid also provide a number of useful features for simulating applications that may require large amounts of time or system resources to run, including shadow execution, memory folding, and off-line simulation by replay of execution traces [13]. We validate our results by comparing application traces produced by SMPI using our network model with those from real world environments. We also compare with traces obtained using models from the literature.

The specific contributions described in this paper are as follows:

- we propose a new flow-based network model that extends previous LogP-based approaches to better account for network topology and message contention;
- we describe SMPI, the simulation platform, and some useful extensions that we have developed to make this tool more useful to developers and researchers alike (e.g., SMPI now implements **all** the collective algorithms and selection logics of both OpenMPI and MPICH for more faithful comparisons);
- we provide a number of experimental results demonstrating how these extensions improve the ability of SMPI to accurately model the behavior of real-world applications on existing platforms, and also show that competing frameworks using previous models from the literature are unlikely to obtain consistently good results;
- we demonstrate the effectiveness of our proposal by making a thorough study of the validity of our models against hierarchical clusters using TCP over Gigabit Ethernet.

This paper is organized as follows: In Section 2 we discuss essential background information in the area of network modeling. In Section 3 we describe SMPI, our chosen implementation framework, along with some key features that make it suitable for simulation of large scale systems, and comparisons to competing simulation platforms. In Section 4 we describe our proposed hybrid network model, focusing particularly on how this model captures the complexities of network topology and message contention. In Section 5 we describe experiments conducted to [in]validate the model, including comparisons of traces from real-world environments as well as traces produced using other network models. In Section 6 we demonstrate the capacity of SMPI to simulate complex MPI applications on a single machine. In Section 7 we discuss related work, including other frameworks for simulating parallel applications and their relevant drawbacks. We conclude in Section 8 and also provide a description of proposed areas of future work.

2 Network Modeling Background

In the LogP model, a parallel machine is abstracted with four parameters: L is an upper bound on the *latency* of the network, i.e., the maximum delay incurred when communicating a word between two machines; o denotes the CPU *overhead*, i.e., the time that a processor spends processing an emission or a reception and during which it cannot perform any other operation; g is the *gap* between messages, whose reciprocal is the processor communication bandwidth; and P represents the number of processors. Assuming that two processors are ready to communicate, the time to transfer a message of size k is then $o + (k - 1) \max(g, o) + L + o$. Ideally, these four parameters should be sufficient to design efficient algorithms. Indeed, this model accounts for computation/communication overlap since for *short* messages, the sender is generally

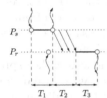

(a) Asynchronous mode ($k \le S$).

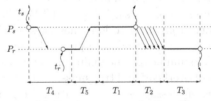

(b) Rendez-vous mode ($k > S$).

Routine	Condition	Cost
MPI_Send	$k \le S$	T_1
	$k > S$	$T_4 + T_5 + T_1$
MPI_Recv	$k \le S$	$\max(T_1 + T_2 - (t_r - t_s), 0) + T_3$
	$k > S$	$\max(o + L - (t_r - t_s), 0) + o +$
		$T_5 + T_1 + T_2 + T_3$
MPI_Isend		o
MPI_Irecv		o

(c) MPI routine costs.

$$T_1 = o + kO_s \qquad T_2 = \begin{cases} L + kg & \text{if } k < s \\ L + sg + (k - s)G & \text{otherwise} \end{cases} \qquad T_3 = o + kO_r$$
$$T_4 = \max(L + o, t_r - t_s) + o \qquad T_5 = 2o + L$$

Fig. 1. The LogGPS model [9] in a nutshell

released before the message is actually received. Unfortunately, it fails to accurately model the transmission of *long* messages that are common in modern parallel applications.

The LogGP model proposed in [7] introduces an additional parameter G to represent the larger effective bandwidth experienced by long messages. The formula for short messages is unchanged but becomes $o + (k - 1)G + L + o$ for long ones. This simple distinction between short and long messages was extended in [8] with the *parameterized LogP* model in which L, o, and g depend on the message size. The rationale is that the overall network performance results from complex interactions between the middleware, the operating system, and the transport and network layers. Hence, performance is generally neither strictly linear nor continuous. This model also introduces a distinction between the sender overhead o_s and the receiver overhead o_r. However, such models may be difficult to use to design algorithms. For instance, they assume that senders and receivers synchronize and include that synchronization cost in the overhead while some MPI implementations use schemes that may not require synchronization, depending on message size.

Finally, Ino *et al.* proposed in [9] the LogGPS model that extends LogGP by adding two parameters s and S to capture the lack of linearity and the existence of a synchronization threshold. Overheads are represented as affine functions $o + kO_s$ where O_s (resp. O_r) is the overhead per byte at the sender (resp. receiver) side. This model is described in Figure 1, where t_s (resp. t_r) is the time at which MPI_Send (resp. MPI_Recv) is issued. When the message size k is smaller than S, messages are sent asynchronously (Figure 1(a)). Otherwise, a *rendezvous* protocol is used and the sender is blocked at least until the receiver is ready to receive the message (Figure 1(b)). The s threshold is used to switch from g to G, i.e., from short to long messages, in the equation. The message transmission time is thus continuously piece-wise linear in message size (Figure 1(c)).

To summarize, the main characteristics of the LogGPS model are: the expression of overhead and transmission times as **continuous piece-wise linear** functions of message size; accounting for **partial asynchrony** for small messages, i.e., sender and receiver are busy only during the overhead cycle and can overlap communications with computations the rest of the time; a **single-port model**, i.e., a sequential use of the network card which implies that a processor can only be involved in at most one communication at a time; and **no topology** support, i.e., contention on the core of the network is ignored as all processors are assumed to be connected through independent bidirectional communication channels. Most of these hypothesis are debatable for many modern computing infrastructures. For example, with multi-core machines, many MPI processes can be mapped to the same node. Furthermore, the increase in the number of processors no longer allows one to assume uniform network communications. Finally, protocol switching typically induces performance modifications on CPU usage similar to those on effective bandwidth, while only the latter are captured by these models.

One alternative to both expensive and difficult-to-instantiate packet-level models and simplistic delay models is flow-level models. These models account for network heterogeneity and have thus been used in simulations of grid, peer-to-peer, and cloud computing systems. Communications, represented by *flows*, are simulated as single entities rather than as sets of individual packets. The time to transfer a message of size S between processors i and j is then given by $T_{i,j}(S) = L_{i,j} + S/B_{i,j}$, where $L_{i,j}$ (resp. $B_{i,j}$) is the end-to-end network latency (resp. bandwidth) on the route connecting i and j. Estimating the bandwidth $B_{i,j}$ is difficult as it depends on the network topology and on interactions with every other flow. This is generally done by assuming that the flow has reached *steady-state*, in which case the simulation amounts to solving a bandwidth sharing problem, i.e., determining how much bandwidth is allocated to each flow. More formally: *Consider a connected network that consists of a set of links $\mathcal{L}$, in which each link l has capacity B_l. Consider a set of flows $\mathcal{F}$, where each flow is a communication between two network vertices along a given path. Determine a "realistic" bandwidth allocation ρ_f for flow f, such that:*

$$\forall l \in \mathcal{L}, \sum_{f \text{ going through } l} \rho_f \le B_l \ .$$

Many different sharing methods can be used and have been evaluated (for example, in [10]). While such models are rather flexible and account for many non-trivial phenomena (e.g., RTT-unfairness of TCP or cross-traffic interferences) [10], they ignore protocol oscillations, TCP slow start, and more generally all transient phases between two steady-state operation points as well as very unstable situations. Therefore, they provide generally a very good upper-bound of what can be achieved with a given network, and can serve as a basis on which to build more accurate models.

3   The SMPI Framework

The goal of our research is to use modeling and simulation to better understand the behavior of real-world large-scale parallel applications, which informs the choice of an appropriate simulation platform. That is, simulations for studying the fine-grain properties of network protocols may have little in common with simulations for studying the scalability of some large-scale parallel computing application. Likewise, models used in algorithm design are expected to be much simpler than those used for performance evaluation purposes. Our choice of SMPI as an implementation environment reflects this goal, as SMPI allows for relatively easy conversion of real-world applications to simulation, and provides a number of useful features for enabling large-scale simulations. SMPI implements about 80% of the MPI 2.0 standard, including most of the network communication related functions, and interfaces directly with the SimGrid simulation toolkit [12]. SimGrid is a *versatile* tool to study the behavior of large-scale distributed systems such as grids, clouds or peer-to-peer systems. It has been shown to be often much more scalable than ad hoc simulators [14,15] and to handle simulations with up to two millions of processes [15] without resorting to a parallel machine. In this section we describe SMPI in greater detail, focusing first on its general approach and then later highlighting some of these features.

Full simulation of a distributed application, including CPU and network emulation, induces high overheads, and for many cases it can be even more resource intensive than direct experimentation. This, coupled with the fact that a major goal in many simulations is to study the behavior of large-scale applications on systems that may not be available to researchers, means that there is considerable interest in more efficient approaches. The two most widely applied of these are off-line simulation and partial on-line simulation, both of which are available through SMPI.

In *off-line simulation* or "post-mortem analysis" the application to be studied is instrumented before being in a real-world environment. Data about the program execution, including periods of computation, the start and end of any communication events, and possibly additional information such as the memory footprint at various points in time, is logged to a trace file. These traces can then be "replayed" in a simulated environment, considering different "what-if?" scenarios such as a faster or slower network, or more or less powerful processors on some nodes. This **trace replay** is usually much faster than direct execution, as the computation and communications are not actually executed but abstracted as *trace events*. A number of tools [16–21], including SMPI, support the off-line approach.

Off-line simulation carries with it a number of caveats: It assumes that programs are essentially deterministic, and each node will execute the same sequence of computation and communication events regardless of the order in which messages are received. A bigger challenge is that it is extremely difficult to predict the result of changing the number of nodes–while there is considerable interest and research in this area [17,22,23], the difficulty of predicting the execution profile of programs in general, and the fact that both applications and MPI implementations are likely to vary their behavior based on problem and message size, suggests that reliably guaranteeing results that are accurate within any reasonable bound may be impossible in the general case. Another problem with this approach is that instrumentation of the program can add delays, particularly if the program carries out large numbers of fine-grained network communications, and if this is not carefully accounted for then the captured trace may not be representative of the program in its "natural" state.

By contrast, the on-line approach relies on the execution of the program within a carefully-controlled real-world environment: computational sections are executed in full speed on the available hardware, but timing and delivery of messages are determined by the simulation environment (in the case of SMPI this is provided by SimGrid). This approach is much faster than full emulation (although slower than trace replay), yet preserves the proper ordering of computation and communication events. This is the standard approach for SMPI, and a number of other simulation toolkits and environments also followed this approach [3,24–26].

To support simulations at very large scale, SMPI allows for **shadow execution** and to trade off accuracy for simulation speed by benchmarking the execution of program blocks a limited number of time, while skipping these blocks later

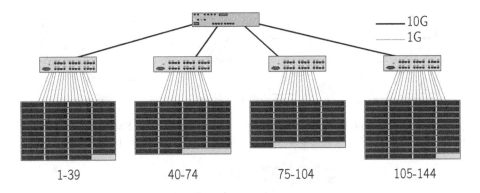

Fig. 2. The graphene cluster: a hierarchical Ethernet-based cluster

on and inserting a computation time in the simulated system clock based on the benchmarked value. This corrupts the solution produced by the application, but for data independent applications (those whose behavior does not depend on the results of the computations) this is likely to result in a reasonably accurate execution profile. A related technique, also provided by SMPI, is **memory folding**, whereby multiple simulated processes can share a single copy of the same malloc'd data structure. Again, this can corrupt results and potentially result in inconsistent or illegal data values, but allows larger scale simulations than what would be possible otherwise, and may be reasonable for a large class of parallel applications. These features are disabled by default, and have to be enabled by an expert user by adding annotations to the application source code. Potential areas for future work include improving this process so that it can be semi-automated, and building more sophisticated models based on benchmarked values.

4   A "Hybrid" Network Model

In this section, we report some issues that we encountered when comparing the predictions given by existing models to real measurement on a commodity cluster with a hierarchical Ethernet-based interconnection network. The observed discrepancies motivate the definition of a new hybrid model building upon Log-GPS and fluid models, that captures all the relevant effects observed during this study. All the presented experiments were conducted on the *graphene* cluster of the Grid'5000 experimental testbed [27, 28]. This cluster comprises 144 2.53GHz Quad-Core Intel Xeon x3440 nodes spread across four cabinets, and interconnected by a hierarchy of 10 Gigabit Ethernet switches (see Figure 2).

4.1   Point-to-Point Communication Model

As described previously in Section 2, models in the LogP family resort to piecewise linear functions to account for features such as protocol overhead, switch

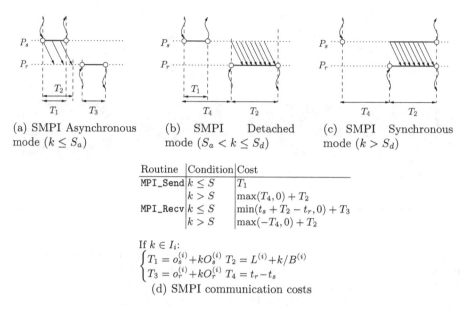

(a) SMPI Asynchronous mode ($k \leq S_a$)

(b) SMPI Detached mode ($S_a < k \leq S_d$)

(c) SMPI Synchronous mode ($k > S_d$)

Routine	Condition	Cost
MPI_Send	$k \leq S$	T_1
	$k > S$	$\max(T_4, 0) + T_2$
MPI_Recv	$k \leq S$	$\min(t_s + T_2 - t_r, 0) + T_3$
	$k > S$	$\max(-T_4, 0) + T_2$

If $k \in I_i$:
$$\begin{cases} T_1 = o_s^{(i)} + kO_s^{(i)} & T_2 = L^{(i)} + k/B^{(i)} \\ T_3 = o_r^{(i)} + kO_r^{(i)} & T_4 = t_r - t_s \end{cases}$$

(d) SMPI communication costs

Fig. 3. The "hybrid" network model of SMPI in a nutshell

latency, and the overlap of computation and communication. In the LogGPS model [9] the time spent in the MPI_Send and MPI_Recv functions is modeled as a **continuous** linear function for small messages ($o + kO_s$ or $o + kO_r$). Unfortunately, as illustrated in Figure 4, this model is unable to account for the full complexity of a real MPI implementation. The measurements presented in Figure 4 were obtained according to the following protocol: To avoid size and sequencing measurement bias, the message size is exponentially sampled from 1 byte to 100MiB. We ran two "ping" and one "ping-pong" experiments. The ping experiments aim at measuring the time spent in the MPI_Send (resp. MPI_Recv) function by ensuring that the receiver (resp. sender) is always ready to communicate. The ping-pong experiment allows us to measure the transmission delay. We ran our analysis on the whole set of raw measurements rather than on averaged values for each message size to prevent behavior smoothing and variability information loss. The rationale is to study the asynchronous part of MPI (from the application point of view) without any a priori assumptions on where switching may occur. This approach allows us to clearly identify different modes interpreted as follows:

- **Small** (when $k \leq 1,420$): this mode corresponds to messages that fit in a TCP packet and are sent asynchronously by the kernel. As it induces memory copies, the duration significantly depends on the message size.
- **Medium** (when $1,420 < k \leq 32,768$ or $32,768 < k \leq 65,536 = S_a$): these messages are still sent asynchronously but incur a slight overhead compared to small messages, hence a discontinuity at $k = 1420$. The distinction at

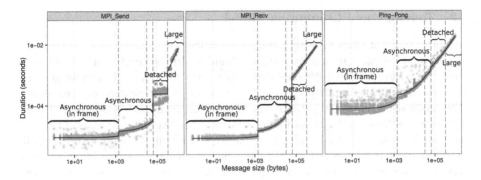

Fig. 4. MPI_Send and MPI_Recv duration as a function of message size

$k = 32,768$ does not really correspond to any particular threshold on the sender side but is visible on the receiver side where a small gap is noticed. Accounting for it allows for a better linear fitting accounting for MPI/TCP peculiarities.

- **Detached** (when $65,536 < k \leq 327,680 = S_d$): this mode corresponds to messages that do not block the sender but require the receiver to post the reception before the communication actually takes place.
- **Large** (when $k > 327,680$): for such messages, both sender and receiver synchronize using a rendez-vous protocol before sending data. Except for the waiting time, the durations on the sender side and on the receiver side are very close.

As illustrated by Figure 4, the duration of each mode can be accurately modeled through linear regression. These observations justify the model implemented in SMPI that is described in Figure 3. We distinguish three modes of operation: asynchronous, detached, and synchronous. Each of these modes can be divided in sub-modes when discontinuities are observed. The "ping" measurements are used to instantiate the values of o_s, O_S, o_r, and O_r for small to detached messages. By subtracting $2(o_r + k.O_r)$ from the round trip time measured by the ping-pong experiment, and thanks to a piece-wise linear regression, we can deduce the values of L and B. It is interesting to note that similar experiments with MPI_Isend and MPI_Irecv show that modeling their duration by a constant term o as was done in [9] is not a reasonable assumption neither for simulation nor prediction purposes[1].

While distinguishing these modes may be of little importance when simulating applications that only send particular message sizes, obtaining good predictions in a wide range of settings, and without conducting custom tuning for every simulated application, requires accurately accounting for all such peculiarities. This will be exemplified in Section 5.

---

[1] More information on how to instantiate the parameters of the SMPI model and about the study of non-blocking operations is available at http://mescal.imag.fr/membres/arnaud.legrand/research/smpi/smpi_loggps.php

4.2 Topology and Contention Model

For most network models, dealing with contention comes down to assuming one of the simple **single-port** or **multi-port** models. In the single-port model each node can communicate with only one other node at a time and messages are queued, while in the multi-port model, each node can communicate with every other node simultaneously without any slowdown. Both models oversimplify the reality. Some flow-level models follow a bounded multi-port approach [29], i.e., the communication capacity of a node is limited by the network bandwidth it can exploit, that better reflects the behavior of communications on wide area networks. However, within a cluster or cluster-like environment the mutual interactions between send and receive operations cannot safely be ignored.

To quantify the impact of network contention of a point-to-point communication between two processors in a same cabinet, we artificially create contention and measure the bandwidth as perceived by the sender and the receiver. We place ourselves in the **large** message mode where the highest bandwidth usage is observed and transfer 4 MiB messages.

In a first experiment we increase the number of concurrent transfers from 1 to 19, i.e., half the size of the first cabinet. As the network switch is well dimensioned, this experiment does not create contention: We observe no bandwidth degradation on either the sender side or the receiver side. Our second experiment uses concurrent `MPI_Sendrecv` transfers instead of unidirectional transfers. We increase the number of concurrent bidirectional transfers from 1 to 19 and measure the bandwidth on the sender (B_s) and receiver (B_r) side. A single-port model, as assumed by LogP-based models, would lead to $B_s + B_r = B$ on average since both directions strictly alternate. A multi-port model, as assumed by other delay models, would estimate that $B_s + B_r = 2 \times B$ since communications would not interfere with each other. However, both fail to model what actually happens, as we observe that $B_s + B_r \approx 1.5 \times B$ on this cluster.

We model this bandwidth sharing effect by enriching the simulated cluster description. Each node is provided with three links: an uplink and a downlink, so that send and receive operations share the available bandwidth separately in each direction; and a specific *limiter* link, whose bandwidth is $1.5 \times B$, shared by all the flows to and from this processor.

Preliminary experiments on other clusters show that this contention parameter seems constant for a given platform, with a value somewhere between 1 and 2. Such value somehow corresponds to the effective limitation due to the card capacity and the protocol overhead. Determining this parameter requires benchmarking each cluster as described in this section. Our set of experiments is available on the previously indicated web page. We are currently working on a more generic benchmarking solution that one could easily use to determine the exact contention factor for any cluster.

This modification is not enough to model contention at the level of the whole *graphene* cluster. As described in Figure 2, it is composed of four cabinets interconnected through 10Gb links. Experiments show that these links become limiting when shared between several concurrent pair-wise communications between cabinets. This effect corresponds to the switch backplane and to the protocol overhead and is captured by describing the interconnection of two cabinets as three distinct links (uplink, downlink, and *limiter* link). The bandwidth of this third link is set to 13 Gb as measured.

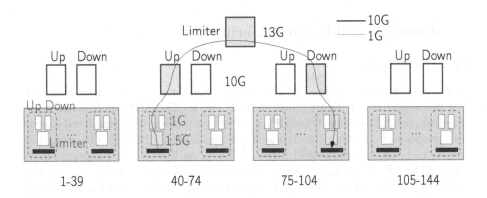

Fig. 5. Modeling the graphene cluster: rectangles represent capacity constraints. Grayed rectangles represent constraints involved in a communication from node to node 40 to node 104.

The resulting topology is depicted on Figure 5 and is easily described in a compact way within SimGrid. Since SimGrid, on which SMPI is based, is a versatile simulator, incorporating further levels of hierarchy or more complex interconnections if needed would be easy [30].

4.3   Collective Communications Model

Many MPI applications spend a significant amount of time in collective communication operations. They are thus crucial to application performance. Several algorithms exist for each collective operation, each of them exhibiting very different performance depending on various parameters such as the network topology, the message size, and the number of communicating processes [31]. A given algorithm can commonly be almost an order of magnitude faster than another in a given setting and yet slower than this same algorithm in another setting. Every widely-used MPI implementation thus provides several algorithms for each collective operation and carefully selects the best one at runtime. For instance, OpenMPI provides a dozen distinct algorithms for the MPI_Alltoall function, and the code to select the right algorithm for a given setting is several thousand lines long. Note that the selection logic of the various MPI implementations is highly dependent on the implementation and generally embedded deep within the source code.

Our [in]validation experiments quickly highlighted the importance of adhering as closely as possible to this logic. Hence SMPI now implements **all** the collective algorithms and selection logics of both OpenMPI and MPICH and even a few other collective algorithms from Star MPI [31]. Deciding which selector and which algorithms are used can be specified from command line, which allows users to test within simulation whether replacing a default algorithm by another may help or not on a particular combination of platform/application.

5   Model [In]Validation Experiments

5.1   Methodology

All the experiments presented hereafter have been done on the *graphene* cluster that was described in the previous section. The studied MPI applications were compiled and linked using OpenMPI 1.6. For comparison with simulated executions purposes, we instrumented these applications with TAU [32]. The simulated executions have been performed either off-line or on-line as SMPI supports both modes. The file describing the simulated version of the *graphene* cluster was instantiated with values obtained independently from the studied applications. We used the techniques detailed in the previous section to obtain these values. In what follows we compare execution times measured on the *graphene* cluster to simulated times obtained with the *hybrid* model proposed in Section 4, the *LogGPS* model that supersedes all the delay-based models, and a *fluid* model that is a basic linear flow-level model whose validation for WAN studies was done in [10].

We did not limit our study to overall execution times as they may hide compensation effects, and do not provide any information as to whether an application is compute or communication bound or how different phases may or may not overlap. Our experimental study makes use of Gantt charts to compare traces visually as well as quantitatively. We rely on CSV files, R, and org-mode to describe the complete workflow going from raw data the graphs presented in this paper, ensuring full reproducibility of our analysis.

5.2   NAS Parallel Benchmarks

The NAS Parallel Benchmarks (NPB) are a suite of programs commonly used to assess the performance of parallel platforms. In this article, we only report results for two of these applications but results for other applications are also available in [33]. The LU benchmark is an iterative computation of a LU factorization. At each iteration, it exhibits a communication scheme that forms a wave going from the first process to the last one and back. The second studied benchmark is CG (Conjugate Gradient). It has a complex communication scheme that is composed of a large number of point-to-point transfers of small messages. Moreover, processors are organized in a hierarchy of groups. At each level communications occur within a group and then between groups. This benchmark is then very sensitive to the mapping of the MPI processes on to the physical processors with regard to network organization, particularly in non-homogeneous topologies. For this series of experiments, we use the off-line simulation capacities of SMPI, i.e., execution traces of the benchmark are first acquired from a real system and then replayed in a simulated context.

Both benchmarks are evaluated with two class of instances, B, and C, where C is the larger instance. A classical goal when studying the performance of an application or of a new cluster is to evaluate how well the application scales for a given instance. Figure 6 shows the speedup as measured on the *graphene* cluster and as obtained with the studied models. For every experiment we ensured that both simulated and real node mapping corresponds to each others.

For the LU benchmark we can see that for the class B instances, the *hybrid* and *LogGPS* model provide an excellent estimation of speedup evolution. As could be expected, the *fluid* model provides an over-optimistic estimation, which can be explained by its poor ability to accurately model transmission time of small messages and computation/communication overlap. For the class C instance, although the *hybrid* model provides a slightly better estimation than the *LogGPS* model, both predict an optimistic scaling of this application. We think, this can be explained by the fact that none of these models include a noise component. Indeed, the communication pattern of LU is very sensitive to noise as each process has to wait for the reception of a message before sending its own data. Such a phenomenon is given by Figure 7 that shows a period of 0.2 seconds of the execution of the LU benchmark with 32 processes. The upper part

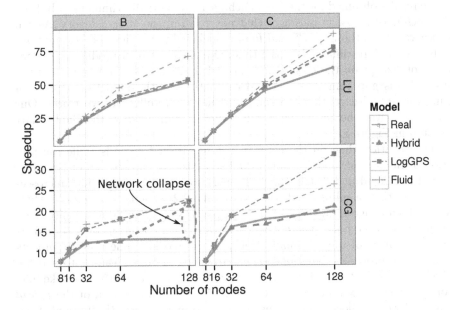

Fig. 6. Comparison between simulated and actual execution times for three NAS parallel benchmarks

of this figure displays the actual execution while the lower corresponds to the simulation of the same phase with the *hybrid* model. Deterministic models such as *LogGPS* or *hybrid* slightly underestimate these synchronization phases and small delay adds up, which hinders the application scalability. However, Figure 7 clearly shows that despite the small time scale, the simulation correctly renders the general communication pattern of this benchmark and that Figure 6 does not hide a bad, but lucky, estimation of each component of the execution time.

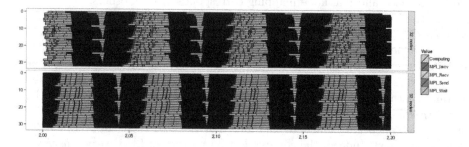

Fig. 7. Part of the Gantt chart of the execution of the LU benchmark with 32 processes. The upper part displays the actual execution while the lower is the simulation with the *hybrid* model. Black areas comprise thousands wave-structured micro messages.

The results obtained for the CG benchmark are more discriminating. Indeed, this benchmark transfers messages that never fall in the *large* category. As can be observed, both the *LogGPS* and *fluid* models fail to provide good estimations and largely underestimate the total time. Our *hybrid* model produces excellent estimation except on the class B instance with 128 nodes. To determine if the source of this gap comes from a bad estimation by the model or a problem during the actual execution, we compared more carefully the two traces. Our main suspect was the actual execution, which is confirmed by the Gantt chart presented in Figure 8.

The execution time on the class B instance is 14.4 seconds while the prediction of the *hybrid* model is only of 9.9 seconds. We can see two outstanding zones of MPI_Send and MPI_Wait. Such operations typically take few microseconds to less than a millisecond. Here they take 0.2 seconds. Our guess is that, due to a high congestion, the switch drops packets and slows down one (or several) process to the point where it stops sending until a timeout of .2 seconds is reached. Because of the communication pattern, blocking one process impacts all the other processes. This phenomenon occurs 24 times leading to a delay of 4.86 seconds. Without this bad behavior, the real execution would take 9.55 seconds, which is extremely close to the 9.85 seconds prediction of the *hybrid* model and would allow the effective speedup to match perfectly its prediction. The same phenomenon is also present for class C although it is less noticeable. In both cases, the speedup shape predicted by the *hybrid* model is non-trivial since it comprises a plateau from 32 to 64 nodes. Such shape can actually be

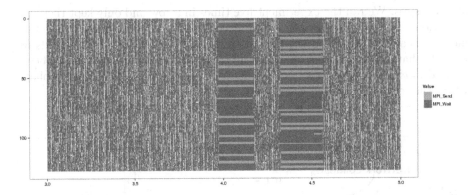

Fig. 8. Two seconds Gantt-chart of the real execution of a class B instance of CG for 128 process

well explained by the hierarchical structure of its communication pattern and how it maps to the network topology. The *LogGPS* model fails at modeling such aspects and would predict an excellent scaling.

Although we do not know for sure yet, we think the timeout issues we encountered could be somehow similar to what is known as the *TCP incast problem* and which has been observed in cloud environments [34]. Such delays are linked to the default TCP re-transmission timeout, which is equal to .2s by default in Linux. Although such value has recently been decreased from 1s to .2s to adapt with recent evolution of Internet characteristics, it remains inadequate for a cluster. Such protocol collapse would clearly need to be fixed in a production environment and we are currently investigating whether decreasing the TCP re-transmission timeout to a drastically smaller value than .2 seconds would help or not as it is not clear that HPC variants of TCP would really help solving such issue.

5.3 Collective Communications

The NAS parallel benchmarks do not heavily rely on MPI collective communication primitives but instead implement a static communication pattern. We conduct the (in)validation with the study of an isolated MPI collective operation at a time. On medium size clusters, simple operations like broadcast only incur minor network contention toward the end of the operation and may thus be correctly predicted with simple models like *LogGPS*. Therefore, although we conducted similar studies for most commonly used operations, we only report the results for the MPI_Alltoall function as it is the most likely to be impacted by network contention. Here we aim at assessing the validity of contention modeling as the message size varies rather than the impact of using different algorithms. To this end, although we extended SMPI so that it implements **all** the collective algorithms and selection logics of both OpenMPI and MPICH, we enforce the use of a single algorithm, i.e., the pairwise-exchange algorithm [35], for all message sizes. We ran the experiment five times in a row and only kept the best execution time for each message size. Indeed, we noticed that the first communication is always significantly slower than the subsequent ones, which tends to indicate that TCP requires some warm-up time. This phenomenon has also been noticed in experiments assessing the validity of the BigSIM simulation toolkit, where the same workaround was applied.

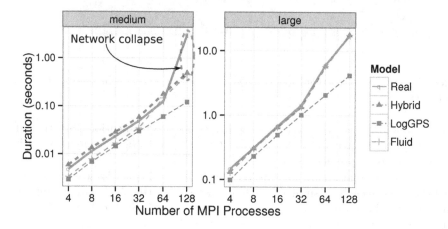

Fig. 9. Comparison between simulated and actual execution times for the MPI_Alltoall operation

Figure 9 shows (in logarithmic scale) the evolution of simulated and actual execution times for the MPI_Alltoall operation when the number of MPI processes varies for the three network models. Results are presented for two message sizes: *medium* messages of 100 kiB and *large* messages of 4 MiB. We can see that for large messages, the *hybrid* and *fluid* models both achieve excellent predictions (within 10%). Unsurprisingly, the *LogGPS* model is overly optimistic in such setting and completely underestimates the effects of network contention. Its prediction error can be **up to a factor of 4** when 128 processors are involved in the All-to-All operation.

For medium messages, the *hybrid* model is again the best contender, with a low prediction error for up to 64 nodes, while the *LogGPS* model is again too optimistic. For such a message size, the lack of latency and bandwidth correction factors in the *fluid* model leads to a clear underestimation of the execution time. Interestingly, when 128 processes are involved in the collective communication, the actual execution time increases dramatically while simulated times continue to follow the same trend. The reason for such a large increase can again be explained by massive packet dropping in the main switch that leads to timeouts, and unexpected re-emissions, hence incurring significant delays compared to usual transmission time. Modeling such phenomenon would probably be quite difficult and of little interest since fixing this problem on the real platform would be much more useful.

6   Simulating a Real Application

Developing a research prototype that allows for simulation of a few benchmarks already requires a lot of efforts and is useful to demonstrate the effectiveness of an idea. However, it does not allow others to build upon it. Therefore, we also ensured SMPI could also be used to simulate complex real applications such as the full LinPACK suite [36], Sweep3D [37], or BigDFT, which is an open-source Density Functional Theory (DFT) massively parallel electronic structure code [38], and the geodynamics application SpecFEM3D [39], which is part of the PRACE benchmark. SMPI also is tested upon 80% of the MPICH2 test suite and against a large subset of the MPICH3 test suite every night. We can thus claim that SMPI is not limited to toy applications but can effectively be used for the analysis of real scientific applications.

In this section we aim at demonstrating the capacity of SMPI to simulate a real, large, and complex MPI application. To this end, we use BigDFT, which is the sole electronic structure code based on systematic basis sets which can use hybrid supercomputers and is able to scale particularly well (95% of efficiency with 4096 nodes on Curie [40]). This is why it is one of the eleven real scientific applications that have been selected in the Mont-Blanc project [2] to assess the potential of low-power embedded components based clusters to address future Exascale HPC needs. One of the objectives of the Mont-Blanc project is thus to develop prototypes of HPC clusters using low power commercially available embedded technology such as ARM processors and Ethernet technologies.

The first Mont-Blanc prototype is expected to be available during the year 2014. It will be using Samsung Exynos 5 Dual Cortex A15 processors with an embedded Mali T604 GPU and will be using Ethernet for communication. In order to start evaluating the applications before 2014, a small cluster of ARM system on chip was built. It is named Tibidabo and is hosted at the Barcelona Supercomputing Center. Tibidabo [41] is an experimental HPC cluster built using NVIDIA Tegra2 chips, each a dual-core ARM Cortex-A9 processor. The PCI Express support of Tegra2 is used to connect a 1Gb Ethernet NIC, and the board are interconnected hierarchically using 48-port 1 GbE switches. The results we present in this section have been obtained using this platform.

For our experiments, we disable the OpenMP and GPU extensions at compile time to study behaviors related to MPI operations. BigDFT alternates between regular computation bursts and important collective communications. Moreover the set of collective operations that is used may completely change depending on the instance, hence the need to use online simulation. In the following experiments, we used MPICH 3.0.4 [35] and Extrae [42] for runtime incompatibility issues between OpenMPI, Tau and BigDFT. Last, while this application can be simulated by SMPI without any modification to the source code, its large memory footprint means that running the simulation on a single machine would

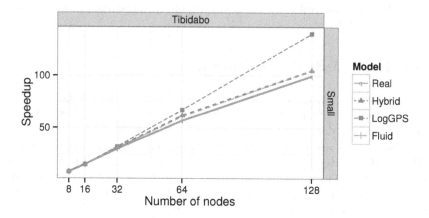

Fig. 10. Evaluating scalability of BigDFT on Tibidabo both through real executions and simulation. The LogGPS model fails to model the slowdown incurred by the hierarchical and irregular network topology.

require an improbably large amount of RAM. Applying the memory folding and shadow execution techniques mentioned in Section 3 and detailed in [11], we were able to simulate the execution of BigDFT with 128 processes, whose peak memory footprint is estimated to 71 GiB, on a single laptop using less than 2.5GB of memory. Such memory requirement could be further improved with additional manual annotations but it was sufficient for our needs.

Figure 10 shows the comparison of the speedup evolution as measured on the *tibidabo* cluster on a small instance. This instance has a relatively low communication to computation ratio (around 20% of time is spent communicating when using 128 nodes and the main used operations are MPI_Alltoall, MPI_Alltoallv, MPI_Allgather, MPI_Allgatherv and MPI_Allreduce) despite the slow computations of tibidabo. This instance is thus particularly difficult to model and is expected to have a limited scalability, which one may want to observe in simulation first to avoid wasting resources or to assess the relevance of upgrading hardware. As expected, the *LogGPS* model predicts an over-optimistic perfect scaling whereas both the *fluid* and the *hybrid* models succeed in accounting for the slowdown incurred by the hierarchical and irregular network topology of this prototype platform. We think this kind of observation really questions the use of the *LogGPS* model for scalability studies.

To further demonstrate the usability of our tool, we want to mention that simulating 64 nodes of tibidabo, which is made of relatively slow ARM processors, on a Xeon 7460 with partial on-line simulation takes twice as less time (10 minutes) than running the code for real (20 minutes).

7   Related Work

Packet-level network simulations are usually implemented as discrete-event simulations with events for packet emission or reception as well as network protocol events. Such simulations reproduce the real-world communication behavior down to movements of individual packets. Some tools following this approach, e.g., NS2, NS3, or OMNet++, have been widely used to design network protocols or understand the consequences of protocol modifications [43]. However, such fine-grain network models are difficult to instantiate with realistic parameter values for large-scale networks and generally suffer from scalability issues. While parallel discrete-event simulation techniques [4, 44] may speed up such simulations, the possible improvements remain quite limited.

Some projects model MPI collective communications with simple analytic formulas [16, 18]. This allows for quick estimations and may provide a reasonable approximation for simple and regular collective operations, but is unlikely to accurately model the complex optimized versions that can be found in most MPI implementations. An orthogonal approach is to thoroughly benchmark collective operations to measure the distribution of communication times with regard to the message size and number of concurrent flows. Then, these distributions are used to model the interconnection network as a black box [45]. This approach has several drawbacks. First, it does not accurately model communication/computation overlap. Second, it cannot take the independence of some concurrent communications into account. Third, it provides little to no information on how the performance of collective operations could be improved. Finally, it does not allow for performance extrapolation on a larger machine with similar characteristics and it provides little insight into the causes of poor performance. A third approach consists in tracing the execution of collective operations and then replaying the obtained trace using one of the aforementioned delay models [4, 16–18]. However, most tools [16–18, 24] use a very basic network topology model that does not account for the complexity of modern platforms. Furthermore, current implementations of the MPI standard dynamically select from up to a dozen different communication algorithms when executing a collective operation depending on message size and on the number of involved nodes. Thus, using the right algorithm becomes critical when trying to predict performance.

Studying the behavior of complex HPC applications or operations and characterizing HPC platforms through simulation has been at the heart of many research projects and tools for decades. Such tools differ by their capabilities, their structure, and by the network models they implement. BigSIM [4], LAPSE [24], MPI-SIM [25], or the work in [26] rely on simple delay models (affine point-to-point communication delay based on link latency and bandwidth). Other tools, such as Dimemas [16], LogGOPSim [17], or PHANTOM [20] use variants of the LogP model to simulate communications. Note that BigSIM also offers an alternate simulation mode based on a complex and slow packet-level simulator. This approach is also followed by MPI-NeTSim [3] that relies on OMNeT++. Finally PSINS [18] and PEVPM [45] provide complex custom models derived from intensive benchmarking to model network contention.

8   Conclusion and Future Work

In this paper, we demonstrated that accurate modeling and performance prediction for a wide range of parallel applications requires proper consideration of many aspects of the underlying communication architecture, including the breakdown of collective communications into their component point-to-point messages, the interconnect topology, and contention between competing messages that are sent simultaneously over the same link. Even relatively minor inaccuracies may compromise the soundness of the simulation, yet none of the models previously used in the literature give due consideration to these factors. We described the implementation of a proposed *hybrid* network model that improves on this situation within SMPI, and showed that SMPI-based simulations do a better job of tracking real-world behavior than those implemented in competing simulation toolkits.

Our priority in this work was the validation of the model at a small scale and for TCP over Ethernet networks. However, we also believe that SMPI will prove very useful to application developers by allowing them to debug parallel applications and study the impact of selecting different collective communication algorithms without wasting cluster resources. It also provides a good comparison point that helps determine whether or not the platform and application behave as expected. Previous models are expected to provide over optimistic evaluations and are thus of little use. Finally, we think this tool will prove very useful to efforts such as the European Mont-Blanc project [2,41], which aims at prototyping exascale platforms using low-power embedded processors interconnected by Ethernet. A next step will be to analyze its adequacy for simulating larger platforms when such machines become available for benchmarking purposes. The study should then extend to other kinds of interconnects (such as InfiniBand) and more complicated topologies (e.g., torus or fat trees).

As a base line, we advocate for an open-science approach, which should enable other scientists to reproduce the experiments done in this paper. For that purpose, the traces and scripts used to produce our analysis are available [46]. Accordingly, SMPI and all the software stack are provided as open-source software available for download from the SimGrid website: http://simgrid.gforge. inria.fr/.

Acknowledgments. This work is partially supported by the SONGS ANR project (11-ANR-INFRA-13), the CNRS PICS $N°$ 5473, the European Mont-Blanc project (European Community's Seventh Framework Programme [FP7/2007-2013] under grant agreement no 288777). Experiments presented in this paper were carried out using a PRACE (European Community funding under grants RI-261557 and RI-283493) prototype and the Grid'5000 experimental testbed, being developed under the INRIA ALADDIN development action with support from CNRS, RENATER and several Universities as well as other funding bodies (see https://www.grid5000.fr). We would also like to thank Luigi Genovese, main developer of BigDFT, who helped us with porting this code on top of SMPI and using interesting problem instances.

References

1. TOP500 supercomputer sites. http://top500.org
2. Mont-Blanc: European Approach Towards Energy Efficient High Performance: Montblanc. http://www.montblanc-project.eu/
3. Penoff, B., Wagner, A., Tüxen, M., Rüngeler, I.: MPI-NeTSim: A network simulation module for MPI. In: Proc. of the 15th IEEE Intl. Conference on Parallel and Distributed Systems, Shenzen, China (December 2009)
4. Zheng, G., Kakulapati, G., Kale, L.: BigSim: A Parallel Simulator for Performance Prediction of Extremely Large Parallel Machines. In: Proc. of the 18th International Parallel and Distributed Processing Symposium, Santa Fe, NM (April 2004)
5. Lucio, G.F., Paredes-farrera, M., Jammeh, E., Fleury, M., Reed, M.J.: Opnet modeler and ns-2: Comparing the accuracy of network simulators for packet-level analysis using a network testbed. In: Proc. of the 3rd WEAS International Conference on Simulation, Modelling and Optimization, ICOSMO, pp. 700–707 (2003)
6. Culler, D., Karp, R., Patterson, D., Sahay, A., Schauser, K.E., Santos, E., Subramonian, R., von Eicken, T.: LogP: Towards a Realistic Model of Parallel Computation. In: Proc. of the fourth ACM SIGPLAN Symposium on Principles and Practice of Parallel Programming (PPOPP), San Diego, CA, pp. 1–12 (1993)
7. Alexandrov, A., Ionescu, M.F., Schauser, K.E., Scheiman, C.: LogGP: Incorporating Long Messages Into the LogP Model - One Step Closer Towards a Realistic Model for Parallel Computation. In: Proc. of the 7th ACM Symp. on Parallel Algorithms and Architectures (SPAA), Santa Barbara, CA, pp. 95–105 (1995)
8. Kielmann, T., Bal, H.E., Verstoep, K.: Fast Measurement of LogP Parameters for Message Passing Platforms. In: Rolim, J.D.P. (ed.) IPDPS-WS 2000. LNCS, vol. 1800, pp. 1176–1183. Springer, Heidelberg (2000)
9. Ino, F., Fujimoto, N., Hagihara, K.: LogGPS: a Parallel Computational Model for Synchronization Analysis. In: Proc. of the eighth ACM SIGPLAN Symposium on Principles and Practices of Parallel Programming (PPoPP), Snowbird, UT, pp. 133–142 (2001)
10. Velho, P., Schnorr, L., Casanova, H., Legrand, A.: On the Validity of Flow-level TCP Network Models for Grid and Cloud Simulations. ACM Transactions on Modeling and Computer Simulation 23(4), 23 (2013)
11. Clauss, P.N., Stillwell, M., Genaud, S., Suter, F., Casanova, H., Quinson, M.: Single Node On-Line Simulation of MPI Applications with SMPI. In: Proc. of the 25th IEEE Intl. Parallel and Distributed Processing Symposium (IPDPS), Anchorage, AK (May 2011)
12. Casanova, H., Legrand, A., Quinson, M.: SimGrid: a Generic Framework for Large-Scale Distributed Experiments. In: Proc. of the 10th IEEE International Conference on Computer Modeling and Simulation, Cambridge, UK (March 2008)
13. Desprez, F., Markomanolis, G.S., Suter, F.: Improving the Accuracy and Efficiency of Time-Independent Trace Replay. In: Proc. of the 3rd International Workshop on Performance Modeling, Benchmarking and Simulation of High Performance Computer Systems (PMBS), Salt Lake City, UT (November 2012)
14. Donassolo, B., Casanova, H., Legrand, A., Velho, P.: Fast and Scalable Simulation of Volunteer Computing Systems Using SimGrid. In: Proc. of the Workshop on Large-Scale System and Application Performance (LSAP), Chicago, IL (June 2010)
15. Quinson, M., Rosa, C., Thiéry, C.: Parallel simulation of peer-to-peer systems. In: Proceedings of the 12th IEEE International Symposium on Cluster Computing and the Grid (CCGrid 2012). IEEE Computer Society Press (May 2012)

16. Badia, R.M., Labarta, J., Giménez, J., Escalé, F.: Dimemas: Predicting MPI Applications Behaviour in Grid Environments. In: Proc. of the Workshop on Grid Applications and Programming Tools (June 2003)
17. Hoefler, T., Siebert, C., Lumsdaine, A.: LogGOPSim - Simulating Large-Scale Applications in the LogGOPS Model. In: Proc. of the ACM Workshop on Large-Scale System and Application Performance, Chicago, IL, pp. 597–604 (June 2010)
18. Tikir, M.M., Laurenzano, M.A., Carrington, L., Snavely, A.: PSINS: An Open Source Event Tracer and Execution Simulator for MPI Applications. In: Sips, H., Epema, D., Lin, H.-X. (eds.) Euro-Par 2009. LNCS, vol. 5704, pp. 135–148. Springer, Heidelberg (2009)
19. Núñez, A., Fernández, J., Garcia, J.D., Garcia, F., Carretero, J.: New Techniques for Simulating High Performance MPI Applications on Large Storage Networks. Journal of Supercomputing 51(1), 40–57 (2010)
20. Zhai, J., Chen, W., Zheng, W.: PHANTOM: Predicting Performance of Parallel Applications on Large-Scale Parallel Machines Using a Single Node. In: Proc. of the 15th ACM SIGPLAN Symp. on Principles and Practice of Parallel Programming, pp. 305–314 (January 2010)
21. Hermanns, M.A., Geimer, M., Wolf, F., Wylie, B.: Verifying Causality between Distant Performance Phenomena in Large-Scale MPI Applications. In: Proc. of the 17th Euromicro International Conference on Parallel, Distributed and Network-based Processing, Weimar, Germany, pp. 78–84 (February 2009)
22. Wu, X., Mueller, F.: ScalaExtrap: trace-based communication extrapolation for SPMD programs. In: Proc. of the 16th ACM Symposium on Principles and Practice of Parallel Programming (PPoPP 2011), pp. 113–122 (2011)
23. Carrington, L., Laurenzano, M., Tiwari, A.: Inferring large-scale computation behavior via trace extrapolation. In: Large-Scale Parallel Processing Workshop (IPDPS 2013) (2013)
24. Dickens, P., Heidelberger, P., Nicol, D.: Parallelized Direct Execution Simulation of Message-Passing Parallel Programs. IEEE Transactions on Parallel and Distributed Systems 7(10), 1090–1105 (1996)
25. Bagrodia, R., Deelman, E., Phan, T.: Parallel Simulation of Large-Scale Parallel Applications. International Journal of High Performance Computing and Applications 15(1), 3–12 (2001)
26. Riesen, R.: A Hybrid MPI Simulator. In: Proc. of the IEEE International Conference on Cluster Computing, Barcelona, Spain (September 2006)
27. Technical specification of the network interconnect in the graphene cluster of grid'5000. https://www.grid5000.fr/mediawiki/index.php/Nancy:Network
28. Bolze, R., Cappello, F., Caron, E., Daydé, M., Desprez, F., Jeannot, E., Jégou, Y., Lantéri, S., Leduc, J., Melab, N., Namyst, R., Mornet, G., Primet, P., Quetier, B., Richard, O., Talbi, E.G., Touche, I.: Grid'5000: a large scale and highly reconfigurable experimental grid testbed. International Journal of High Performance Computing Applications 20(4), 481–494 (2006)
29. Hong, B., Prasanna, V.K.: Adaptive Allocation of Independent Tasks to Maximize Throughput. IEEE Transactions on Parallel and Distributed Systems 18(10), 1420–1435 (2007)
30. Bobelin, L., Legrand, A., Márquez, D.A.G., Navarro, P., Quinson, M., Suter, F., Thiery, C.: Scalable Multi-Purpose Network Representation for Large Scale Distributed System Simulation. In: Proc. of the 12th IEEE/ACM International Symposium on Cluster, Cloud and Grid Computing (CCGrid), Ottawa, Canada, pp. 220–227 (May 2012)

31. Faraj, A., Yuan, X., Lowenthal, D.: STAR-MPI: self tuned adaptive routines for MPI collective operations. In: Proc. of the 20th Annual International Conference on Supercomputing, ICS 2006, pp. 199–208. ACM, New York (2006)
32. Shende, S., Malony, A.D.: The Tau Parallel Performance System. International Journal of High Performance Computing Applications 20(2), 287–311 (2006)
33. Bedaride, P., Genaud, S., Degomme, A., Legrand, A., Markomanolis, G., Quinson, M., Stillwell, Mark, L., Suter, F., Videau, B.: Improving Simulations of MPI Applications Using A Hybrid Network Model with Topology and Contention Support. Rapport de recherche RR-8300, INRIA (May 2013)
34. Chen, Y., Griffith, R., Liu, J., Katz, R.H., Joseph, A.D.: Understanding tcp incast throughput collapse in datacenter networks. In: Proc. of the 1st ACM Workshop on Research on Enterprise Networking, WREN 2009, pp. 73–82. ACM (2009)
35. Thakur, R., Rabenseifner, R., Gropp, W.: Optimization of collective communication operations in MPICH. International Journal of High Performance Computer Applications 19(1), 49–66 (2005)
36. Dongarra, J.J., Luszczek, P., Petitet, A.: The linpack benchmark: Past, present, and future. concurrency and computation: Practice and experience. Concurrency and Computation: Practice and Experience 15 (2003)
37. Baker, R.S., Koch, K.R.: An s_n algorithm for the massively parallel CM-200 computer. Nuclear Science and Engineering 128(3), 312–320 (1998). http://wwwc3.lanl.gov/pal/software/sweep3d/
38. Genovese, L., Neelov, A., Goedecker, S., Deutsch, T., Ghasemi, S.A., Willand, A., Caliste, D., Zilberberg, O., Rayson, M., Bergman, A., Schneider, R.: Daubechies Wavelets as a Basis Set for Density Functional Pseudopotential Calculations. Journal of Chemical Physics 129, 014109 (2008)
39. Peter, D., Komatitsch, D., Luo, Y., Martin, R., Le Goff, N., Casarotti, E., Le Loher, P., Magnoni, F., Liu, Q., Blitz, C., Nissen-Meyer, T., Basini, P., Tromp, J.: Forward and Adjoint Simulations of Seismic Wave Propagation on Fully Unstructured Hexahedral Meshes. Geophysical Journal International 186(2), 721–739 (2011)
40. The curie supercomputer. http://www-hpc.cea.fr/en/complexe/tgcc-curie.htm
41. Rajovic, N., Puzovic, N., Vilanova, L., Villavieja, C., Ramirez, A.: The low-power architecture approach towards exascale computing. In: Proc. of the Second Workshop on Scalable Algorithms for Large-Scale Systems, ScalA 2011. ACM (2011)
42. Barcelona Supercomputer Center: Extrae. http://www.bsc.es/computer-sciences/extrae/
43. Minkenberg, C., Rodriguez, G.: Trace-Driven Co-Simulation of High-Performance Computing Systems Using OMNeT++. In: Proc. of the 2nd International Conference on Simulation Tools and Techniques (SimuTools), Rome, Italy (2009)
44. Mubarak, M., Carothers, C.D., Ross, R., Carns, P.: Modeling a million-node dragonfly network using massively parallel discrete-event simulation. In: High Performance Computing, Networking Storage and Analysis, SC Companion, pp. 366–376 (2012)
45. Grove, D.A., Coddington, P.D.: Communication benchmarking and performance modelling of mpi programs on cluster computers. Journal of Supercomputing 34(2), 201–217 (2005)
46. Companion of the PMBS'13 publication on SMPI. Hosted on Figshare. http://dx.doi.org/10.6084/m9.figshare.833851, Online version of this article with access to the experimental data and scripts (in the org source)

SESH Framework: A Space Exploration Framework for GPU Application and Hardware Codesign

Joo Hwan Lee[1](✉), Jiayuan Meng[2], and Hyesoon Kim[1]

[1] School of Computer Science, Georgia Institute of Technology, Atlanta, GA, USA
{joohwan.lee,hyesoon}@gatech.edu
[2] Argonne National Laboratory, Leadership Computing Facility, Argonne, IL, USA
jmeng@alcf.anl.gov

Abstract. Graphics processing units (GPUs) have become increasingly popular accelerators in supercomputers, and this trend is likely to continue. With its disruptive architecture and a variety of optimization options, it is often desirable to understand the dynamics between *potential* application transformations and *potential* hardware features when designing future GPUs for scientific workloads. However, current codesign efforts have been limited to manual investigation of benchmarks on microarchitecture simulators, which is labor-intensive and time-consuming. As a result, system designers can explore only a small portion of the design space. In this paper, we propose SESH framework, a model-driven codesign framework for GPU, that is able to automatically search the design space by simultaneously exploring *prospective* application and hardware implementations and evaluate *potential* software-hardware interactions.

Keywords: SESH framework · SW/HW co-design · GPGPU · Space exploration

1 Introduction

As demonstrated by the supercomputers Titan and Tianhe-1A, graphics processing units (GPUs) have become integral components in supercomputers. This trend is likely to continue, as more workloads are exploiting data-level parallelism and their problem sizes increase.

A major challenge in designing future GPU-enabled systems for scientific computing is to gain a holistic understanding about the dynamics between the workloads and the hardware. Conventionally built for graphics applications, GPUs have various hardware features that can boost performance if carefully managed; however, GPU hardware designers may not be sufficiently informed about scientific workloads to evaluate specialized hardware features. On the other hand, since GPU architectures embrace massive parallelism and limited L1 storage per thread, legacy codes must be redesigned in order to be ported to GPUs.

© Springer International Publishing Switzerland 2014
S. Jarvis et al. (Eds.): PMBS 2013 Workshops, LNCS 8551, pp. 182–202, 2014.
DOI: 10.1007/978-3-319-10214-6_9

Even codes for earlier GPU generations may have to be recoded in order to fully exploit new GPU architectures. As a result, an increasing effort has been made in codesigning the application and the hardware.

In a typical codesign effort, a set of benchmarks is proposed by application developers and is then manually studied by hardware designers in order to understand the potential. However, such a process is labor-intensive and time-consuming. In addition, several factors challenge system designers' endeavors to explore the design space. First, the number of hardware configurations is exploding as the complexity of the hardware increases. Second, the solution has to meet several design constraints such as area and power. Third, benchmarks are often provided in a specific implementation, yet one often needs to attempt tens of transformations in order to fully understand the performance potential of a specific hardware configuration. Fourth, evaluating the performance of a particular implementation on a future hardware may take significant time using simulators. Fifth, the current performance tools (e.g., simulators, hardware models, profilers) investigate either hardware or applications in a separate manner, treating the other as a black box and therefore, offer limited insights for codesign.

To efficiently explore the design space and provide first-order insights, we propose SESH, a model-driven framework that automatically searches the design space by simultaneously exploring *prospective* application and hardware implementations and evaluate *potential* software-hardware interactions. SESH recommends the optimal combination of application optimizations and hardware implementations according to user-defined objectives with respect to performance, area, and power. The technical contributions of the SESH framework are as follows.

1. It evaluates various software optimization effects and hardware configurations using decoupled workload models and hardware models.
2. It integrates GPU's performance, area, and power models into a single framework.
3. It automatically proposes optimal hardware configurations given multi facet metrics in aspects of performance, area, and power.

We evaluate our work using a set of representative scientific workloads. A large design space is explored that considers both application transformations and hardware configurations. We evaluate potential solutions using various metrics including performance, area efficiency, and energy consumption. Then, we summarize the overall insights gained from such space exploration.

The paper is organized as follows. In Section 2, we provide an overview of our work. In Section 3, we introduce the integrated hardware models for power and area. Section 4 describes the space exploration process. Evaluation methodology and results are described in Sections 5 and 6, respectively. After the related work is discussed in Section 7, we conclude.

2 Overview and Background

The SESH framework is a codesign tool for GPU system designers and performance engineers. It recommends the optimal combination of hardware configurations and application implementations. Different from existing performance models or architecture simulators, SESH considers how applications may transform and adapt to potential hardware architectures.

2.1 Overall Framework

As Figure 1 shows, the major components of the SESH framework include (i) a workload modeling and transformation engine, (ii) a hardware modeling and transformation engine, and (iii) a projection engine. Using the framework involves the following work flow:

1. The user abstracts high level characteristics of the source code into a *code skeleton* that summarizes control flows, potential parallelism, instruction

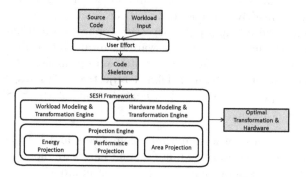

Fig. 1. Framework Overview

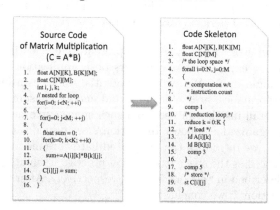

Fig. 2. A pedagogical example of a code skeleton in the case of matrix multiplication. A code skeleton is used as the input to our framework.

mix, and data access patterns. An example code skeleton is shown in Figure 2. This step can be automated by SKOPE [1], and the user can amend the output code skeleton with additional notions such as `for_all` or `reduction`.

2. Given the code skeleton and the specified power and area constraints, SESH explores the design space by automatically proposing potential application transformations and hardware configurations.

3. SESH projects the energy consumption and execution time for each combination of transformations and hardware configurations, and recommends the best solution according to user-specified metrics, without manual coding or lengthy simulations. Such metrics can be a combination of power, area, and performance. For example, one metric can be "given an area budget, what would be the most power efficient hardware considering potential transformations?".

The SESH framework is built on top of existing performance modeling frameworks. We integrated GROPHECY [2] as the GPU workload modeling and transformation engine. We also adopted area and power models from previous work on projection engine. Below we provide a brief description about them.

2.2 GROPHECY-Based Code Transformation Engine

GROPHECY [2], a GPU code transformation framework, has been proposed to explore various transformations and to estimate the GPU performance of a CPU kernel. Provided with a code skeleton, GROPHECY is able to transform the code skeleton to mimic various optimization strategies. Transformations explored include spatial and temporal loop tiling, loop fusion, unrolling, shared memory optimizations, and memory request coalescing. GROPHECY then analytically computes the characteristics of each transformation. The resulting characteristics are used as inputs to a GPU performance model to project the performance of the corresponding transformation. The best achievable performance and the transformations necessary to reach that performance are then projected.

GROPHECY, however, relies on the user to specify a particular hardware configuration. It does not explore the hardware design space to study how hardware configurations would affect the performance or efficiency of various code transformations. In this work, we extend GROPHECY with parameterized power and area models so that one can integrate it into a larger framework that explores hardware configurations together with code transformations.

2.3 Hardware Models

We utilize the performance model from the work of Sim et al. [3]. We make it tunable to reflect different GPU architecture specifications. The tunable parameters are *Register file entry count, SIMD width, SFU width, L1D/SHMEM size* and *LLC cache size*. The model takes several workload characteristics as its inputs, including the instruction mix and the number of memory operations.

We utilize the work by Lim et al. [4] for chip-level area and power models. They model GPU power based on McPAT [5] and an energy introspection interface (EI) [6] and integrate the power-modeling functionality in MacSim [7], a trace-driven and cycle-level GPU simulator. McPAT enables users to configure a microarchitecture by rearranging circuit-level models. EI creates pseudo components that are linked to McPAT's circuit-level models and utilizes access counters to calculate the power consumption of each component. We use this model to estimate the power value for the baseline architecture configuration. Then we adopt simple heuristics to estimate the power consumption for different hardware configurations.

3   Exploratory, Multi Facet Hardware Model

In order to explore the hardware design space and evaluate tradeoffs, the SESH framework integrates performance, power and area models, all parameterized and tunable according to the hardware configuration. In this section, we first describe the process to prepare the reference models about the NVIDIA GTX 580 architecture. These models include power and area models for chip. We then integrate these models and parameterize them so that they can reflect changes in hardware configurations.

3.1   The Reference Model for Chip-Level Power

To get reference values for chip-level power consumption, we use the detailed power simulator in Section ??. As Hong and Kim [8] showed, the GPU power consumption is not significantly affected by the dynamic power consumption except the DRAM power values. Furthermore, the static power is often the dominant factor for on-chip power consumption. Hence, to get the first-order approximation of the GPU power model, we focus on the static power only.

To estimate the static power for a baseline architecture of NVIDIA GTX 580, we collect power statistics from a detailed power simulator [4]. The Sepia benchmark [9] is used as an example input for the simulation. Note that the choice of the benchmark does not affect significantly the value of static power. In Sepia's on-chip power consumption, the static power consumes 106.0 W while the dynamic power consumes 50.0 W. The DRAM power is 52.0 W in Sepia, although it is usually more than 90.0 W in other benchmarks. As a result, the dynamic power accounts for 24.0% of Sepia's the total power consumption of the chip and DRAM. Taking the dynamic power into account will be included in our future work.

The variation in power consumption caused by thermal changes is not modeled for the purpose of simplicity. As measured in [8], we assume a constant temperature of 340 K (67 °C) in the power model, considering that this operation-time temperature is higher than the code-state temperature of 57 °C [8].

Figure 3 shows how much total power is consumed by each component according our model. The GPU's on-chip power is decomposed into two categories;

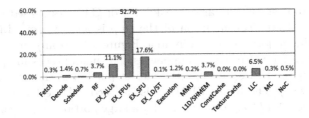

Fig. 3. Power consumption for non-DRAM components

SM-private components and SM-shared components. The total on-chip power consumption is 156.0 W. SM-private components accounts for 93 % (144.7 W) of the overall power, and shared components between SMs account for 7% (11.4 W) of the overall power. From all the SM-private components we model EX_ALUs and EX_FPUs consume the most power (52.7% and 11.1%, respectively). SFU (17.6%), LLC (6.5%), and RF (3.7%) also account for large portions of the overall power consumption.

3.2   The Reference Model for Chip-Level Area

For the area model, we utilize the area outcome from energy introspection integrated with MacSim [4]. The energy introspection interface in MacSim utilizes area size to calculate power. It also estimates area sizes for different hardware configurations. we use the area outcomes that are based on NVIDIA GTX 580.

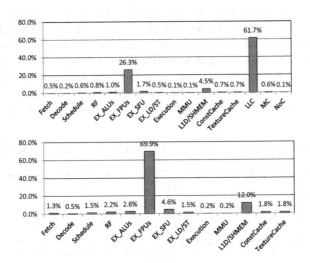

Fig. 4. Area consumption for all non-DRAM components(top) and for SM-private components(bottom)

Figure 4 (top) shows the area breakdown of GTX 580 based on our area model. The total area consumption of the chip is 3588.0 mm^2. LLC (61.7%) accounts for the majority of the chip area. Figure 4 (bottom) shows the breakdown of the area for SM-private components. The main processing part, 32 SPs (EX_ALUs and EX_FPUs), occupy the largest portion of the area (69.9% and 2.6%, respectively). The L1D / SHMEM is the second largest module (12.0%). SFU (4.6%) and RF (2.2%) also account for a large portion of area consumption.

3.3 Integrated, Tunable Hardware Model

$$Area_{target} = Area_{baseline} \times \frac{knob_{target}}{knob_{baseline}} \tag{1}$$

$$Power_{target} = Power_{baseline} \times \frac{knob_{target}}{knob_{baseline}} \tag{2}$$

To estimate how changes in hardware configurations affect the overall power consumption, we employ a heuristic that the per-component power consumption and area scales linearly with the size and the number of components (e.g., doubling the shared memory size would double its power consumption and also area). Given a target hardware's configuration, we can compute the per-component area and power according to Equations (1) and (2), respectively, where $knob$ refers to the size or number of the component in the corresponding architecture. The baseline data is collected as described in Sections 3.1 and 3.2. The per-component metrics are then aggregated to project the system-level area and power consumption.

According to our analysis in Figures 3 and 4, the major components consuming power and area include the register files, ALUs, FPUs, SFUs, L1 cache size, and the last level cache size. The quantities of these components become tunable variables, or knobs, in the integrated model. Table 1 lists the knobs and the value of $knob_{baseline}$ in Equations (1) and (2). The area and power consumption of other components are approximated as constant values obtained from modeling NVIDIA GTX 580. These components are summarized in Table 2.

Table 1. Hardware components that are modeled as tunable knobs

Stage	KNOB	Default(NVIDIA GTX 580)
Per-SM		
RF	Register file entry count	32,768 / SM
ALU	SIMD width	32 / SM
FPU	SIMD width	32 / SM
SFU	SFU width	4 / SM
L1D/SHMEM	L1D size + SHMEM size	64KB / SM
Shared		
LLC	L2 Cache size	768KB

Table 2. Hardware components that are modeled with constant area and power consumption

Category	Stage
Per-SM(w/ fixed number of SMs)	Fetch, Decode, Schedule, Execution(except ALU, FPU, SFU), MMU, Const$, Tex$
Shared	1 MemCon, 1 NoC, 1 DRAM

3.4   DRAM Power Model

DRAM power depends on memory access patterns; the number of DRAM row buffer hits/misses can affect power consumption noticeably. However, these numbers can be obtained only from the detailed simulation, which often takes several hours for each configuration (100s of software optimizations × 10s of hardware configurations easily create 1000s of different configurations). To mitigate the overhead, we use a simple empirical approach to compute the first-order estimation of DRAM power consumption values.

$$P_{DRAM} = MaxDynP \times \frac{Trans\_Intensity}{Max\_Trans\_Intensity} + StatP \qquad (3)$$

The total DRAM power (P_{DRAM}) is computed by adding up the static power ($StatP$) and dynamic power [8]. The dynamic power is computed as a fraction of the maximum dynamic power ($MaxDynP$), which can only be reached in the theoretical condition where every instruction generates a DRAM transaction. The number of DRAM transactions per second on each SM is referred to as *DRAM transaction intensity*, whose value is $Max\_Trans\_Intensity$ under the aforementioned theoretical condition.

$$Trans\_Intensity = \frac{\#DRAM\_Accesses}{Exec\_time} \qquad (4)$$

In this work, the actual DRAM transaction intensity, $Trans\_Intensity$, is approximated by Equation (4). The total number of DRAM transactions per SM ($\#DRAM\_Accesses$) and the execution time in seconds ($Exec\_time$) are estimated values given by the performance model.

In order to construct Equation (3) as a function of the workload characteristics, the values of $StatP$ and $\frac{MaxDynP}{MAX\_Trans\_Intensity}$ need to be obtained as constant coefficients. We therefore use the power simulator to obtain the DRAM power for SVM and Sepia in the Merge benchmarks [9] and solve for the values of these two coefficients. Equation (5) represents the resulting DRAM model.

$$P_{DRAM} = \alpha \times Trans\_Intensity + \beta \qquad (5)$$

where $\alpha = 1.6 \times 10^{-6}$ and $\beta = 24.4$.

4   Space Exploration

Application transformations and hardware configurations pose a design space that is daunting to explore. First, they are inter-related; different hardware configurations may prefer different application transformations. Second, there are a gigantic number of options. In our current framework, we explore each of them independently and then calculate which combination yields the desired solution. Note that this process is made possible largely because of the fast evaluation enabled by modeling.

The application transformations explored include spatial and temporal loop tiling, unrolling, shared memory optimizations, and memory request coalescing. The hardware configurations explored include SIMD width and shared memory size, which play significant roles in performance, area, and power. We plan to explore more dimensions in our future work.

To compare different solutions, we utilize multiple objective functions that represent different design goals. Those objective functions include the followings.

1. Shortest execution time
2. Minimal energy consumption
3. Largest performance per area

5   Methodology

5.1   Workloads

The benchmarks used for our evaluation and their key properties are summarized in Table 3. HotSpot and SRAD are applications from the Rodinia benchmark suite [10]. Stassuij is extracted from a DOE INCITE application performing Monte Carlo calculations to study light nuclei [11,12]. It has two kernels: IspinEx and SpinFlap. We separately evaluate each kernel of Stassuij and also evaluate both kernels together. The sizes of matrices in Stassuij are according to real input data. To reduce the space of code transformations to explore, for each benchmark we set a fixed thread block size large enough to saturate wide SIMD.

HotSpot: HotSpot is an ordinary differential equation solver used in simulating microarchitecture temperature. It has a stencil computation kernel with

Table 3. Workload properties

Benchmark	Key Properties	Input Size
HotSpot	Structured grid. Iterative, self-dependent kernels. A deep dependency chain among dependent kernels	1024 X 1024
SRAD	Structured grid. Data dependency involves multiple arrays; each points to different producer iterations	4096 X 4096
IspinEx	Sparse linear algebra, A X B	A : 132 X 132, B : 132 X 2048
SpinFlap	Irregular data exchange similar to spectral methods	132 X 2048
Stassuij	Nested loops. Dependent parallel loops with different shapes. Dependency involves indirectly accessed arrays	-

structured grid. Kernels are executed iteratively, and each iteration consumes a neighborhood of array elements. As a result, each iteration depends on the previous one. Programmers can utilize shared memory(ShM) by caching neighborhood data for inter-thread data sharing. Folding, which assigns multiple tasks to one thread, improves data reuse by allowing a thread to process more neighborhood-gathering tasks. Fusing loop partitions across several iterations can be applied to achieve better locality and reduce global halo exchanges. We also provide a hint that indicates only one of the arrays used in double buffering is the necessary output for the fused kernel. In our experiments, we fuse two dependent iterations and use a 16 × 16 partition for the consumer loop. The thread block size is set to 16 × 16.

SRAD: SRAD performs spectral removal anisotropic diffusion to an image. It has two kernels: the first generates diffusion coefficients and the second updates the image. We use a 16 × 16 thread block size and indicate the output array that needs to be committed.

IspinEx: IspinEx is a sparse matrix multiplication kernel which multiplies a 132 × 132 sparse matrix of real numbers with a 132 × 2048 dense matrix of complex numbers. We provide a hint that the average number of nonzero elements in one row of the sparse matrix is 14 in order to estimate the overall workload size. Because the numbers of elements associated with different rows may vary. we force a thread to process all elements in columns to balance the workload among threads. We treat the real part and imaginal part of the complex number as individual numbers and employ a 1 × 64 thread block size in our evaluation. Due to irregularity in sparse data accesses, we provide a hint about the average degree of coalescing, which is obtained from offline characterization of the input data.

SpinFlap: SpinFlap exchanges matrix elements in groups of four. Each group is scattered in a butterfly pattern in the same row, similar to spectral methods. Which columns are to be grouped together is determined by values in another array. SpinFlap is a memory-bounded kernel. By utilizing shared memory, programmers can expect performance improvement. There is data reuse by multiple threads on the matrix, which are used for indirect indices for other matrices. The performance can also be improved by folding. Performance is highly dependent on the degree of coalescing, and it varies according to values of indirect indices. To assess the degree of coalescing, we profiled the average data stride of indirect indices and provide this hint to the framework. We assume a 12 × 16 thread block size with no folding.

Stassuij(Fused): Fusion increases the reuse in shared memory. But since data dependency caused by indirect indices in SpinFlap requires IspinEx to be partitioned accordingly, the loop index in IspinEx now becomes a value pointed by indirect accesses in the fused kernel, introducing irregular strides that can become un-coalesced memory accesses. We assume a thread block size of 16 × 4 × 2 and provide a hint that indicates the output array.

5.2   Evaluation Metric

To study how application performance is affected by code transformations and architectural changes, we utilize metrics from previous work [3] to understand the potential optimization benefits and the performance bottlenecks.

1. B_serial : Benefits of removing serialization effects such as synchronization and resource contention.
2. B_itilp : Benefits of increasing inter-thread instruction-level parallelism (ITILP). ITILP represents global ILP (ILP among warps).
3. B_memlp : Benefits of increasing memory-level parallelism (MLP)
4. B_fp : Benefits of improving computing efficiency. Computing efficiency represents the ratio of the floating point instructions over the total instructions.

6   Evaluation

While we have explored a design space with both code transformations and hardware configurations, we present our results according to SIMD widths and shared memory sizes in order to shed more light on hardware designs. We model 64 transformations for HotSpot, 64, 128 transformations for two kernels of SRAD, 576, 1728 and 2816 transformations for IspinEx, SpinFlap and Stassuij(Fused) respectively.

6.1   SIMD Width

We evaluate different SIMD widths from 16 to 128. Figure 5 represents the execution time, energy consumption, possible benefits and performance per area

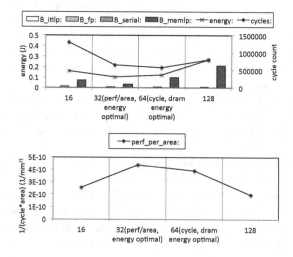

Fig. 5. Execution time, energy consumption, possible benefits and performance per area for optimal transformation for HotSpot on increasing SIMD width

for optimal transformation for HotSpot with increasing SIMD width. The performance-optimal SIMD width is 64 and the optimal SIMD width for minimal energy consumption and maximal performance per area is 32, which is the same as for NVIDIA GTX 580. The reason is that the increased inefficiency in power and area is bigger than the benefit of shorter execution time, even though minimal execution time helps reduce the energy consumption in general. Performance increases from 16 to 64 but decreases from 64 to 128. The application becomes more memory bound with increased SIMD width, and the benefit of less computation time becomes smaller, which we can see from increasing B_memlp.

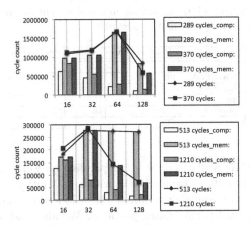

Fig. 6. Comparison between optimal transformation with increasing SIMD width for IspinEx(top) and SpinFlap(bottom)

For HotSpot, SRAD, and Stassuij, the optimal transformation remains the same regardless of SIMD width and objective function. However, depending on SIMD width, optimal transformation changes from 289 (16, 32, 64) to 370 (128) for IspinEx and from 513 (16, 32) to 1210 (64, 128) for SpinFlap. Figures 6 compares the optimal transformation with increasing SIMD width for IspinEx and SpinFlap. The optimal transformation on a narrow SIMD width is selected because it incurs less computation, even though it incurs more memory traffic due to un-coalesced access on a wide SIMD width than optimal transformation on a wide SIMD width. However, the application becomes more memory bound with increased SIMD width, therefore reducing the benefit of less computation.

The transformation ID we use in this paper can be different depending on the degree of loop tiling, loop fusion, unrolling, shared memory optimizations, and memory request coalescing. Figure 7 compares transformations 289 and 370 for IspinEx. Those two have same code structure; the only difference is the decision of which loads to be cached or not. Transformation 370 utilizes shared memory for the load $ld\ cr[njp][ir]$, while transformation 289 doesn't. The difference between transformations 513 and 1210 for SpinFlap is also which loads utilize shared memory or not.

```
 1  def ispinex() {
 2    ...
 3    forall j=0:nt, ir=0:ns*2 {
 4      ...
 5      reduce (float, +) n = 0:avg_j_ntdt {
 6        ...
 7        ld cr[njp][ir]    // Different on 289 & 370
 8        ...
 9      }
10    ...
11    }
12  }
```

Fig. 7. Comparison of transformations 289 & 370 for IspinEx

Table 4. Optimal SIMD width regarding minimal execution time, minimal energy consumption and maximal performance per area

Benchmark	Performance	Energy	Perf/Area
HotSpot	64	32	32
SRAD(first)	32	32	32
SRAD(second)	32	16	16
IspinEx	128	16	16
SpinFlap	128	16	128
Stassuij	32	16	32

The optimal SIMD width is different depending on workload objective functions. Table 4 represents optimal SIMD width for HotSpot, SRAD, IspinEx, SpinFlap and Stassuij regarding minimal execution time, minimal energy consumption and maximal performance per area. We also find strong correlation between minimal energy consumption and largest performance per area. Except for SpinFlap and Stassuij, the optimal SIMD width for minimal energy consumption and the one for largest performance per area are the same.

Considering source code transformation or not changes the optimal SIMD width for SpinFlap. Table 5 compares the optimal SIMD width for SpinFlap when using optimal transformation on NVIDIA GTX 580 or using optimal transformation on each SIMD width. The optimal SIMD width for performance and performance per area is 128 and the energy optimal SIMD width is 16 when we consider source code transformation. However, 16 is the optimal SIMD width for all objective functions when we do not consider source code transformation and use the optimal transformation on NVIDIA GTX 580 instead. Figure 8 compares the execution time, energy consumption and possible benefits for SpinFlap with increasing SIMD width considering source code transformation or not.

In summary, increasing SIMD width helps performance. But the benefit of large SIMD width degrades because of increased inefficiency in power and area,

Table 5. Optimal SIMD width for SpinFlap using fixed transformation or optimal transformation on each SIMD width

Benchmark	Performance	Energy	Perf/Area
Fixed	16	16	16
Variable	128	16	128

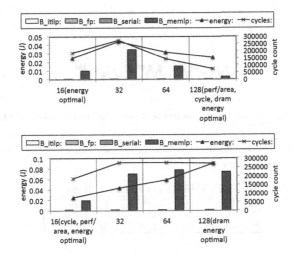

Fig. 8. Execution time, energy consumption and possible benefits for optimal transformation for SpinFlap with increasing SIMD width: (top) considering source code transformation; (bottom) using fixed transformation

and the application becomes more memory bound with increased SIMD width. The optimal SIMD width is depends on workload objective functions, with strong correlation between minimal energy consumption and largest performance per area. The optimal transformation changes depend on SIMD width for IspinEx and SpinFlap. Considering source code transformation or not changes the optimal SIMD width for SpinFlap.

6.2 Shared Memory Size

GPU's shared memory is a software-managed L1 storage on an SM. A larger shared memory would enable new transformations with more aggressive caching. We evaluate shared memory sizes from 16 KB to 128 KB. The values of other parameters remain constant.

The optimal transformation for HotSpot, SRAD and Stassuij and their performance remain the same regardless of shared memory size. The reason is that shared memory usage per SM for optimal transformations for these applications is already less than 16 KB. Therefore, the performance per area for these applications decreases with increasing shared memory size.

For HotSpot and SRAD, none of the transformations are disabled even when the shared memory size per SM is reduced to 16 KB. Such is not the case for IspinEx, SpinFlap and Stassuij. Figure 9 presents the shared memory requirement for all transformations for Stassuij. Some transformation require less than 20 KB of shared memory, but other transformations require more than 80 KB of shared memory. Therefore the number of valid transformations is different

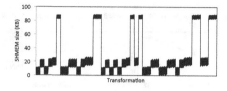

Fig. 9. Shared memory requirement for transformations for Stassuij

Table 6. Number of transformations available for IspinEx, SpinFlap, and Stassuij depending on shared memory size

Benchmark	16 KB	48 KB	64 KB	128 KB
IspinEx	120	192	192	288
SpinFlap	432	1304	1304	1728
Stassuij	2240	2240	2240	2816

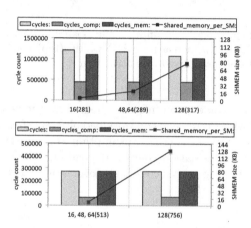

Fig. 10. Comparison between the optimal transformations when increasing shared memory size for IspinEx(top) and SpinFlap(bottom)

depending on the shared memory size. Table 6 presents the number of transformations available for IspinEx, SpinFlap and Stassuij depending on shared memory size.

The optimal transformation for Stassuij remains the same regardless of shared memory size since shared memory usage per SM for the optimal transformation is less than 9 KB. However, the optimal transformation changes depending on shared memory size for IspinEx and SpinFlap. New transformations become available as we increase the shared memory size. The optimal transformation changes from 281 (16 KB) to 289 (48, 64 KB), 317 (128 KB) for IspinEx, and it changes from 513 (16, 48, 64 KB) to 756 (128 KB) for SpinFlap. Figure 10 compares the optimal transformation with increasing shared memory size for IspinEx and SpinFlap. The difference between those transformations is which loads utilize shared memory.

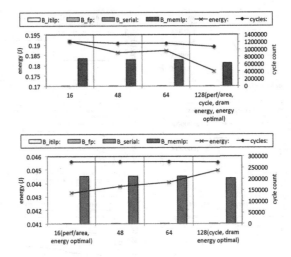

Fig. 11. Execution time, energy consumption and possible benefits for optimal transformation on increasing shared memory size for IspinEx(top) and SpinFlap(bottom)

Figure 11 represents the execution time and energy consumption for the optimal transformations of IspinEx and SpinFlap with increasing shared memory size. When we consider code transformations, the optimal shared memory size for all objective function for IspinEx is 128 KB. Without considering transformations however, the optimal shared memory size is 48 KB. For SpinFlap, the optimal shared memory size for energy and performance per area is 16 KB and the performance-optimal shared memory size is 128 KB when we consider source code transformation. Without considering transformations, the optimal shared memory size remains 16 KB for all objective functions.

In summary, shared memory sizes determine the number of possible transformations in terms of how the shared memory is used. For IspinEx, SpinFlap and Stassuij, some transformations are disabled because of limitation of shared memory size. These applications prefer either small shared memory or very large shared memory, as we can see in Figure 9. For IspinEx and SpinFlap, the optimal transformation changes depending on shared memory size since new transformations become available with increased shared memory size. Considering source code transformations or not changes the optimal shared memory size for IspinEx and SpinFlap.

6.3 Discussion

The findings from our model-driven space exploration is summarized below.

1. For a given hardware, the code transformation with minimal execution time often leads to minimal energy consumption as well. This can be observed

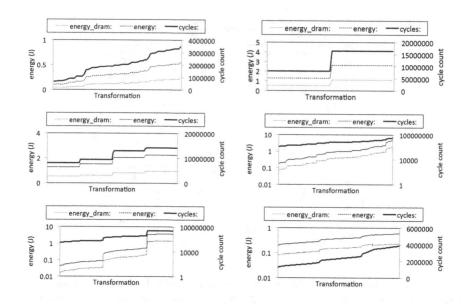

Fig. 12. Execution time and energy consumption of possible transformations of each application on NVIDIA GTX 580. From top to bottom, HotSpot, SRAD (first) SRAD (second), IspinEx, SpinFlap and Stassuij (Fused).

from Figure 12, which represents execution time and energy consumption of possible transformations of each application on NVIDIA GTX 580.

2. The optimal hardware configuration depends on the objective function. In general, performance increases with more resources (wider SIMD width or bigger shared memory size). However, the performance benefit of more resources may be outweighed by the cost of more resources in terms of energy or area. Therefore, the SIMD width and shared memory size that are optimal for energy consumption and performance per area are smaller than those for performance. We also observe that the SIMD width and shared memory size that minimize energy consumption also maximize performance per area.

3. The optimal transformation can differ across hardware configurations. The variation in hardware configuration has two effects on code transformations: it shifts the performance bottleneck, or it enables/disables potential trans-formations because of resource availability. In the examples of IspinEx and SpinFlap, a computation-intensive transformation becomes memory-bound with wide SIMD; a new transformation that requires large L1 storage is enabled when the shared memory size increases.

4. The optimal hardware configuration varies according to whether code trans-formations are considered. For example, when searching for the performance-optimal SIMD width for SpinFlap, the legacy implementation would suggest a SIMD width of 16, while the performance-optimal SIMD width is 128 if transformations are considered and would perform 2.6 × better. The optimal

shared memory size would also change for IspinEx and SpinFlap by taking transformations into account.

5. In order to gain performance, it is generally better to increase the SIMD width rather than the shared memory size. Larger SIMD width increases performance at the expense of area and power consumption. Larger shared memory size does not have a significant impact on performance until it can accommodate a larger working set, therefore enabling a new transformation; however, we found that a shared memory size of 48 KB is already able to accommodate a reasonably sized working set in most cases. This coincides with GPU's hardware design trends from Tesla [13] to Fermi [14] and Kepler [15]. Moreover, we found that energy-optimal shared memory size for all evaluated benchmarks is less than 48 KB, which is the value for current Fermi architecture.

Our work can be improved to enable broader space exploration in less time. A main challenge in space exploration is the large number of possible transformations and architectural parameters. Instead of brute-force exploration, we plan to build a feedback mechanism to probe the space judiciously. For example, if an application is memory bound, the SESH framework can try transformations that result in fewer memory operations but more computation, or hardware configurations with large shared memory and smaller SIMD width.

7 Related Work

Multiple software frameworks are proposed to help GPU programming [16, 17]. Workload characterization studies [18,19] and parallel programming models including PRAM, BSP, CTA and LogP are also relevant to our work [20,21]. These techniques do not explore the hardware design space.

To the best of our knowledge, there has been no previous work to study the relationships between GPU code transformation and power reduction. Valluri et al. [22] performed quantitative study of the effect of the optimizations by DEC Alpha's cc compiler. Brandolese et al. [23] explored source code transformation in terms of energy consumption using the SimpleScalar simulator.

Modeling power consumption of CPUs has been widely studied. Joseph's technique relies on performance counters [24]. Bellosa et al. [25] also used performance counters in order to determine the energy consumption and estimate the temperature for a dynamic thermal management. Wu et al. [26] proposed utilizing phasic behavior of programs in order to build a linear system of equations for component unit power estimation. Peddersen and Parameswaran [27] proposed a processor that estimates its own power/energy consumption at runtime. CAMP [28] used the linear regression model to estimate activity factor and power; it provides insights that relate microarchitectural statistics to activity factor and power. Jacobson et al. [29] built various levels of abstract models and proposed a systematic way to find a utilization metric for estimating power numbers and a scaling method to evaluate new microarchitecture. Czechowski and Vuduc [30] studied relationship between architectural features and algorithm characteristics. They proposed a modeling framework that can be used for tradeoff analysis of performance and power.

While architectural studies and performance improvements with GPUs have been explored widely, power modeling of GPUs has received little attention. A few works use functional simulator for power modeling. Wang [31] extended GPGPUSim with Wattch and Orion to compute GPU power. PowerRed [32], a modular architectural power estimation framework, combined both analytical and empirical models; they also modeled interconnect power dissipation by employing area cost. A few GPU power modeling works use a statistical linear regression method using empirical data. Ma et al. [33] dynamically predicted the runtime power of NVIDIA GeForce 8800 GT using recorded power data and a trained statistical model. Nagasaka et al. [34] used the linear regression method by collecting the information about the application from performance counters. Tree-based random forest method was used on the works by Chen et al. [35] and by Zhang et al. [36]. Since those works are based on empirical data obtained from existing hardware, they do not provide insights in terms of space exploration.

Simulators have been widely used to search the hardware design space. Generic algorithms and regression have been proposed to reduce the search space by learning from a relatively small number of simulations [37]. Our work extends their work by considering code transformations, integrating area and power estimations, and employing models instead of simulations. Nevertheless, their learning-based approach is complementary to our approach and may help SESH framework prune the space as well.

8   Conclusions

We propose the SESH framework, a model-driven framework that automatically searches the design space by simultaneously exploring *prospective* application and hardware implementations and evaluate *potential* software-hardware interactions. It recommends the optimal combination of application optimizations and hardware implementations according to user-defined objectives with respect to performance, area, and power. We explored the GPU hardware design space with different SIMD widths and shared memory sizes, and we evaluated each design point using four benchmarks, each with hundreds of transformations. The evaluation criteria include performance, energy consumption, and performance per area. Several codesign lessons were learned from the framework, and our findings point to the importance of considering code transformations in designing future GPU hardware.

References

1. Meng, J., Wu, X., Morozov, V.A., Vishwanath, V., Kumaran, K., Taylor, V., Lee, C.-W.: SKOPE: A Framework for Modeling and Exploring Workload Behavior. Argonne National Laboratory, Tech. Rep. (2012)

2. Meng, J., Morozov, V., Kumaran, K., Vishwanath, V., Uram, T.: GROPHECY: GPU Performance Projection from CPU Code Skeletons. In: SC 2011 (2011)
3. Sim, J.W., Dasgupta, A., Kim, H., Vuduc, R.: GPUPerf: A Performance Analysis Framework for Identifying Performance Benefits in GPGPU Applications. In: PPoPP 2012 (2012)
4. Lim, J., Lakshminarayana, N., Kim, H., Song, W., Yalamanchili, S., Sung, W.: Power Modeling for GPU Architecture using McPAT. Georgia Institute of Technology. Tech. Rep. (2013)
5. Li, S., Ahn, J.H., Strong, R.D., Brockman, J.B., Tullsen, D.M., Jouppi, N.P.: McPAT: an integrated power, area, and timing modeling framework for multicore and manycore architectures. In: MICRO 42
6. Song, W.J., Cho, M., Yalamanchili, S., Mukhopadhyay, S., Rodrigues, A.F.: Energy introspector: Simulation infrastructure for power, temperature, and reliability modeling in manycore processors. In: SRC TECHCHON 2011 (2011)
7. MacSim, http://code.google.com/p/macsim/
8. Hong, S., Kim, H.: IPP: An Integrated GPU Power and Performance Model that Predicts Optimal Number of Active Cores to Save Energy at Static Time. In: ISCA 2010 (2010)
9. Linderman, M.D., Collins, J.D., Wang, H., Meng, T.H.: Merge: a programming model for heterogeneous multi-core systems. In: ASPLOS XIII
10. Che, S., Boyer, M., Meng, J., Tarjan, D., Sheaffer, J.W., Skadron, K.: A performance study of general-purpose applications on graphics processors using CUDA. Journal of Parallel and Distributed Computing (2008)
11. Pieper, S.C., Wiringa, R.B.: Quantum Monte Carlo calculations of light nuclei. Annu. Rev. Nucl. Part. Sci. **51**, 53 (2001)
12. Pieper, S.C., Varga, K., Wiringa, R.B.: Quantum Monte Carlo calculations of A=9,10 nuclei. Phys. Rev. C **66**, 044310-1:14 (2002)
13. NVIDIA Corporation: GeForce GTX 280 specifications (2008), http://www.nvidia.com/object/product_geforce_gtx_280_us.html
14. NVIDIA, Fermi: Nvidia's next generation cuda compute architecture, http://www.nvidia.com/fermi
15. NVIDIA's next generation CUDA compute architecture: Kepler GK110. NVIDIA Corporation (2012)
16. Jablin, T.B., Prabhu, P., Jablin, J.A., Johnson, N.P., Beard, S.R., August, D.I.: Automatic CPU-GPU communication management and optimization. In: PLDI 2011 (2011)
17. Jablin, T.B., Jablin, J.A., Prabhu, P., Liu, F., August, D.I.: Dynamically managed data for cpu-gpu architectures. In: CGO 2012 (2012)
18. Spafford, K., Vetter, J.: Aspen: A domain specific language for performance modeling. In: SC 2012 (2012)
19. Williams, S., Waterman, A., Patterson, D.: Roofline: an insightful visual performance model for multicore architectures. Communications of the ACM - A Direct Path to Dependable Software (2009)
20. Valiant, L.G.: A bridging model for parallel computation. Commun. ACM (1990)
21. Karp, R.M., Ramachandran, V.: A survey of parallel algorithms for shared-memory machines. EECS Department, University of California, Berkeley, Tech. Rep. (1988)
22. Valluri, M., John, L.: Is Compiling for Performance == Compiling for Power. In: INTERACT-5
23. Brandolese, C., Fornaciari, W., Salice, F., Sciuto, D.: The Impact of Source Code Transformations on Software Power and Energy Consumption. Journal of Circuits, Systems, and Computers (2002)

24. Joseph, R., Martonosi, M.: Run-time power estimation in high performance micro-processors. In: ISLPED 2001 (2001)
25. Bellosa, F., Kellner, S., Waitz, M., Weissel, A.: Event-driven energy accounting for dynamic thermal management. In: COLP 2003 (2003)
26. Wu, W., Jin, L., Yang, J., Liu, P., Tan, S.-D.: A systematic method for functional unit power estimation in microprocessors. In: DAC 2006 (2006)
27. Peddersen, J., Parameswaran, S.: CLIPPER: Counter-based Low Impact Processor Power Estimation at Run-time. In: ASP-DAC 2007 (2007)
28. Powell, M., Biswas, A., Emer, J., Mukherjee, S., Sheikh, B., Yardi, S.: CAMP: A technique to estimate per-structure power at run-time using a few simple parameters. In: HPCA 2009 (2009)
29. Jacobson, H., Buyuktosunoglu, A., Bose, P., Acar, E., Eickemeyer, R.: Abstraction and microarchitecture scaling in early-stage power modeling. In: HPCA 2011 (2011)
30. Czechowski, K., Vuduc, R.: A theoretical framework for algorithm-architecture co-design. In: IPDPS 2013 (2013)
31. Wang, G.: Power analysis and optimizations for GPU architecture using a power simulator. In: ICACTE 2010 (2010)
32. Ramani, K., Ibrahim, A., Shimizu, D.: PowerRed: A Flexible Power Modeling Framework for Power Efficiency Exploration in GPUs. In: GPGPU 2007 (2007)
33. Ma, X., Dong, M., Zhong, L., Deng, Z.: Statistical Power Consumption Analysis and Modeling for GPU-based Computing. In: HotPower 2009 (2009)
34. Nagasaka, H., Maruyama, N., Nukada, A., Endo, T., Matsuoka, S.: Statistical power modeling of GPU kernels using performance counters. In: IGCC 2010 (2010)
35. Chen, J., Li, B., Zhang, Y., Peng, L., kwon Peir, J.: Tree structured analysis on gpu power study. In: ICCD 2011 (2011)
36. Zhang, Y., Hu, Y., Li, B., Peng, L.: Performance and Power Analysis of ATI GPU: A Statistical Approach. In: NAS 2011 (2011)
37. Wu, W., Lee, B.C.: Inferred Models for Dynamic and Sparse Hardware-Software Spaces. In: MICRO 2012 (2012)

Optimal Checkpointing Period: Time vs. Energy

Guillaume Aupy[1](✉), Anne Benoit[1], Thomas Hérault[2],
Yves Robert[1,2], and Jack Dongarra[2]

[1] Laboratoire LIP, École Normale Supérieure de Lyon, Lyon, France
guillaume.aupy@ens-lyon.fr
[2] University of Tennessee, Knoxville, USA

Abstract. This short paper deals with parallel scientific applications using non-blocking and periodic coordinated checkpointing to enforce resilience. We provide a model and detailed formulas for total execution time and consumed energy. We characterize the optimal period for both objectives, and we assess the range of time/energy trade-offs to be made by instantiating the model with a set of realistic scenarios for Exascale systems. We give a particular emphasis to I/O transfers, because the relative cost of communication is expected to dramatically increase, both in terms of latency and consumed energy, for future Exascale platforms.

1 Introduction

A significant research effort is focusing on the characteristics, features, and challenges of High Performance Computing (HPC) systems capable of reaching the Exaflop performance mark [1,2]. The portrayed Exascale systems will necessitate billion way parallelism, resulting not only in a massive increase in the number of processing units (cores), but also in terms of computing nodes. Considering the relative slopes describing the evolution of the reliability of individual components on one side, and the evolution of the number of components on the other side, the reliability of the entire platform is expected to decrease, due to probabilistic amplification. Even if each independent component is quite reliable, the Mean Time Between Failures (MTBF) is expected to drop drastically. Executions of large parallel applications on these systems will have to tolerate a higher degree of errors and failures than in current systems. The de-facto general-purpose error recovery technique in high performance computing is checkpoint and rollback recovery. Such protocols employ checkpoints to periodically save the state of a parallel application, so that when an error strikes some process, the application can be restored into one of its former states. The most widely used protocol is coordinated checkpointing, where all processes periodically stop computing and synchronize to write critical application data onto stable storage. Coordinated checkpointing is well understood, at least in its blocking form (when no computing activity takes place during checkpoints), and good approximations of the optimal checkpoint interval exist; they are known as Young's and Daly's formula [3,4].

© Springer International Publishing Switzerland 2014
S. Jarvis et al. (Eds.): PMBS 2013 Workshops, LNCS 8551, pp. 203–214, 2014.
DOI: 10.1007/978-3-319-10214-6_10

While reliability is a major concern for Exascale, another key challenge is to minimize energy consumption, both for economic and environmental reasons. One of the most power-consuming components of today's systems is the processor: even when idle, it dissipates a significant fraction of the total power. However, for future Exascale systems, the power dissipated to execute I/O transfers is likely to play an even more important role, because the relative cost of communication is expected to dramatically increase, both in terms of latency and consumed energy [5].

In this short paper, we investigate trade-offs between execution time and energy consumption for the execution of parallel applications on future Exascale systems. The optimal period $\mathcal{T}_{\text{Time}}^{\text{opt}}$ given by Young's and Daly's formula [3,4] will minimize (expected) execution time. However, this period $\mathcal{T}_{\text{Time}}^{\text{opt}}$ will not minimize energy consumption, mainly because the fraction of power $\mathcal{P}_{\text{Cal}}$ spent when computing (by the CPUs) is not the same as the fraction of power $\mathcal{P}_{\text{I/O}}$ spent when checkpointing. In particular, we revisit the work of Meneses, Sarood and Kalé [6] for checkpoint/restart, where formulas are given to compute the time-optimum and energy-optimum periods. However, our model is more precise: (i) we carefully assess the impact of the power consumption required for I/O activity, which is likely to play a key role at the Exascale; (ii) we consider non-blocking checkpointing that can be partially overlapped with computations; (iii) we give a more accurate analysis of the consumed energy.

Altogether, this short paper provides the following main contributions:

- We provide a refined analytical model to compute both the execution time and the consumed energy with a given checkpoint period. The model handles the case where checkpointing activity can be non-blocking, i.e., partially overlapped with computations.
- We provide analytical formulas to approximate the optimal period for time $\mathcal{T}_{\text{Time}}^{\text{opt}}$ as well as the optimal period for energy $\mathcal{T}_{\text{Energy}}^{\text{opt}}$, thereby refining and extending Daly [4] and Meneses, Sarood and Kalé [6] results to non-blocking checkpoints.
- We assess the range of time/energy trade-offs to be made by instantiating the model with a set of realistic scenarios for Exascale systems.

2   Model

In this section, we introduce all the model parameters. We start with parameters related to resilience (checkpointing) before moving to parameters related to energy consumption.

2.1   Checkpointing

We model coordinated checkpointing [7] where checkpoints are taken at regular intervals, after some fixed amount of work units have been performed. This corresponds to an execution partitioned into periods of duration T. Every period, a checkpoint of length C is taken.

An important question is whether checkpoints are blocking or not. On some architectures, we may have to stop executing the application before writing to the stable storage where the checkpoint data is saved; in that case checkpoint is fully blocking. On other architectures, checkpoint data can be saved on the fly into a local memory before the checkpoint is sent to the stable storage, while computation can resume progress; in that case, checkpoints can be fully overlapped with computations. To deal with all situations, we introduce a slow-down factor ω: during a checkpoint of duration C, the work that is performed is ωC work units. In other words, $(1 - \omega)C$ work units are wasted due to checkpoint jitter disrupting the progress of computation. Here, $0 \leq \omega \leq 1$ is an arbitrary parameter. The case $\omega = 0$ corresponds to a fully blocking checkpoint, while $\omega = 1$ corresponds to a checkpoint totally overlapped with computations. All intermediate situations can be represented.

Next we have to account for failures. During t time units of execution, the expectation of the number of failures is $\frac{t}{\mu}$, where μ is the MTBF (Mean Time Between Failures) of the platform. Note that if the platform if made of N identical resources whose individual mean time between failures is μ_{ind}, then $\mu = \frac{\mu_{\text{ind}}}{N}$. This relation is agnostic of the granularity of the resources, which can be anything from a single CPU to a complex multi-core socket. When a failure strikes, there is a downtime of length D (time to reboot the resource or set up a spare), and then a recovery of length R (time to read the last stored checkpoint). The work executed by the application since the last checkpoint and before the failure needs to be re-executed. Clearly, the shorter the period T, the less work to re-execute, but also the more overhead due to frequent checkpoints in a failure-free execution. The best trade-off when $\omega = 0$ (blocking checkpoint) is achieved for $T = \sqrt{2C\mu} + C$ (Young's formula [3]) or $T = \sqrt{2C(\mu + D + R)} + C$ (Daly's formula [4]). Both formulas are first-order approximations and valid only if all checkpoint parameters C, D and R are small in front of μ (and these formulas collapse if they become negligible). In Section 3, we show how to extend these formulas to the case of non-blocking checkpoints (see also [8] for more details).

2.2   Energy

To compute the energy consumption of the application, we need to consider the energy consumption of the different phases, and hence the power consumption at each time-step. To this purpose, we define:

- $\mathcal{P}_{\text{Static}}$: this is the base power consumed when the platform is switched on.
- $\mathcal{P}_{\text{Cal}}$: when the platform is active, we have to consider the CPU overhead in addition to the static power $\mathcal{P}_{\text{Static}}$.
- $\mathcal{P}_{\text{I/O}}$: similarly, this is the power overhead due to file I/O. This supplementary power consumption is induced by checkpointing, or when recovering from a failure.
- $\mathcal{P}_{\text{Down}}$: for coordinated checkpointing, when one processor fails, the rest of the machine stays idle. $\mathcal{P}_{\text{Down}}$ is the power consumption overhead when one machine is down, that may be incurred for instance by rebooting the machine. In general, we let $\mathcal{P}_{\text{Down}} = 0$.

Meneses, Sarood and Kalé [6] have a simpler model with two parameters, namely L, the base power (corresponding to $\mathcal{P}_{\text{Static}}$ with our notations), and H, the maximum power (corresponding to $\mathcal{P}_{\text{Static}} + \mathcal{P}_{\text{Cal}}$ with our notations). They use $\mathcal{P}_{\text{I/O}} = \mathcal{P}_{\text{Down}} = 0$.

In Section 3, we show how to compute the optimal period that minimizes the energy consumption. In Section 4, we instantiate the model with expected values for power consumption of Exascale platforms.

3   Optimal Checkpointing Period

We consider a parallel application whose execution time is T_{base} without any overhead due to the resilience method or the occurrence of failures. We compute the expectation T_{final} of the total execution time (accounting both for checkpointing and for failures) in Section 3.1, and the expectation $\mathcal{E}_{\text{final}}$ of the total energy consumed during this execution of length T_{final} in Section 3.2. We will compute the optimal period T that minimizes the objective, either T_{final} or $\mathcal{E}_{\text{final}}$.

3.1   Execution Time

The total execution time T_{final} of the application depends on two sources of overhead. We first compute T_{ff}, the time taken by a fault-free execution, thereby accounting only for the overhead due to periodic checkpointing. Then we compute T_{fails}, the time lost due to failures. Finally, $T_{\text{final}} = T_{\text{ff}} + T_{\text{fails}}$. We detail here both computations:

- The reasoning to derive T_{ff} is simple. We need to execute a total amount of work equal to T_{base}. During each period of length T, there is an amount of time $T - C$ where only computations take place, and an amount of time C of checkpointing, where only a work ωC is done. Therefore, the total number of work units executed during a period of length T is $T - C + \omega C = T - (1 - \omega)C$, and

$$T_{\text{ff}} = T_{\text{base}} \frac{T}{T - (1 - \omega)C}.$$

- The reasoning to compute T_{fails} is the following. Since the mean time between two failures is μ, the average number of failures during execution is $\frac{T_{\text{final}}}{\mu}$. For each failure, the time lost is expressed as:
  - $D + R$ for downtime and recovery;
  - a time ωC for the work that was done during the previous checkpoint and that has to be redone because it was not checkpointed (because of the failure);
  - with probability $\frac{T-C}{T}$, the failure happens while we are not checkpointing, and the time lost is on average $A = \frac{T-C}{2}$;
  - otherwise, with probability $\frac{C}{T}$, the failure happens while we are checkpointing, and the time lost is on average $B = T - C + \frac{C}{2} = T - \frac{C}{2}$.

The time lost for each failure is

$$D + R + \omega C + \frac{T-C}{T}A + \frac{C}{T}B = D + R + \omega C + \frac{T}{2}.$$

Finally,

$$T_{\text{fails}} = \frac{T_{\text{final}}}{\mu}\left(D + R + \omega C + \frac{T}{2}\right).$$

We are now ready to express the total execution time:

$$
\begin{aligned}
T_{\text{final}} &= T_{\text{ff}} + T_{\text{fails}} \\
&= T_{\text{base}}\frac{T}{T - (1-\omega)C} + \frac{T_{\text{final}}}{\mu}\left(D + R + \omega C + \frac{T}{2}\right) \\
&= \frac{T}{(T - (1-\omega)C)\left(1 - \frac{D+R+\omega C+T/2}{\mu}\right)}T_{\text{base}} \\
&= \frac{T}{(T - a)\left(b - \frac{T}{2\mu}\right)}T_{\text{base}},
\end{aligned}
$$

where $a = (1-\omega)C$ and $b = 1 - \frac{D+R+\omega C}{\mu}$.

This equation is minimized for

$$T_{\text{Time}}^{\text{opt}} = \sqrt{2(1-\omega)C(\mu - (D + R + \omega C))}. \tag{1}$$

When $\omega = 0$, we obtain an expression close to that of Young and Daly, but slightly different because they have less accurately approximated the total execution time. In the following, we let ALGOT be the checkpointing strategy that checkpoints with period $T_{\text{Time}}^{\text{opt}}$.

3.2 Energy Consumption

In order to compute the total energy consumption of the execution, we consider the different phases during which the different powers introduced in Section 2.2 are used:

- First, we consume $\mathcal{P}_{\text{Static}}$ during each time-step of the execution. Indeed, even when a node fails and is shutdown, we still pay for the power of all the other nodes, for the cooling system, etc. The corresponding energy cost is $T_{\text{final}}\mathcal{P}_{\text{Static}}$.
- Next, let T_{Cal} be the time during which the CPU is used, inducing a power overhead $\mathcal{P}_{\text{Cal}}$. T_{Cal} includes the base work T_{base}, and $T_{\text{re-exec}}$, the work that must be re-executed after each failure (which we multiply by the number of failures T_{final}/μ):
  - with probability $\frac{T-C}{T}$, the failure does not happen during a checkpoint, and the work to re-execute is $A = \omega C + \frac{T-C}{2}$;

- with probability $\frac{C}{T}$, the failure happens during the execution of a check-point, and the work to re-execute is $B = \omega C + T - C + \frac{\omega C}{2}$.

We derive $\mathcal{T}_{\text{re-exec}} = \frac{T-C}{T} A + \frac{C}{T} B$, hence

$$\mathcal{T}_{\text{re-exec}} = \omega C + \frac{T^2 - C^2}{2T} + \frac{\omega C^2}{2T}.$$

Finally, we have:

$$\mathcal{T}_{\text{Cal}} = \mathcal{T}_{\text{base}} + \frac{\mathcal{T}_{\text{final}}}{\mu} \left(\omega C + \frac{T^2 - C^2}{2T} + \frac{\omega C^2}{2T} \right).$$

The corresponding energy consumption is $\mathcal{T}_{\text{Cal}} \mathcal{P}_{\text{Cal}}$.

- Let $\mathcal{T}_{\text{I/O}}$ be the time during which the I/O system is used, inducing a power overhead $\mathcal{P}_{\text{I/O}}$. This time corresponds to checkpointing and recovery from failures.
  - The total number of checkpoints that are taken in a fault-free execution is equal to the number of periods, $\frac{\mathcal{T}_{\text{base}}}{T-(1-\omega)C}$, and the time taken by checkpoints is therefore $\frac{\mathcal{T}_{\text{base}} C}{T-(1-\omega)C}$.
  - For each failure, there is an additional overhead:
    1. the system needs to recover, which lasts R time-steps;
    2. with probability $\frac{T-C}{T}$, the failure does not happen during a check-point, and there is no additional I/O overhead;
    3. however, with probability $\frac{C}{T}$, the failure happens during a check-point, and the I/O time wasted is (in average) $\frac{C}{2}$.

Altogether, we obtain

$$\mathcal{T}_{\text{I/O}} = \frac{\mathcal{T}_{\text{base}} C}{T - (1-\omega)C} + \frac{\mathcal{T}_{\text{final}}}{\mu} \left(R + \frac{C^2}{2T} \right).$$

The corresponding energy consumption is $\mathcal{T}_{\text{I/O}} \mathcal{P}_{\text{I/O}}$.

- Finally, let $\mathcal{T}_{\text{Down}}$ be the total down time, incurring a power overhead $\mathcal{P}_{\text{Down}}$. We have

$$\mathcal{T}_{\text{Down}} = \frac{\mathcal{T}_{\text{final}}}{\mu} D,$$

and the corresponding energy cost is $\mathcal{T}_{\text{Down}} \mathcal{P}_{\text{Down}}$. This term is only included for full generality, as we expect to have $\mathcal{P}_{\text{Down}} = 0$ in most scenarios.

The final expression for the total energy consumed is

$$\begin{aligned}
\mathcal{E}_{\text{final}} &= \mathcal{T}_{\text{Cal}} \mathcal{P}_{\text{Cal}} + \mathcal{T}_{\text{I/O}} \mathcal{P}_{\text{I/O}} + \mathcal{T}_{\text{Down}} \mathcal{P}_{\text{Down}} + \mathcal{T}_{\text{final}} \mathcal{P}_{\text{Static}} \\
&= \left(\mathcal{T}_{\text{base}} + \frac{\mathcal{T}_{\text{final}}}{\mu} \left(\omega C + \frac{T^2 - C^2}{2T} + \frac{\omega C^2}{2T} \right) \right) \mathcal{P}_{\text{Cal}} \\
&\quad + \left(\frac{\mathcal{T}_{\text{final}}}{\mu} \left(R + \frac{C^2}{2T} \right) + C \frac{\mathcal{T}_{\text{base}}}{T - (1-\omega)C} \right) \mathcal{P}_{\text{I/O}} \\
&\quad + \frac{\mathcal{T}_{\text{final}}}{\mu} D \mathcal{P}_{\text{Down}} + \mathcal{T}_{\text{final}} \mathcal{P}_{\text{Static}}.
\end{aligned}$$

It is important to understand that $\mathcal{T}_{\text{final}} \neq \mathcal{T}_{\text{Cal}} + \mathcal{T}_{\text{I/O}} + \mathcal{T}_{\text{Down}}$, unless $\omega = 0$. Indeed, CPU and I/O activities are overlapped (and both consumed) when checkpointing. To ease the derivation of the optimal period that minimizes $\mathcal{E}_{\text{final}}$, we introduce some notations and let $\mathcal{P}_{\text{Cal}} = \alpha \mathcal{P}_{\text{Static}}$, $\mathcal{P}_{\text{I/O}} = \beta \mathcal{P}_{\text{Static}}$, and $\mathcal{P}_{\text{Down}} = \gamma \mathcal{P}_{\text{Static}}$. Re-using parameters $a = (1-\omega)C$ and $b = 1 - \frac{D+R+\omega C}{\mu}$ from Section 3.1, we obtain:

$$\frac{\mathcal{T}'_{\text{final}}}{\mathcal{T}_{\text{base}}} = \frac{-ab + \frac{T^2}{2\mu}}{(T-a)^2 \left(b - \frac{T}{2\mu}\right)^2}, \quad \text{and}$$

$$\frac{\mathcal{E}'_{\text{final}}}{\mathcal{P}_{\text{Static}}} = \frac{\mathcal{T}'_{\text{final}}}{\mu} \left(\alpha \omega C + \beta R + \gamma D + \frac{\alpha T}{2} - \frac{\alpha(1-\omega)C^2}{2T} + \frac{\beta C^2}{2T} + \mu\right)$$
$$+ \frac{\mathcal{T}_{\text{final}}}{2\mu} \left(\alpha + \frac{\alpha(1-\omega)C^2}{T^2} - \frac{\beta C^2}{T^2}\right) - \frac{\beta C \mathcal{T}_{\text{base}}}{(T-(1-\omega)C)^2}.$$

Then, letting $K = \frac{(T-a)^2 \left(b - \frac{T}{2\mu}\right)^2}{\mathcal{P}_{\text{Static}} \mathcal{T}_{\text{base}}}$, we have:

$$K\mathcal{E}'_{\text{final}} = \frac{-ab + \frac{T^2}{2\mu}}{\mu} \left((\alpha \omega C + \beta R + \gamma D + \mu) + \frac{\alpha T}{2} + \frac{\alpha(1-\omega)C^2}{2T} + \frac{\beta C^2}{2T}\right)$$
$$+ \frac{(T-a)(b - \frac{T}{2\mu})}{2\mu} \left(\alpha + \frac{\alpha(1-\omega)C^2 - \beta C^2}{T}\right) - \beta C \left(b - \frac{T}{2\mu}\right)^2$$
$$= T^3 \left(\frac{1}{4\mu} - \frac{1}{4\mu}\right) + T^2 \left(\frac{\alpha \omega C + \beta R + \gamma D}{2\mu^2} + \frac{b + \frac{a}{2\mu}}{2\mu} - \frac{\beta C}{4\mu^2} + \frac{1}{2\mu}\right)$$
$$+ T \left(-\frac{ab}{2\mu} - \frac{ab}{2\mu} + \frac{\beta C b}{\mu} - 2\frac{(\alpha(1-\omega)-\beta)C^2}{4\mu^2}\right) - \beta C b^2$$
$$- \frac{ab(\alpha \omega C + \beta R + \gamma D + \mu)}{\mu} - \left(\frac{b}{2\mu} - \frac{a}{4\mu^2}\right)(\alpha(1-\omega) - \beta)C^2$$
$$+ \frac{1}{T} \left((\alpha(1-\omega) - \beta)\frac{C}{2\mu} - (\alpha(1-\omega) - \beta)\frac{C}{2\mu}\right)$$
$$= T^2 \left(\frac{\alpha \omega C + \beta R + \gamma D}{2\mu^2} + \frac{b}{2\mu} + \frac{a - \beta C}{4\mu^2} + \frac{1}{2\mu}\right)$$
$$+ T \left(\frac{(\beta C - a)b}{\mu} - 2\frac{(\alpha(1-\omega)-\beta)C^2}{4\mu^2}\right)$$
$$- \frac{ab(\alpha \omega C + \beta R + \gamma D + \mu)}{\mu} - \beta C b^2$$
$$+ \left(\frac{b}{2\mu} + \frac{a}{4\mu^2}\right)(\alpha(1-\omega) - \beta)C^2.$$

Let $\mathcal{T}^{\text{opt}}_{\text{Energy}}$ be the only positive root of this quadratic polynomial in T: $\mathcal{T}^{\text{opt}}_{\text{Energy}}$ is the value that minimizes $\mathcal{E}_{\text{final}}$. In the following, we let AlgoE be the checkpointing strategy that checkpoints with period $\mathcal{T}^{\text{opt}}_{\text{Energy}}$.

As a side note, let us emphasize the differences with the approach of Meneses, Sarood and Kalé [6] when restricting to the case $\omega = 0$ (because they only consider the blocking variant). For each failure, they consider that:

- energy lost due to re-execution is $\frac{T-2C}{2}\mathcal{P}_{\text{Cal}}$, while we have

$$\left(\frac{T-C}{T}\left(\frac{T-C}{2}\right) + \frac{C}{T}(T-C)\right)\mathcal{P}_{\text{Cal}} = \frac{T^2 - C^2}{2T}\mathcal{P}_{\text{Cal}};$$

- energy lost due to I/O is $C\mathcal{P}_{\text{I/O}}$, while we have $\frac{C^2}{2T}\mathcal{P}_{\text{I/O}}$.

Theses differences come from our more detailed analysis of the impact of the failure location, which can strike either during the computation phase, or during the checkpointing phase, of the whole period.

4   Experiments

In this section, we instantiate the previous model with scenarios taken from current projections for Exascale platforms [1,2,5,9]. We choose realistic values for all model parameters: this includes all types of power consumption ($\mathcal{P}_{\text{Static}}$, $\mathcal{P}_{\text{Cal}}$, $\mathcal{P}_{\text{I/O}}$ and $\mathcal{P}_{\text{Down}}$), all checkpoint parameters (C, R, D and ω), and the platform MTBF μ. We start with a word of caution: our choices for these parameters may be somewhat arbitrary, and do not cover the whole range of scenarios that can be investigated. However, a key feature of our model is its robustness: as long as μ is reasonably large in front of checkpoint times, the model is able to accurately predict the best period for execution time and for energy consumption.

The power consumption of an Exascale machine is capped to 20 Mega-watts. With 10^6 nodes, this represents a nominal power of 20 watts per node. Let us express all power values in watts. A reasonable scenario is to assume that half this power is used for operating the platform, hence to let $\mathcal{P}_{\text{Static}} = 10$. The overhead due to computing would represent the other half, hence $\mathcal{P}_{\text{Cal}} = 10$. As for communications and I/Os, which are expected to cost an order of magnitude more than computing [5], we take an overhead of 100, hence $\mathcal{P}_{\text{I/O}} = 100$. A key parameter for the experimental study is the ratio

$$\rho = \frac{\mathcal{P}_{\text{Static}} + \mathcal{P}_{\text{I/O}}}{\mathcal{P}_{\text{Static}} + \mathcal{P}_{\text{Cal}}} = \frac{1 + \beta}{1 + \alpha}. \qquad (2)$$

With our values, we get $\rho = 5.5$. Note that if we used $\mathcal{P}_{\text{Static}} = 5$ and kept the same overheads 10 and 100 for computing and I/O respectively, we would get $\mathcal{P}_{\text{Cal}} = 10$, $\mathcal{P}_{\text{I/O}} = 100$, and $\rho = 7$. These two representative values of ρ ($\rho = 5.5$ and $\rho = 7$) are emphasized by vertical arrows in the plots below on Figure 1. As for $\mathcal{P}_{\text{Down}}$, the power during downtime, we use $\mathcal{P}_{\text{Down}} = 0$, meaning that during downtime we only account for the static power $\mathcal{P}_{\text{Static}}$ of the processors that are idle.

The Jaguar platform, with $N = 45,208$ processors, is reported to have experienced about one fault per day [10], which leads to an individual (processor) MTBF μ_{ind} equal to $\frac{45,208}{365} \approx 125$ years. Therefore, we set the individual (processor) MTBF to $\mu_{\text{ind}} = 125$ years. Letting the total number of processors N vary from $N = 219,150$ to $N = 2,191,500$ (future exascale platforms), the platform MTBF μ varies from $\mu = 300$ min (5 hours) down to $\mu = 30$ min. The experiments use resilience parameters that are representative of current and forthcoming large-scale platforms [9,11]. We take $C = R = 10$ min, $D = 1$ min, and $\omega = 1/2$.

On Figures 1 and 2, we evaluate the impact of the ratio ρ (see Equation (2)) on the gain in energy and loss in time of AlgoE with respect to AlgoT.

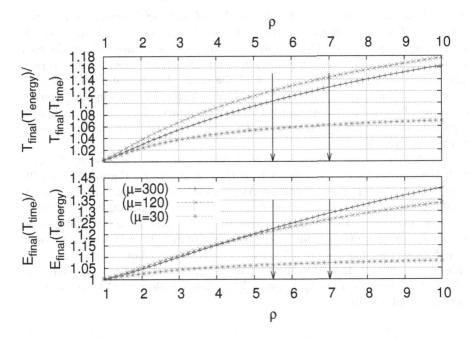

Fig. 1. Time and energy ratios as a function of ρ, with $C = R = 10$ min, $D = 1$ min, $\gamma = 0$, $\omega = 1/2$, and various values for μ

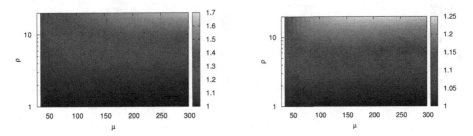

(a) Energy ratio of ALGOT over ALGOE

(b) Execution time ratio of ALGOE over ALGOT

Fig. 2. Ratios of the different strategies with $C = R = 10$ min, $D = 1$ min, $\gamma = 0$, $\omega = 1/2$ as a function of μ and ρ

The general trend is that using ALGOE can lead to significant gains in energy at the price of a small increase in execution time.

We then study in Figure 3 the scalability of the approach on forthcoming platforms. We set the duration of the complete checkpoint and rollback (C and R, respectively) to 1 minute, independently of the number of processors, and we let the downtime D equal to 0.1 minutes. It is reasonable to consider that checkpoint storage time will not increase with the number of nodes in the future, but on the contrary will remain constant. Indeed, system designers are studying a couple of alternative approaches. One consists of providing each computing node with local storage capability, ensuring through hardware mechanisms that this storage will remain available during a failure of the node. Another approach consists iof using the memory of the other processors to store the checkpoint, pairing nodes as "buddies", thus allowing to take advantage of the high bandwidth capability of the high speed network to design a scalable checkpoint storage mechanism [12–15].

The MTBF for 10^6 nodes is set to 2 hours, and this value scales linearly with the number of components. Given these parameters, Figures 3a and 3b shows (i) the execution time ratio of ALGoE over ALGoT, and (ii) the energy consumption ratio of ALGoT over ALGoE, both as a function of the number of nodes. Figures 3a and 3b confirm the important gain in energy that can be achieved, namely up to 30% for a time overhead of only 12%. When the number of nodes gets very high (up to 10^8), then we observe that both energy and time ratios converge to 1. Indeed, when C becomes of the order of magnitude of the MTBF, then both periods $\mathcal{T}_{\text{Time}}^{\text{opt}}$ and $\mathcal{T}_{\text{Energy}}^{\text{opt}}$ become close to C to account for the higher failure rate.

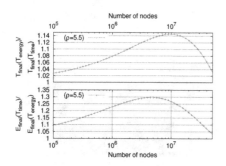

(a) Time and energy ratios, as a function of the number of nodes, when $\rho = 5.5$

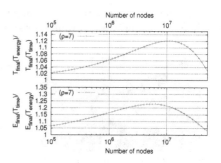

(b) Time and energy ratios, as a function of the number of nodes, when $\rho = 7$

Fig. 3. Ratios of total energy and time for the two period strategies, as a function of the number of nodes, with $\mu = 120$ min for 10^6 nodes, $C = R = 1$ min, $D = 0.1$ min, $\gamma = 0$, $\omega = 1/2$

5   Conclusion

In this short paper, we have provided a detailed analysis to compute the optimal checkpointing period, when the checkpointing activity can be partially overlapped with computations. We have considered two distinct objectives: either the goal is to minimize the total execution time, or it is to minimize the total energy consumption. Because of the different power consumption overheads due to computations and I/Os, we obtain different optimal periods.

We have instantiated the formulas with values derived from current and future Exascale platforms, and we have studied the impact of the power overhead due to I/O activity on the gains in time and energy. With current values, we can save more than 20% of energy with an MTBF of 300 min, at the price of an increase of 10% in the execution time. The maximum gains are expected for a platform with between 10^6 and 10^7 processors (up to 30% energy savings).

Our analytical model is quite flexible and can easily be instantiated to investigate scenarios that involve a variety of resilience and power consumption parameters.

Acknowledgments. This work was supported in part by the ANR *RESCUE* project and by DOE grant # DE-SC0006733. A. Benoit and Y. Robert are with the Institut Universitaire de France.

References

1. Dongarra, J., Beckman, P., Aerts, P., Cappello, F., Lippert, T., Matsuoka, S., Messina, P., Moore, T., Stevens, R., Trefethen, A., Valero, M.: The international exascale software project: a call to cooperative action by the global high-performance community. Int. Journal of High Performance Computing Applications **23**, 309–322 (2009)
2. Sarkar, V., et al.: Exascale software study: Software challenges in extreme scale systems (2009), White paper available at; http://users.ece.gatech.edu/mrichard/ExascaleComputingStudyReports/ECSS%20report%20101909.pdf
3. Young, J.W.: A first order approximation to the optimum checkpoint interval. Comm. of the ACM **17**, 530–531 (1974)
4. Daly, J.T.: A higher order estimate of the optimum checkpoint interval for restart dumps. FGCS **22**, 303–312 (2004)
5. Shalf, J., Dosanjh, S., Morrison, J.: Exascale computing technology challenges. In: Palma, J.M.L.M., Daydé, M., Marques, O., Lopes, J.C. (eds.) VECPAR 2010. LNCS, vol. 6449, pp. 1–25. Springer, Heidelberg (2011)
6. Meneses, E., Sarood, O., Kalé, L.V.: Assessing Energy Efficiency of Fault Tolerance Protocols for HPC Systems. In: Proceedings of the 2012 IEEE 24th International Symposium on Computer Architecture and High Performance Computing (SBAC-PAD 2012), New York, USA (2012)
7. Chandy, K.M., Lamport, L.: Distributed snapshots: Determining global states of distributed systems. Transactions on Computer Systems **3**(1), 63–75 (1985)
8. Bosilca, G., Bouteiller, A., Brunet, E., Cappello, F., Dongarra, J., Guermouche, A., Hérault, T., Robert, Y., Vivien, F., Zaidouni, D.: Unified model for assessing checkpointing protocols at extreme-scale. Concurrency and Computation: Practice and Experience (2013) (to be published); Also available as INRIA research report 7950 at http://graal.ens-lyon.fr/~yrobert
9. Ferreira, K., Stearley, J., Laros, J.H.I., Oldfield, R., Pedretti, K., Brightwell, R., Riesen, R., Bridges, P.G., Arnold, D.: Evaluating the Viability of Process Replication Reliability for Exascale Systems. In: Proc. of the ACM/IEEE SC Conf. (2011)

10. Zheng, G., Ni, X., Kalé, L.V.: A scalable double in-memory checkpoint and restart scheme towards exascale. In: Dependable Systems and Networks Workshops (DSN-W) (2012)
11. Cappello, F., Casanova, H., Robert, Y.: Preventive migration vs. preventive checkpointing for extreme scale supercomputers. Parallel Processing Letters **21**, 111–132 (2011)
12. Zheng, G., Shi, L., Kalé, L.V.: FTC-Charm++: an in-memory checkpoint-based fault tolerant runtime for Charm++ and MPI. In: Proc. 2004 IEEE Int. Conf. Cluster Computing. IEEE Computer Society (2004)
13. Ni, X., Meneses, E., Kalé, L.V.: Hiding checkpoint overhead in HPC applications with a semi-blocking algorithm. In: Proc. 2012 IEEE Int. Conf. Cluster Computing. IEEE Computer Society (2012)
14. Dongarra, J., Hérault, T., Robert, Y.: Revisiting the double checkpointing algorithm. In: 15th Workshop on Advances in Parallel and Distributed Computational Models, APDCM 2013. IEEE Computer Society Press (2013)
15. Rajachandrasekar, R., Moody, A., Mohror, K., Panda, D.K.D.: A 1 PB/s file system to checkpoint three million MPI tasks. In: Proceedings of the 22nd International Symposium on High-Performance Parallel and Distributed Computing, HPDC 2013, pp. 143–154. ACM, New York (2013)

Performance Optimization

Tuning HipGISAXS on Multi and Many Core Supercomputers

Abhinav Sarje[1]([✉]), Xiaoye S. Li[1],
and Alexander Hexemer[2]

[1] Computational Research Division, Lawrence Berkeley National Laboratory,
Berkeley, CA, USA
asarje@lbl.gov
[2] Advanced Light Source, Lawrence Berkeley National Laboratory,
Berkeley, CA, USA

Abstract. With the continual development of multi and many-core architectures, there is a constant need for architecture-specific tuning of application-codes in order to realize high computational performance and energy efficiency, closer to the theoretical peaks of these architectures. In this paper, we present optimization and tuning of HipGISAXS, a parallel X-ray scattering simulation code [9], on various massively-parallel state-of-the-art supercomputers based on multi and many-core processors. In particular, we target clusters of general-purpose multi-cores such as Intel Sandy Bridge and AMD Magny Cours, and many-core accelerators like Nvidia Kepler GPUs and Intel Xeon Phi coprocessors. We present both high-level algorithmic and low-level architecture-aware optimization and tuning methodologies on these platforms. We cover a detailed performance study of our codes on single and multiple nodes of several current top-ranking supercomputers. Additionally, we implement autotuning of many of the algorithmic and optimization parameters for dynamic selection of their optimal values to ensure high-performance and high-efficiency.

1 Introduction

Multi-core and many-core processors are ubiquitous these days, driving most of the electronics available. These emerging architectures are designed to deliver higher computing power by exploiting multiple levels of parallelism. In high-performance scientific computing (HPC), these architectures play a central role in delivering the much needed compute and memory resources to the wealth of scientific codes and are used on a daily basis. In this paper, we consider one such application code developed by us recently, HipGISAXS, which is a massively parallel X-ray scattering simulation code [5,9]. This code targets one particular kind of X-ray scattering, called the Grazing Incidence Small-Angle X-ray Scattering (GISAXS). This, available at numerous Synchrotron Light-source facilities, is a widely used tool by scientists for the characterization of macromolecules and nano-particle systems based on their structural properties, such as their

© Springer International Publishing Switzerland 2014
S. Jarvis et al. (Eds.): PMBS 2013 Workshops, LNCS 8551, pp. 217–238, 2014.
DOI: 10.1007/978-3-319-10214-6_11

shape and size, at the micro/nano-scales. Some of the major applications of these include the characterization of materials for the design and fabrication of energy-relevant nanodevices, such as photovoltaic cells and energy storage devices, and development of high-density storage media. Although current high-throughput synchrotron light-sources can generate tremendous amounts of raw data at a high rate, analysis of this data for the characterization processes remains the primary bottleneck, demanding large amounts of computational resources. HipGISAXS was developed to address this challenge through the use of massive parallelism.

This X-ray scattering pattern simulation code is based on the Distorted Wave Born Approximation (DWBA) theory, and involves a large number of compute-intensive *form-factor* calculations. Scattered light intensity at a point in inverse space is proportional to the form-factor at that point. A form-factor is computed as an integral over the shape functions of the nanoparticles in a given sample. A simulated sample structure is taken as an input in the form of discretized shape-surfaces, such as a triangulated surface. Intensities are determined at a set of q-points which form a 3D grid. Resolutions of shape-surface discretization, as well as of this spatial 3D grid involved also contribute toward the compute-intensity of the simulations. For computational purposes, the form-factor at a single point is described through a summation over the discretized shape-surface:

$$F(\boldsymbol{q}) = -\frac{i}{|\boldsymbol{q}|^2} \sum_{t=1}^{n_t} e^{i\boldsymbol{q}\cdot\boldsymbol{r}_t} q_{n,t} s_t \qquad (1)$$

where $\boldsymbol{q}$ is a point in the inverse space where light intensity is to be determined, and the summation is over all the n_t triangles of the discretized input sample, $\mathcal{T} = \{t_0 \cdots t_{n_t-1}\}$. Such form factors are computed for all q-points in the 3D grid termed as the Q-grid. We represent it by $\mathcal{Q}$ in the following. $\mathcal{Q}$ is a grid of size $n_x \times n_y \times n_z$ and is described by three vectors, one for each spatial dimension, $q_\alpha = \langle p_0 \cdots p_{n_\alpha-1} \rangle, \alpha \in \{x, y, z\}$. This form factor computational kernel is the focus of our tuning and optimization study in this paper.

Although the various emerging architectures are able to deliver high computational power, they require intensive architecture-aware code tuning in order to do so. This gap between the performance of a straight-forward implementation and that of a highly-optimized code, is described quite well in [7,10] where they call it the *"ninja gap"*. In the work presented in this paper, we address the challenge of adapting HipGISAXS to various parallel architectures through intensive optimizations specific to the systems under consideration. These optimizations involve efficient mapping of computations and data transfers on to a given processor architecture. These architectures have a high-degree of parallelism at various levels ranging from instruction level parallelism to multiple NUMA regions on one processor. Such processors form an integral part of todays supercomputers [4]. Many of these processors are built to be generic enough to be used for general-purpose computing. These are majorly the ubiquitous multi-core CPUs. Some of the processors are designed as highly specialized to deliver computing power for specific types of computations. These processors generally are many-core and typically work in conjunction with a main general-purpose host CPU. The most common examples of these are graphics processors and Intel's Many Integrated Cores architecture.

Contributions. The goal of HipGISAXS optimizations described in this paper is to take advantage of various high-performance capabilities offered by the different emerging architectures, and make it truly a "high-performance" code. The work presented in our previous paper [9] includes the parallelization and initial implementation of HipGISAXS on Nvidia Fermi GPU clusters, as well as generic multi-core CPU clusters. In our current work presented this paper, we:

- implement additional architecture-specific optimizations on Nvidia Fermi and Kepler GPUs;
- parallelize and optimize HipGISAXS on the Intel MIC architecture;
- optimize HipGISAXS on the AMD Magny Cours and Intel Sandy Bridge processors;
- implement auto-tuning of many of the compute and optimization parameters involved; and
- present a detailed performance study on supercomputers based on these four architectures and discuss a comparison.

We conduct our study on the following supercomputers which are based on the above architectures (the rankings below were correct as of the June 2013 Top500 list [4]):

1. *Titan*, ranked 2nd, is a Cray XK7 system which gets most of its performance from the Nvidia Kepler K20X cards available on each node.
2. *Stampede*, ranked 6th, is a cluster with an Intel Phi coprocessor, which are based on the Intel MIC architecture, available on each node.
3. *Hopper*, ranked 24th, is a Cray XE6 system which has dual 12-core AMD Magny Cours processors on each of its compute nodes.
4. *Edison* Phase I, an under development system, is a Cray XC30 system which currently has dual Intel Sandy Bridge processors on each compute node.

2   HipGISAXS Overview

HipGISAXS has been implemented in C++ and uses several capabilities of the C++11 standard. It is a highly modularized code which allows for easy access to various routines for optimization, as well as try and compare different optimizations. Depending on the architecture it is compiled for, it calls the GPU, MIC, AMD, or Intel specific codes for the main computational kernel: the numerical form factor calculations. In the following we give a brief overview of this computational kernel. For more details on its basic parallelization and implementation, refer to [9].

The form factor computation at a single q-point involves accessing data and performing independent calculations for each of the input shape triangles, followed by a reduction over all the triangles. This is done for all the q-points in the problem under consideration. The output matrix $\mathcal{F}$ of size same as the Q-grid

$\mathcal{Q}$, is constructed with the results of these computations. This is summarized in the following equation:

$$\mathcal{F}: f(\boldsymbol{q}) = -\frac{i}{|\boldsymbol{q}|^2} \sum_{t=1}^{n_t} e^{i\boldsymbol{q}\cdot\boldsymbol{r}_t} q_{n,t} s_t, \quad \forall \boldsymbol{q} \in \mathcal{Q}. \tag{2}$$

The computational complexity of this kernel is simply the product of all the four dimensions, . A basic implementation of this kernel can be done with four nested loops, with an outer-most loop iterating over all the triangles defining the input shapes and three inner loops iterating over each of the x, y and z dimensions of the q-points, representing the computation over $\mathcal{Q}$. This is then followed by a sum-reduction operation over all the triangles for each q-point. To make referring to these loops easier, let us denote each of them with L_t, L_x, L_y and L_z, respectively. A pseudocode of the kernels is given below. This is how the form factor kernel was originally implemented in HipGISAXS. The definition of a single triangle consists of seven real numbers representing its surface area, three components of its face normal and three components of its centroid. Note that the computations are performed on complex numbers, where re and im represent the real and imaginary parts of a complex number in the following.

```
procedure PHASE1FORMFACTOR(Q, T)
    Input n_x, n_y, n_z, n_t
    Input Q-grid: Q = Q_α{q_α0, · · · , q_α(n_α−1)}, α ∈ {x, y, z}
    Input Shape triangles: T = {t_0, · · · , t_{n_t−1}}
    Output F'_{n_x×n_y×n_z×n_t}
    for each l ∈ {0...(n_t − 1)} do                                    ▷ Loop L_t
        s ← T[l].s                                         ▷ triangle surface area
        p_x ← T[l].p_x, p_y ← T[l].p_y, p_z ← T[l].p_z      ▷ triangle face normal
        c_x ← T[l].c_x, c_y ← T[l].c_y, c_z ← T[l].c_z          ▷ triangle centroid
        for each k ∈ {0...(n_z − 1)} do                                ▷ Loop L_z
            q_k ← Q_z[k]
            for each j ∈ {0...(n_y − 1)} do                            ▷ Loop L_y
                q_j ← Q_y[j]
                for each i ∈ {0...(n_x − 1)} do                        ▷ Loop L_x
                    q_i ← Q_x[i]
                    q_c ← (c_x q_i + c_y q_j + c_z q_k)/(q_i² + q_j² + q_k²)
                    q_p ← p_x q_i + p_y q_j + p_z q_k
                    F'[i, j, k, l] ← s q_p e^{q_{c,im}}(cos(q_{c,re}) + i sin(q_{c,re}))
                end for
            end for
        end for
    end for
end procedure
procedure PHASE2REDUCTION(F')
    Input n_x, n_y, n_z, n_t
    Input F'
    Output F_{n_x×n_y×n_z}
    for each k ∈ {0...(n_z − 1)} do
        for each j ∈ {0...(n_y − 1)} do
            for each i ∈ {0...(n_x − 1)} do
                f ← 0 + i0
                for each l ∈ {0...(n_t − 1)} do
                    f ← f + F'[i, j, k, l]
                end for
                F[i, j, k] ← −if
            end for
        end for
    end for
end procedure
```

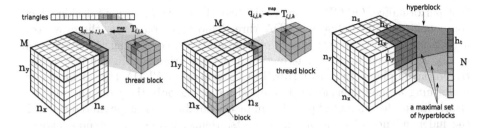

Fig. 1. Problem decomposition schemes. (Left) Phase 1 kernel maps a thread block to a subset of q_y, q_z and $\mathcal{T}$. (Center) Reduction phase kernel maps a thread block to a unique submatrix of $\mathcal{Q}$. (Right) Hyperblocking scheme to handle memory limitations. Graphics taken from [9].

Since the problem under study is embarrassingly parallel, a basic parallelization of the code is quite straightforward. A tiling scheme is used to distribute computations among all the available nodes through MPI. On one node, in order to handle any limitations on the required memory for computations, as well as to increase efficiency, HipGISAXS has a blocking scheme where the computations are decomposed along each of the four dimensions, t, z, y and x, into *hyperblocks*. Computation of hyperblocks is generally performed one after the other. This blocking scheme also has the advantage of making memory transfer and computation overlap, as well as data prefetching, possible. This is specially of essential importance on systems which use an offloading model to transfer computations to a coprocessor. A GPU version is also a part of HipGISAXS, which also incorporates computation decomposition at the level of thread blocks. Fig. 1 shows this existing tiling, hyperblocking, and thread blocking schemes.

In the following we present our performance optimizations and tuning, as well as performance analysis, on each of the four architectures under consideration: Nvidia GPUs, Intel Phi coprocessors, AMD Magny Cours CPUs and Intel Sandy Bridge CPUs.

3   Graphics Processors

We start by giving a description of various optimizations performed on HipGISAXS for the Nvidia Fermi and Kepler architecture based GPUs [1]. The starting point for these optimizations is the code developed earlier as mentioned above. In the following, we describe our additional optimizations and autotuning work tailored to the Nvidia GPUs.

3.1   Nvidia GPU Optimizations

Algorithmic Optimizations. For parallelizing the computations on Fermi and Kepler architectures, we encounter a number of choices to make. Each of these choices affects the performance, some greatly and some marginally. Goal of any performance optimization is to make the choices which would give the best performance. On GPUs, one of the first choices to make is to decide which components should define a CUDA thread block. In our case, there are two kernels for each of the two phases of computations: computing the inner term in Eq. 2, followed by a sum reduction along the triangles. In the first phase, the initial implementation of HipGISAXS generated CUDA thread blocks by performing a one-dimensional decomposition along only the t dimension. This clearly limits the amount of parallelism by the number of triangles and disregards the independence of each of the q-points. Hence, it does not expose enough parallelism for cases where Q is large but the shape definition is small. This kernel was therefore updated to decompose the computations along the three y, z and t dimensions. Recall that the x dimension is typically small, most often being equal to one. This *loop reordering* and *new decomposition scheme* solved the limitations of the initial kernels. To maintain independence in computations, the reduction phase decomposed the domain along the spatial dimensions but not along the triangles since this dimension needs to be reduced. The choice of the sizes of both the hyperblocks and CUDA thread blocks also plays a crucial role in delivering high-performance. We will deal with these choices later in Section 3.1.

One of the main performance disadvantages with the above two kernels is the generation of 4-dimensional intermediate data. Each computed hyperblock is stored by the first kernel in the device memory and then read by reduction kernel. We can eliminate this step of writes and reads by *kernel fusion*. The idea is to keep reducing the computed components and generate only 3-dimensional output which is written to the device memory. This also has the advantage of using less amount of device memory. Parallelization implemented earlier is hence modified: We generate CUDA thread blocks by decomposition along the y and z dimensions and introduce sequentiality along the t dimension. Hence, each thread now executes a loop over the hyperblock triangles and reduces the computed data on the fly. This kernel fusion improved the code's performance on average by about 87%.

Memory Optimizations. Computation of each hyperblock generates partial output corresponding to a submatrix of $\mathcal{F}$. This computed data is copied to the host, reduced with previously computed data corresponding to the same submatrix, and placed at its appropriate position in the larger $\mathcal{F}$. This work is performed by the host CPU while the GPU carries on computations on next hyperblock. Double-buffering is commonly used to hide such memory transfer latencies. We explored, going one step ahead, the use of k-buffering. It was interesting to note that while the performance of triple-buffering was around 5% better than double-buffering, the performance of k-buffering for $k \geq 3$ was about the same (we tried until $k = 32$). Since the memory copy latency is much smaller than the compute duration for each hyperblock, once the latency was completely hidden with triple-buffering, increasing the number of buffers did not have any affect. We verified this against profiler trace data. Usage of the fast on-chip shared memory on each SM of a GPU is critical to obtain good performance. In our case, shared memory can be used to store the input Q-grid and shape triangles information as well as the computed output. Storing input makes data reuse possible, minimizing the amount of memory transfers taking place. Storing the output in shared memory first and then writing to the device memory provides good memory coalescing, increasing the data transfer bandwidth. Storing both input and output on-chip can be expensive since shared memory usage may limit the number of simultaneously scheduled thread blocks on an SM, thereby limiting parallelism and hence, performance. A tradeoff comes into place. After experimentation with the possible cases, our choice was to use shared memory only for the input data: parts of the vectors q_y and q_z defining a particular thread block, and the triangles definition data. All threads in a thread block collectively load the required input to the shared memory in minimum possible number of load operations, and then perform computations on them, storing the results directly into the device memory.

Low-Level Optimizations. As described earlier, the definition of a single shape-surface triangle consists of seven real numbers, representing its surface area, three components of its surface normal, and three components of its centroid coordinates. Since this size (7) does not provide efficient memory-alignment, we padded each triangle definition by one more number to make the count as 8 real numbers. In single-precision, this represents 32 bytes. Doing so aligns each triangle definition to a 32-byte line, making memory transfers more efficient. Further, a manual analysis of the PTX code generated by the compiler for the innermost loop L_t of the kernel revealed that the shared memory address calculation for the 7 components consisted of about one multiply and two adds each. This code is shown below on the left side:

```
mul.wide.u32 %rd35, %r101, 4;     mul.wide.u32 %rd1, %r91, 4;
add.s64 %rd37, %rd11, %rd35;      add.s64 %rd2, %rd1, 4;
add.s32 %r75, %r101, 1;           add.s64 %rd3, %rd1, 8;
mul.wide.u32 %rd38, %r75, 4;      add.s64 %rd4, %rd1, 12;
add.s64 %rd39, %rd11, %rd38;      add.s64 %rd5, %rd1, 16;
add.s32 %r76, %r101, 2;           add.s64 %rd6, %rd1, 20;
mul.wide.u32 %rd40, %r76, 4;      add.s64 %rd7, %rd1, 24;
add.s64 %rd41, %rd11, %rd40;      ld.shared.f32 %f40, [%rd1];
add.s32 %r77, %r101, 3;           ld.shared.f32 %f41, [%rd2];
mul.wide.u32 %rd42, %r77, 4;      ld.shared.f32 %f42, [%rd3];
add.s64 %rd43, %rd11, %rd42;      ld.shared.f32 %f43, [%rd4];
add.s32 %r78, %r101, 4;           ld.shared.f32 %f44, [%rd5];
mul.wide.u32 %rd44, %r78, 4;      ld.shared.f32 %f45, [%rd6];
add.s64 %rd45, %rd11, %rd44;      ld.shared.f32 %f46, [%rd7];
add.s32 %r79, %r101, 5;
mul.wide.u32 %rd46, %r79, 4;
add.s64 %rd47, %rd11, %rd46;
add.s32 %r80, %r101, 6;
mul.wide.u32 %rd48, %r80, 4;
add.s64 %rd49, %rd11, %rd48;
ld.shared.f32 %f72, [%rd37];
ld.shared.f32 %f42, [%rd39];
ld.shared.f32 %f25, [%rd41];
ld.shared.f32 %f34, [%rd43];
ld.shared.f32 %f27, [%rd47];
ld.shared.f32 %f36, [%rd49];
ld.shared.f32 %f39, [%rd45];
```

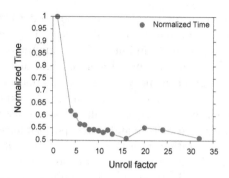

Fig. 2. The effect of loop unrolling on performance. Unroll factor means that the loop is unrolled that many times. Note that best performance is achieved for unroll factors 16 and 32.

In order to reduce the number of operations, and instructions, in L_t, we replaced this code with hand-written PTX code. This code takes advantage of the fact that the memory location offset for each of the 7 triangle components is already known beforehand. Hence, 6 of the 7 multiplies and half of the adds could be eliminated. This code is shown above on the right side. Since each thread in a thread block loops over all the triangles in the corresponding hyperblock, we can take advantage of loop unrolling. Interestingly, the execution time of the kernel reduced by almost 50% on using an unroll factor of 16. In Fig. 2 is shown the trend of execution time (normalized) with the unroll factor.

Nvidia GPUs provide hardware support for single-precision sine and cosine functions at the cost of accuracy. In our optimizations, we take advantage of them since this code does not require high-precision. We implement our own optimized functions for complex number operations and use intrinsics whenever possible to improve performance.

Autotuning Decomposition Parameters. In Section 3.1 we talked about various decomposition parameters, such as the hyperblock size and the CUDA block size. Making an optimal choice of these parameters is crucial to obtaining good performance. These parameters are architecture dependent, and are generally independent of the problem instance. Hence, the code needs to be tuned for optimal parameters only once for a given system. In the following, we study the behavior of the execution time with respect to the possible parameter values.

Recall that a hyperblock size is defined primarily by the dimensions y (h_y), z (h_z) and t (h_t). Each parameter has a tradeoff attached to it. For instance, a larger value of h_y (or h_z) means smaller number of resulting hyperblocks. Computation of each such hyperblock would require larger amount of system memory, resulting in larger volume of each memory transfer (although fewer number of transfers). Depending on how much of these data transfer latencies can be hidden with computations dictates the performance. Also, a fewer number of hyperblocks means less overlap for border cases, which might be significant given the

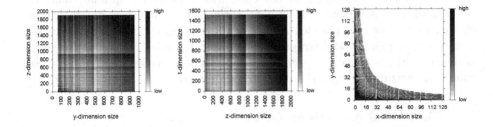

Fig. 3. (Left and Center) The variation in execution time with change in hyperblock sizes. Low is better (yellow regions). (Right) Variation of performance with the choice of CUDA thread block size. The x and y dimensions here correspond to the thread block dimensions.

large size of the hyperblocks. Similarily, a smaller value of h_y (or h_z) would generate a larger number of smaller hyperblocks. The size of a hyperblock needs to be sufficient to occupy all the SMs on the GPU. Too small a size will not provide enough parallelism and, hence, result in under-utilization of the SMs.

Fig. 3 (left) shows an example of the variation in performance as a heatmap with varying values of h_y and h_z, given a constant CUDA thread block size. The first thing we notice in this figure is its banded nature. Also note that the performance is not symmetrical for y and z dimensions. We attribute this primarily to the data organization in memory. We have taken $n_x = 1$, and follow a row-major order storage scheme, which groups the y values together. Each hyperblock is decomposed into thread blocks and each vertical band corresponds to the same number of warps for a given h_z. The change in runtime with h_z is more gradual. Suppose for a given h_z, the matrix $\mathcal{F}$ is perfectly decomposed into equal sized hyperblocks, and we observe good performance. If we increase this h_z by one, an offset in decomposition is created due to which the last set of hyperblocks are partly empty, decreasing performance a little. Further increments of h_z result in this empty region to grow, continually decreasing performance. When h_z reaches a value where $\mathcal{F}$ is perfectly decomposed, we observe a higher performance. This is exactly what we observe in the heat-map. Similarly, Fig. 3 (center) shows a heat-map, with varying h_z and h_t values. Increasing h_t creates a similar situation as we saw for h_z above. Hence, this looks more symmetric along h_z and h_t.

The choice of CUDA thread block sizes poses different criteria. Firstly, the total number of threads in a CUDA thread block, i.e. the product of thread block dimension sizes, is limited to 1024 on Fermi and Kepler. Fig. 3(right) shows the trend in execution times with respect to variation in the sizes of the two dimensions of a thread block. It can be clearly seen that the sizes which are multiple of 32 give the best performances. This is because a warp size is 32, and a full warp would give better performance due to better utilization than the one which is partially empty.

We implement autotuning in our code which makes an optimal choice of these block size parameters. It is done through an exhaustive search within the parameter space in parallel. As we mentioned above, these parameters are architecture dependent and not problem instance dependent, hence setting them once is enough on a given system. All executions of the code can then use these values, amortizing their auto-tuning computation cost.

3.2 Theoretical Analysis on GPUs

To compute the number of floating-point operations (FLOPs) on GPUs, we refer to the generated PTX code. We count each of the special functions of reciprocal, exponent and sine-cosine as one floating-point operation each since the hardware provides support for these functions. Each operation on complex numbers is composed of one or more floating-point operations. The main kernel consists of total of 22 FP multiply operations, 3 FP additions, 3 FP subtractions, 9 FP FMA operations, 2 FP reciprocal, 2 FP absolutes, 1 exponent, 1 sine and cosine operations. Of these 1 multiply and 1 FMA lie outside the loop L_t. Hence, we have a total of 42 FLOPs in a single iteration of L_t, giving a total of $42n_t + 2$ FLOPs for the form factor computation at one q-point. The total FLOPs in the computation of the kernel among all hyperblocks is therefore $n_x n_y n_z (42n_t + 2)$.

To compute the arithmetic intensity (flop/byte ratio), let us consider the computation performed by a single CUDA thread block. For ease of representation, let the CUDA thread block dimension sizes be n_x, n_y, n_z and n_t. In the optimized version of the code, there are a total of $4(n_x + n_y + 7n_t) + 8n_z$ bytes read and $8n_x n_y n_z$ bytes written. Hence, the arithmetic intensity is linear in number of triangles, $O(n_t)$. The kernel is clearly compute bound.

3.3 Performance Analysis on Titan

In the following, we first cover the performance analysis of our GPU optimized code on both Fermi and Kepler architectures. Specifically, we consider the M2090 and the K20X GPUs. M2090 has a theoretical peak performance of 1331 GFLOP/s in single-precision, while K20X has almost 3950 GFLOP/s. In Table 1 we show the performance of our code on a single GPU node. Our code obtains about 814 GFLOP/s on the M2090, and about 2,172 GFLOP/s on K20X GPUs. The former is 61.2% of the theoretical peak and the latter is about 55% of the theoretical peak.

We also perform scaling study on the Titan supercomputer, which is a Cray XK7 with an Nvidia Tesla K20Xm available on each of its nodes. In Fig. 4 we show the strong scaling of our code for an input data consisting of 2M and 8M q-points and 7.5M triangles defining the shape of an organic photovoltaic (OPV) sample. It can be seen that our code scales well. For the case with 2M q points, there is not enough parallelism in the problem instance to efficiently utilize more than 1,024 GPU nodes and, hence, we see flattening in its performance. For the second case with 8M q-points, this is not the case and the code scales up to the

Table 1. Single node execution times in seconds for various input sizes on M2090 and K20X GPUs

$\mathcal{T}$	$\mathcal{Q}$	M2090	GFLOP/s	K20X	GFLOP/s
6,600	2M	0.68	813.6	0.25	2172.2
6,600	8M	2.73	813.2	1.02	2167.2
91,753	2M	9.47	813.4	3.56	2159.1
91,753	8M	37.9	813.4	14.25	2161.5

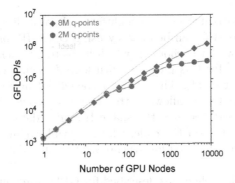

Fig. 4. Strong scaling on the Titan supercomputer. Data is shown for two different Q-grid sizes, and 7.5M triangles. Note how the Q-grid size affects the performance. The code achieves 1.25 PetaFLOPs of sustained performance when using 8,192 GPU nodes.

available 8,192 GPU nodes. It attains a performance of about 1.25 PetaFLOP/s when using 8,192 nodes.

4   Many Integrated Cores (MIC)

The second architecture we consider is Intel's Many Integrated Cores (MIC) architecture. Intel Xeon Phi processors [2] are based on this architecture. This platform acts as a coprocessor connected to a host CPU. Although codes can run in native mode on MIC without the intervention of the host CPU, in our case we use the offload model where the host offloads the kernel computations onto the coprocessor. We chose this model due to three major reasons: HipGISAXS uses certain third-party libraries such as imaging and parallel I/O libraries which either are not available for the MIC architecture or perform best on generic multi-core CPUs, the host in our case, since a single core performance of the host CPU is generally higher than single core performance of this many-core coprocessor. Secondly, by offloading the compute intensive kernels to the coprocessor, the host is available to perform other computations simultaneously, which is beneficial in the case of HipGISAXS since it can perform computations such as structure-factor computation independent of the form-factor computations. In addition to these, offloading also enables overlay computations for large problems since the main memory on the coprocessor is limited while the host may have much larger capacity, enabling offloading one hyperblock at a time which would fit into the coprocessor memory.

4.1   Intel MIC Optimizations

In the following, we present some of our optimizations performed on the form factor kernel of HipGISAXS to adapt it to the Intel MIC architecture.

Algorithmic Optimizations. A straightforward parallelization of form factor computations on the MIC can be done by using OpenMP for the nested loops. We are again faced with the choice of which loops to parallelize, and we choose the loops L_y and L_z for this purpose, with loop L_t being the innermost loop executed by all the threads. This choice is beneficial in our case due to two primary reasons. Firstly, it allows better non-local cache utilization by data reuse since each thread requires the shape triangles data. Secondly, it allows for a better vectorization of the code, which we will explain in Section 4.1. In addition, it eliminates the need for synchronization in reduction operation over the triangles.

We follow a similar scheme as described for GPUs previously for parallelization. Hyperblocking decomposes the computations into smaller subproblems, each of which is computed one at a time using all the available cores on the processor. Since we are using the offload model, this also allows us to exploit data transfer latency hiding through overlap with computations with the use of asynchronous kernel offloading and data copying features available on this coprocessor.

To implement the kernel, we use kernel fusion to merge the reduction step along with the first phase of computing the inner terms.Further, an obvious optimization on the two loops L_y and L_z under consideration is *loop collapsing*. This enables availability of high parallelism for efficient work distribution among the various threads.

Memory Optimizations. In implementing the code using the offload model, we minimize the number of data transfers by using the `nocopy`, `alloc_if` and `free_if` features, as well as asynchronous data copy. With these features, we implement triple-buffering scheme for offloading hyperblock computations and computed submatrix data transfers. This enables a perfect data transfer latency hiding, similar to our case for GPUs. All the data buffers used are aligned to 64-bytes (cache line), and padded to maintain this alignment in order to maximize performance.

We perform detailed performance profiling of our code using the Intel VTune Amplifier profiling tool. The obtained data was used to guide our optimizations. One of the major bottlenecks revealed by the profiler was in loading of the shape triangle data. The data in the triangles buffer is originally organized according to the format of the data read from the input shape definition file. This consists of data for each triangle appearing consecutively. As we mentioned

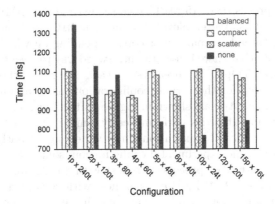

Fig. 5. The performance of various possible configurations on the Intel Phi coprocessor. A configuration is represented by number of MPI processes running on the host (p) and number of OpenMP threads belonging to each MPI process (c) running on the coprocessor. Data is shown for the four different possible affinities: balanced, compact, none and scatter.

previously, this definition consists of 7 real numbers. Hence, the data was stored as such. Since the compiler performed automatic vectorization of the kernel, it had to use gather instructions such as vgatherdps to obtain data corresponding to each component of the triangles definition, which had large stride values spanning over multiple triangles. These gather operations are expensive, and proved to be a major bottleneck in the code. Hence, we performed data reorganization to eliminate such operations. While constructing the triangles buffer, we grouped each component of all triangles together. This allowed to have unit stride values for accessing the data to facilitate automatic vectorization. With this optimization we observed a performance improvement of about 33%.

Environmental Optimizations. Intel compilers provide a wealth of options to perform optimizations. We took advantage of these, along with those provided by environment variables. The VTune profiler also showed that a significant amount of time was being spent in thread waiting routines of OpenMP. Fortunately, setting the environment variable KMP_BLOCKTIME to 0 reduced this overhead. We also employed high pages by setting the value of the environment variable MIC_USE_2MB_BUFFERS to 4K. We also set MIC_KMP_AFFINITY = granularity = fine, compact, which performed the best among other affinity configurations with our code.

Since we use offload model with MPI processes running on the host, and 240 hardware threads (4 threads per core) on the MIC, it is natural to explore various possible configurations in terms of number of MPI processes running on the host and the number of threads each process creates on the MIC. In our case, the host is a dual 8-core processor providing total of 16 cores. Hence, we explore various configurations ranging from 1 MPI process on the host with 240 OpenMP threads on the coprocessor to 15 MPI processes with 16 OpenMP threads each with different affinities. We employed the variable MIC_KMP_PLACE_THREADS to explicitly pin the threads to particular cores depending on which MPI process they belong to. Note that there is no straightforward way to specify the case of 16 MPI processes with 15 OpenMP threads since each core runs 4 threads. The performances we observed for the various configurations using affinities balanced, compact, none and scatter are shown in Figure 5. It can be seen that balanced, scatter and compact affinities perform nearly similar. The default affinity of none performs erratically: the execution times varied significantly between different runs with the same experimental configuration, sometimes even by 200%. The configurations of 6 MPI processes on host with 40 threads (10 cores) each on the coprocessor and 12 MPI processes on host with 20 threads (5 cores) each on the coprocessor and compact affinity are our choices on this platform.

Vectorization and Complex Operations. Intel compilers are capable of automatically vectorizing parts of the code in order to utilize the 512-bit vector registers (floating-point and integer). Keeping the loop L_t as innermost, for each thread to execute, is helpful in vectorization since multiple triangles can be processed simultaneously through SIMD parallelism. Analysis of assembly code of the kernel generated by the compiler showed good vectorization, but not perfect. Since most of the computations in our kernel are operations on complex numbers (i.e. each entity consisting of two floating-point numbers), it is not straightforward for the compiler to vectorize them effectively.

The MIC architecture does not support Intel MMX, SSE or AVX vector instruction sets. It implements its own vector instructions (Initial Many Core Instructions [6]) on 512-bit vectors due to the availability of 512-bit integer and floating-point registers. Hence it can perform operations on 16 single-precision or integer data via SIMD. To address the compiler's failure to efficiently vectorize complex number operations, we implemented our own vectorization by using a combination of the low-level vector intrinsics and assembly code. Before we do that, we need to make a choice on how to represent complex number vectors. A straightforward way is to represent one 512-bit vector by 8 single-precision complex numbers, with the real and imaginary components of a complex number stored next to each other. In practice, this approach does not work well in parallel since to perform operations, the real and imaginary components are treated separately and performing operations on interleaved data is not an efficient way to vectorize. Hence, we follow the "structure-of-arrays" schema and define a complex vector by two 512-bit vector components, one for real part and other for the imaginary part as follows:

```
typedef struct {
  __m512 _xvec;
  __m512 _yvec;
} __m512c;
```

Hence, one complex vector holds 16 complex numbers. This way, we can make full use of the SIMD capabilities on MIC. We implement all our operations on vectorized complex numbers using this datatype using the real number intrinsics and instructions. For example, a simple complex-complex multiplication can be written as follows using 4 multiply, 1 add and 1 subtract intrinsics:

```
static inline __m512c _mm512_mul_pc(__m512c a, __m512c b) {
    __m512c vec;
    __m512 t1 = _mm512_mul_ps(a.xvec, b.xvec);
    __m512 t2 = _mm512_mul_ps(a.yvec, b.yvec);
    vec.xvec = _mm512_sub_ps(t1, t2);
    t1 = _mm512_mul_ps(a.xvec, b.yvec);
    t2 = _mm512_mul_ps(a.yvec, b.xvec)
    vec.yvec = _mm512_add_ps(t1, t2);
    return vec;
}
```

We manually vectorize the entire form factor kernel using such intrinsics and assembly code. Since MIC does not provide hardware support for functions such as sine and cosine, they are implemented in software and their vectorized versions are available through libraries such as SVML. We use such functions from SVML in our code. Compared to the compiler generated vectorization, our manual vectorized code showed about 22% performance improvement.

With the above optimizations, the main bottlenecks in our code were now the two SVML functions we used: exponent and sine-cosine. About 80% of the time was spent together in these functions. Hence, we decided to use our own optimized functions for these operations. We obtained a basic implementation of exp and sincos functions from [8] and performed extensive optimizations (such as instruction re-ordering, arithmetic optimizations, minimize add and multiply instructions through the use of fused-multiply-add). Using these functions in our kernel gave a further overall performance improvement of about 25%. Through micro-benchmarking of the kernel we computed that our exponent function was about 3.57× faster than the SVML implementation. Similarly, our sine-cosine function was about 1.5× faster than the SVML implementation.

Autotuning Decomposition Parameters. Similar to our GPU optimization case, we implement autotuning for optimal choice of the computational decomposition parameters. For the MIC version of the code, we primarily need to tune the hyperblock sizes. An example of the trend of execution time observed for various values of h_y and h_z is shown in Fig. 6. Another example with varying values of h_z and h_t is also shown in the same figure.

Quite different to the behavior we saw in the case of GPUs, here all the small hyperblock sizes should be avoided. Although from the figure it is tempting to choose the largest hyperblock size from the top right corner of the plot, it should be noted that the data for these graphs was obtain through extrapolation, and those configurations with large values of all h_y, h_z and h_t are actually not possible due to memory limitations on the coprocessor. Hence, most of the yellow region we see in the figures should be removed, and we should be able to choose parameter values from the center of the heat maps. Again, the optimal values of these parameters is independent of the problem instance, unless the

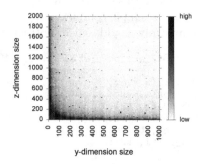

Fig. 6. Variation in performance with change in hyperblock dimension sizes. Low is better (yellow regions). Note that most of the top right parts are not possible due to memory limitations on the coprocessor.

optimal values are larger than the corresponding sizes in the given problem, the autotuner needs to be executed only once on a system, and all subsequent runs of HipGISAXS will use these values and amortize the cost.

4.2   Theoretical Analysis on Intel MIC

We refer to our kernel implementation for MIC architecture, done using vector intrinsics and assembly language, to count the number of floating-point operations. In this case we do not consider the special functions as 1 FLOP because they are implemented using the basic arithmetic operations. We do not count floating-point comparisons in our calculations. For operations on complex numbers, we count the number of real FP operations they are built upon. Hence, a real-complex add is just 1 FLOP, complex-complex add is 2 FLOPs, and so on. Our implementation of `exp` contains 26 FLOPs, and `sincos` contains 23 FLOPs. Adding up these and all remaining operations, we obtain $78n_t + 18$ FLOPs for a single q-point, making the overall total to be $n_x n_y n_z (78n_t + 18)$ FLOPs for the entire problem instance. In this case as well, the arithmetic intensity is a function of number of triangles, $O(n_t)$ making this kernel compute bound for MIC architecture also.

4.3   Performance Analysis on Stampede

We now present some of the performance results we were able to obtain on the Stampede system in the limited time of access and limited number of nodes. We plan to get access to more time and larger number of nodes in order to perform much in depth performance analysis and scaling in the next couple of months. In Table 2 we list the performance on a single MIC node of the Stampede system with various input sizes. The theoretical peak performance of a MIC card is 2,021 GFLOP/s in single-precision. Our codes were able to achieve 484 GFLOP/s, which is about 24% of the peak.

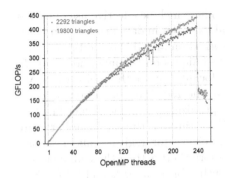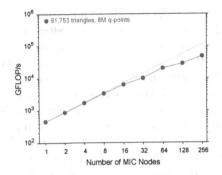

Fig. 7. (Left) Strong scaling is shown for a single node, with varying number of threads. (Right) Strong scaling on multiple nodes of Stampede. Each node has one MIC coprocessor. On 1,024 nodes, we achieved 0.1 PetaFLOPs of performance.

Table 2. Single node execution times in seconds for various input sizes on Stampede, containing the Intel Phi coprocessors (MIC)

# Triangles	# q-points	Time [s]	GFLOP/s
6,600	2M	2.27	453.58
6,600	8M	8.769	469.67
91,753	2M	30.767	465.22
91,753	8M	118.49	483.19
7,514,364	2M	2565.18	456.98

In Fig. 7, we show strong scaling of our code – on a single node, and across multiple nodes upto 256 nodes of the Stampede system. We were unable to get access to larger number of nodes except for one run on 1,024 nodes of Stampede. It can be seen that the code scales quite well. On 1,024 nodes we ran a problem instance with $n_t = 7,514,364$ and 2M q-points, and the code was able to achieve about 0.1 PetaFLOP/s (1024 nodes).

5 On Multi-core CPUs

Next we consider general-purpose multi-core CPU architectures for optimizing HipGISAXS. Due to various similarities with previous cases, and space limitations, we will keep this brief.

5.1 AMD Magny Cours and Intel Sandy Bridge

Cray XE6 and Cray XC30 are built using AMD Magny Cours and Intel Sandy Bridge processors, respectively. These are both general-purpose multi-core processors, the former with 12 cores and the latter with 8 cores. L1, L2 and LLC caches are all system managed. Although it is relatively simple to implement codes for such processors, obtaining high-performance necessitates adapting the code to their specific architectural features. These include effective use of caches through exploitation of spatial and temporal localities in data accesses, and low-level instruction optimizations such as vectorization and ILP exploitation.

We implement data and loop blocking techniques on the innermost loop L_t of our form factor kernel in order to exploit localities on both architectures. We use fused kernel in this case as well, hence, the reduction operation over the triangles minimizes synchronization. Our optimizations of the kernel function on these processors was guided using PAPI [3] through the available hardware counters. AMD Magny Cours provides 128-bit vector registers and supports SSE2 and SSE4a vector instructions. To perform better than the compiler generated vectorization, we implemented the entire form factor kernel using SSE2 vector intrinsics. Intel Sandy Bridge, on the other hand, provides 256-bit vector registers and supports AVX vector instructions. Hence, for this architecture we implemented our kernel using AVX vector intrinsics. In both the cases, we implemented our own optimized versions of operations on complex numbers as well as the special functions `exp` and `sincos`. On Sandy Bridge, since AVX intrinsics do not include integer operations, we implemented them using 128-bit SSE2 vectors. Also, we performed the input shape triangles data reorganization similar to the MIC case explained earlier in order to facilitate efficient vectorization and avoid expensive memory stalls. In addition, this data reorganization includes data blocking to take advantage of localities through available cache as mentioned earlier. Furthermore, we also unrolled the vector loop by a factor of 2 in order to hide instruction latencies. Further, we also incorporate autotuning of the hyperblock decomposition parameters into these codes as well. The trend of the execution time with varying hyperblock dimension sizes was quite similar to that we saw for the MIC architecture previously, hence we do now show it here.

5.2 Theoretical Analysis on Multi-core CPUs

We count the number of floating-point operations in the form factor kernel for our implementations on these multi-core CPUs. These implementations are quite similar (but with different instruction sets: SSE2, AVX). We also count the basic operations for each of the exponent and sine-cosine functions. The total number of floating-point operations in the kernel for a single q-point turns out to be $68n_t + 20$ on Magny Cours and $85n_t + 16$ on Sandy Bridge. Hence, overall FLOP counts on the two architectures are $n_x n_y n_z (68n_t + 20)$ and $n_x n_y n_z (85n_t + 16)$, respectively. Again, similar to the case with MIC and GPU implementations, the arithmetic intensity in this case is also a linear function of the number of triangles, $O(n_t)$.

5.3 Performance Analysis on Hopper and Edison

A single node of Hopper is dual socket containing two AMD Magny Cours processors, providing a total of 24 cores. This XE6 node has 4 NUMA regions, consisting of 6 cores each. In this environment, we have the liberty of choosing

Table 3. Single node execution times in seconds for various input sizes (number of triangles and number of q-points) on AMD Magny Cours processors of Cray XE6 and Intel Sandy Bridge processors of Cray XC30, and corresponding GFLOP/s

T	Q	XE6	GFLOP/s	XC30	GFLOP/s
6,600	2M	6.34	141.7	2.97	378.2
6,600	8M	25.28	142.1	11.87	378.3
91,753	2M	88.16	141.7	41.0	379
91,753	8M	352.0	142	164.1	380

the number of MPI processes and the number of OpenMP threads per process while using all the 24 cores. Through experimentation, we determined that for our code, 4 MPI processes with 6 OpenMP threads each on a node performs the best, and we use this configuration in all subsequent experiments on the Hopper system. These processes and threads are pinned to their respective locations in each NUMA region. In contrast, an XC30 node is dual socket with two Sandy Bridge processors, but with only 2 NUMA regions. This processor also supports Hyper-Threading, providing a total of 16 physical and 32 logical cores. On this system, we observed that the configuration consisting of single threaded 16 MPI processes per node, and without Hyper-Threading, performs the best. Hence, we use this configuration for our experiments on the Edison system. In Table 3 we list single node performance on both systems for several input sizes. The theoretical peak performance of one node of XE6 in single-precision is 403 GFLOP/s, and that of XC30 node is 664 GFLOP/s. With our optimized codes, on a single node of the XE6, we achieved 142 GFLOP/s which is 35.2% of the peak, while on a single node of the XC30, we achieved 380 GFLOP/s which is 57.2% of the peak performance.

Moving on to multiple nodes, in Fig. 8 we show the performance scaling of our optimized code on the Hopper and Edison systems. We utilized up to 6,000 nodes on Hopper (144,000 cores) reaching 0.63 PetaFLOP/s, and 512 nodes on Edison (8,192 cores) reaching 0.19 PetaFLOP/s.

6   Comparisons

In the following we discuss a brief comparison of the optimizations and performance of our codes on the different systems presented in this paper. Both Nvidia GPUs and Intel MIC provide a high-degree of fine grained parallelism, which was beneficial in our case due to the independent nature of computations involved in the form factor kernel. Although comparing the different systems is not an easy task, in our case we plot the performances obtained on the three systems on the same number of nodes. Hence, on Titan, one node provides one K20X GPU, on Stampede, one node provides one Intel Phi coprocessor, on Hopper, one node provides dual socket AMD Magny Cours processors with a total of 24 cores, and on Edison, one node is dual socket with Intel Sandy Bridge with a total of 16 physical cores. On a single node of the four systems, our code achieved

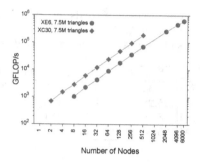

Fig. 8. Strong scaling on the Hopper system, a Cray XE6, and Edison, a Cray XC30. The former is built with AMD Magny Cours processors, each node with 24 cores, making a total of 144,000 cores for 6,000 nodes. The latter consists of Intel Sandy Bridge processors, each node with 16 physical cores, making a total of 8,192 cores for 512 nodes. Our code achieves 0.63 PetaFLOPs on 6,000 nodes of Hopper, and 0.19 PetaFLOPs on 512 nodes of Edison.

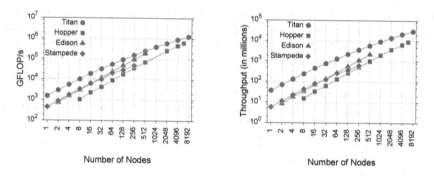

Fig. 9. Comparison of performance of our codes on Titan, Stampede, Hopper and Edison. (Left) Performance in GFLOP/s is shown. (Right) Throughput in TQP/s (number of triangle-q-points processed per second, i.e. one iteration of the loop L_t).

142 GFLOP/s on Magny Cours, 380 GFLOP/s on Sandy Bridge, 484 GFLOP/s on MIC and 2172 GFLOP/s on K20X, the building blocks of the four systems. The graphs shown in Fig. 9 compare the performance of our codes on all the four systems for comparison, with the same number of nodes on each. It can be seen that the performance of Edison and Stampede are very comparable. Scaling on Hopper and Edison is better than on Titan and Stampede. It should be noted that Nvidia GPUs considered above are the only processors among these which provide hardware support for approximate sine-cosine computations. This made a lot of difference since on other systems, these functions had to be implemented in software using basic mathematical operations.

Although developing a bare-bones working code with acceptable performance is easier on multi-core CPUs like the AMD Magny Cours and Intel Sandy Bridge, than on GPUs or MIC, since they are general-purpose processors, extraction of high-performance from them is no easier than the implementations on graphics processors or the MIC architecture. In an attempt to quantify the effort required by each of these architectures to extract the raw computational power, we note that basic code development person-hours was least for the multi-core CPUs, and highest for GPUs. But taking all together the optimization efforts, the effort went into them is quite comparable. In terms of power, we note that the performance per watt achieved by our codes on each of K20X GPU, MIC, Magny Cours and Sandy Bridge architectures are respectively, 8.98 GFLOP/s/Watt, 1.98 GFLOP/s/Watt, 1.3 GFLOP/s/Watt, and 3.3 GFLOP/s/Watt.

7 Conclusions

In this paper we described in detail our efforts on optimizing HipGISAXS, a high-performance X-ray scattering simulation code. In our work targeted four specific architectures: Nvidia GPUs (Fermi/Kepler), Intel MIC (Phi processor), AMD Magny Cours and Intel Sandy Bridge CPUs. These different architectures form the basic building block of four of the top supercomputers: Titan, Stampede, Hopper and Edison, respectively. We presented detailed optimization strategies and analyzed the code performance on these supercomputers. On each of these architectures, our code achieved 55% of peak on Nvidia K20X, 24% of peak on Intel MIC, 35.2% of peak on dual AMD Magny Cours, and 57.2% of peak on dual Intel Sandy Bridge. On the scale of the supercomputers used, our code was able to achieve 1.25 PetaFLOP/s on 8,192 nodes of Titan, 0.1 PetaFLOP/s on 1,024 nodes of Stampede, 0.63 PetaFLOP/s on 6,000 nodes of Hopper and 0.19 PetaFLOP/s on 512 nodes of Edison.

Acknowledgments. The authors thank Samuel Williams for the many helpful discussions, and Nvidia for donating several Kepler GPU cards used in the development of HipGISAXS. The authors also thank the rest of the HipGISAXS development team, Slim Chourou and Elaine Chan. This work was supported by the Director, Office of Science, of the U.S. Department of Energy under Contract No. DE-AC02-05CH11231. This work was also supported by DOE Early Career Award granted to Alexander Hexemer. This research used resources of the National Energy Research Scientific Computing Center (NERSC), which is supported by the Office of Science of the U.S. Department of Energy under Contract No. DE-AC02-05CH11231, of the Oak Ridge Leadership Computing Facility (OLCF) at the Oak Ridge National Laboratory, which is supported by the Office of Science of the U.S. Department of Energy under Contract No. DE-AC05-00OR22725. The authors further acknowledge the Texas Advanced Computing Center (TACC) at The University of Texas at Austin for providing HPC resources that have contributed to the research results reported within this paper.

References

1. Tesla Kepler GPU Accelerators. Datasheet (2012)
2. Intel Xeon Phi Coprocessor. Developer's Quick Start Guide. Version 1.5. White Paper (2013)

3. Performance Application Programming Interface (PAPI) (2013), http://icl.cs.utk.edu/papi
4. Top500 Supercomputers (June 2013), http://www.top500.org
5. Chourou, S., Sarje, A., Li, X., Chan, E., Hexemer, A.: HipGISAXS: A High Performance Computing Code for Simulating Grazing Incidence X-Ray Scattering Data. Submitted to the Journal of Applied Crystallography (2013)
6. Intel Corp.: Intel Xeon Phi Coprocessor Instruction Set Architecture Reference Manual (September 2012)
7. Kim, C., Satish, N., Chhugani, J., et al.: Closing the Ninja Performance Gap through Traditional Programming and Compiler Technology. Tech. Rep. (2011)
8. Pommier, J.: SIMD implementation of sin, cos, exp and log. Tech. Rep. (2007), http://gruntthepeon.free.fr/ssemath
9. Sarje, A., Li, X., Chourou, S., Chan, E., Hexemer, A.: Massively Parallel X-ray Scattering Simulations. In: Supercomputing (SC 2012) (2012)
10. Satish, N., Kim, C., Chhugani, J., et al.: Can traditional programming bridge the Ninja performance gap for parallel computing applications? SIGARCH Computer Architecture News 40(3), 440–451 (2012). http://doi.acm.org/10.1145/2366231.2337210

Multi Objective Optimization of HPC Kernels for Performance, Power, and Energy

Prasanna Balaprakash[1,2], Ananta Tiwari[3], and Stefan M. Wild[1(✉)]

[1] Argonne National Laboratory, Mathematics and Computer Science Division,
Argonne, IL, USA
[2] Argonne National Laboratory, Leadership Computing Facility, Argonne, IL, USA
[3] Performance Modeling and Characterization (PMaC) Lab, San Diego
Supercomputer Center, La Jolla, CA, USA
pbalapra@mcs.anl.gov, tiwari@sdsc.edu, wild@anl.gov

Abstract. Code optimization in the high-performance computing realm has traditionally focused on reducing execution time. The problem, in mathematical terms, has been expressed as a single objective optimization problem. The expected concerns of next-generation systems, however, demand a more detailed analysis of the interplay among execution time and other metrics. Metrics such as power, performance, energy, and resiliency may all be targeted together and traded against one another. We present a multi objective formulation of the code optimization problem. Our proposed framework helps one explore potential tradeoffs among multiple objectives and provides a significantly richer analysis than can be achieved by treating additional metrics as hard constraints. We empirically examine a variety of metrics, architectures, and code optimization decisions and provide evidence that such tradeoffs exist in practice.

1 Introduction

The race to exascale is rapidly changing supercomputer architecture designs. Shrinking circuit sizes and a growing push toward heterogeneous architectures is yielding systems with processors with many cores, sometimes differing vastly in their capabilities. From a user's standpoint, these changes fundamentally alter the way one interacts with these systems. System resiliency, which traditionally was "free," will no longer be so. Lower voltage, a larger number of elements within a node, and elements' shrinking feature sizes are expected to decrease the mean time between failures [1]. Adding extra logic into the hardware to address the resiliency issue takes up valuable chip real estate; the burden of making sure the application ran to a successful and correct completion may be shifted—at a performance/energy price—to the software.

Another challenge the new architecture designs expose is the power wall problem. As an example, [1] recommends the power wall for exascale systems be 20 MW, a limit that is already being flirted with by current-generation petaflop

© Springer International Publishing Switzerland 2014
S. Jarvis et al. (Eds.): PMBS 2013 Workshops, LNCS 8551, pp. 239–260, 2014.
DOI: 10.1007/978-3-319-10214-6_12

systems[1]. Hardware architects are consequently working closely with application scientists to design systems that can deliver more FLOPs per Watt. Hardware-based solutions alone cannot, however, address all the different stress scenarios that software phases might put on hardware. Part of the solution has to come from the software side as well; these solutions can be addressed by *autotuning*. Autotuning is the systematic process of navigating the space defined by the software and hardware parameters that impact a metric related to the performance of the system. Next-generation autotuning strategies should efficiently identify and obtain high-performance code optimizations that can help reduce the power demands of key computational pieces of the scientific applications and carefully orchestrate hardware-provided configuration options to reduce the power draw. Exascale systems will also provide massive concurrency; billions of cores are projected. Writing an application that can take advantage of the available compute resources will provide substantial challenges to today's high-performance computing (HPC) application developers.

Traditionally, the autotuning problem has been expressed as a single-objective (execution time) minimization problem (see, e.g., [3]). Given current and projected changes in architecture designs, however, this formulation of the problem is insufficient for a wide variety of emerging autotuning problems. Execution time will be one among several, possibly competing, system-related metrics such as system resiliency and energy consumption that must be optimized. Ramping up the speed of the processor to complete the application execution, for example, can jeopardize system resiliency because the increase in chip temperature can make it more vulnerable to failures. Similarly, launching an application to utilize more cores than its computational phases need, or can exploit, wastes energy. Therefore, a *multi objective formulation of the autotuning problem is needed*.

Multi objective optimization concerns the study of optimizing two or more objectives simultaneously. Even if there is a unique optimal (software/hardware) decision when any of the objectives is considered in isolation, there may be an entire set of solutions when the objectives are considered collectively. This set is referred to as a Pareto front (formally described in Section 3) and plays an integral role in a wide variety of decision problems in HPC. Two examples relevant to this paper are the following:

1. HPC administrators increasingly must balance financial costs associated with energy consumption with the need for users to obtain results in a timely manner. In some cases it may be possible to quantify a price on time and thereby obtain a single, weighted objective comprising both energy and time costs. However, such *a priori* weights are typically unknown, and minimizing such a single objective does not provide information when these weights (or the price of energy) change. A Pareto front in the time-energy space provides optimal solutions for all possible weights/prices.
2. For hardware design and thermal considerations, power capping—where one must perform a computation while satisfying a specified power limit/

---

[1] For example, the Tianhe-2 computer requires 17.8 MW of power to achieve 33.8 LINPACK petaFLOP/s [2].

budget—is increasingly done. Performance tuning in this context could minimize the single objective of run time subject to a constraint on power. However, such a single-objective optimization will not identify the implications associated with that particular power limit. A one watt increase in this limit could be deemed acceptable if it allowed for a 20% reduction in time. Similarly, a decrease in the power limit could result in a negligible performance loss, and thus placing less thermal stress on the hardware would come at minimal cost. A Pareto front in time-power space provides valuable information on the performance consequences of setting power limits.

Hence, multi objective optimization studies provide significantly richer insight than do single-objective and constrained optimization approaches. The related work summarized in Section 2 provides further examples where considering several metrics simultaneously is of interest.

In Section 3, we present a mathematical formulation of the multi objective performance tuning problem. In Section 4 we bridge the terminologies used by the mathematical optimization and performance-tuning communities for the specific case of time, power, and energy metrics. We establish conditions when problems using these metrics benefit from a multi objective formulation and when the number of objectives of interest can effectively be reduced. To illustrate the relationship between tuning decisions and multiple, simultaneous objectives, we consider a set of problems based on common HPC kernels. Section 5 presents decision spaces consisting of different loop optimization techniques (e.g., loop tiling, unrolling, scalar replacement, register tiling), clock frequencies, and parallelization (e.g., thread and node counts). We use these problems to conduct an experimental study on multiple objectives on several novel architectures. To the best of our knowledge, this is the first detailed work on empirical analysis of run time, power, and energy tradeoffs on an Intel Xeon Phi coprocessor (Section 6.1), an Intel Xeon E5530 (Section 6.2), and an IBM Blue Gene/Q (Section 6.3). Our results show that tradeoffs exist in practice under a number of different settings.

Although current architectures expose only a limited set of energy and power-related parameters (e.g., CPU clock frequency) to the software, we anticipate that exascale architectures may admit a richer set of hardware parameters (e.g., power gating of different hardware components) that have power and energy implications. Therefore, we believe that presenting a framework that shows how tradeoffs can be explored is an important contribution to the HPC community. Furthermore, the existence of these tradeoffs can motivate hardware designers to expose a richer set of configuration knobs to future administrators and software designers. This framework and our analysis are sufficiently general and can be easily extended to incorporate new hardware- and software-based power and energy configuration options as they become available.

2   Related Work

Several recent works have examined metrics based on performance and power/ energy models. An energy-aware compilation framework was developed in [4].

The framework can estimate and optimize energy consumption of a given code taking as input the architectural and technological parameters, energy models, and energy/performance constraints. A performance-adaptive algorithm for optical interconnects was proposed in [5] and used to optimize power consumption, throughput, and latency for various traffic patterns. A multi objective algorithm based on game theory was proposed in [6] for mapping tasks onto multi core architectures in order to optimize performance and energy. An integrated architecture-circuit optimization framework was used by Azizi et al. [7] to study the tradeoff between energy and performance; the authors showed that voltage scaling plays a crucial role in this tradeoff while the choice of an optimal architecture and circuitry does not have a significant impact. The authors in [8] adopted machine-learning techniques to build predictive models for power draw, execution time, and energy usage of computational kernels. A "roofline" model for energy that takes into account algorithm characteristics (e.g., operations, concurrency, and memory traffic) and machine characteristics (time and energy costs per operation or per word of communication) was developed in [9]; using this model, the authors also analyzed the conditions for tradeoffs between time and energy.

Objectives based on architectural simulations have also been used. A multi objective exploration of the mapping space of a mesh-based network-on-chip architecture was performed in [10]; using evolutionary computing techniques, the authors obtained the mappings on a performance-power Pareto front. Performance, power and resource usage objectives were treated by the design space tool in [11] to explore the vast design space of the Grid ALU Processor and its post-link optimizer.

Closer to the presented work are exploratory studies using empirical performance data in conjunction with power or energy. The impact of energy constraints for multithreaded applications on multiprocessor applications was studied in [12] and synchronization-aware algorithms were proposed to save energy with a user-acceptable loss in speedup. Power-monitoring device, PowerMon2, was developed in [13] to enable the analysis of performance and power tradeoffs. The authors in [14] used a power-aware performance prediction model of hybrid MPI/OpenMP applications to develop an algorithm to optimize energy consumption and run time. An automated empirical tuning framework that can be configured to optimize both performance and energy efficiency was proposed in [15]. Energy and performance characteristics of different parallel implementations of scientific applications on multi-core systems were investigated in [16], and interactions between power and application performance were explored. The empirical performance tuning tool Active Harmony [17] was used in [18] to explore the tradeoff between energy consumption and performance for HPC kernels. The effects of CPU and network bandwidth tuning from a whole-system-level perspective were analyzed in [19]; in demonstrating opportunities for energy savings, tradeoffs between power and run times were found.

Researchers have also explored search algorithms for multi objective problems. In addition to execution time, many of these works involve objectives that are simpler to evaluate, e.g., code size; and none have looked at power or energy objectives. Performance and code size were considered in a multi objective approach in [20] when an unroll factor was varied. A multi objective evolutionary algorithm was adopted in [21] to find Pareto-optimal (for combinations of code size, compilation time, and execution time) compiler optimization levels. Evolutionary search algorithms were also used in the adaptive compiler framework [22] to find compiler optimization sequences that minimize code size, average run time, and worst-case run time. Automated tuning of a just-in-time compiler through multi objective evolutionary search was performed in [23]. The tuning identified optimization plans that are Pareto-optimal in terms of compilation time and a measure of code quality. Milepost GCC [24] is a self-tuning optimization infrastructure that supports general multi objective optimization where a user can choose to minimize execution time, code size and compilation time. A multi objective autotuning framework that adopts differential evolution algorithms as a search methodology was developed in [25]. The authors demonstrated the proposed approach by optimizing run time and parallel efficiency when varying loop tiling and thread-count parameters for parallel codes.

3 Multi Objective Optimization: Background and Notation

We consider the multi objective (sometimes called "multi criteria" [26]) mathematical optimization problem

$$\min_{x \in \mathcal{X}} F(x) = [F_1(x), \ldots, F_p(x)], \tag{1}$$

where $p > 1$ objectives are simultaneously minimized. In this paper, we assume that the n-dimensional decision space $\mathcal{X} \subset \mathbb{R}^n$ is a finite collection of discrete points of size $|\mathcal{X}|$. The assumption of a discrete and finite decision space can be relaxed. We assume that each of the p objectives is bounded from below but can take on the extended value "$+\infty$" (e.g., corresponding to an infeasible code transformation within the space $\mathcal{X}$ or a—ideally, reproducible—runtime failure) and that there is at least one point in the decision space $\mathcal{X}$ at which all p objectives are finite.

Many of the standard properties from single-objective optimization have analogies in the multi objective setting. For example, objectives f that should be maximized can be brought into the framework (1) by defining $F_i(x) = -f(x)$. Similarly, the units of the component objectives F_i do not matter since the solution set of (1) is invariant to shift and positive-scale transformations[2].

In the case of minimizing a single objective f, the idea of (global) optimality is simple: $\hat{x} \in \mathcal{X}$ is optimal if and only if $f(\hat{x}) \leq f(x)$ for all $x \in \mathcal{X}$. For multiple objectives, however, we must alter this notion of optimality. The following definitions are standard in multi objective mathematical optimization (see, e.g., [26]).

---

[2] The solution set for $\min_x F(x)$ is exactly that for $\min_x \{\alpha + \text{diag}(\beta)F(x)\}$ for any $\alpha \in \mathbb{R}^p$ and any positive $\beta \in \mathbb{R}^p$.

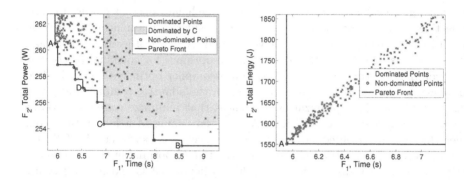

Fig. 1. Illustration of Pareto fronts when minimizing two objectives (fdtd kernel, input size 512, Intel Xeon E5530; see Section 6.2). Left: The points A, B, C, and D are non dominated and hence belong to the Pareto front. Right: The Pareto front is a single point, A, which dominates all other points.

Definition 1. *We say that $F(x) \leq F(y)$ if $F_i(x) \leq F_i(y)$ for all $i = 1, \ldots, p$, and $F(x) \neq F(y)$; in this case we have that y is <u>dominated</u> by x. We say that a point $x \in \mathcal{X}$ is Pareto optimal for (1), or <u>non dominated</u>, if there is no $y \in \mathcal{X}$ with $F(y) \leq F(x)$. We denote the <u>set of Pareto-optimal points</u> by $\mathcal{X}^* \subseteq \mathcal{X}$. The set of objective function values of all Pareto-optimal points, $\mathcal{F}^* = \{F(x) : x \in \mathcal{X}^*\}$, is called the <u>Pareto front.</u>*

The concepts introduced in Definition 1 are perhaps best illustrated by an example. Figure 1 (left) considers the case when the $p = 2$ objectives of time, F_1, and total power, F_2, are simultaneously minimized. The $F_1 \times F_2$ objective space shown is not to be confused with the decision space $\mathcal{X}$ (which in this example corresponds to parameter values defining loop unrolling and other code transformations, see Section 5). For the examples in Fig. 1, we assume that the objective values of every feasible decision $x \in \mathcal{X}$ are shown. The shaded area represents the region in $F_1 \times F_2$ space that is dominated by the point C; all points in this region are inferior to C in both objectives. The set of non dominated points form the Pareto front $\mathcal{F}^*$.

If the objective F_1 (F_2) is minimized in isolation, then we obtain the point A (B), which necessarily belongs on the Pareto front. Similarly, the minimizers of the single objective $f_\lambda(x) = F_1(x) + (1 - \lambda)F_2(x)$, for $\lambda \in [0, 1]$, corresponding to a convex combination of the objectives, will lie on the Pareto front. However, not all points on the Pareto front necessarily correspond to minimizers of a linear combination of the objectives (e.g., point D in Fig. 1 (left)).

Hence, the Pareto front contains significantly richer information than one obtains from single-objective formulations. For example, if one were to minimize time subject to a constraint on power, $F_2(x) \leq \overline{P}$, the Pareto front provides the solution for all possible values of the cap $\overline{P}$. In Fig. 1 (left), we see that caps of 260 W, 257 W, and 254 W would result in minimal times of 6 s, 6.5 s, and 8 s, respectively.

In some cases, the multiple objectives may not be competing. For the same decision space $\mathcal{X}$ considered in Fig. 1 (left), Fig. 1 (right) has a second objective of energy consumption, which is strongly correlated with the objective F_1. In fact, the Pareto front now corresponds to a single point, which simultaneously minimizes both objectives.

As evidenced in these examples, only certain regions of the objective space are of interest. Typically, search algorithms for efficiently finding Pareto fronts focus on a hyperrectangle defined by two points formally defined below.

Definition 2. *The* ideal objective point $F^I = [F_1^I, \dots, F_p^I]$ *for (1) is defined component wise by* $F_i^I = \min\limits_{x \in \mathcal{X}} F_i(x)$. *The* nadir objective point $F^N = [F_1^N, \dots, F_p^N]$ *for (1) is defined component-wise by* $F_i^N = \max\limits_{x \in \mathcal{X}^*} F_i(x)$.

The ideal point represents the best possible value in isolation for each objective. The ideal point can be attained only if the Pareto front consists of a single point as in Fig. 1 (right). The nadir point is the extreme point defined by the Pareto front. In the example in Fig. 1 (left), the ideal and nadir points are at (5.97 s, 252.5 W) and (8.57 s, 260.5 W), respectively. Together, the ideal and nadir points define the range of objective values that decision makers may encounter if they are interested in all possible optimal tradeoffs.

Before directing our focus to three specific metrics, we note that hard constraints, including those involving an objective of interest, can also be incorporated in (1). We assume that these constraints define the decision space $\mathcal{X}$ and that the choice of this decision space can directly affect the objective space, and hence the ideal and nadir points.

4   Optimization of Time, Power, and Energy

In this section we focus on the particular *bi objective* cases where either time and power or time and energy are simultaneously minimized. We could just as easily examine more than two simultaneous objectives. However, interpretation/visualization of the empirical results presented in Section 6 would be less straightforward. Furthermore, though our experimental focus is on objectives defined by empirical evaluation, our framework can also include objectives defined by model or simulator evaluation.

For clarity, we denote the time, power, and energy objectives by T, P, and E, respectively. Since power corresponds to a rate of energy, these two problems (which we can write as $F = [T, P]$ and $F = [T, E]$) are clearly related, with $E = PT$.

One can exploit other properties of these three objectives in their simultaneous optimization. For example, since T, P, E are strictly positive, we can freely multiply/divide by T, P, E without changing inequalities. Similarly, for many problems of interest one can assume that the objective values of two different decision points are different (i.e., for all $x, y \in \mathcal{X}$ with $x \neq y$, $T(x) \neq T(y)$).

This property ensures that there is a one-to-one correspondence between Pareto-optimal decision points $\mathcal{X}^*$ and the Pareto front $\mathcal{F}^*$.

Furthermore, we may have *a priori* knowledge about the relationship between some decision parameters and some objectives. For example, for many architectures it is safe to assert that power is monotonically increasing in the number of nodes employed. Such relationships can be exploited by both exploratory studies and search algorithms to reduce the number of distinct decision points evaluated.

Because of the relationship between power and energy, we have a simple relationship between the two objective spaces considered here.

Definition 3. *Let $\underline{\mathcal{X}^{*P}} \subseteq \mathcal{X}$ denote the set of Pareto-optimal points for $F = [T, P]$, and let $\underline{\mathcal{X}^{*E}} \subseteq \mathcal{X}$ denote the set of Pareto optimal points for $F = [T, E]$.*

Proposition 1. *All points on the energy-time Pareto front have a corresponding point on the power-time Pareto front: $\mathcal{X}^{*E} \subseteq \mathcal{X}^{*P}$.*

Proof. Let $\hat{x} \in \mathcal{X}^{*E}$ denote a point on the energy-time Pareto front (and hence there is no point $x \in \mathcal{X}$ that dominates $\hat{x}$ for the objectives T and E). Now suppose that $\hat{x} \notin \mathcal{X}^{*P}$, and hence there is some $\tilde{x} \in \mathcal{X}$ that dominates $\hat{x}$. If $T(\tilde{x}) < T(\hat{x})$ and $P(\tilde{x}) \leq P(\hat{x})$, then $E(\tilde{x}) = T(\tilde{x})P(\tilde{x}) < T(\hat{x})P(\hat{x}) = E(\hat{x})$, and hence $\tilde{x}$ is strictly better in both T and P. On the other hand, if $T(\tilde{x}) \leq T(\hat{x})$ and $P(\tilde{x}) < P(\hat{x})$, then $E(\tilde{x}) < E(\hat{x})$. In both cases, $T(\tilde{x}) \leq T(\hat{x})$ and $E(\tilde{x}) < E(\hat{x})$, which contradicts the definition of $\hat{x}$ being non dominated for the T and E.

Proposition 1 says that the number of non dominated points for energy-time is bounded by the number of non dominated points for power-time.

Definition 4. *Let $x^{(1)} \in \mathcal{X}^{*P}$ denote a non dominated point on the T-P front that minimizes time: $x^{(1)} \in \arg\min_{x \in \mathcal{X}^{*P}} T(x)$ (where the inclusion is done in case there is not a unique minimizer).*

Proposition 2. *A necessary condition for $x \in \mathcal{X}$ to be a non dominated point on the T-E Pareto front is that*

$$P(x) \leq \frac{P(x^{(1)})T(x^{(1)})}{T(x)}. \tag{2}$$

Proof. By the definition of $x^{(1)}$, $T(x^{(1)}) \leq T(x)$ for all $x \in \mathcal{X}$. Hence, $x \in \mathcal{X}$ can be on the T-E Pareto front only if $E(x) \leq E(x^{(1)})$, which can be rewritten as (2) since $T(x) > 0$ for all $x \in \mathcal{X}$.

Many necessary bounds exist in addition to (2), but (2) is especially useful because it provides a convenient bound that requires only a minimizer of a single objective (time). Furthermore, it offers a mathematical relationship for the conditions needed in order for the energy-time Pareto front to comprise

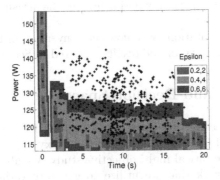

Fig. 2. Illustration of the points comprising a relaxed Pareto front for different values of ϵ (SPAPT adi problem, Intel Xeon Phi; see Section 6.1). The points within each shaded region belong the relaxed Pareto front obtained from (4).

more than one point. Clearly this inequality does not hold for the example in Fig. 1.

Proposition 2 can also be used to look at the effect of idle power. If we decompose the power into a constant idle power and a varying difference above idle power, $P(x) = P_I + \Delta P(x)$, then (2) is equivalent to

$$\Delta P(x^{(1)})T(x^{(1)}) - \Delta P(x)T(x) \geq \left(T(x) - T(x^{(1)})\right) P_I. \tag{3}$$

A necessary condition for (3) is that the power savings must outpace the product of idle power and relative slow-down,

$$P(x^{(1)}) - P(x) \geq \frac{T(x) - T(x^{(1)})}{T(x^{(1)})} P_I.$$

Hence, for fixed times $T(x)$ and $T(x^{(1)})$, it becomes more unlikely that tradeoffs exist as the idle power P_I grows (since there's always an upper bound to peak available power).

For many time-power-energy multi objective problems, one may need to acknowledge the measurement error in each objective. Assuming that there is a fixed error margin $\epsilon_i \geq 0$ for the ith objective, if $F_i(x)$ is within ϵ_i of $F_i(y)$, then we cannot say that x is truly better than y (or vice versa) with respect to the objective F_i. The notion of non dominance in Definition 1 would thus need to be modified so that x dominates y if $F(x) \neq F(y)$ and

$$F_i(x) + \epsilon_i \leq F_i(y) \quad \text{for all } i = 1, \ldots, p. \tag{4}$$

As a result, one would arrive at a *relaxed Pareto front* that potentially consists of a cloud of points. This is illustrated in Fig. 2 for different multiples of the measurement error margin ($\epsilon_1 = .2\text{s}, \epsilon_2 = 2\text{W}$). In practice, one often knows what the ϵ_i should be. For example, we know what the measurement resolution of power and time are for each of our experiments; see the measurement descriptions in Section 6.

To simplify the presentation, we follow the convention in Definition 1 (which takes $\epsilon_i = 0$ for $i = 1, \ldots, p$) for the results reported in Section 6.

5   Problem Sets and Decision Spaces

We now describe the set of problems, consisting of HPC kernels from SPAPT [27], TORCH [28], and CSPARSE [29], and the proxy application miniFE [30], that we used for our empirical multi objective study. We also describe the code transformation framework that we utilize to generate variants with different flavors of compiler optimizations.

Each search problem in the SPAPT [27] suite is a specific combination of a kernel, an input size, a set of tunable decision parameters, a feasible set of possible parameter values, and a default configuration of these parameters for search algorithms. These problems are expressed in an annotation-based language that can be readily processed by Orio [31]. The tunable decision parameters are loop unroll/jamming, cache tiling, register tiling, scalar replacement, array copy optimization, loop vectorization, and multi core parallelization using OpenMP. The kernels in SPAPT are grouped into four groups: elementary dense linear algebra kernels, dense linear algebra solver kernels, stencil code kernels, and elementary statistical computing kernels. This work considers problems from three groups: matrix-matrix multiplication (mm), matrix transpose and vector multiplication (atax), and triangular matrix operations (trmm) from the basic dense linear algebra kernels; bi conjugate gradient (bicgkernel) and lu decomposition kernels from the dense linear algebra solver kernels; and matrix subtraction, multiplication, and division (adi), 1-D Jacobi computation (jacobi), finite-difference time domain (fdtd), and matrix factorization (seidel) kernels from the stencil code kernels.

To generate and evaluate a set of points in the SPAPT decision space, (which can be further extended to include different compiler optimization parameters), we must use a source-to-source transformation framework. We use Orio [31], which is an extensible and portable software framework for empirical performance tuning. It takes an Orio-annotated C or Fortran implementation of a problem along with a tuning specification that consists of various performance-tuning directives as inputs, generates multiple transformed code variants of the annotated code, empirically evaluates the performance of the generated codes, and has the ability to select the best-performing code variant using various search algorithms. We refer the reader to [31] for a detailed account of annotation parsing and code generation schemes in Orio.

On multi core architectures, larger core counts reduce the ratio of peak memory bandwidth to peak floating-point performance. To analyze such behavior, we include two bandwidth-limited problems: a sparse matrix multiplication kernel and a quick sort kernel that sorts n items in $O(n \log n)$ time. The reference implementation of the sparse matrix multiplication kernel is based on CSPARSE, a concise sparse matrix package in C [29], and takes sparse matrix triplets as input. For the quick sort kernel, we use the implementation from the TORCH Computational Reference Kernels [28], a collection of core problems in scientific computing. While in the sparse matrix multiplication kernel the number of nonzero elements in the matrix leads to floating-point operations, the quick sort kernel performs only comparisons without any significant floating-point operations.

For large-scale multi node experiments, we use a proxy application from the Mantevo project, which was designed to explore the capabilities of emerging architectures [30]. miniFE is a finite-element mini-application that implements kernels representative of unstructured, implicit finite-element applications. It assembles a sparse linear system from a steady-state heat conduction problem on a brick-shaped domain of linear, 8-node hex elements. It then solves the linear system using a simple (unpreconditioned) conjugate gradient (CG) algorithm. Thus the kernels that miniFE contains are computation of element-operators (diffusion matrix, source vector), assembly (scattering element-operators into sparse matrices and vectors), sparse matrix-vector products (during the CG solve), and vector operations (level-1 BLAS: axpy, dot, norm). Running miniFE with a fixed set of dimensions and varying the number of MPI ranks is a commonly used strong scaling test.

To illustrate the wide applicability of our framework, we use different HPC platforms in the experimental study (platforms are described in the next Section). For each platform, we use a subset of the problems described above that can exercise the unique and important aspects of that platform. The decision-making process for selecting the benchmarks for experimental evaluation of the proposed framework had one more important dimension – choosing kernels and applications that are well known to the HPC community, so that the results can be evaluated and assimilated within the larger context of what the community already knows about the behaviors (e.g., performance consequences of different compiler optimizations) of those kernels.

6   Experimental Results

We now summarize the findings from our empirical evaluations on three markedly different platforms. The Intel Xeon Phi's Many Integrated Core (MIC) architecture serves as a platform that allows us to explore the tradeoffs among concurrency, power, and performance on nodes with many simple cores, a characteristic that we anticipate will be increasingly common in next-generation large-scale systems. The Intel Xeon E5530 architecture allows us to explore the tradeoffs among power, energy, and performance in a current-generation architecture. The availability of clock frequency scaling on the Xeon E5530 allows us to enrich our decision space $\mathcal{X}$ (see Section 3) with hardware-provided, power-related configuration options. Our measurement setup on the Xeon E5530 also provides us with more detailed power measurement capabilities. IBM's BG/Q was chosen as a way to demonstrate our framework's applicability on a vastly different processor architecture and to explore the tradeoffs among concurrency, power, and performance on a large, multi nodal scale.

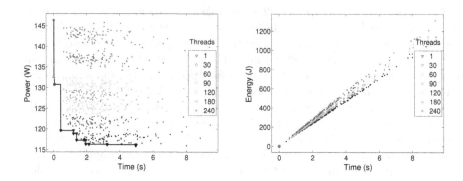

Fig. 3. Power, energy, and time for the fdtd SPAPT kernel on Intel Xeon Phi (includes both thread count and code transformation variants)

6.1   Intel Xeon Phi

The experiments described in this section are carried out on a first-generation Intel Xeon Phi coprocessor (based on the Intel Many Integrated Core (MIC) architecture) [32], consisting of 60 standard cores clocked at 1090 MHz and with full cache coherency across all cores. Each core offers four-way simultaneous multithreading (SMT) and 512-bit-wide SIMD vectors, which corresponds to 8 double-precision or 16 single-precision floating-point numbers. Each core has a fully coherent 32 KB L1 instruction cache, a 32 KB L1 data cache, and a 512KB unified L2 cache. The coprocessor card contains 8 GB of memory, and is connected via a PCI Express bus to a Westmere host running CentoOS 6.3 and with 64 GB of host main memory.

Setup and Measurement. For power measurement, we relied on the system management utility `micsmc` (v. 4346-16) designed for monitoring and managing Xeon Phi coprocessors. Currently, `micsmc` has a time resolution of 0.5 seconds and power measurement resolution of 1 W. The `icc` compiler (version 13.0.0 20120731), with `-mmic` (for native MIC libraries) and `-O3` optimization flags, was used to compile the code variants.

We configure each variant to run k times, where k is selected (separately for each kernel) so that the total run time is at least 50 seconds. Let $r_1(x), \ldots, r_k(x)$ denote a sequence of k run times for the variant x and let $(t_1(x), p_1(x)), \ldots, (t_m(x), p_m(x))$ denote a time-stamped sequence of power measurements obtained from the `micsmc` utility. To calculate power draw for the variant, we consider all power readings $(t_i(x), p_i(x))$ with $r_2(x) \leq t_i(x) \leq 50$ (with $r_1(x)$ omitted to remove any cold-cache effect and the time needed for memory allocation on the card). A 10-second sleep interval in between two successive executions ensures that the processor returns to a normal temperature and power state.

Results. Figure 3 shows the results obtained on the SPAPT problem `fdtd` (with an input size of 500×500). In these plots, we show the average run time, average power, and average energy required by the code variants. The results show a clear

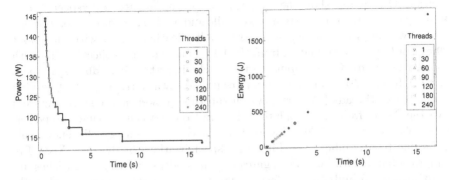

Fig. 4. Power, energy, and time for the sparse matrix multiplication kernel on Intel Xeon Phi

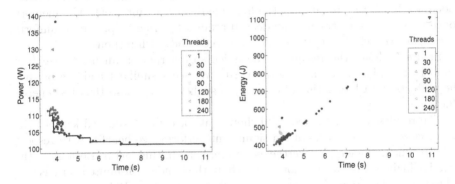

Fig. 5. Power, energy, and time for the quick sort kernel on Intel Xeon Phi

tradeoff between run time and power and the number of threads. The number of threads adopted has the largest impact on the power draw whereas the code transformation decisions have the largest impact on run time. We observe that the code variants are clustered based on the number of threads. The power draw increases by approximately 5 W with an increase of 30 threads. The corresponding energy plot does not show a tradeoff; it exhibits a race-to-idle condition [33]. Similar trends were seen for other SPAPT problems.

When there is no activity, the coprocessor enters into a complete idle state (PC-state), where it has an efficient power management module to save power and energy by power gating [34]. Currently, the power draw we observe is approximately 60 W. After transitioning from an idle state to the normal operating state, however, we observe high idle power (currently between 80 W and 90 W). Consequently, even a small run time reduction results in significant energy savings. We note that some previous works (e.g., [35,36]) subtract idle power from the power drawn during the normal operating state in order to consider only the increase in the power draw that can be attributed to a given workload's execution. Our figures show the view from a system operator's perspective and take into account the total system power (idle and workload computation power).

Next we focus on the sparse matrix multiplication kernel with the input trdheim, a large, sparse matrix from the UFL sparse matrix collection [37] with 1,935,324 nonzeros. Other inputs tested (including std1_Jac3_db, biplane-9, and t3dl from [37]) produced similar results. We study the impact of varying the number of threads (concurrency) on run time, power, and energy. Figure 4 shows the Pareto front. Although there is a tradeoff between run time and power, we can observe race-to-idle behavior when it comes to energy efficiency. This can be due to a number of architectural specializations of the Intel Xeon Phi to improve bandwidth [32]. The aggregate bandwidths of L1 and L2 caches are approximately 15 and 7 times faster than the aggregate memory bandwidth, respectively. A 16-stream hardware prefetcher is used to improve the cache hits. It uses a special instruction called "streaming store" that allows the cores to write an entire cache line without reading it first. The interconnect has a 64-byte-wide data block ring to support the high bandwidth requirement. The memory controllers are symmetrically interleaved around the ring to provide a uniform access pattern, which eventually increases the bandwidth response.

Figure 5 shows the results of the quick sort kernel on an input size (the number of random integers to sort) of 10^7. We see a similar trend except that the variants with larger thread counts are slightly slower and thus less energy efficient.

The results from Intel Xeon Phi show that for compute-limited kernels, the use of large core counts results in significant performance benefits with respect to both time and energy. Nevertheless, power is a limiting factor. Because of the effective high-bandwidth memory subsystem, the bandwidth-limited kernels also exhibit a similar trend. We note that in all our Intel Xeon Phi experiments, we observe that the maximum power is between 140 W and 145 W, irrespective of the type of kernel tested. The average power draw is determined by the number of threads used rather than the type of computation. This observation underscores the importance of developing workload-aware parallelization schemes for the next-generation systems with many cores, so that one uses only the number of cores (or threads) that the workload can actually exploit.

6.2   Intel Xeon E5530

We now describe our results on an Intel Xeon E5530 workstation with two quad-core processors. Each core has its own 32 KB L1 cache and 256 KB L2 cache; each of the quad-core processors has a shared 8 MB L3 cache (for a total of 16 MB of L3 for the 8 cores). The processors can be clocked at 1.60, 1.73, 1.86, 2.00, 2.13, 2.26, or 2.39 GHz. Processor clock frequency is changed by using the cpufreq-utils package [38] that is available with many popular Linux distributions.

Setup and Measurement. Component-level (CPUs and DIMMs) power measurements are collected by using a PowerMon2 apparatus [13]. PowerMon2 is a hardware and software framework designed to obtain fine-grained (up to 1,024 samples per second) current and voltage measurements for different components of a target system (e.g., CPUs, memory subsystem, disks, GPUs). We measure the system-level power draw using the WattsUp Pro power meter [39]. The power meter is a fairly inexpensive device, costing less than $150 at the time of this writing. Although the device is easy to use, it provides relatively coarse-grained measurements, roughly one reading per second. We implemented a command-line interface on top of the WattsUp driver to monitor and calculate the overall energy usage of an application.

Since we can measure system level power only at 1-second granularity, we configure the main computational loops to run k times, where k is selected (separately for each kernel/input) so that the total run time at the highest CPU frequency is more than five seconds. This ensures that we collect a sufficient number of power readings that can be attributed to the main computation of the kernels. The execution time reported in the paper is for these k iterations of the computation kernel. A post processing step sweeps through the data to attribute portions of the power measurements to the actual kernel loops. These power measurements are then averaged to determine the power draw for a single execution. To account for the unavoidable noise in this empirical data collection process, we measure each variant three times. The execution time and the power draw reported here are averages of these three runs.

Here we discuss results for the fdtd, jacobi, and bicgkernel SPAPT kernels. For fdtd, we selected two different input sizes: 512×512 (henceforth referenced as fdtd512) and 4096×4096 (fdtd4096). The selection decision was driven by our desire to ensure that we have test cases that stress the CPU and memory subsystem in different ways. Indeed, the last level cache misses per instruction for the base SPAPT case (no transformations) ranges from 1.8×10^{-4} for bicgkernel (making it a very compute-bound kernel) to 0.03 for fdtd4096 (making it a memory-bound kernel).

The code transformations applied to the kernels and the transformation spaces are taken as in [27]. However, we supplement the SPAPT decision spaces with a CPU clock frequency parameter. For each of the kernels, we select 300 (a number chosen simply to limit the time required for data collection) randomly selected variants from the code transformation space. Each of these variants is evaluated on all available clock frequencies.

Results. Figure 6 shows the Pareto fronts for the objectives time and total system power (as measured at the wall). The first observation that demonstrates the richness of the decision space is that, for a given hardware frequency parameter, the power range for the code variants is large. Tradeoffs between time and system-level power draw are evident. The power draw is lower for slower clock speeds, but this comes with a slow-down of the computation. Especially interesting is that the Pareto fronts show cases where one can reduce the power draw and not impact the performance substantially. Such behavior should be of high interest to co-design centers designing power-limited hardware targeted to specific types of computations.

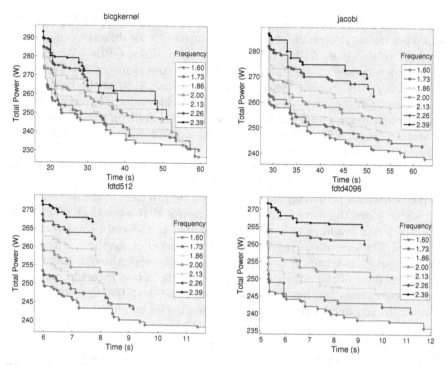

Fig. 6. Pareto fronts (for each clock frequency) for SPAPT kernels on Intel Xeon E5530 for the objectives time and total system power. The shaded area shows the Pareto front across all frequencies.

We can also examine particular transformation variants. Figure 7 shows the energy and time for the five highest-performing (as measured at the fastest clock rate) variants. This figure shows some interesting tradeoff decisions that we can explore. For example, for variant v1 of the memory-bound fdtd4096 kernel, we see that we can trade 0.8% loss in performance with 7.5% decrease in the energy consumption by running the kernel at the lowest frequency. The energy savings amount is not as significant for the compute-bound bicgkernel, where one can trade 1.2% loss in performance with 2.8% decrease in the energy consumption by running variant v1 at clock frequency 2.12GHz.

Figure 8 shows the Pareto fronts for each clock frequency for component-level power draws of the fdtd4096 kernel. When we analyze each of the fronts for different clock frequencies in isolation, we see a clear tradeoff between DIMM and CPU power draws for different code variants. We attribute this behavior intuitively to the optimizations that impact data motion. Code variants that have better data motion behavior reduce the stress on DIMMs thereby lowering the DIMM power. At the same time, better data motion leads to more compute work for the CPU, thereby raising its power demand. Such tradeoffs are of interest in studies for future architectures where one may consider constraining CPU draw

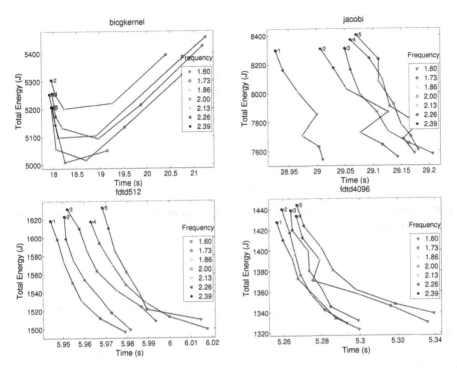

Fig. 7. Energy and time on Intel Xeon E5530 for the five highest-performing variants (v1–v5) from the SPAPT transformation space. The curves illustrate the tradeoff behavior as clock frequency is changed.

(e.g., for thermal/fault considerations) and/or DIMM draw (e.g., as a proxy for effective memory footprint or simulator of memory-starved systems).

6.3   Vesta IBM Blue Gene/Q

Vesta is a developmental platform for Mira, a 10-petaflop IBM Blue Gene/Q supercomputer [40] at Argonne. Vesta's architecture is the same as Mira's except that it has two compute racks (Mira has 48 racks). A rack has 32 node boards, each of which holds 32 compute cards. Each compute card comprises 16 compute cores of 1600 MHz PowerPC A2 processors with 16 GB RAM (1GB/core). In total, Vesta has 2,048 nodes (32,768 compute cores). The nodes are connected via a proprietary 5-D torus network. The compute nodes are water-cooled for thermal efficiency and run on CNK, a proprietary, lightweight kernel that minimizes OS noise.

Setup and Measurement. For the power measurements in BG/Q, we use a power profiling code that periodically samples power draw [41]. Because of cabling and control system limitations, the code requires a minimum partition size of 128 nodes, which spans 4 node boards. The profiler code runs one thread

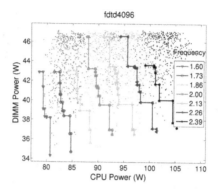

Fig. 8. Pareto fronts (for each clock frequency) on Intel Xeon E5530 for component-level power draws

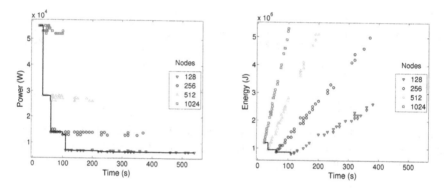

Fig. 9. Power, energy, and time for `miniFE` on BG/Q

on each node board and records the power on all the domains every 0.25 seconds along with a time stamp. We refer the reader to [41] for further details on the power profiling in BG/Q.

We set the input size (controlling the box domain from which a finite-element problem is assembled and solved) of `miniFE` to $n_x = n_y = n_z = 1000$. We considered a decision space with four parameters: two generic parameters that control the scaling behavior and two application-specific parameters. The generic parameters are the number of nodes ({128, 256, 512, 1024}) and the number of threads per core (either 8 (one thread every other core) or 16 (one thread per core)). The two `miniFE` specific parameters are the percentage of unbalance in the decomposition ({5, 10, 20, 30, 40, 50, 60, 70, 80, 90}) and a Boolean decision parameter ({Yes, No}) that controls whether matrix-vector products are performed with overlapping communication and computation. In total, we had 160 code variants for the experimental analysis.

Results. The results in Figure 9 show that there are tradeoffs between time to completion and both power and energy. As expected, increasing the node count decreases the time to completion but increases the power draw. In addition to the workload power, the significant increase in the power draw can be attributed to the fact that each node board consumes an idle power of roughly 1500 W [41]. The node count of 1024 uses 32 node boards, but 128 uses only 4 node boards. Concerning energy, the best parameter configuration within each node count provides a tradeoff between time to completion and energy consumption. Within a given node count, however, the fastest code variant consumes the least energy.

7 Conclusions and Outlook

In this paper we have provided a formalism for multi objective optimization studies of broad applicability in autotuning, architecture design, and other areas of HPC. With a focus on time, power, and energy, we illustrated that a multi objective analysis provides richer insight than do constrained and single-objective formulations. We have also contributed a significant empirical study, spanning a diverse set of platforms, power measurement technologies, kernels, and decision spaces. Our findings showed that in some settings objectives are strictly correlated and there is a single, "ideal" decision point; in others, significant tradeoffs exist.

A key component in most autotuning frameworks is the search algorithm that carefully orchestrates the selection and evaluation of various parameters to optimize given (multiple) objectives. Measuring the quality of a parameter configuration in the decision space is crucial for any search algorithm. Our multi objective optimization framework can enable the search algorithm to compare the quality of the parameter configurations in the context of conflicting multiple objectives.

Future work includes characterizing settings where empirical tradeoffs agree with those predicted by models (e.g., the roofline work in [9]) and where relationships between objectives are not as well understood. Significant opportunities exist for studying the tradeoffs among additional objectives; we especially mention resiliency since its relationship to power-based and temperature-based objectives is expected to be a prime concern in future extreme-scale systems [1].

Acknowledgments. Support for this work was provided through the Scientific Discovery through Advanced Computing (SciDAC) program funded by the U.S. Department of Energy, Office of Science, Advanced Scientific Computing Research. This research used the computational resources of the Argonne Leadership Computing Facility under a Director's discretionary allocation. We thank Paul Hovland and Laura Carrington for valuable discussions and Kazutomo Yoshii for insights on the power monitoring systems of BG/Q and Intel Xeon Phi and valuable feedback.

References

1. Kogge, P.: The tops in flops. IEEE Spectrum **48**(2), 48–54 (2011)
2. TOP500 List: June 2013 Report, http://www.top500.org

3. Balaprakash, P., Wild, S.M., Hovland, P.D.: Can search algorithms save large-scale automatic performance tuning? Procedia Computer Science **4**, 2136–2145 (2011)
4. Kadayif, I., Kandemir, M., Vijaykrishnan, N., Irwin, M., Sivasubramaniam, A.: EAC: A compiler framework for high-level energy estimation and optimization. In: Proceedings of the Design, Automation and Test in Europe Conference and Exhibition, pp. 436–442. IEEE (2002)
5. Kodi, A., Louri, A.: Performance adaptive power-aware reconfigurable optical interconnects for high-performance computing (HPC) systems. In: Proceedings of the 2007 ACM/IEEE Conference on Supercomputing (SC), pp. 1–12 (2007)
6. Ahmad, I., Ranka, S., Khan, S.U.: Using game theory for scheduling tasks on multi-core processors for simultaneous optimization of performance and energy. In: IEEE International Symposium on Parallel and Distributed Processing (IPDPS), pp. 1–6. IEEE (2008)
7. Azizi, O., Mahesri, A., Lee, B.C., Patel, S.J., Horowitz, M.: Energy-performance tradeoffs in processor architecture and circuit design: A marginal cost analysis. In: ACM SIGARCH Computer Architecture News, vol. 38, pp. 26–36. ACM (2010)
8. Tiwari, A., Laurenzano, M.A., Carrington, L., Snavely, A.: Modeling power and energy usage of HPC kernels. In: IEEE 26th International Parallel and Distributed Processing Symposium Workshops & PhD Forum (IPDPSW), pp. 990–998. IEEE (2012)
9. Choi, J.W., Bedard, D., Fowler, R., Vuduc, R.: A roofline model of energy. In: 2013 IEEE 27th International Symposium on Parallel Distributed Processing (IPDPS), pp. 661–672. IEEE (May 2013)
10. Ascia, G., Catania, V., Palesi, M.: Multi-objective mapping for mesh-based NoC architectures. In: Proceedings of the 2nd IEEE/ACM/IFIP International Conference on Hardware/Software Codesign and System Synthesis, pp. 182–187. ACM (2004)
11. Jahr, R., Ungerer, T., Calborean, H., Vintan, L.: Automatic multi-objective optimization of parameters for hardware and code optimizations. In: International Conference on High Performance Computing and Simulation (HPCS), pp. 308–316. IEEE (2011)
12. Park, S., Jiang, W., Zhou, Y., Adve, S.: Managing energy-performance tradeoffs for multithreaded applications on multiprocessor architectures. In: ACM SIGMETRICS Performance Evaluation Review, vol. 35, pp. 169–180 (2007)
13. Bedard, D., Lim, M.Y., Fowler, R., Porterfield, A.: PowerMon: Fine-grained and integrated power monitoring for commodity computer systems. In: IEEE SoutheastCon 2010, pp. 479–484 (2010)
14. Li, D., de Supinski, B.R., Schulz, M., Cameron, K., Nikolopoulos, D.S.: Hybrid MPI/OpenMP power-aware computing. In: IEEE International Symposium on Parallel & Distributed Processing (IPDPS), pp. 1–12. IEEE (2010)
15. Rahman, S.F., Guo, J., Yi, Q.: Automated empirical tuning of scientific codes for performance and power consumption. In: Proceedings of the 6th International Conference on High Performance and Embedded Architectures and Compilers, pp. 107–116. ACM (2011)
16. Lively, C., Wu, X., Taylor, V., Moore, S., Chang, H.C., Cameron, K.: Energy and performance characteristics of different parallel implementations of scientific applications on multicore systems. International Journal of High Performance Computing Applications **25**(3), 342–350 (2011)

17. Tăpuş, C., Chung, I.H., Hollingsworth, J.K.: Active harmony: towards automated performance tuning. In: Proceedings of the 2002 ACM/IEEE conference on Supercomputing, Supercomputing 2002, pp. 1–11. IEEE Computer Society Press, Los Alamitos (2002)
18. Tiwari, A., Laurenzano, M.A., Carrington, L., Snavely, A.: Auto-tuning for energy usage in scientific applications. In: Alexander, M., et al. (eds.) Euro-Par 2011, Part II. LNCS, vol. 7156, pp. 178–187. Springer, Heidelberg (2012)
19. Laros III, J.H.: Measuring and tuning energy efficiency on large scale high performance computing platforms. Technical Report SAND2011-5702, Sandia National Laboratories (August 2011)
20. Heydemann, K., Bodin, F.: Iterative compilation for two antagonistic criteria: Application to code size and performance. In: Proceedings of the 4th Workshop on Optimizations for DSP and Embedded Systems (2006)
21. Hoste, K., Eeckhout, L.: Cole: Compiler optimization level exploration. In: Proceedings of the 6th Annual IEEE/ACM International Symposium on Code Generation and Optimization, pp. 165–174. ACM (2008)
22. Lokuciejewski, P., Plazar, S., Falk, H., Marwedel, P., Thiele, L.: Multi-objective exploration of compiler optimizations for real-time systems. In: 13th IEEE International Symposium on Object/Component/Service-Oriented Real-Time Distributed Computing (ISORC), pp. 115–122 (2010)
23. Hoste, K., Georges, A., Eeckhout, L.: Automated just-in-time compiler tuning. In: Proceedings of the 8th Annual IEEE/ACM International Symposium on Code Generation and Optimization (CGO), pp. 62–72. ACM (2010)
24. Fursin, G., Kashnikov, Y., Memon, A.W., Chamski, Z., Temam, O., Namolaru, M., Yom-Tov, E., Mendelson, B., Zaks, A., Courtois, E., et al.: Milepost gcc: Machine learning enabled self-tuning compiler. International Journal of Parallel Programming 39(3), 296–327 (2011)
25. Jordan, H., Thoman, P., Durillo, J.J., Pellegrini, S., Gschwandtner, P., Fahringer, T., Moritsch, H.: A multi-objective auto-tuning framework for parallel codes. In: Proceedings of the International Conference on High Performance Computing, Networking, Storage and Analysis (SC), pp. 10:1–10:12. IEEE Computer Society Press, Los Alamitos (2012)
26. Ehrgott, M.: Multicriteria Optimization. 2nd edn. Springer (2005)
27. Balaprakash, P., Wild, S.M., Norris, B.: SPAPT: Search problems in automatic performance tuning. Procedia Computer Science 9, 1959–1968 (2012)
28. Kaiser, A., Williams, S., Madduri, K., Ibrahim, K., Bailey, D., Demmel, J., Strohmaier, E.: TORCH computational reference kernels: A testbed for computer science research. Technical Report UCB/EECS-2010-144, EECS Department, University of California, Berkeley (December 2010)
29. Davis, T.A.: Direct methods for sparse linear systems, vol. 2. SIAM (2006)
30. Heroux, M.A., Doerer, D.W., Crozier, P.S., Willenbring, J.M.: Improving performance via mini-applications. Technical Report SAND2009-5574, Sandia National Laboratories (September 2009)
31. Norris, B., Hartono, A., Gropp, W.: Annotations for productivity and performance portability. In: Petascale Computing: Algorithms and Applications. Computational Science, pp. 443–462. Chapman & Hall/CRC Press (2007)
32. Intel Xeon Phi Coprocessor - the Architecture: http://software.intel.com/en-us/articles/intel-xeon-phi-coprocessor-codename-knights-corner
33. Albers, S., Antoniadis, A.: Race to idle: New algorithms for speed scaling with a sleep state. In: Proceedings of the 23rd Annual ACM-SIAM Symposium on Discrete Algorithms (SODA), pp. 1266–1285. SIAM (2012)

34. Intel Xeon Phi Coprocessor System Software Developers Guide: http://software.intel.com/en-us/articles/ intel-xeon-phi-coprocessor-system-software-developers-guide
35. Alonso, P., Dolz, M.F., Igual, F.D., Mayo, R., Quintana-Orti, E.S.: Saving energy in the LU factorization with partial pivoting on multi-core processors. In: 20th Euromicro International Conference on Parallel, Distributed and Network-Based Processing (PDP), pp. 353–358. IEEE (2012)
36. Springer, R., Lowenthal, D.K., Rountree, B., Freeh, V.W.: Minimizing execution time in MPI programs on an energy-constrained, power-scalable cluster. In: Proceedings of the Eleventh ACM SIGPLAN Symposium on Principles and Practice of Parallel Programming, pp. 230–238. ACM (2006)
37. Davis, T.A., Hu, Y.: The University of Florida sparse matrix collection. ACM Transactions on Mathematical Software **38**(1) 1:1–1:25 (2011)
38. CPU Freq. Scaling, https://wiki.archlinux.org/index.php/Cpufrequtils
39. WattsUp? Meters, https://www.wattsupmeters.com/
40. IBM System Blue Gene Solution - Overview, http://www-03.ibm.com/systems/ technicalcomputing/solutions/bluegene/
41. Yoshii, K., Iskra, K., Gupta, R., Beckman, P., Vishwanath, V., Yu, C., Coghlan, S.: Evaluating power-monitoring capabilities on IBM Blue Gene/P and Blue Gene/Q. In: IEEE International Conference on Cluster Computing (CLUSTER), pp. 36–44. IEEE (2012)

Performance Tuning of Fock Matrix and Two-Electron Integral Calculations for NWChem on Leading HPC Platforms

Hongzhang Shan[1]([✉]), Brian Austin[1], Wibe De Jong[1], Leonid Oliker[1], N.J. Wright[1], and Edoardo Apra[2]

[1] CRD and NERSC Lawrence Berkeley National Laboratory,
Berkeley, CA 94720, USA
{hshan,baustin,wadejong,loliker,njwright}@lbl.gov
[2] WR Wiley Environmental Molecular Sciences Laboratory, Pacific Northwest
National Laboratory, Richland, WA 99352, USA
edoardo.apra@pnnl.gov

Abstract. Attaining performance in the evaluation of two-electron repulsion integrals and constructing the Fock matrix is of considerable importance to the computational chemistry community. Due to its numerical complexity improving the performance behavior across a variety of leading supercomputing platforms is an increasing challenge due to the significant diversity in high-performance computing architectures. In this paper, we present our successful tuning methodology for these important numerical methods on the Cray XE6, the Cray XC30, the IBM BG/Q, as well as the Intel Xeon Phi. Our optimization schemes leverage key architectural features including vectorization and simultaneous multithreading, and results in speedups of up to 2.5x compared with the original implementation.

1 Introduction

NWChem [18] is an open source computational chemistry package for solving challenging chemical and biological problems using large scale ab initio molecular simulations. Since its open-source release three years ago, NWChem has been downloaded over 55,000 times world wide and played an important role in solving a wide range of complex scientific problems. The goal of NWChem is to not only provide its users a computational chemistry software suite, but also to provide fast time to solution on major high-performance computing (HPC) platforms. It is essential for a software tools like NWChem to effectively utilize a broad variety of supercomputing platforms in order for scientists to tackle increasingly larger and more complex problem configurations.

Moden HPC platforms represent diverse sets of architectural configurations, as clearly seen in different processor technologies and custom interconnects of the current top five fastest computers in the world [17]. The No.1 system employs Xeon E5-2682 and Xeon Phi (Intel MIC) processors while the No. 2 system uses

© Springer International Publishing Switzerland 2014
S. Jarvis et al. (Eds.): PMBS 2013 Workshops, LNCS 8551, pp. 261–280, 2014.
DOI: 10.1007/978-3-319-10214-6_13

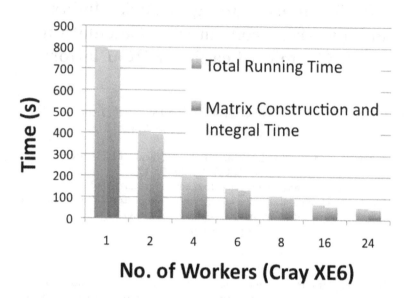

Fig. 1. The total running times and the corresponding fock matrix construction and integral calculation times on Hopper

Opteron 6274 and Tesla K20X processors. These two platforms follow similar host+accelerator design patterns. The No. 3 and 5 systems use IBM PowerPC A2 processors (IBM BG/Q), and No. 4 uses SPARC64 processors. The diversity of the high performance computing architectures poses a great challenge for NWChem to make efficient use of these designs.

In this work, we address this issue by tuning the performance of NWChem on three currently deployed HPC platforms, the Cray XE6, the Cray XC30, the IBM BG/Q, and the Intel MIC. Although NWChem provides extensive capabilities for large scale chemical simulations, we focus on one critical component: the effective evaluation of two-electron repulsion integrals with the TEXAS integral module that are needed for the construction of the Fock matrix needed in the Hartree-Fock (HF) and Density Functional Theory calculations [7]. This capability consists of about 70k lines of code, while the entire NWChem distribution includes more than 3.5 million lines. Figure 1 shows the total running times of our NWChem benchmark c20h42.nw on the 24-core node of Hopper, the Cray XE6 platform. This benchmark is designed to measure the performance of the Hartree-Fock calculations on a single node with a reasonable runtime for tuning purposes. Each worker is a thread created by the Global Array Toolkit [4], which is responsible for the parallel communication within NWChem. The total running times are dominated by the Fock matrix construction and primarily the two-electron integral evaluation.

By exploring the performance on these four platforms, our goal is to answer the following questions and infer guidelines for future performance tuning.

Table 1. The Important Node Characteristics of the Four Platforms

	Cray XE6	Cray XC30	Intel Xeon Phi	IBM BG/Q
Node	Two 12-core AMD Opteron (24) Two Sockets	Two 8-core Intel Xeon (16) Two Sockets	60 Intel MICs 5110P Multi Sockets	16 IBM Power A2 SMP
Memory	32GB DDR3 800MHz 51.2 GB/s	64GB DDR3 1666MHz 106 GB/s	8GB GDDR5 2500MHz 352 GB/s	16GB DDR3 1333MHz 42.6 GB/s
Core	2.1 GHz 1 Thread 8.4 GF/s SSE	2.6 GHz 2 Hyper Threads 20.8 GF/s 4-way SIMD	1.05 GHz 4 Hyper Threads 16.8 GF/s 8-way SIMD	1.6 GHz 4 Hyper Threads 12.8 GF/s Quad FU
Cache	L1: 64KB L2: 512KB L3: 6MB/6 Cores	L1: 32KB L2: 256KB L3: 20MB/8 Cores	L1: 32KB L2: 512KB	L1: 16KB L2: 32MB(shared)

(I) What kind of optimizations are needed? *(II)* How effective are these optimizations on each specific platforms? *(III)* How should the code be adapted to take maximum advantage of the specific hardware features, such as vectorization and simultaneous multithreading? *(IV)* Is there a consistent approach to optimize the performance across all four platforms? Our insights to these questions are discussed and summarized in Sections 8 and 10.

The rest of the paper is organized as follows. In Section 2, we describe the four experimental platforms and in Section 3 we briefly introduce the background for Fock matrix construction and two electron repulsion integral calculations. The tunning processes and the corresponding performance improvements on the four platforms are discussed in Sections 4, 5, 6, 7 individually. We summarize the tuning results in Section 8. Related work is discussed in Section 9. Finally we summarize our conclusions and outline future work in Section 10.

2   Experimental Platforms

To evaluate the impact of our optimizations, we conduct experiments on four leading platforms, the Cray XE6, the Cray XC30, the Intel MIC, and the IBM BG/Q. Below, we briefly describe the four platforms we used and Table 1 summarizes the important node characteristics of these four different architectures.

2.1   The Cray XE6, Hopper

The Cray XE6 platform, called Hopper [8], is located at NERSC and consists of 6,384 dual-socket nodes connected by a Cray Gemini high-speed network. Each socket within a node contains an AMD "Magny-Cours" processor with 12 cores running at 2.1 GHz. Each Magny-Cours package is itself a MCM (Multi-Chip Module) containing two hex-core dies connected via HyperTransport. Each die has its own memory controller that is connected to two 4-GB DIMMS. This means each node can effectively be viewed as having four chips and there are large potential performance penalties for crossing the NUMA domains. Each node has 32GB DDR3-800 memory. The peak data memory bandwidth is 51.2GB/s. Each core has 64KB L1 cache and 512KB L2 cache. The six cores on the same die share 6MB L3 cache. The compiler is PGI Fortran 64-bit compiler version 13.3-0.

2.2 The Cray XC30, Edison

The Cray XC30 platform, called Edison [2], is also located at NERSC. The first stage of the machine contains 664 compute nodes connected together by the custom Cray Aries high-speed interconnect. Each node is configured with 64GB DDR3-1666 memory. The peak memory bandwidth is 106 GB/s. Each node has two 8-core intel Sandy Bridge processors (16 cores total) running at the speed of 2.6 GHz. Each core supports two hyper threads and supports 4-way SIMD vector computations. Each core has 64KB L1 cache and 256KB L2 cache. The 8-core processor has 20MB L3 cache shared by all eight cores. The compiler we used is Intel Fortran 64 Compiler XE version 13.0.1.

2.3 The Intel MIC, Babbage

The Intel MIC platform, called Babbage [12], is a new test platform located at NERSC. There are total 45 compute nodes connected by the Infiniband interconnect. Each node contains two MIC cards and two Intel Xeon host processors. Each MIC card contains 60 cores running at the speed of 1.05 GHz and 8 GB GDDR5-2500 memory. The peak memory bandwidth is 352GB/s. However, using STREAM benchmark, the best achievable bandwidth is only around 170GB/s. Each core supports 4 hardware threads and an 8-way SIMD vector processing unit capable of delivering 16.8 GF/s floating-point computations. Each core has 32KB L1 cache and 512KB L2 cache. The compiler we used is Intel Fortran 64 Compiler XE version 13.0.1.

2.4 The IBM BG/Q, Mira

The IBM BG/Q platform, called Mira [13], is located at Argonne National Laboratory. Each node contains 16 compute cores (IBM Power A2) and 1 supplemental core to handle operating system tasks. The memory size on a node is 16 GB DDR3-1333 with 42.6 GB/s peak memory bandwidth. Each core supports 4-way simultaneous multithreading and a QUAD SIMD floating point processing unit capable of 12.8 GF/s computing speed. Each core has 16KB L1 data cache and all 16 cores share the 32MB L2 cache. The memory on the node follows SMP (symmetric multiprocessing) not NUMA (nonuniform memory access) architecture. The compiler is IBM XL fortran compiler for BG/Q version 14.1.

3 Background for Fock Matrix Construction and Two-Electron Integral Evaluation

In quantum physics or chemistry, the Hartree-Fock method [7] is a fundamental approach to approximate the solution of Schrödinger's equation [5,20,21]. During this approach, a matrix called the Fock matrix (F) needs to be repeatedly constructed. It is a two-dimensional matrix and its dimensional size is determined by the number of basis functions, N. Elements of the Fock matrix are computed by the following formula [3]:

$$F_{ij} = h_{ij} + \sum_{k=1}^{N} \sum_{l=1}^{N} D_{kl}((ij|kl) - \frac{1}{2}(ik|jl))$$

where h is one-electron Hamiltonian, D is the one-particle density matrix, and $(ij|kl)$ is a two-electron repulsion integral. The time to construct the Fock matrix is dominated by the computation of these integrals. In NWChem, the most heavily used module to calculate the integrals is called TEXAS [19]. Given this equation, the total number of quartet integrals to build the matrix F could reach $O(N^4)$ making it computationally prohibitive. However, by applying molecular and permutation symmetry as well as screening for small values, the complexity can be reduced to $O(N^2 - N^3)$.

The computation of each single or block of integrals is an independent operation that can be easily parallelized. However, the computational cost of each individual integral differs substantially depending on the angular momentums of the corresponding basis functions. Therefore, a dynamic load balancing method is used to ensure that all parallel workers perform equal amounts of integral computations. The Fortran pseudo-code of this approach is shown in Listing 1. The algorithm utilizes a global task counter to distribute work to a parallel worker that is available. To avoid network pressure on the global task counter, in each iteration a runtime determined block of tasks gets assigned to a parallel worker.

Listing 13.1. Dynamic Load Balancing Method

```
my_task      = global_task_counter(task_block_size)
current_task = 0
do ijkl = 2*ntype, 2, -1
  do ij = min(ntype, ijkl-1), max(1, ijkl-ntype), -1
    kl = ijkl - ij
    if (my_task .eq. current_task) then
        call calculate_integral_block()
        call add_intgrals_to_Fock()
        my_task = global_task_counter(task_block_size)
    endif
    current_task = current_task + 1
  enddo
enddo
```

For efficiency, blocks of integrals with similar characteristics are passed to TEXAS integral package. The goal is to enable sharing and reuse of temporary data for integrals in the same block. However, the number of integrals can efficiently be performed concurrently is limited by the cache size and memory requirements. Therefore, we implement two levels of blocking. The higher level is used to assign a block of integrals to the parallel workers. The lower level is used to decide how many integrals can actually be done at the same time in the TEXAS integral package. The integrals are calculated according to the Obara-Saika (OS) method [14]. The algorithm [19,22] also uses the method proposed by Tracy Hamilton (TRACY) to shift angular momenta from electron 1 (centers 1, 2) to electron 2 (centers 3,4). If the sum of the angular momentum of the quartet shells is less than two, the integrals are handled by a special fast path.

Our performance tuning work focused on the intra-node performance. The inter-node communication of NWChem is handled by a separate software package called the Global Array Toolkit [4]. Optimizing the inter-node communication performance is out of the scope of this paper. Actually, each integral calculation does not involve any communication. Only constructing the Fock matrix does.

4   Performance Tuning on Hopper

The initial performance of building the Fock matrix and calculating the integrals for the benchmark and the expected perfect linear scaling performance are shown in Figure 2. We note that as the number of workers increases, the running time is reduced linearly. However, for large number of workers scaling performance deteriorates, especially when utilizing all 24 cores/node of the NERSC Hopper system.

4.1   Task Granularity for Dynamic Load Balancing

Profiling results indicate that the non-perfect linear scaling behavior is related with the dynamic load balancing approach. In order to reduce the number of task requests, we assign a chunk of tasks to each worker (instead of just one). There is a thus a balance between the request overhead and the assigned task granularity (smaller granularities result in higher overheads to request those tasks). The baseline version NWChem computes the task granularity using an algorithm based on the number of workers, the request overhead, and the problem characteristics. However, developing a perfect algorithm is challenging due to two reasons. First, the time to finish a task may differ substantially, sometimes even by orders of magnitude. Second, a chunk of tasks assigned to a worker together may further exacerbate the situation.

The granularity size selected by the default algorithm shows inefficiencies when relatively large number of parallel workers are applied. The selected chunk size tends to be too big, leading to the load imbalance. To improve the performance, we modify the default algorithm so that a smaller granularity size can be chosen. Fortunately, the overhead for requesting the tasks increased only

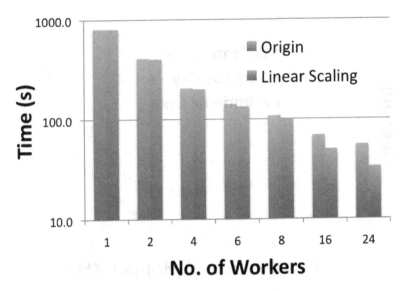

Fig. 2. The initial performance of building Fock matrix and evaluating two-electron integrals on Hopper

slightly. The performance improvement is shown in Figure 3 labeled with Task Granularity. For a fully saturated node of 24 workers, our optimization approach improves performance by over 40%.

4.2 Data Locality

As mentioned in Section 3, the TEXAS integral code does not compute the two-electron integrals one by one. Instead, integrals with similar types are organized in one block and computed together so that intermediate results can be reused. There are some overheads to create the related data structures and perform preliminary computations. If the number of integrals in the block is small, the overhead cannot be effectively amortized. More importantly, array access performance is directly related to this number; small sizes may cause runtimes to suffer due to poor spatial data locality.

By examining the profiling analysis we found that there exist many cases with small block sizes. In extreme cases, the block size is equal to one, leading to poor data locality and low efficiency of the blocking structure. This occurs with the special handling of integrals consisting of only s, p, and sp basis functions. To improve the data locality and the efficiency of the block structure, we updated the code to avoid generating block lengths of one. The performance improvement results are shown in Figure 3 labeled with Data Locality. Results show that performance has been further improved by 10-18% for all configurations. Note that the graph displays cumulative performance improvements.

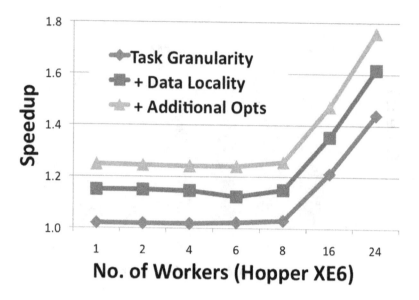

Fig. 3. The cumulative performance improvement relative to the original code on the Cray XE6

4.3   Other Optimizations

We additionally performed several other optimizations. Although the effect of each individual optimization is not significant, the combined effect results in an additional 10% improvement, seen in Figure 3 as "Additional Opts". First, we examined function *uniq_pairs*, which is used to compute the unique ij or kl pairs appeared in a block of integrals and sort them in ascending order. The original implementation first collects all pairs, sorts them using a algorithm similar to quicksort, and stores the unique pairs in an array. However, we found that many pairs are redundant, and therefore developed a simple hash algorithm to partially remove the redundant data first and then sort the remaining data. The number of pairs to be sorted has thus been reduced greatly, resulting in a 75% running time reduction for this function, which accounted for 2-3% of the total program run time.

Other optimizations focused on applying loop transformations to several time-consuming loops. Techniques include loop un-rolling and blocking and data pre-fetching. Although compilers may perform these optimizations automatically, our goal was to help compilers generate more efficient code. The performance impact varied across the loops, sometimes leading to additional small improvements. Finally, we optimized several statements to remove redundant computations.

By combining all these optimization efforts, overall performance improved significantly, by 25-75% relative to the original implementation, as shown in Figure 3.

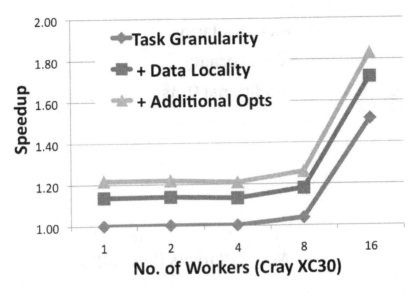

Fig. 4. The cumulative performance improvement relative to the original code on the Cray XC30

5 Performance Tuning on Edison

The same set of optimization were also applied to Edison. Figure 4 shows the cumulative performance improvement of our optimization schemes. Similar to Hopper, when more than eight workers are active, the original implementation suffers from load imbalance. By reducing the task granularity, the performance improves up to 50% when 16 workers are used. Optimizing data locality further improved the performance by approximately 13-20%. Finally, other specific optimizations discussed in Section 4 resulted in performance gains of another 8%. On Edison, results show that loop transformations, such as unrolling and blocking, has a much smaller performance impact compared with Hopper. This is encouraging for application developers, since these kind of optimizations are not only difficult but also result in less readable code. Overall, the final accumulative performance improvement for all optimizations on Edison resulted in an improvement of 1.2 – 1.8x compared to the original version.

5.1 Simultaneous Multi-threading

One major architectural difference between Edison and Hopper is that Edison uses Intel Sandy Bridge processors that supports hyper-threading. Each physical core can thus be treated as two logical cores, running two threads concurrently, allowing us to run up to 32 workers per node. Using the optimized implementation with hyper-threading, with 32 workers per node, results in an additional

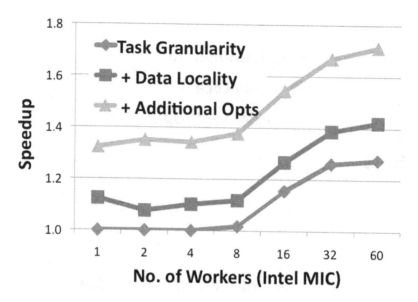

Fig. 5. The cumulative performance improvement relative to the original code on the Intel MIC

performance improvement of approximately 14% compared with 16 workers (in single-threaded mode).

6   Performance Tuning on Babbage

The Intel MIC architecture supports two programming modes, allowing either execution on the host with selected code sections offloaded to the Intel MIC accelerator (offload mode) or native execution on the Intel MIC architecture (native mode). In this work, we focus our effort to the native mode.

Figure 5 shows the performance improvement on the Intel MIC architecture, which contains 60 physical cores per card. Load balancing is once again a significant bottleneck, and adjusting the task granularity, allows a performance improvement of up to 28% when 60 workers are used. Increasing data locality is additionally effective, further improving the performance about 10% across all shown configurations. Finally, the performance effect of additional optimizations become much more prominent, delivering 20 - 30% performance gains, due mainly to their effects on compiler-driven vectorization. Similar to the Edison platform, manual loop transformations do not show a performance impact.

6.1   Vectorization

One important feature of the Intel MIC architecture is its vector processing unit. Each core has 32 512-bit-wide vector registers and its vector unit can execute

Table 2. The total running times for NWChem with and without vectorization on the Intel MIC

No. of Workers	1	2	4	8	16	32	60
With Vec	4170	2080	1050	517	261	133	72
Without Vec	5380	2610	1310	665	333	167	92

8-wide double precision SIMD instructions in a single clock, providing 1TFlops/s peak floating-point performance per card. Making effective use of the vector processing unit is the key to obtain high-performance on this architecture, and can be obtained via two approaches. The first is the use of low-level intrinsic functions to explicitly implement vectorization, while the second leverages the compilers and compiler directives to vectorize the code. We focus on the second approach to maintain a general and portable code version (although more extensive vectorization is likely possible via the intrinsic approach). Note that there are some loops that are not vectorizable due to serialization, data dependence, complex code structures, or other reasons. By adding directives or transforming the loop bodies, the compiler is able to vectorize certain key loops. (The effectiveness of the transformations was determined from the vectorization report generated by the Intel compiler's -vec-report6 option.) The transformations include using temporary arrays to assemble data for vectorization, splitting the loop body to separate the vectorizable and non-vectoriable codes.

One important parameter that effects the performance of the vector processing units is the vector length. Recall that in the TEXAS implementation, the number of quartet integrals that can be computed together is decided by a block size. This number is carefully decided by TEXAS based on cache size and shell characteristics. It is also the length of a several important data arrays. Increasing this number may potentially improve the vector units performance, while simultaneously degrade data reuse and cache efficiency. We experimented with different sizes and found that the best overall performance is obtained when the default size is quadruped. Further increasing this number causes the cache performance to degrade significantly, especially for the recursive OBASAI functions.

Table 2 shows impact of vectorization for NWChem by comparing vectorized results with compiler disabled vectorization via the no-vec option. Results show that vectorization improves performance by approximately 22%. For a more detailed analysis, we explored the sequential running times of the top ten subroutines in the TEXAS integral package with and without vectorization in Figure 6, which account for about 73% of the total running times. Function *erintsp* is used to compute the integrals when the sum of the angular momentum of the quartet shells is less than two. The other functions, except *destbul*, are used to implement the OBASAI and TRACY algorithms, which are applied when the sum is not less than two. The *destbul* function is used to put the non-zero integral results and corresponding shell labels from a selected block of quartets of shells into a buffer.

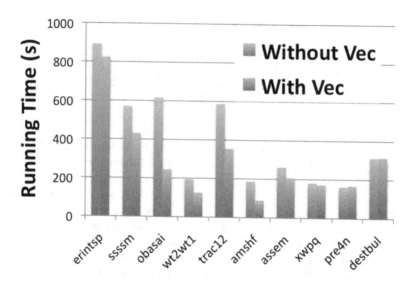

Fig. 6. The running times for the top ten functions in TEXAS integral package with and without vectorization on the Intel MIC

- ERINTSP: Most of its time is spent on the FM function which returns the incomplete gamma function fm(x). Based on the value of its input variable x, FM jumps to different branches depending on conditionals. The complex code structure cannot be vectorized directly. By profiling, we discovered that the most often executed branch is the one with time-consuming computation $\frac{1}{\sqrt{(x)}}$. Our optimization thus performed the inverse square root for all the input variables in advance and stored the results in a temporary array. Therefore the results can be directly accessed from the temporary array. The advantage is that the compiler can automatically apply a vectorized implementation of the inverse square root operation. Unfortunately, for some input values, the computation is unnecessary. The final performance results indicate that overall this change is a valuable optimization on the MIC platform.
- SSSSM: Calculates the integrals of the form $(s, s|s, s)(m)$ using the FM function. Compared with `erintsp`, its running time is more heavily dependent on the performance of the inverse square root operations. A similar optimization as in `erintsp` has been performed.
- OBASAI: Computes the integrals of the form $(i + j + k + l, s|s, s)(m)$ or $(s, s|i + j + k + l, s)(m)$ based on the results of `ssssm`. Among the top ten functions, this one benefits most from vectorization, showing an improvement of 2.5x. The innermost loops are dominated by uni-stride data access and can be automatically vectorized by compiler.
- WT2WT1, AMSHF: Are dominated by data movement with segmented uni-stride data access, and require compiler directives to vectorize the code.

- TRAC12: Calculates the integrals of the form $(i + j, s|k + l, s)(m)$ based on **obasai** results by shifting angular momenta from position 1 to 3 or 3 to 1. The innermost loops can be fully vectorized with uni-stride data access. However, some code transformations are required.
- XWPQ, PRE4N, ASSEM: Preprocess or postprocess data for Obasai and Tracy algorithms. Though most loops inside these functions can be vectorized, the data access is dominated by indirect, scattered data access due to integral screening. Memory performance is the bottleneck, not the floating-point operations, thus vectorization has little impact on performance. The improved performance of vectorized **assem** comes from some loops with uni-stride data access patterns.
- DESTBUL: Returns the results of non-zero integrals and corresponding labels. The code can not be easily vectorized due to data dependence.

Of the top ten functions, four routines (**obasai, wt2wt1, trac12, and amshf**) with uni-stride data access benefit directly from vectorization as the compiler can automatically vectorize the code. Some routines require compiler directives to guide the vectorization or perform source level loop transformations. Two other subroutines (**ssssm and erintsp**) need the introduction of temporary arrays to take advantage of the vectorized inverse square root function. Three other subroutines (**assem, xwpq, pre4n**) suffer from indirect, scattered data access and can not easily benefit from vectorization. The final function (**destbul**) cannot be vectorized due to data dependence.

Overall, significant effort has been dedicated to vectorizing each individual subroutine. Our observation is that the process of leveraging vectorization is not only time consuming but also extremely challenging to fully leverage. Future research into new algorithms that are better structured to utilize wide vector units could significantly improve the behavior of the two-electron integral evaluation algorithms.

6.2 Simultaneous Multi-threading

The Intel MIC architecture features many in-order cores on a single die, where each core also supports 4-way hyper-threading (4 hardware threads). However, the front-end of the pipeline can only issue up to 2 instructions per cycle, where the two instructions are issued by different threads. Therefore, at least two hardware threads are necessary to achieve the maximum issue rate. By running two workers per physical core (120 threads), using the optimized implementation, the running time can be reduced from 72 to 56 seconds — a 30% improvement. Unfortunately, we can not run more than two workers per physical core due to memory limitation. There is only 8GB memory per card, which seriously limits the total number of workers that can be run concurrently.

7 Performance Tuning on Mira

On the Mira BG/Q, the Global Array Toolkit [4] is built using communication network ARMCI-MPI. As a result, dynamic load balancing becomes very

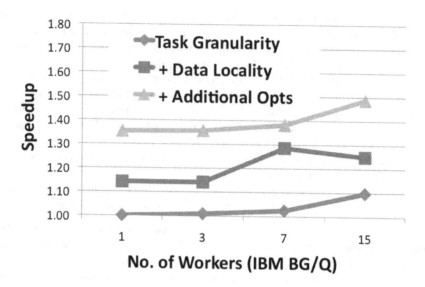

Fig. 7. The cumulative performance improvement relative to the original code on the IBM BG/Q

expensive. Initial results showed that more than 30% of the running time is spent on requesting tasks. This is related with MPI-2 RMA operation which does not support atomic operations. To reduce the overhead, we developed a PAMI (Parallel Active Message Interface [11]) interface using PAMI_Rmw function to request tasks. The overhead was therefore reduced to around 10%, however this is still a significant cost compared with other platforms. Using the MU (messaging unit) SPI (system programming interface) may improve performance and will be the subject of future investigation. Instead, we adopt a master-slave approach, which devotes one worker to responding to the task requests and not performing integral calculations. In this way, the overhead of requesting tasks becomes trivial. However, this is offset by the cost of lossing one worker for the integral calculation.

The performance improvement of our optimizations on the 16-core per node platform is shown in Figure 7. Recall that given the dedicated master thread, only an odd number of workers is available. Additionally we successfully applied all previously discusssed optimizations, resulting in an overall performance improvement of 35 - 49%.

7.1   Vectorization

The BG/Q architecture supports vectorization, where each core has a quad-vector double precision floating point unit called IBM QPX capable of 8 floating point operations per cycle. Compiler directives are provided to inform the compiler the conditions of data dependence and data alignment. However, we

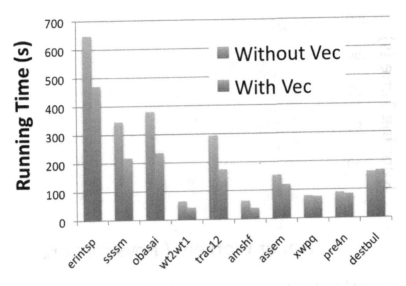

Fig. 8. The running times for top ten functions in TEXAS integral package with and without vectorization on the IBM BG/Q

observed that the requirements of BG/Q compiler derived vectorization is even more strict than on the Intel MIC architecture. The loops with indirect data access can not be automatically vectorized by the IBM compiler. Nonetheless, comparing the results of vectorized version and non-vectorized version, results show that the vectorized code delivers a 25% improvement compared with the non-vectorized version. Figure 8 shows the running times for top ten subroutines in the TEXAS integral package with and without vectorization on the BG/Q. The pattern of vectorization effect on these subroutines is similar to that on the Intel MIC architecture. The first two subroutines benefit from the vectorization of inverse square root operation, The next four subroutines benefit from vectorization of the uni-stride data access. The next three subroutines suffer from indirect, scattered data access. The last one can not be vectorized due to data dependence. Note that the impact of vectorization also differs depending on the subroutine and architecture (BG/Q versus MIC).

7.2 Simultaneous Multi-threading

Similar to the Intel MIC architecture, each BG/Q core also supports four hardware threads. Each cycle two instructions can be issued selected from two different threads with one to the XU units and another to the AXU units [1]. XU handles all branch, integer, load/store instructions while AXU executes floating-point instructions. Therefore, at least two threads are needed to maximize the instruction issue rate. Figure 9 displays the NWChem running times when

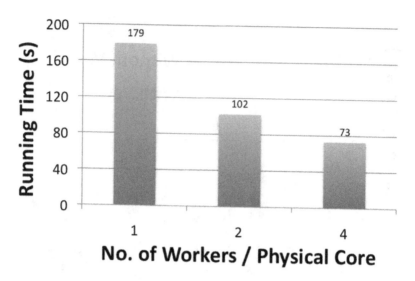

Fig. 9. The performance of running 1, 2, and 4 hardware threads per core on a full IBM BG/Q node

1, 2, and 4 hardware threads per core are used on a full node. Running 2 workers per core (32 per node) improves performance by a factor of 1.7x, while running 4 workers per core (64 per node) results in a significant improvement of 2.2x — thus demonstrating the effective impact of simultaneous multithreading for NWChem on the BG/Q platform.

8   Results and Discussion

The goal of our study is to understand the performance effect of different optimization techniques and find a consistent tuning approach that enables NWChem to perform efficiently on a variety of leading scientific platforms. The architectural diversity of high-end computing systems make this a significant challenge, which was tackled on four important platforms: the Cray XE6, the Cray XC30, the Intel MIC, and the IBM BG/Q.

Experimental results show that improving load balance is the most efficient approach to accelerate NWChem performance on all four platforms, followed by increasing data locality. Developing more intelligent algorithms based on application insights (such as the hash sorting algorithm) is also effective across all platforms. However, those optimizations and directly related loop transformations, such as loop unrolling and data prefetching, and are only effective on some of the platforms. This is actually a good sign for application developers, as compiler maturity and emerging auto-tuning techniques may relieve users of these burdensome transformations.

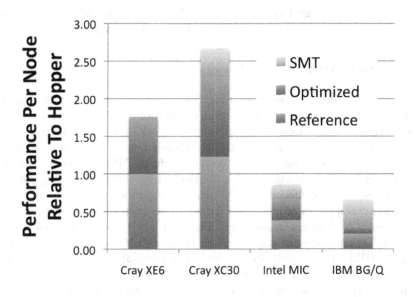

Fig. 10. The node performance relative to Cray XE6

Simultaneous multi-threading and vectorization are key architectural features that increasingly are driving high node performance. Our results show that multi-threading is effective in improving NWChem performance. On the IBM BG/Q platform, running 2, and 4 tasks per core can improve performance by 1.7x and 2.2x, respectively. While, on the Intel MIC, running two tasks per core can improve the performance 1.3x. The limited memory size (8GB) prohibited us from running 4 tasks per core (240 threads per node) on MIC. From the design of the instruction issue on the IBM BG/Q and the Intel MIC, two instructions issued in a clock cycle must come from different threads, necessitating multi-threading to achieve high performance.

Vectorization has long been supported by many processor families. However, as recent architectures have moved to higher SIMD lengths, vectorization has become a more critical component of extracting high performance from the underlying hardware. Our experimental results showed that the performance difference between the vectorized code (using compiler directives) and the non-vectorized code is about 22% and 25% MIC and BG/Q respectively. The key to extracting performance from vectorization is to develop uni-stride data access or use vectorized library functions. For NWChem, simply focusing on each individual subroutines and attempting to vectorize the loops is not enough to extract full potential from the vector processing units. A better approach is to develop new algorithmic designs that can maximize the advantages of vectorization.

Finally, Figure 10 presents a summary comparison normalized to the Cray XE6, which highlights original, optimized, and multi-threaded performance (where appropriate). Overall our approach consistently improves the Fock matrix construction and integral calculation for NWChem across all four platforms, attaining up to 2.5x speedup compared with the original version.

9   Related Work

There are numerous studies examining NWChem optimization schemes. The importance of vectorization for integral calculations had been recognized by Hurley, Huestis, and Goddard [9] in previous work. They described a vectorized procedure to transform integrals over atomic symmetry orbitals into integrals over molecular orbitals on a vector platform Alliant FX8/8. Foster et al. [3] presented scalable algorithms for distributing and constructing the Fock matrix in SCF problems on several massively parallel processing platforms. They also developed a mathematical model for communication cost to compare the efficiency of different algorithms. Tilson et al. [16] compared the performance of TEXAS integral package with the McMurchie-Davidson implementation on IBM SP, Kendall Square KSR-2, Cray T3D, Cray T3E, and Intel Touchstone Delta systems. Ozog et al. [15] explored a set of static and dynamic scheduling algorithms for block-sparse tensor contractions within the NWChem computational chemistry code. Similar algorithms may also be applied for integral calculations. Hammond et al. [6] studied the performance characteristics of NWChem using TAU. However, the focus was on communication. In addition, Jong et al. [10] provided a review of the current state of parallel computational chemistry software utilizing high-performance parallel computing platforms. The major difference of our work is that we focus on performance tuning (as opposed to algorithm development), and developed an effective strategy across four modern HPC platforms.

10   Summary and Conclusions

In this paper, we examined the performance tuning processes for the Fock matrix construction and integral calculations of NWChem on four deployed high performance computing platforms. The results indicate that load balancing has significant potential for improving performance, and attains up to 50% speedup. When combined with our additional optimization strategies, an overall speedup of up to 2.5x was achieved.

On platform that supports simultaneous multithreading, running multiple threads can improve the performance significantly. On the IBM BG/Q platform, running 2 and 4 threads per core can improve performance by 1.7x and 2.2x, respectively.

Finally, extracting the full performance potential from the vector processing units is a significant challenge for NWChem. Via substantial programming effort, we obtained a vectorized version running approximately 25% faster compared to non-vectorization mode on the MIC and BG/Q platforms. However, the current code can not be fully vectorized due to complex code structures, indirect non-continuous data access, and the true data dependence and serialization. Our future work will focus on developing new algorithms which can more effectively harness the potential of the vector processing units and multithreading on next-generation supercomputing platforms.

Acknowledgments. All authors from Lawrence Berkeley National Laboratory were supported by the Office of Advanced Scientific Computing Research in the Department of Energy Office of Science under contract number DE-AC02-05CH11231. This research used resources of the National Energy Research Scientific Computing Center (NERSC), which is supported by the Office of Science of the U.S. Department of Energy under Contract No. DE-AC02-05CH11231.

References

1. A2 Processor User's Manual for BlueGene/Q, http://www.alcf.anl.gov/user-guides/ibm-references#a2-processor-manual
2. Edison Cray XC30, http://www.nersc.gov/systems/edison-cray-xc30/
3. Foster, I., Tilson, J., Wagner, A., Shepard, R., Harrison, R., Kendall, R., Littlefield, R.: Toward High-Performance Computational Chemistry: I. Scalable Fock Matrix Construction Algorithms. Journal of Computational Chemistry 17, 109–123 (1996)
4. Global Arrays Toolkit, http://www.emsl.pnl.gov/docs/global/
5. Gill, P.M.W.: Molecular Integrals Over Gaussian Basis Functions. Advances in Quantum Chemistry 25, 141–205 (1994)
6. Hammond, J., Krishnamoorthy, S., Shende, S., Romero, N.A., Malony, A.: Performance Characterization of Global Address Space Applications: A Case Study with NWChem. Concurrency and Computation: Practice and Experience, 1–17 (2010)
7. Harrison, R., Guest, M., Kendall, R., Bernholdt, D., Wong, A., Stave, M., Anchell, J., Hess, A., Littlefield, R., Fann, G., Nieplocha, J., Thomas, G., Elwood, D., Tilson, J., Shepard, R., Wagner, A., Foster, I., Lusk, E., Stevens, R.: Toward high-performance computational chemistry: II. a scalable self-consistent field program. Journal of Computational Chemistry 17, 124–132 (1996)
8. Hopper Cray XE6, http://www.nersc.gov/systems/hopper-cray-xe6/
9. Hurley, J.N., Huestis, D.L., Goddard, W.A.: Optimized Two-Electron-Integral Transformation Procedures for Vector-Concurrent Computer Architecture. The Journal of Physical Chemistry 92, 4880–4883 (1988)
10. Jong, W.A., Bylaska, E., Govind, N., Janssen, C.L., Kowalski, K., Muller, T., Nielsen, I.M., Dam, H.J., Veryazov, V., Lindh, R.: Utilizing High Performance Computing for Chemistry: Parallel Computational Chemistry. Physical Chemistry Chemical Physics 12, 6896–6920 (2010)
11. Kumar, S., Aamidala, A.R., Faraj, D.A., Smith, B., Blocksome, M., Cernohous, B., Miller, D., Parker, J., Ratterman, J., Heidelberger, P., Chen, D., Steinmacher-Burrow, B.: PAMI: A Parallel Active Message Interface for the Blue Gene/Q Supercomputer. In: The 26th International Parallel and Distributed Processing Symposium (May 2012)
12. The Intel MIC, http://www.intel.com/content/www/us/en/architecture-and-technology/many-integrated-core/intel-many-integrated-core-architecture.html
13. Mira IBM Bluegene/Q, http://www.alcf.anl.gov/user-guides/mira-cetus-vesta
14. Obara, S., Saika, A.: Efficient Recursive Computation of Molecular Integrals Over Cartesian Gaussian Functions. The Journal of Chemical Physics 84, 3963–3975 (1986)

15. Ozog, D., Shende, S., Malony, A., Hammond, J.R., Dinan, J., Balaji, P.: Inspector-Executor Load Balancing Algorithms for Block-Sparse Tensor Contractions. In: Proceedings of the 27th International ACM Conference on International Conference on Supercomputing (May 2013)

16. Tilson, J.L., Minkoff, M., Wagner, A.F., Shepard, R., Sutton, P., Harrison, R.J., Kendall, R.A., Wong, A.T.: High-Performance Computational Chemistry: Hartree-Fock Electronic Structure Calculations on Massively Parallel Processors. International Journal of High Performance Computing Applications **13**, 291–306 (1999)

17. Top500 Supercomputer Sites, http://www.top500.org/lists/2013/06/

18. Valiev, M., Bylaska, E., Govind, N., Kowalski, K., Straatsma, T., van Dam, H., Wang, D., Nieplocha, J., Apra, E., Windus, T., de Jong, W.: Nwchem: a comprehensive and scalable open-source solution for large scale molecular simulations. Computer Physics Communications **181**, 1477–1489 (2010)

19. Wolinski, K., Hinton, J.F., Pulay, P.: Efficient Implementation of the Gauge-Independent Atomic Orbital Method for NMR Chemical Shift Calculations. Jounal of the American Chemical Society **112**, 8251–8260 (1990)

20. Helgaker, T., Olsen, J., Jorgensen, P.: Molecular Eletronic-Structure Theory. Wiley (2013), www.wiley.com

21. Helgaker, T., Taylor, P.R.: Gaussian Basis Sets and Molecular Integrals. In: Modern Electronic Structure Theory (Advances in Physical Chemistry). World Scientific (1995), www.worldscientific.com

22. Lindh, R., Ryu, U., Liu, B.: The Reduced Multiplication Scheme of the Rys Quadrature and New Recurrence Relations for Auxiliary Function Based Two Electron Integral Evaluation. The Journal of Chemical Physics **95**, 5889–5892 (1991)

Performance Analysis of the NWChem TCE for Different Communication Patterns

Priyanka Ghosh[1], Jeff R. Hammond[2]([✉]), Sayan Ghosh[1],
and Barbara Chapman[1]

[1] Department of Computer Science, University of Houston,
Houston, TX 77004, USA
{pghosh06,sgo,chapman}@cs.uh.edu
[2] Leadership Computing Facility, Argonne National Laboratory,
Lemont, IL 60439, USA
jhammond@alcf.anl.gov

Abstract. One-sided communication is a model that separates communication from synchronization, and has been in practice for over two decades in libraries such as SHMEM and Global Arrays (GA). GA is used in a number of application codes, especially NWChem, and provides a superset of SHMEM functionality that includes remote *accumulate*, among other features. Remote *accumulate* is an active-message operation that applies $y+ = a * x$ at the target rather than just $y = x$ (as in Put) which gives the programmer additional choices with respect to algorithm design. In this paper, we discuss and evaluate communication scenarios for dense block-tensor contractions, one of the mainstays of the NWChem computation chemistry package. We show that apart from the classical approach involving dynamic scheduling of data blocks for load balancing, reordering one-sided Get and Accumulate calls affects the performance of tensor contractions on leadership-class machines substantially. In order to understand why this reordering affects the performance, we develop a proxy application for the NWChem Tensor Contraction Engine (TCE) module. We utilize this proxy application to compare different implementations with a focus on communication.

Keywords: NWChem · One-sided communication · Global Arrays · MPI-3 · Tensor contractions

1 Introduction

NWChem [3,17] is one of the best-known applications that relies heavily upon one-sided communication, having employed the Global Arrays (GA) since the outset and never explicitly adopted the ubiquitous MPI model[1]. GA [11] is a PGAS (Partitioned Global Address Space) programming model in library form that includes a much richer set of functionality than SHMEM, which has existed

---

[1] The exception to this statement is not relevant to this paper.

© Springer International Publishing Switzerland 2014
S. Jarvis et al. (Eds.): PMBS 2013 Workshops, LNCS 8551, pp. 281–294, 2014.
DOI: 10.1007/978-3-319-10214-6_14

for approximately the same amount of time. SHMEM provides a set of remote memory access (RMA) primitives that are implementable in hardware, thereby enabling efficient implementations that can – at least in theory – consume no processing resources except when processing elements make SHMEM calls. On the other hand, the design of GA exposes features that the programmer needs to implement mathematical algorithms found, for example, in quantum chemistry, which frequently include multidimensional array accesses and floating-point accumulate (Acc)[2]. Generalized noncontiguous access (i.e., beyond simple strided access) and remote floating-point accumulate are rarely implemented in network hardware (except when the "network" is shared-memory). Consequently, GA consumes processing resources in the background - frequently in the form of a communication helper thread but occasionally as remote interrupts - that can have a nontrivial impact on performance in some cases [5]. However, the overall application performance benefits despite this overhead because of greater algorithmic flexibility in the application design. For example, eliminating remote accumulate in favor of remote writes reduces parallelism because, unlike the former, the latter cannot occur concurrently on the same remote buffer within a synchronization epoch.

Parallel performance optimization of NWChem is much like any other code in most respects; one attempts to reduce load-imbalance [1, 12, 16], use caching to avoid communication if not a memory bottleneck [9], and reduce the cost of remote data lookup [8], etc. Just as in MPI programs, one can trade a set of communication operations for another equivalent set. For example, in MPI one pads arrays in FFT to replace `MPI_Alltoallv` with `MPI_Alltoall`, which is more efficient if the padding overhead is low; on the other hand, trading `MPI_Alltoallv` for many send-recv calls will be more efficient in the sparse case (many processes send no data). Transforming communication patterns are not always about reducing data movement, of course; reducing synchronization overhead is essential for scalable algorithms.

A widely-held view is that one-sided communication is less synchronous than two-sided communication, but the practical differences between *Put/Get* and *Send/Recv*, for example, are primarily due to their implementation. If *Put/Get* use only network hardware while *Send/Recv* use network hardware plus processing on both sides, then the processing overhead may be a noticeable difference. Within the one-sided regime, *Put* and *Get* differ with respect to local completion, since this entails a round-trip in the case of *Get* (since the data must arrive for the buffer to be used), while in *Put*, local completion can be strictly local. Remote accumulate *(Acc)* is similar to *Put*, at least from the perspective of the initiator.

In GA programs, there are two types of synchronization overheads: explicit and implicit. Obviously, explicit synchronization overheads are the well-known ones (e.g., global synchronization via a barrier, as in `ga_sync`). Implicit synchronization is required when issuing a *Get*, for example, as the request for remote

---

[2] We emphasize all instances involving calls to (GA, MPI)_Get, (GA, MPI)_Accumulate with *Get* and *Acc* in this paper.

data must be delivered to the remote node[3], acted upon, and the data delivered back to the initiator. On the other hand, *Put* and *Acc* will complete locally without any explicit remote activity. Additional latency for *Get* with respect to *Put* or *Acc* can arise from contention on the network, waiting in the remote active-message queue, and the cost of the active-message itself, which might entail a strided memory copy that crosses multiple levels of the memory hierarchy. *Put* and *Acc* see all of these same effects but the cost is mostly hidden from the application, at least with respect to direct measurement of their costs, because the initiator proceeds without waiting on their remote completion. In aggregate, however, the sum of the remote processing costs are visible unless the associated resources would otherwise be idle. For this reason, *Acc* is more expensive than *Put*, since it requires floating-point computation. What is not clear is whether - in terms of aggregate parallel performance - one should favor *Get* or *Acc*. One of the goals of this paper is to determine the answer to this question experimentally.

One of the more popular methods in NWChem is the quantum many-body method known as coupled cluster (CC) theory, which is used heavily for solving chemical problems requiring quantitative accuracy for chemical bond-breaking, e.g. combustion. Given its steep computational cost – $O(N^7)$ in the case of the most commonly used CC variant, CCSD(T) – simulations running on thousands of cores for many hours are rather common, hence even modest performance improvements in the scalability and efficiency of these methods pay off significantly. Given that much of the floating-point computation in CC simulations is performed using the BLAS3 subroutine DGEMM, which usually runs at more than 80% of peak for the dimensions used in NWChem, the most obvious place for optimization in NWChem CC codes is in the communication, synchronization, and load balancing.

Past approaches to improve performance involve efficient strategies to reduce the amount of load imbalance in the CCSD module [12]. In this paper, our focus is the design space of the Tensor Contraction Engine (TCE) module to evaluate the performance behavior observed for CCSD block tensor contractions when restructuring *Get* and *Acc* calls. We consider two types of optimizations: (1) reordering of the loops over tiles to trade *Get* calls for *Acc* calls and (2) reduction in *Get* calls by fetching multiple blocks at a time into a cache. The individual tensor contractions in NWChem are very complex, supporting a range of dimensions (up to 8-dimensional arrays) with both permutation symmetry and block sparsity (which arises from point-group symmetry - see [12] for details) and containing a number of optimizations that are opaque to non-chemists. Therefore, we implemented a stripped down proxy application that exposes only the essential features of an individual tensor contraction implemented using the TCE

---

[3] Different node resources may be involved in processing these requests depending on the implementation strategy and the nature of the request itself; contiguous requests may be processed in hardware while noncontiguous requests often require processor intervention to pack messages to be large enough to saturate the network bandwidth.

template. The proxy considers only the cases of 2-dimensional arrays[4] and uses regular tiling, which reduces some of the issues associated with load balancing. Thus, the proxy is most useful for understanding the trade-offs associated with restructuring the communication operations, which is exactly the purposes for which it was designed. We did not implement a proxy version of optimization (2) since it was not necessary to understand the results for that case.

The primary contributions of this paper are: (1) design and implementation of two new variants of the NWChem TCE tensor contraction template that are demonstrated empirically to be significantly faster than the original for real-world chemistry problems on the primary hardware platform for NWChem (x86/InfiniBand); (2) development of a proxy application to model the different communication pattern found in one of these variants; and (3) implementation of the proxy application in the original GA programming model and MPI (3.0 standard [10]) to evaluate any potential differences between the communication infrastructure therein. The differences in the behavior of the full NWChem application and the proxy demonstrate the shortcomings of the proxy and reveal the downsides of eliminating domain-specific application complexity.

2   Implementation and Design

The Tensor Contraction Engine (TCE) [2,7] is a project to automate the derivation and parallelization of quantum many-body methods such as CC. A large number of procedures are necessary because of many different types of contractions possible between tensors of various rank. All tensors are decomposed using tiling, where each tile falls into a single symmetry class (see [7] for details) and these tiles define the granularity of all tensor contractions.

2.1   Algorithms Implemented in NWChem

Algorithm 1 provides an overview of the default implementation of a distributed tensor contraction in TCE. *NXTVAL* represents the centralized dynamic load balancer inherited from TCGMSG, a communication library which predates MPI, that queries a global counter and runs over all possible tasks in a given contraction. The *Symmetry* function is a condensation of a number of logical tests in the code that determine whether a particular tile will be nonzero. In Algorithms 1, 2, and 3, the indices given for the local buffer contraction are the tile indices where each tile index represents a set of contiguous indices and where each tile is grouped in such a way that the symmetry properties of all its constitutive elements are identical.

---

[4] A tensor contraction involving 2-dimensional arrays is just a matrix-matrix multiplication and optimal algorithms for these are known, but we are trying to model arbitrary dimensionality and the benefit to the proxy of supporting this is not justified given the additional complexity required to implement it explicitly.

Algorithm 1 illustrates the *Original* (default) version of the tensor contraction template, wherein all the *Gets* are performed in the innermost loop repeatedly for fetching every tile into local buffers. This approach entails redundant calls to *TCE_Get* since the same tile is fetched multiple times during subsequent iterations. The calls to *GA_Accumulate* are, however, sparse due to the aggregation of dense inner loop, computations satisfying a set of symmetry conditions into a single task. *TCE_Get* is shorthand for a small number (between 1 and 8) of *GA_Get* operations combined with the accumulation of the resulting buffers from these onto a single buffer, as described in [8].

Algorithm 1. Pseudocode for *Original* version of TCE-CCSD implementation

---

Tiled Global Arrays: A, B, C
Local buffers: a, b, c;
forall the $h1, h2, p3, p4 \in O, V$ tiles **do**
  if $NXTVAL(my\_pe)=True$ **then**
    if $Symmetry(h1,h2,p3,p4)=True$ **then**
      Allocate c for C(h1,h2,p3,p4) tiles
      for $p5, p6 \in V$ tiles **do**
        if $Symmetry(h1,h2,p5,p6)=True$ **then**
          if $Symmetry(p5,p6,p3,p4)=True$ **then**
            TCE_Get A(h1,h2,p5,p6) into a
            TCE_Get B(p5,p6,p3,p4) into b
            c(h1,h2,p3,p4) += a(h1,h2,p5,p6) * b(p5,p6,p3,p4)
          end
        end
      end
      GA_Acc c into C(h1,h2,p3,p4)
    end
  end
end

Algorithm 2 illustrates the *Inverted* version of the TCE-CCSD method where the number of calls to *Gets* are drastically reduced by transferring the *Get* call to the outer loop. Therefore, once a tile is fetched into the local buffer *b*, it is reused in all computations of the dense inner loop satisfying the set of symmetry conditions. The penalty on the hand mandates the need for excessive number of calls to *Accumulate*, after it is moved inside the innermost loop in order to maintain the symmetry criterion.

In quantum chemistry applications, such as NWChem, a usually large molecular system lacking any spatial symmetry produces set of tiles which align well to the number of processors and can be used to obtain high scalability. In such a scenario, we encounter lesser load imbalance among tasks owing to the proper distribution of the dense computations and thus stand to gain performance benefit if we were to reduce the cost of communication, by minimizing the number of

Algorithm 2. Pseudocode for *Inverted* version of TCE implementation

```
Tiled Global Arrays: A, B, C
Local buffers: a, b, c;
forall the p3, p4, p5, p6 ∈ V, V tiles do
    if Symmetry(p3,p4,p5,p6)=True then
        if NXTVAL(my_pe)=True then
            TCE_Get B(p5,p6,p3,p4) into b
            for h1, h2 ∈ O tiles do
                if Symmetry(h1,h2,p3,p4)=True then
                    if Symmetry(h1,h2,p5,p6)=True then
                        Allocate c for C(h1,h2,p3,p4) tiles
                        TCE_Get A(h1,h2,p5,p6) into a
                        c(h1,h2,p3,p4) += a(h1,h2,p5,p6) * b(p5,p6,p3,p4)
                        GA_Acc c into C(h1,h2,p3,p4)
                    end
                end
            end
        end
    end
end
```

calls to *Gets* and *Accumulates*. Algorithm 3 illustrates such an approach wherein we strip the outer loop and save the blocks obtained from a *Get* call for multiple reuse later. This approach (*Cache* version) guarantees fewer calls to *Get* compared to both the *Original* and *Inverted* versions as well as fewer calls to *Accumulate* in comparison to the *Inverted* version.

2.2 TCE Proxy Applications

We designed a proxy application replicating the TCE module functionality for both the *Original* and *Inverted* versions. We implemented this using two programming models namely GA and MPI. Apart from revealing software overheads between MPI and GA versions of the block tensor contraction kernel, the RMA implementation of MPI is fundamentally different to that of ARMCI and by extension, GA. As the RMA implementation of MPI has substantially improved, we expected better results for the *Original* version (lesser accumulates with local completion semantics [passive target synchronization]) for most of the test data sizes, than the *Inverted* version, which requires a request handle for waiting (local completion) on outstanding accumulates.

The *Inverted* version incorporates a *double-buffering* scheme, wherein two local buffers for the same array are maintained, one for communication and the other for computation. Data is transferred using the communication buffer, and local computations proceed with the compute buffer (a wait is issued prior to using the compute buffer, to ascertain completion of previous task). The buffers are swapped at the end of an iteration. MPI request based accumulate

---

Algorithm 3. Pseudocode for *Cache* version of TCE implementation

---

Tiled Global Arrays: A, B, C
Local buffers: a, b, c;
Local Hash Table: Htable;
forall the $h1, h2, p3, p4, p5, p6 \in O, V, V$ *tiles, unroll U* **do**
  if *NXTVAL(my_pe)=True* **then**
    forall the $h1i, h2i, p5i, p6i \in U, U$ *tiles* **do**
      if *Symmetry(h1i,h2i,p5i,p6i)=True* **then**
       | TCE_Get A(h1i,h2i,p5i,p6i) and save into Htable
      end
    end
    forall the $p3i, p4i, p5i, p6i \in U, U$ *tiles* **do**
      if *Symmetry(p3i,p4i,p5i,p6i)=True* **then**
       | TCE_Get B(p5i,p6i,p3i,p4i) and save into Htable
      end
    end
    forall the $h1i, h2i, p3i, p4i \in U, U$ *tiles* **do**
      Allocate c for C(h1i,h2i,p3i,p4i) tiles
      for $p5i, p6i \in U$ *tiles* **do**
        if *Symmetry(h1i,h2i,p3i,p4i)=True* **then**
          if *Symmetry(h1i,h2i,p5i,p6i)=True* **then**
            Fetch block(h1i,h2i,p5i,p6i) from Htable into a
            Fetch block(p5i,p6i,p3i,p4i) from Htable into b
            c(h1i,h2i,p3i,p4i) += a(h1i,h2i,p5i,p6i) *
            b(p5i,p6i,p3i,p4i)
          end
        end
      end
      GA_Acc c into C(h1i,h2i,p3i,p4i)
    end
  end
end

(`MPI_Raccumulate` with `MPI_Wait`) and ARMCI non-blocking operation (`ARMCI_NbAccS` with `ARMCI_Wait`) are used for taking advantage of this overlap in computation and communication.

3   Experimental Results

We have performed all our experiments on an InfiniBand cluster Tukey, a 96-node, 16-core, 2-way SMP AMD processor with 64 GB memory per node at Argonne National Laboratory. The system is running Linux kernel 2.6.32 (x86_64). NWChem was compiled with GCC 4.4.6 and linked against Goto-BLAS 2 1.13[4]. Because BLAS calls dominate the computation in NWChem, compiler optimizations do not significantly affect the performance (this has been confirmed experimentally in the past by one of the present authors). For the proxy applications (GA/MPI), BLAS from ATLAS library[18] is used. The high-performance interconnect is InfiniBand QDR with a theoretical throughput of 4 GB/s per link and ~ 2 μs latency. The communication libraries used were ARMCI from GA 5.1, which is heavily optimized for InfiniBand, with MVA-PICH2 1.8 (for NWChem and GA proxy) and MVAPICH2-X 2.a (for MPI proxy). We have launched all our NWChem experiments with eight MPI processes per node, whereas for the proxy applications, we have four MPI processes per node.

3.1 Full Application Tests

Figures 1a and 1b represent the comparison in terms of performance obtained for a 8-H_2O and 9-H_2O CCSD simulation respectively, with the aug-cc-pvdz basis running on the Tukey cluster. CC simulations can be categorized as symmetrically sparse or asymmetrically dense. We find the problems falling in the latter category (characteristic to the water molecule), a more suitable candidate to perform the cache optimization. In both figures we notice the strong scalability of the *Inverted* version in comparison to the *Original* version. This is attributed to fewer *Get* operations performed in the *Inverted* version. Since *Gets* in NWChem have to satisfy several symmetry constraints, it is a far costlier operation compared to *Accumulate*. The *Cache* version accounts for a 27% reduction in the total number of *Gets* compared to *Inverted* and a 72% reduction compared to *Original* (as seen in Table 1). This contributes towards an average performance improvement of 20% and 10% for *Original* and *Inverted* respectively, due to the reduction in the overall network communication.

The percentage of improvement is subject to change based on the size and symmetry of the molecule being used in the simulation. With smaller molecules, which lead to fewer tasks, the dynamic load balancer (NXTVAL) will add some overhead for the *Cache* version and in case of molecules with high symmetry, we may not encounter a reduction in the total number of *Gets*.

Table 1. Results comparing the number of *Gets* and *Accumulates* encountered for the three TCE-CCSD implementations

Input Data Molecule		Total Number	
8-H_2O		Get	Accumulate
	Original	84700	682
	Inverted	32065	71632
	Cache	23353	21582
9-H_2O		Get	Accumulate
	Original	119448	810
	Inverted	45072	101196
	Cache	32904	25650

Table 1 draws a comparison based on the number of *Gets* and *Accumulates* recorded for the various implementations of TCE-CCSD module in NWChem. These results have been acquired using a TCE profiling interface (TPI) constructed within the TCE framework.

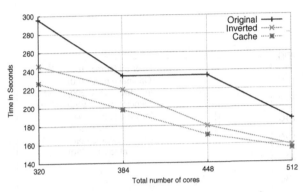

(a) Results comparison for water w8 aug-cc-pvdz

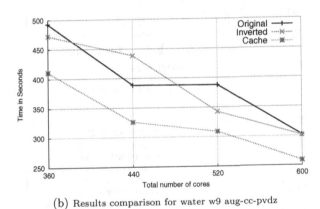

(b) Results comparison for water w9 aug-cc-pvdz

Fig. 1. Results obtained for *Original, Inverted* and *Cache* versions for the water w8 and w9 molecules

3.2 Proxy Applications Using GA and MPI

GA. The results obtained for the proxy application using GA depicted in Figures 2a and 2b representing square matrix sizes of 24K and 32K respectively, clearly indicate that the *Original* version surpasses the *Inverted* version in terms of performance. In contrast to NWChem, this behavior is expected since the *Get* operations in the proxy application are computationally less expensive in comparison to the *TCE_Get*'s in NWChem resulting in *Accumulates* becoming more costly. Since the *Original* version performs the least number of *Accumulates*, it clearly wins in terms of performance. However, the *Original* version demonstrates weaker scalability compared to *Inverted* especially for cases with larger block sizes as seen in Figure 2b with block size of 1200. We suspect this is owing to the creation of fewer number of tasks in case of *Original*, where the lack of core count saturation results in higher load imbalance. *Inverted* scales better than *Original* due to creation of more tasks, increase in core saturation resulting in better load balance.

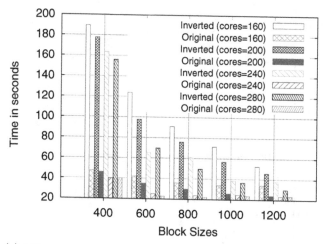

(a) 24K square matrix with ppn=4 and nodes=40,50,60 and 70 using GA

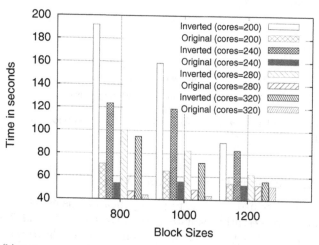

(b) 32K square matrix with ppn=4 and nodes=50,60,70 and 80 using GA

Fig. 2. Results obtained for *Original, Inverted* versions of the GA proxy application

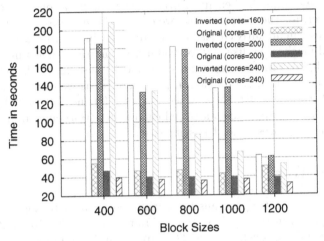

(a) 24K square matrix with ppn=4 and nodes=40,50 and 60 using MPI

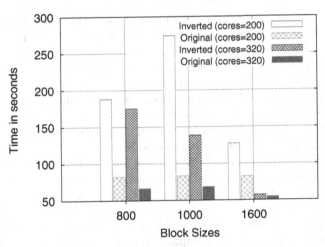

(b) 32K square matrix with ppn=4 and nodes=50 and 80 using MPI

Fig. 3. Results obtained for *Original, Inverted* versions of the MPI-3 proxy application

MPI. Since the domain decomposition technique for MPI proxy-app versions rely on dimensions being perfectly divisible by the total number of processes, we have chosen only the cases which satisfy this criteria. The performance of *Inverted* versions are subpar compared to that of *Original*, which could be attributed to a greater number of *Accumulates*. However, the *Inverted* versions for larger processes were observed to be better in terms of scalability. This pattern is observed from execution on 240 processes for 24K matrices as shown in Figure 3a and 32K matrices using 320 processes in Figure 3b. This indicates that for larger data sizes (with coarser block sizes) on proportionally large number of processes, we obtain the benefit of overlapping computation with communication. However, for the *Original* case, we observe from Figures 3a and 3b that execution times remain fairly consistent with different block sizes, and transitions between small block sizes (like 600 to 1000 in 24K matrices shown in Figure 3a) is almost negligible. In this case too, large block sizes (and a larger number of processes) have a positive impact on performance, as we could observe from Figure 3b (12 secs difference between block sizes 1600 and 800 on 320 processes for 32K matrices), as opposed to a trivial change in performance from 800-1600 block sizes on 200 processes for the same case.

4 Related Work

Fundamentally different algorithms for distributed-memory tensor contractions have been explored in the Cyclops Tensor Framework (CTF) [15]. The relative merits of the CTF approach and the TCE approach depend upon the details of the architecture and the degree of irregularity (e.g., block-sparsity) in the computation. The Cyclops tensor framework exploits the challenges of high dimensional symmetry in coupled cluster by employing a cyclic distribution to decompose tensor contractions with a redistribution kernel, which transposes tensors of any dimension minimizing communication by increasing computation. Redistribution of data permutes the dimensions such that the subsequent contraction phase may apply a matrix-martix multiplication algorithm (Recursive SUMMA) in an effort to minimize the amount of data communicated for each tensor. Sadayappan and coworkers have attempted to bring together the best of CTF and TCE in the CAST project [14], but the lack of integration into NWChem means we cannot compare directly with our full application results.

The Inspector-Executor model [13] employs low-overhead static partitioning techniques for reducing the load imbalance encountered for block-sparse tensor contractions within NWChem to mitigate the ovehead and dynamic scheduling algorithms for block-sparse tensor contractions within NWChem (alternative to the dynamic global load balancer NXTVAL). Additionally, with the use of a "Dynamic Buckets" design, tasks are split into buckets which are then associated with groups of processors thereby minimizing the effect of variation in task execution time.

Our work, on the other hand, focuses on minimizing the cost of communication across the network by limiting the number of calls to *Get* and *Accumulate* in NWChem's TCE. By employing strategies to store data locally (within a processor), we curtail the cost of redundant one-sided communication evident particularly in dense nonsymmetric molecules with regular task sizes. Similar to the ideas discussed in [6], we also designed self-contained application proxies for exploring algorithmic design choices pertaining to NWChem TCE, estimating the performance trade-off between the different communication patterns and varying communication runtime libraries.

5   Conclusions and Future Work

We identified two new implementations of the TCE template that improve the performance of NWChem by more than 10%. One of these is based upon inverting communication to reduce *Get* in favor of *Accumulate* while the other reduces *Get* using caching. To understand how the different communication patterns affect performance, we developed a simple proxy application and tested it using both GA and MPI. However, the simple proxy was unable to reproduce the quantitative results of the full application, although some of the basic trends were the same. We are developing more complex proxies with the intent of reconciling their behavior to the full application. Once more accurate proxies are developed, we can employ them to understand a variety of one-sided programming models, including GA, MPI, OpenSHMEM, and PGAS languages such as UPC and CAF. We will also expand our experimental studies to other architectures and to many thousands of cores. We also intend to further optimize the *Cache* variant by incorporating static partitioning so that we can implement it on accelerator systems (Intel MIC and GPU). The *Cache* version is ideal for accelerator offload model since it has higher compute intensity per task.

Acknowledgments. This research used resources of the Argonne Leadership Computing Facility at Argonne National Laboratory, which is supported by the Office of Science of the U.S. Department of Energy under contract DE-AC02-06CH11357.

References

1. Aprà, E., Rendell, A.P., Harrison, R.J., Tipparaju, V., de Jong, W.A., Xantheas, S.S.: Liquid water: obtaining the right answer for the right reasons. In: Proceedings of the ACM/IEEE SC Conference on High Performance Networking and Computing, pp. 1–7. ACM, New York (2009)
2. Auer, A.A., Baumgartner, G., Bernholdt, D.E., Bibireata, A., Choppella, V., Cociorva, D., Gao, X., Harrison, R., Krishnamoorthy, S., Krishnan, S., Lam, C.-C., Lu, Q., Nooijen, M., Pitzer, R., Ramanujam, J., Sadayappan, P., Sibiryakov, A.: Automatic code generation for many-body electronic structure methods: the tensor contraction engine. Molecular Physics **104**(2), 211–228 (2006)
3. Bylaska, E.J., de Jong, W.A., Govind, N., Kowalski, K., Straatsma, T.P., Valiev, M., van Dam, H.J.J., Wang, D., Aprà, E., Windus, T.L., Hammond, J., Autschbach, J., Nichols, P., Hirata, S., Hackler, M.T., Zhao, Y., Fan, P.-D., Harrison, R.J., Dupuis, M., Smith, D.M.A., Nieplocha, J., Tipparaju, V., Krishnan, M., Vazquez-Mayagoitia, A., Wu, Q., Voorhis, T.V., Auer, A.A., Nooijen, M., Crosby, L.D., Brown, E., Cisneros, G., Fann, G.I., Früchtl, H., Garza, J., Hirao, K., Kendall, R., Nichols, J.A., Tsemekhman, K., Wolinski, K., Anchell, J., Bernholdt, D., Borowski, P., Clark, T., Clerc, D., Dachsel, H., Deegan, M., Dyall, K., Elwood, D., Glendening, E., Gutowski, M., Hess, A., Jaffe, J., Johnson, B., Ju, J., Kobayashi, R., Kutteh, R., Lin, Z., Littlefield, R., Long, X., Meng, B., Nakajima, T., Niu, S., Pollack, L., Rosing, M., Sandrone, G., Stave, M., Taylor, H., Thomas, G., van Lenthe, J., Wong, A., Zhang, Z.: NWChem, a computational chemistry package for parallel computers, version 6.0 (2010)

4. Goto, K.: Gotoblas. Texas Advanced Computing Center, University of Texas at Austin, USA (2007), http://www.otc.utexas.edu/ATdisplay.jsp
5. Hammond, J.R., Krishnamoorthy, S., Shende, S., Romero, N.A., Malony, A.D.: Performance characterization of global address space applications: a case study with NWChem. Concurrency and Computation: Practice and Experience **24**, 135–154 (2011)
6. Heroux, M.A., Doerfler, D.W., Crozier, P.S., Willenbring, J.M., Edwards, H.C., Williams, A., Rajan, M., Keiter, E.R., Thornquist, H.K., Numrich, R.W.: Improving performance via mini-applications. Sandia National Laboratories, Tech. Rep. SAND2009-5574 (2009)
7. Hirata, S.: Tensor contraction engine: Abstraction and automated parallel implementation of configuration-interaction, coupled-cluster, and many-body perturbation theories. The Journal of Physical Chemistry A **107**(46), 9887–9897 (2003)
8. Kowalski, K., Hammond, J.R., de Jong, W.A., Fan, P.-D., Valiev, M., Wang, D., Govind, N.: Coupled cluster calculations for large molecular and extended systems. In: Reimers, J.R. (ed.) Computational Methods for Large Systems: Electronic Structure Approaches for Biotechnology and Nanotechnology. Wiley (2011)
9. Liu, X., Patel, A., Chow, E.: A new scalable parallel algorithm for fock matrix construction, pp. 1–12 (May 2014)
10. MPI Forum. MPI: A message-passing interface standard. Version 3.0 (November 2012)
11. Nieplocha, J., Harrison, R.J., Littlefield, R.J.: Global arrays: A portable "shared-memory" programming model for distributed memory computers. In: Supercomputing (SC) (1994)
12. Ozog, D., Hammond, J.R., Dinan, J., Balaji, P., Shende, S., Malony, A.: Inspector-executor load balancing algorithms for block-sparse tensor contractions. In: International Conference on Parallel Processing (ICPP) (October 2013)
13. Ozog, D., Shende, S., Malony, A.D., Hammond, J.R., Dinan, J., Balaji, P.: Inspector/executor load balancing algorithms for block-sparse tensor contractions. In: ICS, pp. 483–484 (2013)
14. Rajbhandari, S., Nikam, A., Lai, P.-W., Stock, K., Krishnamoorthy, S., Sadayappan, P.: Framework for distributed contractions of tensors with symmetry. Ohio State University (2013) (Preprint)
15. Solomonik, E., Matthews, D., Hammond, J., Demmel, J.: Cyclops tensor framework: reducing communication and eliminating load imbalance in massively parallel contractions. In: Proceedings of the International Parallel and Distributed Processing Symposium (IPDPS) (2013)
16. Straatsma, T.P., McCammon, J.A.: Load balancing of molecular dynamics simulation with NWChem. IBM Systems Journal **40**(2), 328–341 (2001)
17. Valiev, M., Bylaska, E., Govind, N., Kowalski, K., Straatsma, T., Dam, H.V., Wang, D., Nieplocha, J., Apra, E., Windus, T., de Jong, W.: NWChem: A comprehensive and scalable open-source solution for large scale molecular simulations. Computer Physics Communications **181**(9), 1477–1489 (2010)
18. Whaley, R.C., Dongarra, J.J.: Automatically tuned linear algebra software. In: Proceedings of the 1998 ACM/IEEE Conference on Supercomputing (CDROM), pp. 1–27. IEEE Computer Society (1998)

Author Index

Printed in the United States
By Bookmasters